Orienting to Chance

Orienting to Chance

Probabilism and the Future of
Social Theory

MICHAEL STRAND AND
OMAR LIZARDO

The University of Chicago Press
Chicago and London

The University of Chicago Press, Chicago 60637
The University of Chicago Press, Ltd., London
© 2025 by The University of Chicago
Published 2025

34 33 32 31 30 29 28 27 26 25   1 2 3 4 5

ISBN-13: 978-0-226-84311-7 (cloth)
ISBN-13: 978-0-226-84313-1 (paper)
ISBN-13: 978-0-226-84312-4 (ebook)
DOI: https://doi.org/10.7208/chicago/9780226843124.001.0001

Library of Congress Cataloging-in-Publication Data

Names: Strand, Michael (Sociologist), author. | Lizardo, Omar, author.
Title: Orienting to chance : probabilism and the future of social theory / Michael
    Strand and Omar Lizardo.
Other titles: Probabilism and the future of social theory
Description: Chicago ; London : The University of Chicago Press, 2025. | Includes
    bibliographical references and index.
Identifiers: LCCN 2025003181 | ISBN 9780226843117 (cloth) | ISBN 9780226843131
    (paperback) | ISBN 9780226843124 (ebook)
Subjects: LCSH: Sociology—Philosophy. | Social sciences—Philosophy. | Probabilities. |
    Chance—Social aspects.
Classification: LCC HM585 .S786 2025 | DDC 301.01/5192—dc23/eng/20250203
LC record available at https://lccn.loc.gov/2025003181

Contents

Enter the Mosaic

> I must premiss that we, all of us, use this word ["probability"] with a degree of lax-
> ity which corrupts and rots our reasoning to a degree that very few of us are at all
> awake to.
>
> CHARLES SANDERS PEIRCE, *Notes on the Doctrine of Chances*

Probability is a core tool of sociology. Contemporary sociologists design their research and carry out their analyses in an environment permeated by probabilistic ideas and techniques. The methods sections of sociology papers brim with references to the number of interviews done, the number of hours of observation completed, and the number of cases examined. Findings are often carefully laid out in tables full of averages, confidence intervals, and standard deviations. The field of sociology has been engaged with probability from the start, and so what we do now might seem like continuity or, even, progress. Classical sociologists like Karl Marx, Emile Durkheim, Max Weber, and W. E. B. Du Bois all pondered the nature of society using concepts like "socially average" and "concomitant variation," but also "rhythm," "Chance" and "*Chance*."[1] Our classical forebears would be puzzled and even disappointed with us, however. To them, we would appear dull and uninspired when it comes to probability, because we seem to limit our understanding of it entirely to *frequency of occurrence*. Even as we insist that our methodological tool kit has achieved levels of sophistication and technical prowess they could have scarcely imagined, they would only rebuff us, unimpressed, and respond with a simple plea: Why have we forgotten what they, particularly Weber and Du Bois, once pursued?

Like most scientific fields today, contemporary sociology pays little explicit attention to probability beyond its methodological applications; frequency and probability are often assumed to be synonymous. Some have sounded alarms, however, about this black-boxed nature of probability. Andrew Abbott observed over three decades ago that sociologists, and presumably all social scientists who rely on linear-regression methods, have little choice but to emphasize "fixed entities with variable attributes" in their research designs and explanatory accounts because of the peculiar dominance of a statistical metaphysics he calls "general linear reality."[2] Statistical tools supply us with a view of the world in which we can carry out our research, and our claims can only be true if that world holds firm. That world can make sociological claims valid, but it is a strange world in which fixed entities are all that exist and the only way they can relate to each other is through a kind of monotonic causal flow. In this linear world (plus error), causes predictably lead to effects, though a temporal dimension is lacking, and so too are sequencing, path dependence, and contingency. For Abbott, statistics camouflages this world and hides its weird metaphysics.[3] Here, he echoes an earlier observation made by sociologist Randall Collins, who argued that far from a mere social-scientific method, statistics comprises a "substantive theory of how chance processes operate in the world."[4]

Their shared point is straightforward enough. The statistics behind the linear regression method contains a hidden ontology, featuring entities, attributes, and causal orders all its own, and generally limiting what reality can be for those who use the method. Much of the substantive theory behind this linear reality was apparent to the classical sociologists. They seem more conversant than social scientists are today with the notion that probability is a concept or substantive theory of what constitutes the world. Probability had not yet been subject to a conquest by method or black-boxed in statistical packages. As a result, these past thinkers can appear to us today as remarkably innovative, or perhaps terribly obscure and hopelessly naive, when they engage with probability. We have thus far lacked a way of understanding that, for some of the most notable classics of sociology, probability presented an open field of conceptual innovation and application—the polar opposite of what sociologists typically presume today.

In this book, we attempt to restore that open field, for reasons we believe go to the very core of the sociological field and the sociological imagination. Because probability is not understood to be translatable into qualitative experience, sociologists have been left with a dichotomy that really exists nowhere else, between interpretation and probability. This dichotomy translates into others: qualitative versus quantitative, or interpretivism versus positivism. The dispute at the basis of these distinctions is over probability, but the reasons why this is so are not apparent at first. To see those reasons requires allowing a new entrant on the scientific scene of the past few decades to enter the conversation.

*

The Latinate origins of the word "data" provide us with a simple definition: Data is "what is given," and in one sense, the definition rings truer now than at any time previous. In recent years, "what is given" has grown in volume and variety, just as the speed of its acquisition and the scale of its recording have grown leaps and bounds over what was previously possible. A comprehensive "datafication" is underway, as if guided by some vision that once appeared only in the dreams of late-Enlightenment figures like physicist Pierre-Simon Laplace, and even then it could only be expressed by an imaginative, distinctly nonhuman form, conjured for the sole purpose of comprehending. This form is Laplace's "demon," a creature able to conceive of a real-time "N = all," in full possession of information past and present, and who thus peers out on a world made fully knowable and predictable in a way that we mere mortals remain desperately incapable of doing. The philosopher Ernst Cassirer once referred to Laplace's vision and its later incarnations as "the Laplacean spirit."[5] It has been alive for well over two hundred years now. But perhaps it is only now, in the twenty-first century, that it has become possible to render it away from a spiritual or devilish medium, as an "ideal" or "demon," to redeem it from being merely a scenario in a Philip K. Dick novella,[6] by turning it into an engineering problem—and one that might be within our human grasp to solve. "Data" holds the key to solving that problem, many believe, and Laplace returns again to life, this time as the muse for these newly christened "data scientists" who develop a machine intelligence for the purpose.

By one definition, a data scientist is one who "liberates and creates meaning from raw data,"[7] typically by using computational tools on large datasets involving enormous numbers of data points. Another definition presents data scientists in more of a service role. Data scientists are those who "[connect] statistical models and computational methods to solve discipline-specific problems."[8] Regardless of what they are defined as doing, data scientists tend to advocate something novel in the world of science writ large: "data-centricity." In its most specific formulation, data-centricity consists of a revision to knowledge that puts data at the center of the scientific process. It becomes a more important player than either theory or method. In our view, the most disruptive aspects of data science can be found here. As if guided by the Laplacean spirit made achievable, data-centricity presents a challenge to a largely settled understanding of the role of data in a science that has persisted for the past seventy years at least.

That settled understanding was provided, above all, by the philosophical sect known as "logical positivism," which was the cardinal form of mid-century philosophy of science and known for making normative recommendations. The positivists forbade any suggestion that data might constitute a "raw product" outside a particular method of recording. Nobody, according to these philosophers, enjoys an immediate revelatory relation to the world, and so everyone needs data in order to *represent* an underlying phenomenon that is accessible in no other way.[9] Data are human-made, and their features are determined by the methods used for collection. It is those methods that make data "objective," and so any scientist worth their salt better have good methods training. A good scientist must try to gather the *right* data with the right method to reveal the phenomenon they intend to represent. That recipe gives any dataset a kind of *fixed* content. It can only serve to represent *this* phenomenon, the one we gathered the data to represent.

The logical positivists saw data as fulfilling a subsidiary function in the research process, one determined by its *instrumental* relation to theory.[10] Data without theory is not only blind in this view; it is also pointless. A good scientist cannot go on an "adventure"[11] of data gathering for its own sake. They may dissect, diagnose, run experiments, and thus generate data; but it must be data they have good reason to think will confirm or disconfirm their theoretically derived hypotheses. A good scientist keeps data in proximity with theory from start to finish. To the ears of a midcentury logical positivist, then, the prospect of a "data science" would probably sound either blandly obvious or a contradiction in terms.

These are normative recommendations, and how far they were ever put into practice is an open question. But the image of science is important here for observations that some have made recently: specifically, that data science fundamentally revises this image, and that it does so essentially by reversing the arrow. A data-driven or data-centric science stands in contrast to the theoretically motivated one offered by logical positivism. Data science *starts* with data. Even if it is unclear what phenomenon a given dataset could possibly represent, data can be continually collected with no research use in mind. Not only that, but the methods also used to gather it are of secondary importance, particularly if machines can do the gathering for us. Tightly controlled sampling methods, the crowning jewel of mid-twentieth-century social science, appear as unnecessary extravagances.[12] More generally, data science commits to data as bearing a sui generis validity, measured by qualities like volume, granularity, and resolution. Data once used is not *exhausted* by that use; it can be picked up and used again for a different analysis, a different question, to access a different phenomenon, even by a different researcher from a different field. Data can become the principal merit of a scientific contribution.[13] A new source of data, a new approach to data cleaning or public availability, even treating a corpus as "data" for the first time—all become valued in their own right, rather than only for the role they play in relation to theory.

Aspirations like these, as far as anyone can tell, first gained traction outside academia and its epistemic cultures.[14] They were born, if anywhere, in the proprietary research departments of the modern tech giants, among people trained in engineering and computer science. The vast corpus of data had been pooling and accumulating for some time, particularly as large swaths of human life moved online; but no one really knew what to do with it. What seemed evident was that having a hypothesis in mind or a theory (of anything) did not seem to make it useful. What could put it to use, however, was some capital investment and machines, particularly those that could wade through the data with an algorithm sufficient to connect a seemingly infinite number of dots—to find its *structure*, that is. Little of this research looked (or looks) like conventional scientific learning in the logical-positivist mold; this fact does not matter. If the new regime has come to stand behind any principle, it is that data should be gathered and circulate freely among those who know how to use it. The practices that place restrictions on data, like characterizing bits of it as "random" or even granting the right of refusal to those whose action generates the data, must be abolished or at least hidden in very small print that nobody reads when they sign up for an app.[15]

There are many indications that, having been born outside of academia, data science is now entering the ivory tower and the business of professing. Data science programs have been founded at universities in growing abundance; to attach the word "computational" to one's approach or CV appears to generate a high probability of being published or hired for a scarce academic job like nothing else can. While we might dismiss an episodic fascination— trendiness runs thick in the history of knowledge and the academy— something is happening here, we believe, that cannot be ignored. Claims that data science will render theory obsolete or finally achieve the fabled alliance between "the two cultures"[16] warrant our skepticism. Yet, to remain oblivious in our silos to all trends associated with data science would be a tragic mistake. While the specter of data science can be haunting, particularly for the more theoretically inclined (who may only see in it a harbinger of their further marginalization or even their professional annihilation), it also presents a unique opportunity to revisit a topic that, for at least a hundred years, has been guarded by impossibly high methodological walls—though a topic that could be remarkably generative and fruitful should those walls finally come down. In our view, that opportunity concerns the meaning and use of probability.

*

Many observers would agree that data science spells changes to probabilistic reasoning in science, because it exposes significant limitations in the frequentist interpretation of probability. That interpretation of probability associates probabilistic claims with a strong necessary condition—specifically, the number of counts of a phenomenon—and it is almost exclusively focused on the quality control of a data sample. It appears in full view in the early twentieth century in the work of figures like Ronald Fisher, who, following in the line of other committed eugenicists like Francis Galton and Karl Pearson, created many of the statistical methods as we know them today, all in mad pursuit of objectivity and its political spoils[17] The quality of a data sample was essential for establishing the significance of findings in a uniquely statistical sense, and with significance came epistemic authority to generate belief.

Data science, for its part, scrambles these barometers of significance. Variables that have gone completely unnoticed or undefined using statistical significance measures become significant within massively large datasets and combed by machine-learning tools. As some critics have noticed, in its apparent displacement of trusted means of significance testing, data science also opens the door for a whole litany of new scientific evils (multiple testing, "p-hacking," etc.) that appear as a subversion of how statistics has come to be treated in science. Many fear that it has become so easy to quantitatively establish significance using data science protocols that proposals have been floated to make statistical (p-value) thresholds far stricter than they have been in the past—perhaps an opening move in a great game of forever-shrinking significance.[18] Given statistical methods' basic commitment to the frequentist interpretation of probability, these challenges to significance testing and, with it, the authority of the scientist, have provided researchers across many fields with enough reason to switch allegiance to what has traditionally been treated as frequentism's main competitor.[19]

Bayesianism, as this competitor is typically known, is historically older than frequentism, as it traces its origins back to the eighteenth-century English minister Thomas Bayes. For some, that history does not really matter. All that Bayes did was put words to a "commonsense" version of probability that everyone (these critics believe) will arrive at sooner or later. On these grounds, Bayesianism offers what some consider to be a novel approach to knowledge, rooted in relative assessments and learning as updating, dependent on neither prior facts nor posterior findings, but *both*.[20] From a Bayesian perspective, probability is entirely conditional, meaning simply that, unless we have data in hand and unless it makes us reach into the future with a belief about further data, we cannot possibly assess probability. Will more data make any difference? For Bayesians, this kind of question not only has the virtue of being straightforward and easy to understand, it is also extremely well-suited for doing science in an era of data abundance.

A Bayesian will not claim any bit of knowledge as final; it all remains provisional on further inputs. Theories are "conditional probability statements" that seek out data not to illustrate or falsify them but to *update* them.[21] Bayesianism typically places few restrictions on prediction, allowing it to take as simple a form as mapping inputs onto outputs with no explanatory hypothesis needed beforehand. Abundant data means ample opportunity to calculate a "prior estimate," or to quantify our beliefs about the future, and a "posterior estimate" becomes a sign of how much our ideas have changed.[22] Knowledge here is more akin to "permanent learning" than it is to rivals like universal law, causality, or interpretive meaning.[23] For many who are persuaded by these views, perhaps the only apparent caveat is that Bayesianism adds a thick layer of insulation between us and the world. This caveat is typically debated as the *subjectivism* of the approach. If every bit of knowledge we have serves only as a precursor to a later updating, seemingly in perpetuity, then presumably we can never reach that proverbial bedrock where we turn our spade.

Even outside statistical applications, Bayesian logic finds broader appeal in sociology these days as a general way of using theory that invites new evidence, with the goal of updating rather than confirming. The broader relevance of Bayesianism for contemporary social science ranges from its connection to the abductive practice of *surprise* to its consistency with a postcolonial critique of paradigmatic model cases and the Eurocentrism of sociology — entirely apart from its extensive computational applications.[24] To know with certainty is to feel the greatest confidence, according to the Bayesian view, and thus to experience no doubt; but perhaps that feeling comes as a result of limited data, or when we ignore what does not confirm our expectations, or when we maintain an epistemic injustice in what we count as knowledge and our conventions for obtaining it.

For our purposes, the challenge that Bayesianism presents to frequentism demonstrates just how much can change should the underlying interpretation of probability in a scientific field be altered ever so slightly. In a sense, we seek to do the same, and while we find lots of common ground with Bayesians, a certain question nevertheless sticks in our craw. If the difference between *updating* and *testing* is that whatever we might have in mind prior to engaging with new data that stands as a mediation between us and what we can only, in a sense, asymptotically approach, then probability must entail something that can *affect* our confidence in that prior belief, with us as the mostly passive partner to the exchange. The question, left unanswered by both Bayesianism and frequentism, is quite simply: *How can probability be something that could ever tell us what to believe?*

*

In the late 1970s, philosopher David Lewis found himself in a similar position.[25] Tired of epistemological debates over probability that had gone stale since Lewis's predecessor, Rudolf Carnap, had formulated the two widely agreed-upon concepts of probability ("degree of confirmation" and "frequency in the long run")[26] a generation earlier, Lewis decided to go back to the basics—all the way back, in fact, to philosopher David Hume and his famous problem of induction. For Hume, knowledge of the future presented a grave question: How can we ever be confident in what the future will be like if all we have access to is our experience of the past? Lewis deviates from the conventional treatments of Hume, however, because he does not frame his approach as a question solely about our subjective knowledge. For Lewis, Hume tells us something more objective. That we *do* know some predictive things about the world based on experience is beyond question. Lewis is primarily interested in *how* our experiential knowledge can give us that capacity in the first place.

Lewis later became famous for endorsing the (much-abused) philosophical construct of "possible worlds" as not only real but commonplace and capable of solving many problems in logic and metaphysics.[27] Here, he offers a portrait of one world, "the Humean world," in which *whatever* we might give credence to as existing (from galaxies to hearts, from bad ideas to good vibes) depends on "localized matters of particular fact" and can thus be dissected into minute points that relate to each other on the smallest distributions of space and time.[28]

Our world can be presumed to be just such a world, according to Lewis, because whatever creatures we might find living in this Humean world (let's just call them *humeans*) would be very much like us (*humans*) in several respects. These humeans would share our capacity for induction by using their sense organs to learn from experience. More generally, both human and humean need induction to survive in their respective worlds because *between* the matters of fact that comprise the bit-by-bit construction of those worlds lies *objective chance*. To cross it, human and humean must build an inferential bridge, though one that will never be quite perfect. If the next moment is just as local and particular as the current one, as Lewis suggests, it only appears as a possibility connected to us by chance. The world itself will update and restructure as we take some chances rather than others. With enough data points, an observer can minimize the departure of the past from the future and reduce the objective chance that lies between those temporal junction points in our stream of action, though even with all the world available as data to them, this observer can never make entirely error-free predictions. Lewis refers eloquently to this portrait of the world as "a vast mosaic."[29] And for both us humans and his humeans, it provides as good a depiction as any of the necessary parameters for our knowledge should *chance*, in Lewis's understanding of it, be *objective*.

In hindsight, Lewis's arguments on these points can appear prescient. Data and computing power in 1980 were minuscule compared to what is possible today. The information requirements to map out a Humean world likely seemed like the stuff of science fiction to Lewis, so he limited himself to drawing it out in principle. Yet another philosopher writing at the same time, Jean-Francois Lyotard, was willing to peer into that future.

Lyotard would associate what he calls "the postmodern condition" with the triumph of data and its complete transformation of the nature of knowledge. Lyotard is well-known for declaring the "incredulity toward metanarratives" as being the token feature of postmodernism in a philosophical and political sense; less well-known is how the decline of those grand stories—ranging from Marxism to enlightenment to progress—corresponds with the resurgence of what had remained latent all along: namely, the value of knowledge as determined strictly by a performance principle, or "performativity," which the metanarratives so consequential to the twentieth century had kept at bay. More commonly, the word "impact" condenses this understanding of knowledge today. "The growth of power, and its self-legitimation, are now taking the route of data storage and accessibility, and the operativity of information," Lyotard argued; "increasingly, the central question is becoming who will have access to the information the machines must have in storage to guarantee that the right decisions are made."[30] Knowledge becomes equivalent to data retrieval, with pedagogy a course of instruction on how to use the "terminals" that give access to it. For Lyotard, writing in 1979, "data banks are the Encyclopedia of tomorrow. They transcend the capacity of each of their users. They are 'nature' for [postmoderns]."[31]

Today, amid growing data volume, the internet of things, artificial intelligence, the prospect of quantum computing, and algorithmic/machine learning—perhaps the datafied mosaic world of Lewis, alongside Lyotard's postmodern horizon, comes fully into view. The measurement, storage, and retrieval of ever more local and particularized matters of fact occurs now on scales that would shock both Lyotard and Lewis. Perhaps they hammered out their arguments on the chunky keyboard of an Apple II—issued in 1977—working at processing speeds about 1500 times slower than that of the first iPhone. Though they appear prophetic in their anticipation of data-centricity, neither Lyotard nor Lewis can explain why big data could have a potentially revolutionary effect on knowledge. One of the first influential advocates of predictive analytics in the social sciences provides more insight on that score.

Economist Susan Athey presents the appeal and epistemic shift marked by data science in the context of a simple and practical question: How can public officials efficiently allocate a limited number of health inspectors to thousands of restaurants in a large city? It is not difficult to imagine the time and energy necessary to meet such a challenge in conditions of data scarcity (past and present). It requires a model based on details sampled from each restaurant; that sampling needs to assume that all the restaurants are comparable to each other and that the data gathered are relevant, which also requires a lot of limiting assumptions. Finally, theory is needed to establish how significant relationships in a statistical sense can conceivably allow for causal inference. Public-health officials need those causal accounts, after all, as it is upon models of causation that health inspection ultimately hinges.

As Athey argues, data abundance—and the data-centricity it affords—changes the approach quite dramatically. With big data, "the decision problem . . . [falls] squarely in the prediction domain," not the causal domain.[32] It becomes possible to work from the starting point of "knowing which establishments are more likely to have violations," and by knowing this, to establish which restaurants "should be inspected" *prior* to making any decisions about inspector allocation. As opposed to extrapolating from an average restaurant, which never exists in reality, a "more realistic setting [that] incorporates heterogeneity across units" is accessible.[33] As the data is localized and particularized, it is not limited by commonsense categorizations. Predicting a health code violation becomes, to a certain extent, possible ex ante. Algorithmic interpolation fills in sequences of initial states that terminate in a health problem. Dedicating inspections to *these* restaurants, we can feel confident that the restaurants not in this pool will only experience health code violations within the slimmest of margins.

For Lyotard, knowledge of this sort does all the things that postmodern knowledge is supposed to do, providing a clear sense of use and increasing the efficiency and speed of a system, regardless of whether the knowledge can be harmonized with human understanding or not. Performative knowledge does not have to make sense, after all. For Lewis, Athey's framework would approach what he calls the "best system" by making it possible to be "perfectly reasonable" in affording us something close to the one belief we *would* have if we were good Laplaceans and knew "all about the course of history up to now (no matter what that course of history actually is, and no matter what time is now)."[34] Both Lewis and Lyotard associate their arguments with Hume's early-modern puzzle of induction, which the modern tools of statistics have never quite been able to extinguish entirely. But in making this connection to the famous skeptic, Lewis and Lyotard unintentionally draw our attention to something that, in our view, can account for the appeal of data science, though it does not entail a strong shift to particularity and locality.

Historian Lorraine Daston has recently pointed out that sociohistorical conditions exist for the kind of induction that Hume is known for, and that we would be helped in interpreting him—and what he means for us today—by considering these conditions.[35] Despite serious doubts that we can ever understand the causes of things, Hume did think that we *can* trust our sense of the future regarding, say, the sun rising tomorrow, or even that there will be milk available in the store, even if we cannot explain how either of these things will come to pass. About other things, like whether our lottery ticket will be the winning one or whether we will stub our toe walking out our front door, induction does not seem to help.[36] For Hume to suggest a heterogeneity in approach is difficult to reconcile with the universal skepticism that is often associated with him. In Daston's view, Hume's biography is not immaterial to this paradox.

The cities (Edinburgh, London, Paris) where this bon vivant spent most of his time testify firsthand to a certain kind of predictability. Between these places, the failures of induction often become readily apparent—who, after all, could predict a collapsed bridge on the turnpike moving between towns? Yet inside them, "pockets of predictability," as Daston calls them, tend to come into existence that allow induction to work. Some pockets have a radius that extends no further than the city limits; others seem to go on forever, like "commerce" in Hume's view of it.[37] For Daston, pockets like these provide a sociohistorical grounding for Hume's sense that induction can be a reliable tool, but not about all things.[38] To see how this reliability might have something to do with an *ontic* rather than epistemic argument, consider Hume's famous example of colliding billiard balls.

Hume asks us to put ourselves in the place of an observer watching one billiard ball about to strike another. It is easy enough for us to imagine a "hundred different events" that might follow (e.g., one ball might shatter into a million pieces; both balls might stop frozen in place; one ball might shoot straight upward on contact, hitting the ceiling).[39] Yet, despite being able to imagine many possibilities, we cannot help but "give preference to one" outcome, specifically the most probable outcome. One billiard ball will strike the other, sending it in the opposite direction at roughly equal force. We do not give preference to this possibility because knowledge is important to us. We do so because we are particularly attuned to what will happen when the *action* begins.

If individual points of color, distributed in a grid-like pattern, constitute the mosaic in Lewis's mind—and seemingly the model for the "machine vision" of contemporary AI—then maybe Lewis and contemporary AI are mistaken about the mosaic, because they perceive it at the wrong distance.[40] To look from such a *close* distance—so locally and particularly—is to forget that mosaics are not actually small points of color. With the right orientation and distance, the small bits gel into wholes, complete pictures.[41] Point distributions are arrayed more irregularly; they are signs of something beyond themselves. The mosaic world we have in mind is a world where our orientation matters. As we perceive the world around us, we are constantly oriented by what it *could* be. We adjust our body. We guess the range where we *should* perceive it. Every move we make, we become aware of where we stand relative to the picture we are looking at. We seem bound by it in some strange way.

A patchwork mosaic resists the notion that data is necessarily better the more particular and local it gets. We can place high epistemic value on probability, yet we can also question whether matters of fact that come to us as the equivalent of pointillist points filling out a grid are the best route to prediction. If a large language model (LLM) can predict word sequences in any given sentence, it does not create connecting links. It only mechanically mimics them with distance metrics and weights. Word frequencies are local and particular matters of fact, which can be quite useful for training a machine to send a text message. But simply counting frequencies does not tell us about the probability of the words, which requires connecting links maintained within a range, and there is wiggle room to consider. The words are probable because of how they are produced: by a *human* text generator in coordination with expectation. Language is not a structure or a matter of use. It is a vast array of repetition.[42] What we want to know about a language is *ontologically* significant: How does it exist in this novel form, as *probability*?

To account for the world as a patchwork requires an unfamiliar style of reasoning. For starters, it requires changing what subjectivity and objectivity typically mean today. To be subjective is to be oriented toward the world in a way that does not create an expectation. "Objective" refers to what the world must be like to create expectations. The objective world, in this case, consists

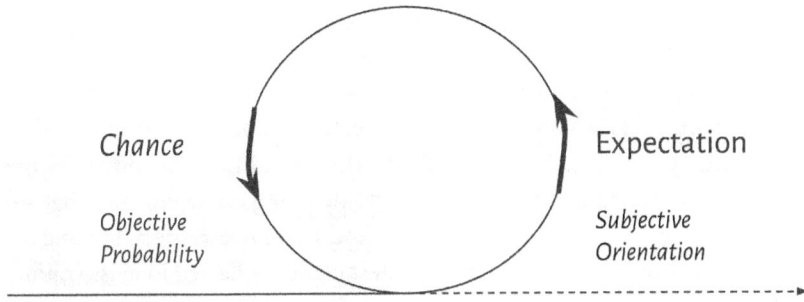

FIGURE 1. The *Chance*/expectation loop

of formations of *Chance*. We draw this unusual word from Max Weber and Johannes von Kries—two key figures in probabilism—who use it to refer to something akin to Daston's pockets of predictability, though with the caveat that all *Chance* requires an orientation—we must *loop into* it for it to exist. The state is a *Chance*, or a collection of them, according to Weber, just as much as a card game is. Both consist of action oriented by distinct probabilities. We might say the same about race, gender, capitalism, a social network— they all exist as *Chance*.

The image shown in figure 1 tries to visualize the meaning of these statements, puzzling as they may sound. Here we can find the loop depicted in which we (humans) play a critical part. *Chance* is the probabilities and possibilities that make up the objective world. Expectations loop us into *Chance*, and those expectations are adequately caused by objective probability, which means they are not subjective. The overall tendency is for expectations to match an average probability we might calculate statistically.

A *looping effect* draws *Chance* from a potential state and at the same time defines our relationship to it. A *probability order* appears from relatively uniform and consistent looping effects between expectation and *Chance*. Such orders remain persistently threatened by dissolution back into subjectivity. When that happens, or when we cannot find a *Chance* to loop into, we rely on our capacity to interpret the world and generate meaning from it, perhaps even to sew and suture it together despite the chaos it presents to us, which is different from having expectations of what the world is basically like. Interpretation is a far more contingent and discontinuous act than expectation, and for that reason one interpretation can potentially change everything, if it can stick.

We will refer to this perspective as "probabilism" because it is rooted in a novel, and some might say illegitimate, interpretation of probability, one that focuses on ontology. Here, "probability" does not refer to frequencies, nor does it refer to an updated belief as the Bayesians might claim. It does not refer to a regression equation, nor even does it refer to, as Lewis would have it, features of the world that could tell us whether what we believe about the world is right or at the very least appropriate. In this book, "probability" refers to something that actually exists in the world, something that comprises the entities we are familiar with in the world, including ourselves, and that we relate to as such. It is very much a Humean world in that respect, but one for which more local and particularized matters of fact, collected in mass volume and high velocity, will actually prohibit us from understanding in the long run. This world was familiar to sociologists like Weber and Du Bois at the turn of the twentieth century, and it would still be familiar to sociologists today if history had taken a different turn. These classical sociologists understood that the social world in particular—from whatever disciplinary perspective we approach it—is a world that stands in dire need of probabilism if we are to understand and work to change it.

*

In the pages that follow, our effort is more genealogical than programmatic. We seek answers of some kind for the following main questions: How did one interpretation of probability come to be the interpretation that rules them all? What does it mean that this interpretation has, nevertheless, been fundamentally challenged? If truth lies in the future, as Peirce once intimated, then having some sense of what that future will entail if we do not act is essential. So, what if we had a different interpretation of probability to guide us? One we can access without frequency counts or prior estimates? What does that mean, more practically, for social research? Can interpreting probability as something that exists in the world, rather than only in our calculations, make any difference?

In this book, we tell the story of probabilism, what it means, why it has been mostly forgotten, and what difference it would make if we permitted it to return. We envision our tangled prose to be more of a tool kit than an authoritative treatment or budding worldview. Readers are invited to pick up, use, interpret, and otherwise engage the concepts for themselves. If we can speak frankly, though, there are really only a couple of concepts, and one particular word, that readers might try to keep in mind even if all the rest, as is likely, should slide away.

The philology of the word *Chance* is not clear. We draw this visually striking word (always capitalized and italicized or, often following the German convention, with each letter spaced—i.e., C h a n c e) from Weber, who himself draws it from Kries. It is not clear when the word entered the German language.[43] As far as anyone can tell, it is a pidgin concoction of Anglo-French origin, with words in those languages like the English *chance* and the old French *cheance* being of much longer provenance. As we recount in chapter 2 below, the word makes sense given the way Kries used it and why he used it, particularly in conjunction with a slightly more commonplace German word, namely *Spielraum* ("play-space" or "action-space"). We are not the only ones to notice *Chance*. Weber's most recent translator, Keith Tribe, takes note of it and makes the important decision *not* to translate it into any English equivalency, as previous translators of Weber, specifically Talcott Parsons and Alexander Henderson, had done before. Anglo-German sociologist Ralf Dahrendorf noticed the integral importance of *Chance* to Weber's sociology in the late 1970s.[44] Others have taken note as well.[45] We discuss this history in chapter 3.

Worth noting here, at the start, is political theorist Carl Schmitt's appraisal of Weber and *Chance* in Schmitt's *Legalität und Legitimität* (or *Legality and Legitimacy*), a text he wrote in 1932 amid the collapse of the Weimar Republic in Germany. A few months later, Schmitt would begin his notorious alliance with the ascendent Nazi Party. Schmitt was, by any measure, a serious student of Weber, attending the last public lectures Weber gave in 1919 and 1920 and even a Saturday seminar that Weber ran. In this text, however, Schmitt calls out Weber, and the Weimar Republic's constitution that Weber helped design, precisely for the critical role it gives to *Chance*. Notably, Schmitt declares that he will not attempt to translate the word *into* German, but he associates it with the "liberal era of free competition and of *expectation*," adding that "it concerns the mixture of fortunate occurrence and conformity with law, freedom and calculability, arbitrariness and culpability, that is characteristic of this era."[46] In Schmitt's estimation, the era of *Chance* is over, and the premise of "equal chance" to possess power, which in Schmitt's view constitutes the democratic foundation of legality, has run aground on its contradictions. As Schmitt adds, "when things have really gone that far," as he believed they had in Germany in the early 1930s, "it ultimately comes down to who holds the reins of power at the moment when the entire system of legality is thrown aside and when power is constituted on a new basis."[47] The sociology of Weber, Schmitt suggests, can help us very little there, for the simple reason that "'Chance' occurs frequently in Max Weber's sociology."[48]

We mention these points here to whet the appetite for what is to come, but also to provide some (loose) definition of this key concept. Schmitt found *Chance* less beguiling than politically passé. He tried to cast it into the dustbin of history, to little avail. Still, Schmitt gives what we find to be a close approximation to what we take the word to mean. *Chance* does have a connection to expectation. It does apply to an institutional arrangement characterized by something like "equal chance." The paradoxical combinations that Schmitt mentions—of fortune with law, freedom with calculation, arbitrariness with culpability—we also find to be relatively in line with the meaning of *Chance*. But Schmitt is mistaken: The concept is not pinned to a liberalism he wished to rid the world of, though we might find *Chance* in liberal institutions. Above all, *Chance* remains integral to Weberian sociology, but it finds approximations in other sociologies, as when Du Bois called for an unhesitant sociology that would talk about "Law" and "Chance"[49] simultaneously, or later on when sociologist Pierre Bourdieu described a sociology built on the idea that "expectations tend universally to be roughly adapted to objective chances."[50]

Notably, when we engage with Charles Sanders Peirce below, it becomes clear that he does not mean the same thing by "chance" as *Chance*, but neither does it seem like Peirce simply means what a typical English sentence might mean by it, as in (perhaps suitably) "this book has no chance to convince me," or "this cluttered book seems to have come together by chance." In our view, Peirce offers something far more valuable than just an argument that admits that "chance" matters in the world. He would say something more profound—like, perhaps, that chance *is* the world. Peirce offers us a concept that he calls "continuum," which is closely tied to our perception of the world, leading us to group qualities of it together and to make predictions about things. As Peirce observes, if rolling a pair of dice "turns up sixes a thousand times running," that would still "not afford the slightest security for a prediction that they would turn up sixes the next time."[51] To say that the dice express "a general rule" is not simply a nominal or semantic expression: "A rule to which future events have a tendency to confirm is *ipso facto* an important thing, an important element in the happening of those events." Thus, the dice offer a range of outcomes. We can count them on each roll. Mere frequency will bring us little, however, if what we are after is probability. For probability lies elsewhere—in *continuum*, "in the general conditions which permit the determination of individuals," in the object-nature of the pair of dice, as *chancy*, as filled, in other words, by chance: a potential that needs a second, like us and our toss, to come into being.[52]

This book attempts to recover the intellectual tradition in which concepts like *Chance* and chance make sense, because they have shared origins and shared application today. The tradition is an old one, but it is one that is sorely needed at present to take advantage of the opportunity data science presents—an opportunity that is all too easy to mistake for something else. Probabilism will only remain alive, just as it has over many years, if scholars from varied fields and backgrounds, with different goals in mind, pick it up and use it for their own purposes. What follows, then, is not limited to one field. Our goal is to make room for the adoption of probabilism possible in the human sciences to help them find a way to remain a lively human endeavor as opposed to a mostly machinic unconscious. Readers can use what they learn here as they see fit, just as we have. Readers can skip around the following chapters as they please. If it helps, the book comes in four parts: Part I is *historical* (or genealogical, to be more precise); part II is *exegetical* (and hopefully mimetic); part III is *an intervention* (or, better, a call for collaboration); and part IV is *application* (or a discussion of the implications of probabilism for how sociologists, in particular, do what they do). There is a logic, a rhyme and reason to what follows what, but we are only wedded to rhythms, not sequences, and so should you be.

PART I

Probability and Probabilism

Take away *probability*, and you can no longer please the world; give *probability*, and you can no longer displease it.

BLAISE PASCAL, *Pensées*

What then is the future path open before Sociology? It must seek a working hypothesis which will include Sociology and Physics. To do this it must be provisionally assumed that this is a world of Law and Chance. That in time and space, Law covers the major part of the universe, but that, in significance, the area left in that world to Chance is of tremendous import. In the last analysis, Chance is as explicable as Law: just as the Voice of God may sound behind physical law, so behind Chance we place free human wills capable of undetermined choices, frankly acknowledging that in both these cases we confront the humanly Inexplicable.

W. E. B. DU BOIS, "Sociology Hesitant"

1

On the Genealogy of Probability

The conclusion which seems to follow from this is that the calculus of probabilities is a useless science, that the obscure instinct which we call common-sense, and to which we appeal for the legitimization of our conventions, must be distrusted. But to this conclusion we can no longer subscribe. We cannot do without that obscure instinct. Without it, science would be impossible.

HENRI POINCARÉ, *Science and Hypothesis*

Probability is not the product of a scientific revolution. It does not appear in a sudden burst of intellectual creativity, ex nihilo, as it were. The consensus view is that it emerges slowly; so slowly, in fact, that it is not clear what should be included as part of its history. What appears innovative in the long arc of probability typically does so only retrospectively, by historians connecting the dots later on. Those who actually did the innovating often had their sights set elsewhere. They happened to contribute to probability while they were seeking to make an argument about religious belief, say, or logic, or to give a bit of gambling advice. It is only in the nineteenth century that the historiography of probability starts to focus on the central intellectual feats that serve as a prelude to statistics.[1]

For philosopher Ian Hacking, the history of probability includes a history of statistics, but it is far from exhausted by that history. Hacking adopts an archaeological perspective to make this point, following the lead of Michel Foucault's *Order of Things*[2] and its concentration on shifts in *epistemes*, or large discursive structures that define what knowledge can be across all disciplines and that are subject to sudden, dramatic transformations. Hacking seeks to recover "the preconditions for the emergence of probability" as they help shape the "space of possible theories about probability."[3] That space initially opened by a shift in the tectonic plates underlying the European intellectual world between the fifteenth and seventeenth centuries. Most pivotally, the Catholic domination of thought ruptured, then waned.

The tenor of the period was a relaxing of absolutism and universalism. The collapse of the scholasticism of St. Thomas Aquinas and the erosion of standard epistemic practices like demonstration by deduction made revealing and abolishing "*opinio*" more difficult to do. Varied interpretations of scripture, alongside discoveries of more early Christian texts not in the Bible, would find sectarian culmination in the Reformation. For Hacking, probability, in the iteration most familiar today, is born here, in this intellectual context. Most of all, it is evidenced by the emergence of "partial signs."[4]

A partial sign is one "possessed of probability, rather than certainty." Its meaning is *discovered* (somehow) rather than given. Such a conundrum provoked a special kind of terror among those accustomed to a given or received meaning, one meant to be memorized. Now they were tasked with filling in the blank themselves. Witch hunts, the brutal violence of the Thirty Years' War, the strikingly elevated religious devotion of some Puritan sects—all unfolded in a symbolic universe haunted by the probability of signs that seemed now to require an interpretive input but unable to remove itself of the taint of arbitrariness, thus cycling easily into political intrigue, mutual accusation, and simple opportunism. It was not nihilism that encroached—we can save that for later—but rather a comparatively massive need for interpretation.

When the church realized it could not stem the tide, it conceded a workaround. Catholic "probabilism" attempted to incorporate partial signs by allowing for the possibility that one could hold a religious view or belief on "probable" rather than absolute grounds, provided some guidelines be followed.[5] First, someone better have a good question with a genuinely indeterminate or puzzling answer; that is, it must require a judgment that only a priest could make, or preferably a number of priests, or even more preferably someone higher up in the church hierarchy. Second, a person should consult more than one religious authority for answers and agree with the majority opinion. Third, if all else fails, the person should ask themselves what is most useful to believe.

In today's academicized intellectual fields, probability and interpretation are two separate pursuits; their difference is fractally replicated in core distinctions like natural versus social science, social science versus humanities, and "hard" fields versus "soft" ones. Hacking's account, as it reveals the significance of something as obscured by the passage of time as Catholic probabilism to the historical trajectory of probability, challenges this *doxa* by insisting that probability is irreducible to statistics. With the right historical lens, it becomes clear that probability and interpretation have been linked all along.

Hacking calls his approach an "archaeology" in the tradition of Foucault; but as Foucault found, archaeology cannot handle evidence that demonstrates continuity with the present.

As far as the ancient documents reveal, the Greek philosopher Aristotle knew of probability, or at least of "the probable."[6] The probable, according to Aristotle, is "what is likely to happen." It also applies to a "generally approved proposition" in more epistemic terms. Aristotle makes a further connection between what is probable and *endoxa*, which is the root word of *doxa* and is generally taken to mean "common opinion," what goes "undiscussed" or is unknowingly believed.[7] Hacking tells us that Aristotle's ideas came about "simply too long ago" to make much of them today. They are antiquarian and have no bearing on the present.[8] For historicism, the risk is always anachronism. Thus, even though Aristotle's probability can seem to mirror a frequentist versus Bayesian distinction, it *cannot* actually be doing so—that distinction would not take shape for another two thousand years. Nevertheless, Hacking must concede that Aristotle's understanding of probability *does* strike us as more straightforward than what appears between the fifteenth and seventeenth centuries. After all, it did not have to deal with the authority of the Catholic Church and bore none of the ecclesiastical controversy over probability.[9]

In this chapter, we build on Hacking's essential account but also deviate from it in a crucial respect—one that, we believe, can account for the shock of recognition we find in Aristotle, and one that can also maintain Hacking's central point about the (re)appearance of probability when and where it happened. Probability of this sort requires that we avoid making it synonymous with contemporary statistical applications. But how? Hacking's archaeology offers one way to do this. His is a history of the present, to be sure, but one in which there is no way out. We offer a different account. We put history to work on probability in order to *escape* from history.

A Genealogical Approach

In the trajectory of Foucault's thought, the shift from archaeology to genealogy reflects a diminished concern with attempting to find coherence among many different disciplinary forms of knowledge and a heightened concern with conflict, power, and subjugation, alongside multiple temporalities and forms of change.[10] Added to these concerns is a focus on the *body*.[11] Thus, to provide a genealogy will find us placing emphasis on fractures and conflict; it will also find us seeking out a kind of *naturalism*. A genealogy finds no paradigm case or essence in this regard; it only finds history. A naturalistic emphasis draws attention to continuity, leveraging the fact that in a genealogy the main characters are always embodied creatures who do not change over time, though their dispositions are called upon and activated differently. For Hacking, that continuity is achieved by making things as varied as Pascal's wager and today's multinomial regression analysis equal parts of an encompassing, discursive structure. For us, the constitutive vagueness of probability invites a different conclusion. Its history demonstrates a certain dispositional stance on the world. We cannot activate that disposition ourselves; something in the world must call it out of us.[12] At the risk of sounding grossly metaphysical, we coin a phrase for this evocation—the *will to prediction*.[13]

Through a genealogical lens, probability refers to a history of appropriations of this will, creating *means of prediction* of normative definition and application. Means of prediction have been devised from varied orientations—from the religious to the hyper-rational, from the actuarial to the scientifically racist—over the years, and for a variety of reasons up to the present day: to give gambling advice, to encourage religious belief, to argue for welfare policy, to sell insurance, to evaluate sports performance.[14] Probability is present in an accumulation of tools and applications; only indirectly does it become a focus itself.

To link signs and their interpretation to probability does not present us with an epistemic question. It should, instead, draw our attention toward ontology. On these terms, probability is what can absorb particularity and make it indistinct and predictable. Hacking coins his own phrase—"taming chance"—for this phenomenon, but he limits it to statistics. For our purposes, chance is tamed when it becomes *expectation*. An early-modern link between interpretation and probability arose from a situation haunted by the realization that some signs might *never* be interpreted and, correspondingly, that we might never know what to expect—about the "chances" of a game of dice, for instance, or more harrowingly, about our fate in some version of the afterlife. These signs pertain to outcomes that, to us, always remain equally likely.[15]

From Parlor Games to Large Numbers

In Paris in 1654, when the so-called Chevalier de Méré asked mathematician Pierre de Fermat to answer some questions about games-playing, and when Fermat turned to his friend Blaise Pascal for help, the two approached the task with mathematical confidence.[16] Their interests were atypical. The distinction between math and morality was still fuzzy, and neither Pascal nor Fermat abided by a modern distinction of objectivity and subjectivity, which, at the time, carried a different meaning than our post-Kantian understandings of them.[17] The chevalier had asked what it is reasonable for a player to do during certain gameplay scenarios, particularly those involving fairness of play. What should happen, for instance, if a game ends prematurely with one player in the lead? How should the potential winnings be divided fairly?

Pascal and Fermat, in providing mathematically rigorous answers to such questions, were not concerned with probability as a knowledge problem. For them, and presumably for the chevalier, games of chance were novel relative to most situations in life because in them players interface directly with they called "*hasard*" or what is typically translated as "chance." The dice could not be wobbly, in this case, and the cards must be uniform enough. Probability could not be found without these conditions having been met. Pascal and Fermat could assume that probability was inherent in things without a second thought, especially when those things were capable of exhibiting fairness. Thus, they made probability conditional on something like actual conditions in the world, on properties that allow for what probability needs above all; principally, the constitution of "*le hasard est égal*" (the equality of chance).[18] Regardless of what the chances are, all players must be able to *expect* them equally if the game is to allow for probability. Thus, while a game of chance may appear to Pascal and Fermat to consist simply of a set of rules, with perhaps some objects mixed in—like symmetrical dice or a uniform pack of cards—the two thinkers cast their attention on the game's equality of chance, as it is the game *as* an equality of chance that more specifically affects the players, from determining the reasonableness of their actions to deciding their impressions of fairness and justice. Likewise, only in a game where equal chances hold can Pascal and Fermat's mathematical calculations apply.

Pascal and Fermat attempt to provide a mathematical defense of predictions the players *can* make, and these possible predictions depend on states of the world outside the players' states of mind or the information they have at their disposal. Even if the players in Pascal and Fermat's games played a million hands, they would not find certain outcomes favored over others, though they would figure out what is *not* possible. Players can learn what a random result is and what falls *outside* of the game's range of possibility. For Pascal, good Catholic that he was, the fascination with these matters seems to revolve around the limits of reason.[19] In situations that present us with equal chances, the only thing we can do in response is to *wager* on the probable. In a bold bit of analogous reasoning for which he has since become famous, Pascal applies the same principles to mortal life and the existence of God, a circumstance which, as far as we can ever know, *is* of equal chance.[20] But for this analogy to be valid at all, as Pascal well understands, there must be something about our passage through this vale of tears that affects us much as a card player is affected by the game and presents us with an equal chance. In the face of such a circumstance, we cannot reason; the best we can do is have faith.

Christiaan Huygens, writing shortly after Pascal and Fermat, would argue that to play a game of "equitable chance" is to play a game that "works to no one's disadvantage."[21] Only in the context of such a game can every player have the expectation, which Huygens understood as interchangeable with hope, that every possible outcome could happen to them. This equality of expectation and the ability of expectations to be "fairly traded for one another" among players is what makes the game a *fair* game. If the aim is to calculate probabilities, the focus must be on specifying (i.e., "putting a value on") expectations for *investment* in games: "By Fair gaming [players can] procure the same Expectation."[22] For expectations to be equitable, the game itself must be structured fairly by ensuring that all possible success "depends entirely on Fortune."[23] Only when these conditions apply can the results be probable and thus lead people to invest in the game, something they could not do outside such distinct contexts. In such conditions of equal chance, people will do what they predict and thus take part in *enacting* the outcome of their predictions.

For most readers today, such arguments conjure up the hyper-rational strategies of decision theory or game theory, which rest upon the deciphering of contingencies and a cost/benefit ratio.[24] Pascal's wager, in particular, appears in a long literature pondering the intricacies of "infinite utility."[25] For us, this kind of analysis misses the forest for the trees. It picks out small nuggets of insight from these theorists, typically those available to mathematical rigor, and ignores what someone like Pascal understood clearly: that his mode of analysis can only apply once certain objective conditions are met. If Pascal applied probability in such different circumstances as mortality and parlor games, he did not do so because he sought to advocate something like the universal application of a proto–decision theory; he did so because both scenarios were available to probability, as they both feature equal chances, though not everything does. For Huygens's part, the investments players could make in games of chance were unlike the investments they could make in anything else. Their distinct *lusiones* were the appeal of games, in his view, due to the opportunities they create and how those chances afford all players "equitable expectation." Yet, an abstract and formalized decision-theoretic or rational-choice perspective, while it can absorb this chance for an individual, was not what Pascal and his ilk had in mind, at least not if such a perspective made probability entirely epistemological, and thus conditional only on certain epistemic criteria (like frequencies or averages).[26]

For historian Lorraine Daston, these classical formulations are premised on the judgments of "reasonable men" (*l'homme éclairé*), a kind of epistemic authority that will later becomes most prominent in the objectivity claimed by statisticians.[27] For classical probability theorists, however, the most logically rigorous deduction tries to read ambiguous signs in the context of gameplay. If we understand these theorists as being concerned with conditions in the world being met such that probability can *then* apply, "the reasonable man" is an abstraction—a collection of dispositions triggered in the heat of the game.[28] We will not find Pascal, Fermat, or Huygens making a clear distinction between probability and expectation. By learning what their mathematics concluded, a player could learn what to expect. Pascal, Fermat, and Huygens were not familiar with large numbers, so it is not surprising that they did not associate their version of probabilistic reasoning with a sample of data. What is more important is that they did not associate probability with anything that we could call "empirical." In classical probability, rather, practical consequences were the principal preoccupation, and to understand them you did not first need to count them.

English minister Thomas Bayes is not commonly discussed as a classical probability theorist alongside someone like Pascal, even though he lived far closer to Pascal than to us. Perhaps he is typically seen differently because Bayes appears to us as more contemporary, at least at the present moment, as he marks the "author" of a discourse whom it still pays to cite. In a pamphlet published posthumously in 1763, we can find Bayes's famous principle: "[The] probability of any event is the ratio between the value at which an expectation, depending on the happening of the event, ought to be computed and the value of the thing expected on its happening."[29] This principle is always read as the statement that makes probability conditional on expectation. Thus, the concept of probability remains undefinable without expectation, which means that no event or outcome can be *absolutely* probable. Bayes appears to have no problem conceiving of this sort of expectation as commonplace to human thinking, even calling it "common sense."[30] But what goes neglected in the Bayesian conversation is how contingent his approach is on something that does align with classical probability theorists like Pascal.

To use Bayes's example as he explains his famous principle: Suppose we find a flat table and roll a series of balls across it.[31] As we do so, Bayes argues, we can treat the first ball and where it lands as a kind of uniform distribution (i.e., a prior) that can help us assess all the rest. Thus, given the trajectories of the later balls and where they land, what does this information tell us about our initial estimate? In other words, how likely was it that that first ball would land where it did? How surprised should we be? As we roll more balls, our initial judgment will change, and it could continue changing in perpetuity so long as we keep rolling the balls.

As those who use the predictive-processing model in cognition, which we consider later in chapter 6, have noticed, Bayes is making a claim here about cognition, a surprisingly useful one. How much do we need to change our initial expectation now that the event that formed it (the initial ball rolling across the table) appears to us *to have been* (the past perfect tense is important here) either predictable or unpredictable? Such a recipe proves useful if we want to infer what the brain fundamentally does from its *own* (neural) point of view.

What goes mostly overlooked in this analysis, however, is what brings Bayes's insights into alignment with those of Pascal, Fermat, and Huygens in their presumption that probability is nothing—it can *be* nothing—without *action*. Without rolling the initial ball, we will have no prior estimate to make. Without rolling subsequent balls, we cannot update that initial estimate and form an expectation. The possession of expectation is the strong presumption made by probability theorists who associate probability with a state of belief or our sense of confidence. All inferences we can make using a comparison of prior and posterior depend on it.

Bayes himself came from a long line of nonconformist ministers who all dissented against the control of the Church of England. He is also like Pascal in that respect. While today the *subjectivism* of his approach (not unlike the decision theory in Pascal) is often highlighted, we must be careful of anachronism. Whatever "subjectivity" we find in Bayes reflects the *unconditional* approach he takes to the will to prediction, as he finds that it has no apparent need for what exists in a state of equal chance, whether it be the fate of a soul after mortal life or a hand of blackjack. Bayes's principle exhibits the will to prediction as cued much more simply by the unexpected information we receive in any given perception. In this way, he differs from Pascal, Fermat, and Huygens and has more in common with the statistics that would soon come. Yet in the attention he gives to action, Bayes is classical like them. It is Bayes's departure on this particular note from contemporary probability, including those perspectives that currently bear his name, that make him appealing to us. We will now develop this point by tracing a genealogy of frequentism as the prevailing understanding of probability across all science today.

The Splintering of Probability

Dutch mathematician Jacob Bernoulli's pamphlet *Ars cconjectandi* was published in 1713.[32] The groundwork for the frequency interpretation can be found here: measurements, counts, repeated observations—all are necessary for the "art of conjecture." Bernoulli's goal would have been recognizable to someone like Bayes. "Probability," according to Bernoulli, is a "degree of certainty . . . To make a conjecture about anything is to measure its probability; therefore, the art of conjecture, or guessing, we define as the art of measuring the probabilities of things as exactly as possible."[33] But unlike those of Bayes and the classical probability theorists, the tenor of Bernoulli's argument is not classical. Even as he searches for the art of conjecturing or guessing, he would seem to search in vain. If he sets his spade to uncover cognition—very much like the classics—he finds it, at least in a certain sense, but Bernoulli adds another layer to the will to prediction, one that will grow enormously in consequence thereafter: namely, *frequency*.

Bernoulli had no problem associating "ratio" with "numeric ratio" and making both concepts carry an empirical significance. For Pascal and Fermat, an equivalent focus would be on fairness; for Bayes, on conditionality. "Observing similar examples of the event many times," Bernoulli argues, "we ought to presume that the event will or will not occur just as often as it has been observed to occur or not to occur previously in similar situations."[34] Thus, to enhance our "subjective certainty" (or "moral certainty"), we can take a large number of observations. There are no worldly preconditions for this technique to be applicable or not. By measuring and recording events with an eye on frequency, the will to prediction can be called upon as an entirely *epistemic* engagement with the world around us. This particular art of conjecturing consists of a recommendation for *how to* conjecture. Bernoulli associates a large number of observations with an epistemic standard—the closer we get the better. One can conjecture all one likes about the future, even about that which eludes one's own personal experience, provided one grounds one's conjectures in sufficiently observed frequencies.

We can see the beginnings of a symbolic power in Bernoulli's prescriptions, claimed now on the grounds of *how to predict*. Gone are the associations of chance (*hasard*) with action; gone too is conditionality, or Bayes's non-absolutism. In lieu of calling upon an authority to interpret partial signs, *frequency* takes over from an objective side. On this new basis, probability will eventually be enshrined as authoritative knowledge by removing any link to interpretation. However, as prediction becomes contained in statistical models, the Bayesian outlook, as we will see, makes a comeback. First, however, Bernoulli's early limit theorem, his law of large numbers, will need to be turned into objectivity.

Turning Frequency into Objectivity

An important entry at this point in the genealogy is the eminent French physicist Pierre Simeon de Laplace and particularly his philosophical essay on probability.[35] Laplace thought he was simply summarizing what had become conventional wisdom at this point, over a hundred years since Bernoulli and a little over sixty since Bayes. Laplace puts probability in the context of a grand failure of the species, specifically our ignorance: "Present events are connected with preceding ones by a tie based upon the evident principle that a thing cannot occur without a cause which produces it."[36] This tenet is what Laplace calls the "principle of sufficient reason." If this principle did not apply in all cases—if, for instance, we were to find "two positions with exactly similar consequences" and see one move without the other also moving—then we would have seen an "effect without a cause," and we would have to erroneously posit the decisive role of "choice" in the phenomenon. Laplace dismisses this stance as mere ignorance: "We ought to regard the present state of the universe as the effect of its anterior state and as the cause of the one which is to follow."[37]

Taking astronomy as his principal paradigm, Laplace makes probability "relative, in part to this ignorance, and relative to our knowledge."[38] For many, the combination signals his Bayesianism, which Laplace had become familiar with sometime after 1781, when his colleague Richard Price, Bayes's literary executor, brought it to France. Laplace therefore insists that we start from a stance of "equal possibility" and proceed to collect data until we can go no further—presumably arriving at a point when "all the cases" we might care to observe are "favorable to [the] event" and we no longer find ourselves in a state of "indecision" among the possibilities.[39] Laplace follows the classical probabilists in referencing a game of chance, though he does not share their ontic focus nor their apparent epistemic-democratic leanings. Laplace's focus is entirely epistemological, by contrast, and also authoritative, defining probability as relative to this state of ignorance rather than to knowledge, thus opening the door for him to use probability as a tool for distinguishing good from bad knowledge—a task he was perfectly willing to do.[40]

A key ambiguity in his formulation arises, however, when Laplace begins to explain his reasons for placing such emphasis on "equal possibility." The calculator of probability requires some safety in the assumption that what they calculate involves events or cases of the same thing. For Laplace, this commonality is straightforwardly defined: "The theory of chance consists in reducing all the events of the same kind to a certain number of cases equally possible, that is to say, to such as we may be equally undecided about in regard to their existence."[41] To use his example, if we want to calculate the speed of Jupiter relative to Saturn, and we notice an irregularity in what we expected to find, this observation would make us "undecided." Waves of possibility would then crescendo in our head. Eventually we would realize that, among the possibilities we have entertained, the passage of Halley's Comet most closely aligns with our expectation of what *should* happen should it, in fact, be the cause of that effect.[42]

Laplace uses the example to further insist upon probability as a lesser knowledge that we must settle for given our state of inevitable ignorance. But what he introduces here assigns a positive value to ignorance—it is what evokes the will to prediction, which here becomes manifest in our effort to arrive at the possibility that we can finally account for our defeated expectation and the ambiguous signs that arise as a result. Because Laplace makes the notion of equal chances provisional, they are only a necessary step on the way to a larger epistemic goal, particularly if the process is to start from a wide range of possibilities and slowly narrow them down to the right one. Such narrowing is what Laplace would emphasize as "succession" and what would eventually come to be labeled as the "rule of succession," which is a bedrock for inferring probability in an unknown domain based on what we have already observed, assuming that all possible inputs are potentially responsible for or predict the results we have observed.[43] If we believe our observations are equally possible relative to another event, then we can at least entertain the idea that whatever happened could have gone another way or could have had different antecedents. For Laplace, reaching a "true possibility" means something pretty close to finding yourself in a state of utter certainty.

The reasoning here is essentially Bayesian, which means that to be "equally undecided" is an epistemic problem. Laplace takes some time at this point in his argument to criticize magic and astrology.[44] They are only believable as a bow to authority, but what is worse for Laplace is that magic and astrology predict (and thus mystify) based on *single cases*. In this regard, it is not hard for us to believe that what happens to us, individually, is "miraculous," and it would probably not take us very long to find an astrologer who would gladly confirm the premonition. For Laplace, such belief is a grievous error, however, and for a specific reason. In such cases, we have allowed for no state of indecision about the event and no equal possibility. If we assume miracles, the only indecision we face is between what happened and what could have *never* happened. We will likely find that, far from being miraculous, the event was typical or *average*; all we needed to do was situate it in the right range of equal possibilities. Experience alone could never teach us to do so, and so the effect is to render highly questionable what we can learn by concentrating on the single cases and events that appear to constitute our lives.

Laplace's approach to probability did not rest on averages or means (*moyenne*); probability was not even critical to his picture of the world, for which uncertainty only stood as a statement of ignorance. In hindsight, such a perspective is extraordinary, as to calculate an average has since become treated as a statement of relative certainty rather than quantified ignorance. Such a calculation also constitutes likely the primary scenario today in which to invoke the will to prediction. To present an average chance to someone whose own fate might be implicated in it—such a calculation can make them orient to chance in a way they had never considered before. Presented with its version of equal chances, they begin to predict. Laplace seems to have understood the novelty of this impression. He appreciates the difference between calculating probability in the "moral sciences," which for him included jury testimony and democracy among its range of topics, and doing the same in the "natural sciences." Such a distinction was not all that common prior to this point, though it would become so in the years to follow, fueled in no small part by recommendations that Laplace was prepared to make.

As Laplace would boldly proclaim: "Let us apply to the political and moral sciences the method founded upon observation and upon calculus, the method which has served us so well in the natural sciences."[45] Such a proclamation came with an evident purpose in mind: to allow those who can use probability to warn us against "sudden changes which in the moral world as well as in the physical world never operate without a great loss of vital force."[46] During Laplace's life, France lost a monarchy, saw the political reinvention of time in the Brumaire, and witnessed the rise and fall of that "world-historical" figure whom Laplace taught the finer arts of projectile-arc calculation when the pupil was a young artillery officer—Napoleon Bonaparte.[47] Probability as tool of sober-minded caution, useful in tempering dreams of total revolution, has remained ever since. It was not Laplace, however, who would pursue this thread the furthest.

Ambitious Belgian astronomer Adolphe Quetelet's arrival in Paris and his meeting with Laplace at the Paris Observatory in December 1823 are consequential events in any history of probability. There, Quetelet absorbed what he had come to learn: how to construct an observatory, as he had gotten approval from the city fathers of Brussels to build one of their own. But he also absorbed probability, or at least Laplace's version of it, as Quetelet tailed the great man of science around. Quetelet would become the most dedicated disciple of Laplace, in particular pursuing the Frenchman's suggestion that the moral sciences could (and should) be rooted in probability calculations, just as much as in a field like astronomy. In the ornate surroundings of the observatory (built originally by Louis XIV and not yet decimated by fire), Quetelet became convinced of this possibility, and the ever inquisitive and ambitious

Belgian would make a further connection that would prove even more consequential.

The kind of limit theorem Laplace proposed could be reached only in one
way: the Bernoullian way of *frequent observation*. On these grounds, Quetelet
would propose a representational view of data as constituted by observations
of the world that, should we record them with enough frequency, can yield
an accurate picture of a phenomenon as it occurs within a distribution. Laplace did not pay much attention to averages. The "avalanche of numbers,"
of government-collected and -recorded statistics—particularly about biopolitical matters of population—had not yet occurred. When it did, Quetelet
would embrace the idea that anything counted often enough had one such
central tendency; single cases were little more than sites for variable attributes and the individuals who exhibit them. For Quetelet, the life and times of
l'homme moyen ("the average man") is the most integral bit of knowledge we
can obtain by following Laplace's decree to make moral science probabilistic,
and what this knowledge can provide us with warrants a new name and a new
scientific field: *physique sociale* ("social physics").[48]

With Quetelet, then, we move from the notion of frequency as *normal*
or normative, as found in Bernoulli's art of conjecturing, to frequency as the
royal road to *objectivity*—from frequency as good reasoning to frequency as
definitive knowledge. As probabilistic inference standardizes individual cases,
Quetelet unveils a reality beyond them,[49] coinciding with the "avalanche of
numbers," which was significant in one sense and incidental in another.[50]
Quetelet did not necessarily need large numbers to see the world as a normal
distribution. But because they provided such an immense volume of observations, about all manner of things, Quetelet and his followers were only too
willing to take up the invitation to apply his tenets to anything they could,
no matter how morbid or "immoral" the subject matter, making it seem as if
everything *could*, at least in principle, be predicted.[51] And because they did
so, their efforts sufficed for those less knowledgeable of their techniques with
satisfaction for a kind metaphysical longing: from predictions made of all
phenomena in the world to the world itself operating on a predictable course,
as evidenced by history.

Such a perspective helped coin the word "determinism" as an early iteration of what we mentioned at the start of this book—what Ernst Cassirer
calls "the Laplacean spirit."[52] Only in mid-nineteenth-century determinism, according to Cassirer, is the spirit made real. For Laplace himself, the
prospect of total knowledge was a limit. We humans could never reach it
due to our incurable ignorance. Nevertheless, the prospect of total knowledge helps us learn by exposing the difference between what we would like

to know and what we do know. That is the "critical" version of determinism. With Quetelet and the response to his efforts, determinism becomes far more metaphysical—a window directly onto the world. Something like "law," and what we understand of it, is not a concept that only serves to reveal how much we don't know. It becomes, rather, a property of the universe itself.

Englishman Henry Buckle would popularize Quetelet's principles in this way in his widely read *History of Civilization in England*, two volumes of which Buckle was able to publish before his premature death in 1862, at the age of forty-one.[53] His texts, which were translated into multiple languages, enjoyed a wide influence. Marx almost certainly read Buckle and from him took to reading Quetelet largely through Buckle's eyes. Quetelet would thereafter have a palpable, if seldom acknowledged, influence on Marx's analysis of capitalism.[54] Quetelet's influence on Durkheim was more direct.[55] The attraction to Quetelet's mean predictions is not simply epistemic; rather, substantive inferences about what is sui generis, "socially average," or appears to follow historical "laws of development" all reveal some debt to Quetelet.

In 1866, English logician John Venn would offer what was, and for some still is, the authoritative treatment of frequentism in his influential *The Logic of Chance*.[56] On these grounds, Venn finds himself largely in agreement with Quetelet, though he expresses some skepticism about inferences made on the basis of an "*homme moyenne*." Venn objects more strongly, however, to something that Marx and Durkheim did not find similarly objectionable in Quetelet. In fact, Venn is created with coining a phrase for it: calling it "Fatalism or Necessitarianism." Using a similar diagrammatic logic as the one that bears his name, Venn argued that for statistical prediction to be fatal would require that "antecedents and consequences, in the case of our volition . . . be supposed to be very nearly immediately in succession . . . whereas in statistical enquiries the data are often widely separate, if indeed they do not apply merely to signal groups of actions or results."[57]

Venn credits Quetelet with establishing probability as a measurable property of the world. Yet in his accusation of fatalism, Venn picks up on the key question at the interface of probability's objectivity and *our* subjectivity. The equivalence of probability and frequency is controversial to those unaccustomed to large numbers.[58] If crimes and suicides appear with regularity in a statistical sense, in an experiential sense they are singular cases that stand out *against* regularity. Suppose we can use the facts compiled over the last several years to predict what will happen in the coming year. Would prediction in this case eradicate moral freedom, or would knowing a statistical rate help to enhance it?

It is not surprising that it was in Germany that Venn's premonition went the furthest, and Venn himself would come around to seeing his own interpretation of probability as most closely in line with the probabilism that appears from Germany and questions the statistical absorption of probability.[59] By "retaining a scientific worldview," Queteletian statistical facts put objective stock in the patterns revealed. As a challenge to moral freedom that became apparent only in single cases, however, this reduction of "lawful" claims to regularities made the meaning of statistics opaque. As some would ask: "What is the *object* of statistical reasoning?"[60]

Laplace never concerned himself with such a question. Meanwhile, Quetelet thought he had found the answer in the "average man." Durkheim mostly agreed with him, seeing the average as the embodiment of the externally constraining "social fact" that did not require translation into common sense. As Gabriel Tarde noted around the same time, however, for sociologists to hand their ontology over to Quetelet would be disastrous, as doing so would lead sociologists to make the same mistake as the Belgian astronomer's social physics in assuming that single cases imitate each other because certain variable factors "spread instantaneously" through them all.[61] Tarde predicted that this mistake would lead sociology to forget the elemental social fact that all a statistical average can only tell us about is what *happens* in single cases. If we persist in incorporating probability in statistical models, then surely, in Tarde's view, sociologists must also attempt to find probability in the single case. Quite the contrary has transpired, however; sociologists have typically treated single cases as radically anti-probabilistic.

The Subjective and the Objective

It was not until a few decades into the twentieth century that associating frequency with objectivity became commonplace across the sciences. Applied mathematician Richard von Mises, for example, uses an example from Laplace to demonstrate the relationship. He asks us to imagine that we are playing a game of cards that requires us to draw fourteen cards at random. Each card features one letter of the alphabet.[62] When we do this, we are astonished to learn that our fourteen randomly drawn cards spell out the word "Constantinople." For Mises, we would assume correctly that "something utterly improbable" has happened. But why? The answer is simple but also demonstrates, for Mises, that any consideration of *improbability*—let alone probability—is illogical without some reference to frequency. Randomly drawing fourteen cards that yield gibberish occurs with far more *frequency* than drawing fourteen that spell out "Constantinople."[63] Because the *lack* of frequency is measurable, we should not expect to draw such a combination of cards—that is, its "objective probability" is low.[64]

To Mises, probability had become a branch of mathematics, a development that led him to restrict its application significantly from even Venn's application of it. Mises did not believe probability could be applied in social science, for instance, because the observation of frequency would be necessarily distorted. The cases could not be similar enough to be called repetitions, which are necessary to make up what Mises calls "a collective" or "attribute space."[65] A drawing of cards is capable of that kind of homogeneity, and thus, Mises can use his example. For Mises, the sheer quantity of repetitions, or what he calls "place selection," is all that can revise our initial sense of chance *into* probability, which in this case is made entirely equivalent to a limiting frequency, or the ratio that will be asymptotically approached should we observe or engage in a repetitive action a large enough number of times.

As Mises made these arguments for connecting probability with frequency, the mathematical ground had been prepared by Soviet mathematician Andrey Kolmogorov and the axioms he derived for probability.[66] Mises unproblematically associates frequency with probability in part because doing so makes probability mathematically tractable; but he also does so because he understands frequency to be en route to objectivity. For Mises, objectivity appears to be associated strictly with *authority over belief*. Probability surpasses chance, a distinction that, in Mises's view, evidently mirrors the distinction between subjectivity and objectivity. The subjective, here, is wholly associated with a limitation on inference.[67]

Mises was not alone in positing this dichotomy or its hierarchy. The same version of objectivity had been prepared by earlier statistical probabilists, among them the famous triumvirate of Francis Galton, Karl Pearson, and Ronald Fisher. It is relevant for the genealogy of probability that the three were prominent eugenicists, with Galton coining the term and establishing the Galton Laboratory, which bore the original title of "Eugenics Research Office," and at which first Pearson and then Fisher would assume the mantle of chief researcher. Galton coined the term "regression," which for him bore a very particular concrete meaning: "regression to the mean" of human characteristics after multiple generations of miscegenation. While the average man was the "purest" type for Quetelet, that version of *homme* became the embodiment of a middling mediocrity in the population in Galton, Pearson, and Fisher's view.[68] To associate probability with the "study of populations" takes some mental gymnastics if we also want to include coin flips and measurement errors. The association derives from eugenics, and it has stuck around ever since.[69]

For reasons that are not unrelated to these politics and that are not at all surprising, Galton, Pearson, and Fisher showed particular disdain for any insistence on a subjective element in probability, casting shade on its proponents and setting up institutional roadblocks for the advancement of those suspected of believing it. These efforts were so effective that Bayesian approaches remained scientifically marginalized for the next several decades.[70] Galton, Pearson, and Fisher appear so insistent on the connection of frequency with objectivity not because this connection constituted anything like a next step in the history of probabilistic reasoning. No one before them had made it, not even Venn, who shared with them the strong assumption that probability *is* frequency. Indeed, venturing into objectivity appeared contradictory to most probability theorists in the past, insofar as they retained a Laplacean view of probability as inferior to determinism.[71] Objectivity in the particular form favored by Galton, Pearson, and Fisher appears fueled by "cognitive interests" that were not prepared by the genealogy of probability to that point. Those interests were consistent, rather, with a move toward professionalization and a claim of expertise, as part of their attempt to bolster a racist eugenics policy with a transfer of scientific capital into the political field, a transfer that made "objectivity" pivotal as demonstration of authoritative knowledge.[72] The objectivity of statistical claims coincided with this professionalizing project, as rooted in establishing a stronghold over prediction that, at least since Quetelet, was understood to have significant political stakes.

The structure that frequentism gave to data provided its own way of generating and then resolving uncertainty—a way that could be broadly convincing to the structured interests of politicians but also to the public at large: both audiences untrained in the discourse of statistics. Such a "trust in numbers" appeals to the highly structured language of math to generate knowledge apparently "removed from the individuality of its makers."[73] In an important sense, then, "the higher the stakes became, the more statistics became reliant on sampling probabilities (the predictive facts, measurable by frequencies)."[74] Frequency must stand for probability if such statistical artifacts as the normal curve distribution can claim to represent something socially *normative* in their mathematical structure. For Fisher, in particular, who arguably took the link between probability and eugenics the furthest, the manner in which probability engaged with uncertainty or ignorance, only to absorb it, was only possible on the basis of frequency counts, and thus any rebuttal to the conclusions of a statistical analysis that did not rely on the same tool kit could be dismissed out of hand as lacking the knowledge necessary to make any claim at all:

> It has often been recognized that any probability statement, being a rigorous statement involving uncertainty, has less factual content than an assertion of certain fact would have, and at the same time has more factual content than a statement of complete ignorance. The *knowledge* required for such a statement refers to a well-defined aggregate, or population of possibilities within which the limiting frequency ratio must be exactly known. The necessary *ignorance* is specified by our inability to discriminate any of the different sub-aggregates having different limiting frequency ratios, such as must exist.[75]

In this logic, frequencies must be "reasonably thought of" as revealing "an objective probability, independent of the state of our evidence."[76]

Even before Fisher made this claim about objective probability, Galton had already taken this same conflation of the tools of logic for the ways of the world perhaps as far as it could go. His Quincunx mechanism (or "Galton board") is a telling artifact of this period in the genealogy of probability: a pinball-like apparatus featuring a pyramidal array of pegs; balls are dropped in from the top and bounce around stochastically as they cascade downward; at the bottom, the balls "normally distribute" by collecting in vertical channels. Here, Galton quite literally *reifies* the normal distribution in a physical mechanism.[77] Echoing the fascination of Quetelet with averages, he demonstrates his own obsession with normal distributions as a recurring pattern in nature and society, everywhere to be discovered with enough collected observations. These distributions appeared to him as nothing less than a "cosmic order."[78]

From these efforts to use probability as a staging ground for authoritative knowledge, frequencies become a royal road to validity and warrantability. In its leverage of "objectivity," this paradigm is impossible to separate from epistemic authority, which keeps in place the version of probability invoked in a political context as scientific capital—authority on what is real and true, at least when you want to prove your point. With the authority of large-N observations over a single case, frequentist probability becomes a tool for demonstrating the hard limits of unassisted human cognition.[79] Such enthronement was responded to just as we would expect of something rooted not in consensus but symbolic power. A heterodox position would entail not associating probability with frequency. To take such a position is to tempt illegitimacy, forcing those perspectives adhering to different interpretations to adapt or else invite contradiction.

John Maynard Keynes's *Treatise on Probability* is a good example. The book was mostly written when Keynes was a student in the early twentieth century, and it was linked to a fellowship application that Keynes ultimately failed to get. It reveals an odd deference to the frequentists, even though Keynes obviously disagrees with them. Thus, "all probabilities must be based on statements of frequency," Keynes argues, though he goes on to reject the idea of "probability as being identical with statistical frequency."[80] To make such a contradictory case, Keynes demonstrates a common tactic in the resistance to the authoritative objectivism of frequencies. The tactic is to cede objectivity to the frequentists, essentially let them have it, and to alternatively double down on the *subjectification* of probability as either a mostly epistemic property (like a propositional claim) or a highly personal trait (like a sense of risk or gamble).

Thus, for Keynes, probability consists of the "proportion of true propositions in a *class*."[81] How "truth-frequent" are some propositions relative to others in a class? According to Keynes, the "fundamental tenet of a frequency theory of probability is . . . that the probability of a proposition always depends upon referring to some class whose truth-frequency is known within wide or narrow limits." Thus, he regarded probability as "the degree of belief which it is *rational* to entertain in given conditions, and not merely with the actual beliefs of particular individuals, which may or may not be rational."[82] The conflation of frequencies with probabilities by the eugenicists made geophysicist Harold Jeffreys even more insistent on the strict epistemic nature of probability. He would argue for a view of probability as a "reasonable degree of belief" that is, strictly following Bayes, always to be considered conditional on some prior possession of relevant information. In his words, "because $P(p|q)$ depends on both p and q it cannot be an objective statement, since different persons with different knowledge would assess different probabilities of p. . . . The probability of a proposition irrespective of the data has no meaning and is simply an unattainable ideal."[83] His colleague E. T. Jaynes regarded objectivity as a possible goal of probability, though any impression of objectivity could only be decided on a kind of consensus or convergence in belief: "Our goal is that inferences are to be completely 'objective' in the sense that two persons with the same prior information must assign the same prior probabilities."[84] Jaynes understood the difficulty of pursuing what he called an "objective Bayesianism," seemingly a contradictory combination, as "there is no single universal rule for assigning priors—the conversion of verbal prior information into numerical prior probabilities is an open-ended problem of logical analysis."[85]

For Keynes, Jaynes, and Jeffreys, then, frequencies could lead to the prob-

ability *of* truth and reasonability, which to them situated probability somewhere between an epistemic principle and logical tool. A personalist approach to the same question introduced different psychological mechanisms
in the space between information and belief, ones that we might consider
irrationalist by nature. Economist Leonard Savage would argue that what we
call "probability" is essentially a reference to "the *confidence* that a particular
individual has in the truth of a particular proposition."[86] Thus, two people
"faced with the same evidence may have different degrees of confidence in
the truth of the same proposition . . . and only by interrogating [themselves],
not by reference to the external world."[87] Likewise, for Italian actuary Bruno
de Finetti, the only true indicator of a probability is our willingness to take a
risk or *make a bet* based on it.[88] Probability calculation can only help render
explicit what, in this sense, remains a personal state of mind, which combines
some information, like frequency counts, but which draws this information
together with something more ineffable: "We could be guided by the hope
of a risky gain and risk everything, or we might prefer the modest tranquil-
ity of those who feel safe from the tricks of fortune. We are perfectly free
with regard to this choice; everyone can do as he wishes. The probability calculus cannot say we are right or wrong."[89] For his part, Finetti offers a bold
proclamation (in all caps): "PROBABILITY DOES NOT EXIST." On grounds
of an ontological nihilism, Finetti compares belief in the objective existence
of probability to belief in "phlogiston, the Cosmic Ether . . . even Fairies and
Witches . . . Probability, too, if regarded as something endowed with some
kind of objective existence, is no less a misleading misconception, an illusory
attempt to exteriorize or materialize our true probabilistic beliefs."[90]

Whether these subjectivists claim allegiance to Bayesianism or not, they
all come to agree that *we* (the knowers) need probability to feel confident in
our belief or safe in our risk, or to achieve truth in our proposition. For the
frequentist, it is our *data* that needs probability in order for it to be trust-
worthy and significant rather than error-prone and random, but also to allow
it the features that generate scientific capital for use in the political field. From
one perspective, it remains unclear how "probability comes to us, and charges
our models with something explanatorily vital." From the other perspective,
a probabilistic model pertains merely to how data was generated when tested
against a "known probability procedure" and found to be significant according to its parameters.[91] And yet how, as some have asked, can the "noise of
the world" be smoothed into something like a probabilistically distributed
outcome? If we don't do it *ourselves*, if this is not what our *data* does, then
what does?[92]

The Present Situation

In one sense, our genealogy of probability must culminate at this point. Activation of the will to prediction remains largely contained to these parameters and within these options. On the one hand, frequentist statistics is alive and well, fully capable of finding probability, even in absence of any apparent causal relationship or observable agency, a problem all too familiar to a generation of sociologists.[93] The will to prediction here operates in the absence of uncertainty. Among other consequences, this certainty ties us to the state, to insurance companies, and even to our own (*amor fati*) seemingly predetermined fates. As Venn would point out: While it is "quite true I have only the opportunity of dying once myself . . . [if] I am a member of a class in which deaths occur with frequency [then] I form my opinion upon evidence drawn from that class."[94]

On the other hand, the subjectivist camp, and specifically Bayesianism, has broadened the horizon of what is typically considered uncertain, or risky, as based on the premise that, if such an evaluation is probabilistic, it must be subjective.[95] With the will to prediction unleashed, a thousand new consumer products appear whose sellers are only too willing to provide a sense of assurance in the face of risk—in exchange, of course, for money.[96] Prediction markets are flourishing, providing a perfect place to demonstrate your sense of risk and confidence (and bravado).[97] But as new as some of these developments seem, the present situation is not all that much different from what Savage took note of in 1954 as he was writing a textbook in part to revive Bayesian reasoning.

Developing a point first raised by French physicist Henri Poincaré, Savage would observe that while "it is unanimously agreed that statistics depends somehow on probability . . . as to what probability is and how it is connected with statistics, there has seldom been such complete disagreement and breakdown of communication since the Tower of Babel."[98] It might seem like we can safely ignore this puzzle, that business can proceed as usual without a clear answer to the "what is probability" question. Or, if we find that we *need* to answer it, we can just say "frequency." Either of these options would be sufficient if probability had nothing to do with the world, if it were merely epistemic, and if the will to prediction could simply be activated unconditionally, in whatever way *we* see fit.

That Savage goes back to Poincaré is fitting in this regard. In the latter's 1903 book *Science and Hypothesis*, we can find an attempt to reconcile subjective and objective probability. To Poincaré, subjective probability is defined most of all by the "necessity of *action*," while the most characteristic feature of objective probability is the *absence* of action.[99] The two are fundamentally different in this regard, though also intimately entangled. Poincaré is famous for proposing what would later be called the "law of arbitrary function," in which he puzzled over the apparent lack of connection between initial states and outcomes even within a deterministic mechanism like an engine.[100] He concluded that only action could be responsible for introducing probability into the system, and for Poincaré this point made probability essential to any mode of scientific reasoning. In this form, probability does not, then, constitute a foolproof way to reduce uncertainty, nor is it a way of determining whether some bit of reasoning or decision-making is truly *rational*.

Poincaré's perspective is not easy to reconcile with the branch of the family tree described in the last section. Regardless of which side one takes, either branch requires a firm adherence to a distinction between subjective and objective, placing the interpretation of probability inside these pincerlike jaws. The two sides meet every so often, though always acrimoniously—in so-called statistics wars, the most recent iteration of which has concerned significance testing.[101]

On a different side of the family tree, a different perspective lies, one that some have drawn into connection with Poincaré's arguments, as the interpretation of probability from this side of the family tree does not quite fit the subjective-versus-objective, epistemic-versus-aleatory, Bayesian-versus-frequentist dichotomies. From this branch, thinkers have gazed skeptically at the quantification and mathematization of probability. They have made arguments that constitute a rejection of what was learned about probability from the "avalanche of numbers." They have marked instead a partial return to the lessons of Pascal and Huygens, who understood probability to be contained and located within the parameters of a game of chance (or the Christian game of life). Thinkers from this branch of the family tree have focused on figuring out the ontology that probability claims need in order to work. This focus has not, however, taken these thinkers in the metaphysical direction pursued by Quetelet and Buckle after him.

Thus, along a third branch in the genealogy of probability, we can find a cousin to both Bayesianism and frequentism: *objective probability*. Unlike its family members once removed, objective probability does not give in to the nineteenth-century tendency to deontologize chance, nor does it move probability out of statistical models and into our own heads or personalities. Two probability theorists can help us understand this omitted chapter in the genealogy of probability: Johannes von Kries and Charles Sanders Peirce.

2

Introducing Objective Probability

And so we come now to the other basic idea to be introduced here. It begins with the
fact that lawful regularity does not cover the real world in all its entirety and in all its
particulars. Rather, the conduct (the action) of things in the real world is not subject to
lawful regularity in every respect; some conduct is discernible only in the concrete. We
need to distinguish nomological from ontological determinants of the action of things
in the world.

JOHANNES VON KRIES, *Principles of the Probability Calculus*

The meanings of "subjective" and "objective" that hover over modern probability theory ultimately derive from the Laplacean formulation visited in the
last chapter. Laplace himself never used those terms, though. He could not
have, at least not in a way we would be familiar with today, as at the time
of his essay, subjective and objective meant nothing particularly philosophical. This situation would soon change.[1] The irony is that the philosopher Immanuel Kant, who more than anyone has given "objective" and "subjective"
their contemporary meanings, himself had pretty definite thoughts about
probability, though in comparison with Laplace, Kant remains the minor figure.[2] For Kant, "in the case of probability . . . the ground of holding-to-be-
true is *objectively valid*." Unlike, "plausibility," probability "lies in the object
itself; in the thing that is to be cognized."[3] For probability to be objectively
valid means that it allows us to make a "disjunctive judgment" in which two
propositions are related not by "logical sequence" but because they both "occupy a part of the sphere of possible knowledge; all of them together occupy
the full sphere."[4] Here, Kant elaborates what it means for probability to lie in
the object, such that it is capable of *affecting* a theory.[5] If the source of probability is epistemic, then a frequency count or a prior/posterior estimation can
establish it. But if the source of probability lies *within* the object, then for Kant
it must reveal the object's "objective possibility."

When we come now to consider the two probability theorists who will frame our discussion in this chapter, we will see that they took a more Kantian route with respect to the objectivity of probability. In doing so, they planted the seeds of an approach to probability that is different from either frequentism or Bayesianism. Johannes von Kries and Charles Sanders Peirce agree with Kant that human knowers are not always or inevitably in a state of indifference about the world, even if they cannot claim to fully know it.[6] It is all a question, rather, of how the world is probabilistically configured. While the nineteenth-century avalanche of numbers made everything "teem with frequencies," Kries and Peirce took a more skeptical approach, ultimately arguing that we must separate probability from statistics, from applied mathematics, and even from quantification altogether, if we want to know how it is possible to be oriented to the world with a certain amount of confidence, absent any definitive way of knowing it. In doing so, they would radically rethink the role of frequencies, statistical significance, and modeling in the scientific endeavor.

A Different Route to Probability

That two figures as different as Kries and Peirce, who knew nothing of each other's existence as far as we can tell, would both be led toward a similar approach to probability is not as much of a surprise once we dig into the details. They followed similar paths. Both became interested in probability not by visiting the government statistics office but in the course of their own data-driven research. For Kries, a physiologist who would likely be considered a neuroscientist today, the inspiration came from medical research, which was just beginning the large-scale use of controlled trials, their reliance on statistical inference, and how this inference compared with the seasoned expertise of practiced physicians.[7] Kries was particularly concerned that the results of clinical trials would supersede the judgment of doctors working with patients by effectively preventing them from noticing case-by-case differences in favor of high-frequency results.[8] For Peirce, the concern was much the same, though it had nothing to do with medicine. His interests in probability were piqued mostly by his experience in astronomical measurement and coastal surveying.[9] Both endeavors demanded such extraordinary precision that Peirce began to ponder the nature of anything being *truly* particular and what it means for a measurement to be precise in a world of process and change.

Beyond these practical concerns, Kries and Peirce were also strident skeptics regarding the issue of psychological measurement, specifically the version that Gustav Fechner had proposed in the 1860s that concerned "just-noticeable differences."[10] Fechner claimed to show that our perceptual capacity to notice differences had a logarithmic relation to the world, which essentially meant that we sense difference in the brightness of light, the loudness of noise, or the intensity of heat in proportion to its stimulus. The more particular the stimulus is, the more *noticeable* it is, and its particularity may be due to something like its apparent rarity (i.e., provoking surprise). Fechner seemed to demonstrate that our capacity to notice these differences revealed an objective, measurable, and systematic (e.g., "logarithmic") relation to the world as a natural fact, regardless of what our prior expectations are.

Peirce agreed with much of what Fechner claims, finding that the "feeling of belief" is related to the "expression of the state of facts which produces the belief" via Fechner's law.[11] This formulation, we would suggest, is ultimately the source of Peirce's concern with abduction, although he had not yet fleshed that idea out fully as a general theory of scientific epistemology. Peirce would go on to try his hand at psychophysical research, developing arguably the most experimental version of psychology at the time.[12] What he found was a little different from Fechner, however, and more generally different from what provoked concern, especially in astronomical observation, over what were referred to as "personal errors" or "personal equations," and how they appeared to contradict the possibility of coherent measurement.[13] If, according to Fechner, the best we can do in terms of registering differences—and how some might be more similar to each other than to others—is the Gaussian or normal distribution, Peirce found that it was possible to actually *improve* our observations (i.e., our "personal equation") and discriminate *better* between chance occurrences and patterned ones, and thus narrow the tails of the distribution with *practice*.

Kries, like Peirce, also agreed with much of Fechner's analysis but asserted that the latter nevertheless omits an important point in formulating his measurement of just-noticeable differences. To know that particular perceptions of different intensities are perceptions of the *same* general phenomena, such that we can group them together, there must be some *equal* baseline of sorts that all the observations share.[14] We do this sort of grouping, for instance, when we mathematically render the difference between particular sensations on a quantitative scale of more or less intensity, thus making the difference between, say, the number one and the number five meaningful. At the baseline, we stop noticing differences because, in Kries's view, what we are trying to notice really *is* the same here, consisting entirely of shared characteristics rather than just-noticeable differences. For Kries, the danger with Fechner's analysis is that this baseline might only be a convention introducing an arbitrary comparability and commonality between what are actually unrelated phenomena—their particularity being something *other* than a difference of intensity.

Beyond these specific arguments, both Kries and Peirce found that Fechner's "law" could be applied to address shortcomings in Laplace's influential view of probability. As noted above, to the degree that Laplace refers to an objective source of probability, he frames it solely as an epistemological problem arising from our state of inevitable ignorance. On these terms, a frequency count or a prior estimation can plausibly (though partially) solve that problem using epistemic tools. For someone like Kant, on the other hand, the source of probability is not a function of our ignorance; it lies instead in the object of our orientation. We can come to know the "real possibility" of what experience tells us about the world around us, even if this knowledge can never fully yield a prediction of which we can be *entirely* confident. Kries and Peirce fall more in line with Kant, not Laplace, on this matter, which helps explain their partial agreement with Fechner's research. This alignment also serves as an invitation to both Peirce and Kries to make a series of wider points about probability—to fill in a gap in the long history of thinking about probability that they both noticed.

Probabilistic Inference: Abduction and Synchysis

For both Kries and Peirce, human knowers are not always or inevitably in a state of indifference or ignorance about the world, and for both thinkers, this point means that there can be *other* forms of probabilistic inference beyond a calculated probability that is meant to overcome an inherent deficiency. As we will see, this argument is the part of their probability theory that, in many ways, resonates the most into the present. Peirce calls this idea "abduction"; Kries's related idea is "synchysis" (or more broadly, the "synchytic formation of concepts").[15] Both concepts refer to cognition that demonstrates "probabilistic reasoning," finding naturalistic roots in line with contemporary cognitive science. Peirce links abduction to "instinct," and the principle was (and remains) part of the resistance to cognition as a form of computation; Kries's notion of synchysis—defined most often in rhetoric as a complicated arrangement of seemingly unrelated words—strongly resembles connectionism in cognitive science. For Kries, synchysis involves the formation of a "concept," while for Peirce abduction is an "explanatory hypothesis" that puts us in an interpretant state, oriented to meaningful signs in the world and available to signification ourselves. Neither of these processes works on the grounds of synthesis or anything analytic, which for both Kries and

Peirce can teach us nothing new. In this sense, neither an abduction nor syn-chytic judgment yields a new category based on merging traits with what is already known.[16] Both are fundamentally probabilistic principles; abduction and synchysis both feature far more leeway and room to maneuver than do analytical categories or deduction alone, with the corresponding subjectivity neither definite nor definitive.

Both synchysis and abduction provide an epistemic principle, though that epistemology is not distinguishable from what they entail about cognition. For Kries, synchysis rests upon the construction of *Spielraum* or "range" of assorted particulars and how they appear to hold together as singular itera-tions of the same thing. Thus, the concept of "red" cannot be limited to pre-cise examples or a strict application. We will encounter single things in the world that strike us as red even though we never achieve a state of complete certainty. They are not definitive tokens of red in an analytic sense; rather, they fall within its range. For Peirce, we infer a "would-be" through abduction based upon an inference drawn from a surprising or particularly noticeable perception. In Peirce's view, this would-be is as close to a direct appearance of *chance* ("firstness") as we will ever get.

As probabilistic inferences, then, abduction and synchysis involve a kind of guessing.[17] At the heart of both processes is an attempt to *loop* into what *could* be out there in the world. In Peirce's words, it would only be on an infinitesimal chance that the nature of our guessing would not reflect "the in-fluence of phenomena," but what those phenomena are is not apparent with-out our guessing contribution.[18] Both synchytic judgment and abduction are triggered by "natural promptings"—of something unexpected or distinctly noticeable. Since neither abduction nor synchysis relies on determinate rules, however, or on the apprehension of single phenomena in their entirety, what-ever states of certainty they provide are strictly provisional. But the implica-tions here are quite different from those of Laplace's agnosticism and, for that matter, Bayesian priority.

In a wide enough range (*Spielraum*) or "continuum," everything can ap-pear probabilistic, even existence itself. Probability becomes objective only in smaller dimensions of space and time. Peirce's abduction and Kries's synchy-sis are fundamentally alike in this respect. The logical form of both is more like a loop than a linear deduction from first principles or an inductive gath-ering of particulars. For both Peirce and Kries, abduction and synchysis have implications that extend beyond epistemic rules or methods. With abduction, we revise a structured expectation based on deviation, and on these grounds draw a further inference. Likewise, to form a concept through synchysis means we do not start with a definition and then hunt for examples. As Kries puts it, "each new item is evaluated with respect to the existing concept by means of a subsumption judgment based on an impression of belongingness." As with abduction, this process can lead either to the revision of a concept or the inclusion of a new example of it.[19] Because they do not associate probability strictly with statistics, Peirce and Kries connect probability to these versions of a novel probabilistic logic. We return to some of these specific points again in chapter 7.

Kries and Peirce on Probability

It is as part of these arguments on synchysis and abduction that we can situate Kries and Peirce's views on probability. Their views are not compartmentalized or isolated from their views of epistemology and ontology. This lack of compartmentalization is partially why Kries and Peirce could find limits in frequentism. They sensed that probability was irreducible to applied mathematics or quantification and thus could not simply become a "method." For these reasons, Kries and Peirce have both been referred to as "quasi-classical" probability theorists because the approaches they devise tell us more about what *probability* is (i.e., a range, a "continuum," a "propensity") than about how it can stand as a secondary measurement for *another* phenomenon.[20] Indeed, the main point that Kries and Peirce draw from their engagement with Fechner is that psychological traits are not measurable, which means that whatever we might assign a sense of probability to, it is not relative to our state of mind or state of information, if by these we understand something that has no relation to the world.

For his part, Kries did not disagree with Laplace on the latter's ideas about the difference between the all-knowing "demon" and the ignorant human mind. For Kries, a deterministic relation is one that extends with full predictable continuity in time and space. Laplace's demon had implied as much: Everything can be known according to the initial states that are its extension in the world. However, Kries added an important addendum to this notion. The demon, in his case, can know "laws" but can "never (neither *ex ante* nor *ex post*) achieve such detailed knowledge of the conditions that a certain event seems to be necessarily connected with them."[21] In Kries's terms, Laplace's demon could know *nomological* laws of the universe, but that same demon would have little to say about *ontological* specifics. Meanwhile, we humans can also "never (neither *ex ante* nor *ex post*) achieve such detailed knowledge of the conditions of a certain event" such that we could readily connect those laws to it, which means that events as we experience them are singular to us.[22] But this singularity does not mean, for Kries, that they constantly surprise us.

Rather, our experience can teach us "that the conditions (in so far as we know them)" for a given event "constitute a certain *possibility* which is more or less large."[23]

For Kries, the frequentist tools of statistics can give us a calculation, but that calculation makes it appear as if whatever they distinguish as an outcome occurred "by chance." All "specific considerations have been dropped as superfluous. They do not impend on the issue whether the relevant outcome could occur in a particular case." In Kries's view, what does "impend" on whether an outcome could occur in a single case are "ontological ranges of behavior" (or *Spielraum* and what we might also translate as "ontological action-spaces"). A range "represents knowledge beyond which we cannot go. It is the object to be determined."[24] The "conditions" that, in an "overall general" manner, constitute a range can be divided into conditions that would create the outcome and conditions that would prevent it.[25] The ranges for which our "probability statements" are most valid are those that we have *designed*, in a physical and mechanical sense, as games of chance. Within these ranges, every event or outcome that occurs is "valid in *all* cases" as they are valid for "anyone who wishes to form an expectation concerning the action in such a case."[26]

From this perspective, a probability statement is rooted in the fact that even if "we do not exactly know the actions of the conditions in an individual case . . . we otherwise definitely know in which size ratio . . . the ranges of the configurations entailed in the realization of one or other outcome are to each other."[27] According to Kries, for a game of chance like roulette, the physical setup makes all possible outcomes capable of appearing *probable*; this randomizing quality is the main attraction of these games.[28] The rules and mechanics of the game generates "ontological action-spaces [*Spielraum*]" with every throw or drawing.[29] An event occurs in the context of the game "if the occurrence or absence depends on the exact ontological determinations of the causal circumstances which are beyond our knowledge."[30] Kries makes a Bayesian point here: A game of chance is the prototype for probability, a way of setting our priors, because our knowledge of these games can never be so perfect or complete that we can easily predict what will follow what. Kries, however, takes this idea in a different direction than contemporary Bayesians tend to. He asks: What *makes* the game of chance such a remarkable venue for probability?

For Kries, probability is not the difference between a prior and posterior estimate; neither is it an absolute or relative frequency. It refers to the objective states of the world that allow for knowledge of specific cases or events (like each toss of the roulette ball) that achieves three specific things:

(1) makes them all part of the same range, (2) gives each case or event leeway to be aligned with the others, though not entirely, and (3) makes the same action relevant for them, and forbids other action from being relevant.[31]

Kries mentions the "ideal gas law" as a further example. The behavior of molecules when trapped in a closed container with a divider in between is a question, associated with physicist Ludwig Boltzmann, that had been in discussion since the 1860s. The conditions are not easily mimicked by nature, and thus the law is considered ideal rather than real. Nevertheless, "the regularity" of the gas law "could be understood in a similar manner and a similar sense as . . . the regularity in the overall result of many cases of games of chance."[32] To Kries, the gas law and the roulette table are analogous as both molecules and roulette balls alike pass through "a quite specifically limited circle of states." Thus, a "great variety of effects can only cause the recurrence of these same actions."

> In the game of dice or when tossing a coin, this limitation of states is given by the finiteness of the orientations possible in the first place, i.e. ultimately by the character of the space. This character implies that whatever number of twists we do with the dice or the coin always only leads to the repetition of the same possible final positions. Something similar can be achieved in some other ways. If, for example, a gas molecule is trapped in a certain space bounded by solid walls, then the probability approach which we can use for its containment in one or other part of the space is based in an entirely similar way on the fact that the great number of completely different effects which the molecule experiences as it collides can also only cause a certain limited circle of action patterns and that therefore, if we think of all the variations of these effects, these [patterns] repeat themselves in steady alternation.[33]

In Kries's study of Boltzmann, gas in a closed container "after a certain period of time . . . fills the whole space uniformly, i.e. the same quanta [of the gas] are contained everywhere in the volume unit; furthermore . . . everywhere the same pressure and the same temperature occur" because a "very specific velocity distribution" of the molecules occurs.[34] What Kries wants to get across, however, is that regardless of the distributions we observe, they tell us about the range that applies to each molecule.

Like Kries, Peirce develops an approach to probability based on a response to Laplace. For those guided by the Laplacean spirit, the future will exhibit a distribution of outcomes that directly resembles the past; Venn would call this part of Laplace "the rule of succession." For Peirce, this rule simply constitutes the reduction of "synthetic to analytic reason."[35] As noted above, his early engagements with probability led him to distinguish induction from abduction.

Here, we can find a similar break from Laplace as the one evident in Kries: leading Peirce not toward a standardized calculation method but toward an interpretation of probability that associates it with a kind of reasoning that reveals new things about the world.[36] Laplace's rule of succession works to forbid and disregard surprise. In more standardized terms, the rule means that little stock is placed in cases or events that appear as errors in a distribution (outliers, uncorrelated). For Peirce, such a rule makes sense statistically, but it encourages a general disregard for the non-normal or "surprising" case at the heart of abduction. We can see a similar pivot from Laplace in another of Peirce's contributions to probability theory.

The rule of indifference is also one of the cornerstones of Laplacean probability, as it marks a continuation of Bernoullian large numbers. A high number of observations produces a distribution of results rather than just one. Frequency, here, incites the will to prediction to find the most probable grouping; the implication, as Peirce notes, is that a high number of observations are both equally possible and equally probable.[37] We can understand two events to be equally possible according to the same initial conditions— say, an ominous dark cloud leading to rain and high winds, or a decrease in wind without rain—but we can also know that they are *not* equally probable. The only situation in which we find a near-perfect overlap between the possible and the probable is in games of chance, and because that is the case, only in such circumstances should we ever expect to witness anything close to our complete indifference about the future. As Peirce suggests, we do not need complete indifference to *abduct*—quite the opposite, in fact.

As many have noted, Peirce's thoughts on probability migrated over the years away from epistemic commitments to frequentism. One example of this shift in Peirce's voluminous writings concerns the nature of a die (or dice) as marking a kind of container of chance—a "chancy object."[38] If we encounter *chance* in a first moment of perception, the rupture of subjectivity in a second moment finds a responsiveness in a third moment as habit, which could only have any constancy for subjectivity by looping into the "habits of the world."[39] Peirce claims that all we can say of a single die is that it "has a certain '*would-be*'; and to say that a die has a 'would-be' is to say that it has a property, quite analogous to any habit." Such a statement "would by no means imply that the habit consists in that action—so to define the die's 'would-be,' it is necessary to say how it would lead the die to behave on an occasion that would bring out the full consequence of the 'would be'; and this statement will not of itself imply that the 'would-be' of the die consists in such behavior."[40] It would appear that, for Peirce, this would-be is a *potential* that may be reserved in the die forever and never be expressed on any occasion. It remains part of the die's objectivity as a continuum, and if we engage in an "endless series of throws" of this die, the data we collect would be significant, but not because of their frequency. The data would be significant because they would reveal the full constitution of the "would-be" of the die, and perhaps that, regardless of what we expect of the die, it is capable of miraculous things.

Thus, for Peirce, a statistical artifact like a limit frequency only stands as a *sign* for which probability is the *object*—not the other way around. His reversal of a standard frequentist framework indicates his commitment to a version of reality not confined to actual (measurable, countable) existence, but one that includes possible qualities and potential effects. Peirce develops another concept for this purpose: *continuum* or *continuity* as "something whose possibilities of determination no multitude of individuals can exhaust." In his neologistically defined metaphysics of "syncheism," Peirce emphasizes the universe's tendency to increase in connectedness by reducing separation and particularity via semiosis.[41] More specifically, with an emphasis on continuity Peirce seeks to explain *how probability emerges from chance* in the general tendency of things to take habits.

In his Cambridge lectures from 1898, Peirce gives the example of drawing a line on a blackboard. By itself, the line appears discontinuous, and though it may set us off abducting toward what it might be, we will have no luck restoring ourselves to any state of belief about it. But then we draw another line close to it, and then another (and so on). From the chance appearance of a single line to now several surrounding it, their interconnections produce a continuity "from chance occurrences."[42] Together, they become something distinguishable. As we extrapolate from one line to another, a composite appears in their continuity. From a mere chance occurrence capable of anything, the lines come to signify to us as *habit*, and thus as predictable and expectable—something we can loop into. The motivation here is not fundamentally different from the one that leads Kries toward the concept of Ranges or *Spielraum*. For Kries, too, within the correct Range, nothing is accidental—there are no "bare particulars." Such a realization should make us attentive to the difference between evoking the will to prediction through epistemic construction versus evoking it through direct engagement with the world in perception and action.

This is what we find at the ontological level. Ontology is only apparent in single cases, and depending on what makes the case "single," it is where we will find objective possibility, as it concerns initial states that *are* alterable (i.e., variable). The nomological, as Kries applies it, indicates initial states that are not alterable and thus maintain continuity across all cases.[43] In the setup of the roulette game, for instance, variability comes mostly from the movement of our hand as we toss the ball onto the spinning wheel. Kries makes a point in line with one that, as mentioned in chapter 1, French physicist Henri Poincaré would arrive at a few years later: The genesis of probability ultimately lies in *action*. Everything else about a roulette game is constant and perfectly mirrored across the initial states and outcomes that bookend the moment of action (when the ball is tossed). Presumably, the more data we acquire on how action plays this role, the more predictable our play will become (e.g., if we toss the ball moving our hand this fast at this angle, it always comes up red). However, the number of possibilities this single moment contains might be so vast that, even if we form reasonably good expectations, we are never able to reconstitute the entire situation.[44]

For Peirce's part, "objective possibility" is more straightforwardly a logical principle that he would embrace after concluding that the universe lacked any determined laws at all, which means that any "first" bit of any experience must be logically categorized as *chance*.[45] For Peirce, such a conclusion demands that a concept like "objective possibility" refer to "that mode of being which is not subject to the principle of contradiction since if it be merely possible that A is B, it is possible that A is not B . . . Possibility is that mode of being in which something is held in reserve, so that actuality is not attained."[46] Nevertheless, it is not simply a figment of the imagination. Absolute chance, in this regard, is not tantamount to accident, which Peirce says is wholly contingent on having unbreakable a priori commitments. On the contrary, there is "pure spontaneity or life as a character of the universe, acting always and everywhere though restrained within narrow bounds by law, producing infinitesimal departures from law continually, and great ones with infinite infrequency." Such a statement is consistent with Peirce's understanding of the ideas of continuity and abduction and overlaps closely with a notion like *Spielraum*. A difference, however, is that Peirce is perfectly willing to draw *chance* into perception itself and the order of signification as first-order ways of interfacing with the world, making its basic content (what Peirce refers to as "percipuum") probabilistic through and through.[47]

For both Peirce and Kries, then, a calculated probability and an expectation are not only different, but we can find no hierarchy between them; the former is without grounds in staking a claim to authoritative knowledge in relation to the latter. Rather, both are versions of a will to prediction, though they are invoked under different circumstances. Most notably, one is epistemically (nomologically, in Kries's words) phrased while the other is ontological (i.e., engaging in *chance*, demonstrating firstness, in Peirce's words).[48] For Kries's and Peirce's probabilism, the mutual effort is to develop a set of concepts for absorbing or taming chance outside the statistical tool kit. This effort

leads them both to draw into question what quantitative probability calculations can signify to us who live in the ontological world. As these calculations
gather particular cases within a kind of total knowledge, what do they tell us
about single cases, which invariably remain sites of action?

Both Kries and Peirce agree that (*pace* Quetelet) statistical predictions do
not convey determinism in particular cases. The most those predictions can
reveal is a non-probabilistic sense of "reality" that stands as a provisional
placeholder inviting further inquiry. In their distinct ways, Kries and Peirce
share a common goal of knowing probability in the formation of expectation and habit, neither of which can assume a numerical form. As Kries puts
it: "Any probability statement requires first of all a list of cases that appear
equally possible to our present and individual state of knowledge. Thus, they
are of a subjective nature. However, since probability statements are only possible in connection with a particular knowledge having an objective meaning,
and since this knowledge contributes to probability expressions, we can say
that probability statements have an objective meaning, too."[49]

Yet Kries argues that far from carrying "objectivity" as a reflection of large
numbers, probability statements only have an objective meaning for the same
reason they have a subjective meaning. "Objective possibility" is a category
that stands as a kind of logical displacement of frequency counts, as it defines
the only ultimately valid way that probability can be objective and a probability calculation be nonarbitrary.[50] Kries liked to reference games of chance
because they made the ontological reality stand out in such stark contrast
to what he refers to as nomological: Even knowing the laws of physics, we
cannot predict precisely where the roulette ball will fall. The same is true, he
thought, for the kinetic movement of gas molecules made famous by Boltzmann.

Peirce would likely consider Kries's efforts at ontology as an attempt to de-
cipher firstness, which is indeed impossible. Nevertheless, neither Kries nor
Peirce follows in the tradition of Bayes by concluding that all we can have is
subjective states of mind or information. Abductive surprises are not subjective according to Peirce, and neither are judgments of objective possibility
subjective according to Kries. For both theorists, part of the problem of calculating probabilities lies in the need to create moments of indecision and
thus inference. The risk is that our calculations can only yield "probabilities
in a figurative sense" because of the *manufactured* nature of those moments.[51]
Here, they once again find an ally in Kant. The only way for probability to be
capable of changing our thinking (non-figuratively) is if it takes the form of
an object: For Kries, this means not a single object but rather a Range, a *Spielraum*; for Peirce, it means a *continuum*.

Pragmatism and Objective Probability

It should not surprise us that the main lines of conversation that Kries and Peirce inspire are carried on mostly by philosophers these days. When Kries and Peirce started their investigations into probability, they found it impoverished—buried under the weight of increasingly technical application, all premised on an interpretation of probability they found largely bankrupt. Philosophers who pick these threads today continue the battle against frequentism, tending to favor either a "propensity" approach (after Peirce) or a "range" approach (after Kries).[52] But the influence of probabilism is far from limited to these conversations. As for their contemporaries, Kries and Peirce's efforts were convincing enough to make probability conceivable and interesting outside of numerical formulation and statistical calculation.[53]

We can start with the influence of Peirce's approach to probability on later pragmatist thought. Peirce is uncontroversially recognized as a founder of pragmatism; yet more central to Peirce's influence on later pragmatist thought than is typically recognized is his probabilism. As noted above, Peirce embraced ideas that would allow him to situate probability in the world. As we will argue, his efforts maintain a throughline in later pragmatist thought, particularly in the connection that Peirce draws, on the grounds of his probabilism, between action and knowledge—specifically what appears at the interface between habit and a chance world.

When Peirce's friend, the psychologist and philosopher William James, argues for replacing "freedom" with "chance" in his argument in support of indeterminism, he is not seeking to make an argument about principles.[54] Rather, as James puts it, chance means "pluralism." It means that "possibilities are really *here*."[55] In fact, James joins the two terms together to create a new word—"chance-possibilities"—to make his point, implying a similar space between actual and potential status as we can find in various elements of Peirce's probabilism, particularly the "would-be" and the notion of objective possibility.[56] George Herbert Mead's approach to the philosophy of the present, for its part, also displays a characteristic emphasis on possibility as an ontological dimension alongside probability, which appears as action-relative. "Present reality is a possibility," according to Mead; "it is what would be if we were there instead of here. Through the mechanism of significant symbols, the organism places itself there as a possibility, which acquires increasing probability as it fits into the spatio-temporal structure and the demands of the whole complex act of which its conduct is a part."[57]

The significance of putting a term like "hypothesis" into action and of engaging with the terms "possibility" and "probability" in a non-epistemic sense is brought to its fullest expression in John Dewey's notion of inquiry. For Dewey, "ends-in-view" are dynamic predictions—or what he calls "predicate-possibilities"—made in the thick of the situation, and the more "problematic the situation . . . the more thorough the inquiry that has to be engaged in."[58] Inquiry is not neatly parceled into, on the one hand, an "objective state of affairs" that could be described with scientific precision by an external observer and, on the other, the "subjective point of view" of the actor to whom prediction does not apply. Instead, the "state of affairs," according to Dewey, is irreducibly composed of an entanglement between what are typically classed as objective and subjective elements.[59] The act of perception on the actor's part introduces such a subjective element. However, perception is not spectatorial and detached; Dewey understands it to be the "initial stage" in a dynamic action cycle.

For Dewey, in a more concrete sense, perceptions are *predictions*, as "projections of possible consequences; they are ends-in-view": "The terminal outcome when anticipated (as it is when a moving cause of affairs is perceived) becomes an end-in-view, an aim, purpose, a prediction usable as a plan in shaping the course of events."[60] The in-viewness of ends is as much shaped by antecedent natural conditions as is perception of contemporary objects "external to the organism."[61] Objects become "potentialities" in this perspective as "sets of qualities treated . . . for specified existential consequences;" but whatever potentialities an object has does not mean it loses others. Rather, objects exist as a range of potentialities (modeled on the form of a "would-be").[62]

The world consists of potentiality and is unsolid, even though it appears frequently in one way rather than another. As Dewey argues, an "organic interaction" with the world "becomes inquiry when existential consequences are anticipated; when environing conditions are examined with reference to their potentialities; and when responsive activities are selected and ordered with reference to actualization of some of the potentialities."[63] Dewey's larger task in delineating the nature of inquiry is to redeem probability as having every bit the same "logical status" as necessity has in an explanation, which among other things means grounding our explanations in potentiality rather than resting them on causation.[64]

Kries's Diffuse Influence on Subsequent Thinking About Probability

For American philosopher and mathematician Arthur Burks, Peirce's probabilism is indeed as elemental to pragmatism as we are suggesting; but Burks, writing in the early 1960s, recognized that Peirce's seemingly singu-

lar views on probability found a comrade-in-arms an ocean away in the figure of Kries.[65] Burks could not delve into this parallel as much as we have.
In part, this is because John Maynard Keynes and his *Treatise on Probability* (mentioned in in chapter 1) remained, for a long time, the only English-
language analysis of Kries.[66] Such a singular conduit of information helps to
explain why Kries could be seemingly so influential among those outside the
Anglophone world, and why this influence became more or less secondhand
(mostly via Keynes) in the Anglophone world. The influence of Kries's approach to probability is therefore more weblike in its diffusion than the more
coherent influence of Peirce on pragmatism.

Keynes's own probabilism is a good example of Kries's indirect, "several
steps removed"—though evident and inextricable—pattern of influence.
Keynes singles out the German scholar for demonstrating a probabilistic style
of reasoning built around the firm position that probability is arbitrarily rendered into numbers.[67] He reserves special praise for Kries's concept of *Spielraum*, which Keynes translates as "field," for how it disentangles probability
from frequency counts. In retrospect, Keynes's impact on those within his
Cambridge milieu at the time—mainly via his introduction of Kries's work
and German probabilism—has turned out to be quite extensive, though his is
not the only line of influence.[68]

Philosopher Ludwig Wittgenstein did not need Keynes's translational and
exegetical work, being a native German speaker himself. Still, it seems as if
Wittgenstein had no prior knowledge of Kries prior to his relationship with
Keynes.[69] Yet the famous philosopher quickly took up the idea that probability refers to a "range." He shared this idea with Frank Ramsey, who later
adapted it to an early version of decision theory.

In Wittgenstein's *Tractatus logico-philosophicus*, he posits that an interval
of time exists between p and q in an *if... then* relationship ($p \rightarrow q$): "The truth-
conditions of a proposition determine the range [*Spielraum*] that it leaves
open to the facts."[70] For his part, Ramsey uses the example of "the probability
of recovery from chickenpox" as occurring with proportions distributed in
a "range."[71] Both Wittgenstein and Ramsey rejected frequentism for similar
reasons as Kries and Peirce, finding that it was less a sign of an object and
more the object we are trying to signify. They both adopt a concept of probability more akin to objective probability than any other. Probability is a possibility set and a distribution of either truth values or outcomes over some set
of elementary propositions or initial states. In these definitions, probability
renders logic "dynamic" as it *contracts* time and maintains something original
over time.[72]

In the 1950s, the statistician and economist Leonard Savage would formalize Ramsey's approach, drawing it together into "expected utility," which has since become the cornerstone of revealed preference, and the mathematical rational action theory at the core of modern microeconomics.[73] For Ramsey's part, he refers to unknowable circumstances spanning over a future period of time to identify the "quantity of belief" or "degree of certainty of belief" that is the equal partner in rationality as the subjective value placed on goods or goals.[74] The value of one good over another is a function not only of desirability but also of the probability of attaining it. Such a schema largely serves as the psychology of modern microeconomics, but it is not the only psychology that appears out of objective probability.

Kries's approach to objective probability would have a fuller influence on the work of psychologists Edward Tolman and Egon Brunswik, the latter of whom would baptize his approach as "probabilistic functionalism."[75] In their collaborative work, with an influence that ranges from Gestalt psychology to contemporary cognitive linguistics, Tolman and Brunswik propose that environments have a "probabilistic" texture, and this texture explains the externality of environments in relation to actors whose action unfolds on the basis of "hypotheses."[76] Tolman and Brunswik understand the probabilism evident here in a fully naturalistic sense. An "organism's task in any given case is to correct whatever hypotheses it brings with it to fit the real probabilities of the actually presented set-up."[77] If the environment is probabilistic, and we establish a hypothetical relation to it, our expectations will be conveyed by our action. Brunswik would pursue these points further in arguing that such "environmental probability" is, in fact, the primary source of the variation exhibited in action.[78]

Arguments like these would later influence Pierre Bourdieu, whose probabilism we will take up specifically in chapter 4 as marking a continuity with Max Weber. But objective probability did not travel through only one path to encourage Bourdieu to adopt heterodox stances on probability, such as the idea that "expectations tend universally to be roughly adapted to objective chances." Elsewhere, we can encounter claims that also influenced Bourdieu in Maurice Merleau-Ponty's emphasis on finding a "phenomenological basis for statistical thought."[79] Michel Foucault borrows the concept of *Spielraum* to define specific "clearings" or spaces that are neither determined nor undetermined but which feature "lee-way" and open a range of possibility.[80] These connected pathways extend back to Edmund Husserl's phenomenology and, through it, to Martin Heidegger's ontology, which informed Merleau-Ponty, Bourdieu, and Foucault.[81] Husserl engaged with Kries quite extensively, most importantly agreeing with him on the distinction between "nomological" and "ontological" and situating phenomenology in the first camp—the side that studies general principles or laws but can tell us nothing specific about single cases.[82] The segue from Husserl to Heidegger largely turns on the notion of what is ontological. Heidegger would draw liberally on the idea of *Spielraum* to define his influential position on the matter, appearing in many ways to establish his departure from Husserl, and open the door to existentialism, on a question Kries would have recognized: What comes into existence with action?[83]

For his part, Kries found theoretical physics to be the field that best engages with his approach, which is not surprising given his own engagement with Boltzmann's ideal gas law. Max Planck—in the acceptance speech for the Nobel Prize in physics in 1918—explains the "elementary quantum of action" as one among two constants in the quantum understanding of physics, describing the "'elementary region' or 'range' of probability'" necessary to give the kinetic movements of particles a "statistical treatment."[84] Planck gives no citation for the quote, but if the formulation is, in fact, drawn from Kries, then the latter would caution such an application. We should not mistake an outcome that is "maximally probable" for one we can expect to be "lawfully determined."

On the question of quantum mechanics, especially the so-called Copenhagen Interpretation, Niels Bohr and Werner von Heisenberg would deviate from Planck's "quantum of action." Their disagreement from Planck meant the notion of action in physics would be given an ontological understanding rather than serve as an epistemic placeholder. In philosopher Ernst Cassirer's words, this moment marked the final death knell of determinism in physical science, well over a hundred years after Laplace seemed to suggest it, and meant that statistical statements necessarily become "inexact" statements that cannot tell you about the "fate" of an individual particle.[85] Historian and philosopher of science Gaston Bachelard also suggested that because the quantum revolution rested on "objective indeterminacy in all physical observation," it "sets limits to the assignment of realistic attributes" to individual particles.[86] The kinetic shifting of gaseous matter, for example, appeared to Bachelard to offer definitive proof that scientific "terminology should reflect the fact that we are describing a collective and not an individual reality."[87]

By confronting what he thought was a problem the new physics had introduced, philosopher Karl Popper was also led toward objective probability, which he found incompatible with frequentism and Bayesianism. The proper understanding of probability, in his view, was lacking from these perspectives because, specifically in the case of physics, they meant that "physicists make use of probabilities without being able to say, consistently, what they mean by 'probability.'"[88] Popper would call his alternative "the *propensity* interpretation of probability."[89] Far from being a claim about the uncertainty of belief, "uncertainty" in quantum theory refers, according to Popper, to the objective uncertainty of "scatter-relations" in which "particles have paths, i.e., momentum and positions, although we cannot predict these, owing to scatter relations."[90] To accept that point, Popper argues, we must accept that "probabilities be 'physically real'—that they must be physical propensities, abstract relational properties of the physical situation," and thus what we take to be real objects are really just "propensities to realize singular events."[91] Popper had earlier used Kries's "range" principle to help formalize his famous principle of falsification, specifically to refer to a "range" of basic statements extending across a "subclass" and having their truth value reflect the "amount of 'free play' between them in reality."[92] In his words, this approach means that "range and empirical content . . . are converse (or complementary) concepts." If we do not abide by this principle, then according to Popper, we miss chance of having our theories loop into the world at all, rendering them unfalsifiable and effectively moot.[93]

Across all these threads, there are many lines of influence, and beyond this influence itself lies a hypothesis that's tricky to establish with any satisfaction. Yet, in one way or another, we claim, the core Kriesian idea—that probability emerges in objective circumstances configured as ranges—is persistent. It is also not a marginal element to these many separate arguments. Despite the successful move by frequentists at the turn of the twentieth century to establish their interpretation of probability as authoritative, there existed a healthy heterodoxy prior to that time, and it was not limited to Bayesianism. So why did this perspective have no apparent influence in sociology, despite the fact that, as we establish in chapter 3, arguably the most influential figure in the history of sociology—Max Weber—went all in?

American Sociology and Objective Probability: A Missed Chance

Sociology's early adoption of statistics was largely filtered via the British line of development following in line with the apparent culmination of probability theory in frequentist statistical principles and methods, as devised in succession by the aforementioned Francis Galton, Karl Pearson, and Ronald Fisher.[94] Accordingly, a key reason that objective probability would be brushed aside in sociology is that in the Anglophone sphere, the field has always been marked by a deep commitment to frequentism, even as this has become less true of its rival discipline, economics, over the last several decades.[95] For some, sociology's frequentism stands out in a bad way, given the popularity of Bayesian approaches in many other (often cutting-edge) fields compared to its lagging absence in sociology.[96] Even when objective probability is glimpsed, however, it is typically filtered through the frequentist lens of "variable" sociology.[97] There are two main reasons for the oversight of objective probability in sociology: The first involves the genealogy of the action concept in American sociology; the second involves the translation of the key sociological text featuring objective probability into English.

In 1963, Roscoe Hinkle attempted to discover the "antecedents of the action orientation" in sociology prior to the publication of Talcott Parsons's *The Structure of Social Action* in 1937. Parson's text had defined in monopolistic fashion the sociological significance of "action" for a couple of academic generations to that point. So what, Hinkle inquired, were the roads not taken? He found that they were nearly all informed by pragmatism.[98]

Hinkle describes Mead as a key influence on other approaches during this pre-Parsonian era.[99] Mead's idea of the relative "disorganization [of] features external" to actors informed a theory as commonly invoked as the one later proposed by William and Dorothy Thomas—namely, that situations had to be "consciously defined" in order to contain reality. Hinkle also found that pre-Parsonian approaches to action did not appear to have a similar principle as *Verstehen*. Rather than an interpretive attribution of subjective meaning, theories of action drew instead on a rival concept like "life-history because it reveals the subject's own view of his situation, his train of experience or life movement."[100]

The marginalization of prior approaches to action by Parsons's influence had a specific effect on probabilism. For Parsons, the element of prediction needed to be kept strictly separate from action because including prediction *in* action would only result in reducing what he sought above all to preserve—namely, the "value element" or values—to nonsubjective *conditions* of action. As Parsons notes, this need to preserve the role of values in what we do is necessary because the idea of an "end" to action is ambiguous. Parsons appreciates the continuous flow of action that proceeds apace, seemingly from the day we are born to the day we die. The end of action might be conceived of as "the subjective anticipation of a desirable future state of affairs." But this conception is not subjective enough; it is as an expression of values that the ends of action might be sought—"the realization of which the action of the individual in question may be thought of as directed."[101]

Ends are thus conceived as future states of affairs in which actors see themselves altering the impersonal flow of events. If action were purely based on predictions, according to Parsons, if all we sought after in action could be read from our anticipations and sense of likelihood, this scenario would squeeze out and exclude value-orientations as the core "voluntaristic" aspect of action—the principal way in which we can say, with validity, that our action is truly ours.[102] But with this argument, Parsons would contribute to the tendency in the midcentury American sociological field to create strict dichotomies, like between interpretive and positivist approaches or between qualitative versus quantitative methods and logics of inquiry. These dichotomies have left a lasting imprint. By rendering a notion like "internalized probability" effectively illegible (and likely nonsensical), Parsonian action theory effectively surrendered probability to the statisticians, who were only too willing to engage in their own protective monopolization of its meaning and use. This set of factors is one reason why objective probability has made no apparent inroads in sociology. The second main reason also involves Parsons and another influential Weber scholar, and it concerns not the task of concept formation but the task of translation, both linguistic and conceptual.

German British sociologist Ralf Dahrendorf once took note of the "more than one hundred places" in the first part of Weber's *Economy and Society* in which Weber "uses chance as a word or a category." However, he adds, "one cannot but be surprised about how little attention the literature on Weber has paid to the term."[103] Keith Tribe more recently remarks upon Weber's "relentless use of *Chance*" to try to capture not only how frequently Weber uses the term but also the significance it carries for his arguments.[104] It is from Parsons, along with the economist Alexander Henderson, that we get the only English translation of Weber's key text until Tribe's translation of *Wirtschaft und Gesellschaft*—the original four-chapter format that Weber originally intended for the text—in 2019–2020. The way in which Parsons and Henderson treat this mysterious word—*Chance*—in their translation, which they could not fail to notice in simply glimpsing at the German-language original, would further contribute to the compartmentalization of probability and interpretation as distinct pursuits in sociology.

On page 100 of Parsons and Henderson's 1947 translation, while still in the first chapter after the eighty-six-page introduction—written by Parsons himself—we can find the following footnote:

> This is the first occurrence in Weber's text of the term *Chance*, which he uses very frequently. It is here translated by "probability," because he uses it as interchangeable with *Wahrscheinlichkeit*. As the term "probability" is used in a technical mathematical and statistical sense, however, it implies the possibility of numerical statement. In most of the cases where Weber uses *Chance*, this is out of the question. It is, however, possible to speak in terms of higher and lower degrees of probability. To avoid confusion with the technical mathematical concept, the term "likelihood" will often be used in the translation. It is by means of this concept that Weber, in a highly ingenious way, has bridged the gap between the interpretation of meaning and the inevitably more complex facts of overt action.[105]

What is significant about this statement is just how much of Weber's original text will need to be modified, in most cases substantially, to successfully
follow this rubric. Not to mention that Weber would have known that Kries
distinguishes between these terms (i.e., *Chance* and *Wahrscheinlichkeit*) and
does not use them interchangeably.

Parsons and Henderson thus notice *Chance* but pivot away from the term
based on what they expect will be a deep confusion in understanding the text.
Weber becomes essentially a frequentist in their version of the text. The sentence to which Parsons and Henderson append the above footnote is, in their
version, translated as: "On the other hand, even the most perfect adequacy on
the level of meaning has causal significance from a sociological point of view
only in so far [*sic*] as there is some kind of proof for the existence of a probability that action in fact normally takes the course which has been held to be
meaningful."[106] The new translation of the same passage by Tribe, who does
not follow Parsons and Henderson's rubric, renders the sentence very differently: "On the other hand, even the most evident meaningful adequacy has
significance for sociological knowledge only to the extent that a correct causal
statement can be given—as proof the existence of a (specifiable) *Chance* that
action does tend to follow an apparently meaningful course with specifiable
frequency, or something close to it (either on average or in a 'pure' case)."[107]

Parsons and Henderson assume that probability must be numerical and
epistemic. They assume that probability requires a frequency count, or it cannot be relevant to sociological knowledge. They also assume (incorrectly) that
Weber would agree with them. We can see something similar in a second
conduit of Weber into American sociology. In this case, translation is not
the critical factor, but exegesis is by someone who seems to have known the
meaning of *Chance* but confuses its significance.

Sociologist Alfred Schutz's phenomenological reading of Weber's interpretive sociology, particularly after the rise of ethnomethodology, is often
touted as an alternative to Parsons by post-functionalist action theorists.[108]
Yet, like Parsons, Schutz ultimately falters on the issue of probability, misunderstanding the key conceptual role of objective probability in Weber's late
sociology. As Schutz (a native German speaker) reads and critiques *Economy
and Society* in the original German, he does not ignore Weber's "relentless use
of *Chance*." But he calls Weber out by accusing him of a fundamental ambiguity, which Schutz emphasizes with what we can assume is a frustrated exas-
peration (italics original): "*For whom does this probability exist—the actor, or
the social scientist who observes him?*"[109]

Thus, for Schutz, probability appears to carry an exclusively epistemic
meaning. Schutzian "objective probabilities" are the subjective probabilities

imputed by an observer to others' actions.[110] For Schutz, the notion of objective probability as external chances existing independently of any observer
strikes him as unimaginable—surely not what Weber is meaning to imply
(and if he is, then Weber is wrong). Schutz insists, instead, that "objective
probability . . . is a category of interpretation."[111]

On a path independent of Parsons, then, we can find a separate source
of the frequentist enshrinement in sociology by those who were not practicing frequentists and were, to some degree, resistant to positivism (Schutz
more than Parsons). Weber became a primary resource in the fight against
positivism and quantitative hegemony in sociology. Influential collected
translations of Weber's work have often provided the main pedagogical coun-
terweights to that vision of the sociology, but notably neither Hans Gerth and
C. Wright Mills's volume from 1949 (*From Max Weber*) nor the Edward Shils
and Henry Finch volume from the same year (*The Methodology of Social Sciences*) features a key essay that Weber published in 1913—an essay in which
we can find his most explicit statements on probabilism before *Economy and
Society*. We analyze this essay at length in the next chapter. That it is missing
from the Shils and Finch volume is particularly noteworthy, because essentially the same set of essays were collected and translated into French in 1965
by the philosopher and sociologist Julien Freund. As we show in chapter 4,
the essay's inclusion in Freund's book likely contributed to Pierre Bourdieu's
being the first sociologist to grasp Weber's probabilism, despite the German
sociologist's canonization and reams of exegesis in the United States.

Weber's use of *Chance* has received some attention by German-language
scholars. Those works have, with few exceptions, not been translated or
otherwise overcome the Anglophone barrier.[112] Dahrendorf is a notable exception; so too are papers in the 1980s by theorist Stephen Turner.[113] With the
pragmatist revival in American sociology over the last few decades, abduction has made its way deeper into the field,[114] though the probabilistic aspects
of pragmatism remain mostly unexplored. What prevails mostly undimmed
is the common idea that actors do not (or cannot and should not) predict and
that someone in the role of a sociologist *can* predict, which goes hand in hand
with the now well-established presumption that when actors predict, they do
so poorly because they lack the right knowledge. Such a perspective presumes
the possession of a means of prediction and has a hard time admitting that we
can take any other form of it seriously.[115]

We have used genealogy to identify this *doxa*—a field-level common
sense, which renders some ideas unthinkable and others heterodox (think-
able but risky). Sociologists did not have to inherit this history, and they are
far from alone in having done so. Even when frequentism is challenged, it has

a way of maintaining its grip. On that score, consider, briefly, the most influential engagement with probability as a concept of the last half-century, and how even it refuses to breach that wall.

Psychologists Amos Tversky and Daniel Kahneman have become wildly influential over the last several decades on the basis of a seeming probabilism and how it has served to apparently reconcile the rationalistic expected utility framework with a behavioral and naturalistic portrait of human decision-making.[116] In their initial research in the 1970s, bearing indicative titles like "On Belief in the Law of Small Numbers," "On the Psychology of Prediction" and "Availability: A Heuristic for Judging Frequency and Probability," Tversky and Kahneman demonstrate their intent to draw frequentist principles out of statistics and into the psychological domain. This stance may seem to indicate a radical move against frequentism and perhaps hint at a revival of Bayesianism. It is nothing of the sort. For Tversky and Kahneman, experiments like asking test subjects (more specifically, the undergraduates and high school students whom they enlisted for the purpose) to make guesses about various things (potential words, identities, or population traits) based on limited or fragmentary evidence only serves to demonstrate how *bad* we are at assessing probabilities.

In the context of genealogy, Tversky and Kahneman reinforce an old Laplacean point about our inevitable ignorance. Our thinking is overdetermined by heuristics and biases that lead us to overemphasize some things and underemphasize others. For Tversky and Kahneman, the range of possibility for when and how to make predictions consists of an opposition between subjective heuristic-versus-objective statistical measures that reveal accurate degrees of probability. They do not question the principle that frequency simply *is* probability. Hence, as they conclude, we humans think in ways that commit "statistical fallacies," as we fail at nearly every measure of being good frequentists by *nature*.[117]

It is no mystery why economics would be so welcoming of this perspective, nor why it could coexist peacefully with expected utility. While critical of some economic principles—hence, the "behavioral" modifier—Tversky and Kahneman maintain a strongly normative orientation that renders their so-called behaviorism shockingly undescriptive.[118] Such an approach could easily gel with an economics from an era revealed in Milton Friedman's 1966 position-taking essay "The Methodology of Positive Economics," in which this leading economist is perfectly willing to entertain unsound (relative to empirical arguments) models if they are normatively valid.[119] From this perspective, just as much as that of Parsons own, quite different, normativity, to treat actors seriously as those who make predictions in the wild would give an undue emphasis to "knowledge" in action. From Parsons and Schutz to contemporary behavioral economics based on Tversky and Kahneman's research, frequentist predictions do, in fact, precede and can cover the individual situation. It can hold up no ontological distinction unless we define it differently, whether as the source of incurable psychological fallacies or as the venue for things unavailable to probability, like values or subjective meaning. But consider now an exception to this rule, from a sociologist whom Hinkle does not mention as a precursor to Parsons—for evident reasons, Hinkle's omission is not surprising and is surely not accurate.[120]

Du Bois and the Probabilist Theory of Action

American sociologist W. E. B. Du Bois is the only figure who straddles both the German and pragmatist traditions of objective probability. As an undergraduate at Harvard, Du Bois was strongly influenced by James.[121] During his two-year (1892–1894) sojourn in Berlin, Du Bois spent much of his time in close contact with political economists Gustav von Schmoller and Adolf Wagner, both of whom came from the same milieu as Kries as critics of frequentism, particularly Quetelet's seeming erasure of moral freedom.[122] It should not surprise us, then, that Du Bois links probabilism as directly to action as he does; it should also not surprise us that the frame of reference for what he is doing has proven elusive, it seems, until now. Du Bois is a fitting bookend to a genealogy of objective probability, not because the story concludes with him. Du Bois might have brought objective probability into sociology and the social sciences over a hundred years ago if not for deeply wrought epistemic injustice.[123]

The themes we can find in Du Bois's seminal "Sociology Hesitant" from 1905 (which remained unpublished until 2000) anticipate much of what Dewey will later discuss as putting prediction into action as part of inquiry. For Du Bois, however, the role of prediction in action contributes to a novel characterization of sociology as a field that attempts "to measure the limits of Chance in human action."[124] Du Bois, both in 1904 and, retrospectively, in 1944, characterizes his sociology as an attempt to "measure the element of Chance in human conduct."[125] At this point, Du Bois views this attempt as a return to James's pragmatism and a turn against the German critique of Quetelet (as represented by Schmoller). Nevertheless, he is conscious of playing the two thinkers off each other, knowing that the pivot from one to the other is not as fundamental as it has only subsequently been made to seem.

In "Sociology Hesitant," however, Du Bois is insistent and clear. He recommends adopting such a focus unhesitatingly because doing so is the only way to avoid the dangers of Comtean positivism and Queteletian "statistical facts." In Du Bois's view, some phenomena can faithfully be categorized as "Laws" but not at the expense of the partiality of Chance. To measure the limits of Chance is to commit to probability as both objective and non-epistemic, and to make such inferences requires nothing like a frequency count.[126] In advocating to bring the "Hypothesis of Law" and the "Assumption of Chance" squarely into the purview of sociologists, Du Bois echoes James's support of indeterminism and his emphasis on the present being "real as [a] possibility." Du Bois makes a substantive claim about free will and Chance that echoes James and is phrased in the context of determinism: "Protagonists of 'free' will are found to be horrified deniers of 'Chance.' And strenuous defenders of orthodox Science are found talking as though the destinies of this universe lie largely in undetermined human action—indeed, they could not avoid such talk and continue talking. Why not then flatly face the Paradox? [Why not] frankly state the Hypothesis of Law and the Assumption of Chance, and seek to determine by study and measurement the limits of each?"[127]

The distinction Du Bois draws here is fully consistent in its application with Kries's core distinction between the nomological ("Hypothesis of Law") and the ontological ("assumption of Chance") as distinguishable components of any analysis that is consistently probabilistic. Thus, an adequate sociological perspective must focus on the joint distribution of both Law and Chance, and as Du Bois makes it a point to emphasize, the latter has everything to do with the study of human action.

In a plan for an unpublished article (and possibly a book) from 1946, Du Bois describes a highly probabilistic approach to a "science of human action," complete with handwritten scribbles that resonate with the finer points of Dewey and Peirce (e.g., "feeling as truth," "art as realization"). He argues that the "outer world" remains contingent on our "assumption" that it exists; we relate to what is external to us on the basis of "hypothesis," which we maintain so long "as it works."[128] For Du Bois, we are constantly torn between safely relying on assumptions and being cast within the "Shadow of Doubt"—the sense of being surrounded by an "unknown world of black Fear and Frustration," because the world is only available to us on the grounds of a successful hypothesis. Much like Du Bois contrasts Chance to Law, here he reiterates the idea that both are involved in any single-case instance. We cannot simply apply what we know in a "Lawful" sense to what unfolds in whatever we characterize as a single case. If our delineation of the singularity of a case is roughly accurate, it will feature leeway or an action space that contradicts its lawful context.[129]

Du Bois's probabilism and the onus he places on Chance occurs independently of, though indirectly aligns with, Weber's own slightly later turn to

Chance via Kries. Only Du Bois had the benefit of participating in the American wing of objective probability that started with Peirce. As we will argue below, in chapter 7, this combination makes Du Bois's probabilistic approach contain certain advantages for sociologists that Weber's probabilism does not. If the chronology Du Bois gives in "Sociology Hesitant" is about right, then both Du Bois and Weber both turn toward objective probability at about the same time independently of each other. Du Bois will later misread his probabilistic turn as a turn against Weber, when it was, in fact, a turn *toward* the German scholar. Such confusion is eminently justified; the independent development of two versions of objective probability across an ocean leaves much room for misapprehension.

Because of the omission of objective probability from the usual history of sociological theory, however, it might appear as heterodox speculation at best (or incomprehensible word salad at worst) about a version of probabilistic inference that hardly seems interested in statistics. Our contention in this first part of the book has been that the more puzzling statements we can retrieve from Du Bois and Weber can be understood by retrieving the history they are part of. Genealogically, we have attempted to rattle the *doxa* in which frequentism is the anchor that prevents sociology from drifting into dangerous shoals. It is an anchor that, perhaps, has come to weigh us down.

PART II

Classical and Contemporary

In chapter 2, we established that Kries evidently borrowed one of his key categories from Kant, specifically "objective possibility." This fact is not a surprise. Kries was a close reader of Kant and even published a book about him.[1] We could say the same about Peirce, who engaged in an "intensive philosophical study" of Kant under his father's watchful eye in his twenties but had been reading him much earlier.[2] Kant was not alone on the philosophical reading list of Kries, the budding neuroscientist, nor was he alone on the list of the American polymath Peirce, who claimed deep knowledge of Baruch Spinoza as well, the seventeenth-century Dutch philosopher, having first read him in his teens. Eventually Peirce would come to see his own pragmatism having been anticipated in Spinoza's work. Kries, meanwhile, read at least certain parts of Spinoza's key text *Ethics* closely. He paid particular attention to the passages where Spinoza describes *adequate ideas*.[3]

As Spinoza describes them, adequate ideas are located somewhere between "God's knowledge" and "hearsay" on the epistemic ladder. If the former sees all, the latter only knows what can be understood from a single point of view. According to Spinoza, adequate ideas constitute an "intuitive knowledge" (or *scientia*), because they are a *third* kind of knowledge that works through and then surpasses both the first ("hearsay" or immediate signs) and second ("God's knowledge") kinds.[4] For Spinoza, however, adequate ideas do not present us with a recipe for good science, if by this we mean an objective science, with the most data, or the best performative knowledge. Rather, the term "adequate" is an invitation to ontology, which, for Spinoza, cannot be separated from what it means *to act*: "I say that we 'act' when something happens, either within us or externally to us, whereof we are the adequate cause—that is (by the foregoing definition) when through our nature something takes place within us or externally to us, which can be clearly and distinctly understood through our nature alone. On the other hand, I say that we are acted on when something happens within us, or something follows from our nature externally, of which we are only a partial cause."[5] To cite an accidental cause for action is inadequate, in this view, because it does not explain according to *action*. An adequate cause, according to Spinoza, tells us where the action is. It tells us about ontology, about what exists, by citing the effects it can have.

What we find in these passages appears as a kind of *rite of passage* for the intellectual tradition we are recovering. Kries, Max Weber and Pierre Bourdieu, likely Peirce himself, and quite possibly even Du Bois—his "first love" being philosophy—all seem to have read these parts of Spinoza.[6] The points Spinoza makes are well-taken by his readers, and they all appear to notice and emphasize the same points. In particular, it is this specific word—"adequate"—that, if they do not use it specifically, sticks in the mind of each thinker. Weber discusses adequate cause using the case of a mother who "boxes" her child on the ears in a fit of anger. The mother then explains how the incident was "out of character"—an accident, in other words, and not *really* an action.[7] For Du Bois, and here we speculate, his focus on Chance, and the toolkit of concepts he sketches out to center in any sociological analysis, is not inconsistent with drawing attention to action as a grounds for making sociological explanations adequate, or—in Du Bois's words—"non-hesitant" in allowing Chance to be part of our equations. A similar premise appears consistent with Bourdieu's practice theory, as we recount more fully in chapter 4, and to link ideas to the "practical consequences" of their objects is the hallmark feature of pragmatism from Peirce forward.

For Kries, the significance of adequate cause becomes clearest in the case of legal responsibility, which is arguably his textbook demonstration of the link between action and ontology.[8] Kries uses the following example: If a coach driver gets drunk before he drives a passenger in his coach, and if he misses a turn, which leads a passenger to be late, and if that passenger then gets struck by lightning, we could not say that the coach driver's drunkenness caused the passenger to get struck by lightning, as this whole antecedent sequence would not be part of its probability. If, however, the coach driver rolls his coach in a ditch and kills the passenger, we could say the antecedent conditions (i.e., drunkenness) *are* part of its probability.

Kries, here, argues against John Stuart Mill and his logic of necessary and sufficient conditions, as "any theory of causation for which there is no other causal connection than the constant ordered sequence of A and B—which bases a causal connection only on an unexceptionable regularity of succession—will, ultimately, prove sterile."[9] For a Millsian, the above sequence finds a causal relation that has been "broken" or "counteracted" by another influence. The coach driver's drunkenness is not a causal factor of the passenger being struck by lightning, although it seems to be. It has been canceled by the lightning. In the Millsian logic, we can only glimpse the ontology that comes through by model construction in multivariate statistics. For Kries, however, a coach driver's drunkenness can kill a passenger, and so too can lightning; we can make nomological arguments for these connections. *Ontologically*, however, they might do nothing to affect the *Chance* of death. For Kries, a regular uniformity between antecedent conditions and outcomes only applies in a nomological sense, but this sense is never adequate. Adequacy, for Kries, only applies in the single case for a very simple reason: because that is where the action is.[10]

Kries's notion of "adequacy" comes, quite directly it seems, from Spinoza. But what does this point tell us about objective probability, that it should it pass through the seventeenth-century Dutch philosopher as it runs its historical course? Unlike some varieties of realism today, ontology (an inference toward what exists) is empirical rather than metaphysical for the objective probabilist. To act, according to Spinoza, is to be the adequate cause of an effect. When the effects of action tell us how its cause *exists*, the field of ontology opens, and all explanation will only come to rest with an ontological statement of what exists. In chapter 5, we explain the significance of this line of reasoning for contemporary social theory. For now suffice it to say that what is capable of action is what exists; but *where* and *when* can it be an adequate cause?

While objective probabilists draw from Spinoza, this is a question they pose that he does not. For Spinoza, we will only find *one* plane of existence ("immanence") in all of creation, and it is God. For the objective probabilist, ontology is more complicated. Action is bound to *Spielraum* or continua: Distinct ontologies ("propensities") appear *there*; new things come to exist within Ranges ("fields") as they become capable of adequate causation. Ideas like these—core elements of Spinoza's "radical enlightenment"[11]—become important for the next part of the story, which finds two prominent sociologists (one following the other) picking up the threads of objective probability and weaving it into their frameworks in subtle but, once detected, significant ways.

3

Max Weber, the Probabilist

The empirical "validity" of an order . . . is the probability (*Chance*) of its being "complied with." That means . . . associates, on the average, count on the probability (*Chance*) of order-oriented behavior on the part of others, just as they also, on the average, regulate their own action according to the same kind of expectations held by others.

MAX WEBER, "Some Categories of Interpretive Sociology"

The word "interpretive" should be used with caution in understanding Weber's sociology. This claim might seem strange; after all, a focus on interpretation might be what Weber is most known for. Actions must be meaningful, and the sociologist cannot explain them without understanding them (*Verstehen*). Rather than a search for explanatory laws, the human sciences engage in the interpretive pursuit of giving charitable explanations for what people do in the world—"charitable" because people are not assumed to be pawns of forceful inevitabilities—either subpersonal or suprapersonal—but are rather seen as *intentional* actors responsive to meaning, who give subjective definitions to qualities of their lives at least enough to "make active persistence appealing."[1]

Since this codification of Weberian sociology, along with Weber's enshrinement in the American sociological field as a "classic" in the postwar period, Weber the interpretivist has been subject to few challenges, despite what can be documented as systematic anomalies. This version of Weber takes *The Protestant Ethic and the Spirit of Capitalism* as his key text, essentially serving as a "model system" for interpretive sociology,[2] with all the necessary and hallmark features: interpretation, historicist and contextual focus, and an emphasis on subjective meanings or reasons as adequate causes of observable action. Thus, the analysis on display in that breakthrough text should be taught and repeated if interpretive sociology and interpretive explanation in sociology are to be more generally sustained and kept valid. The Parsons and Schutz reception and mediation of Weber's later work, as documented in the previous chapter, help account for how this image of Weber became solidified.

For contemporary paradigms built on this reading of Weber—from social constructionism to ethnomethodology, cultural sociology, and interpretivism, among many others—his interpretive sociology finds its place secured, but this Weber is one who has been retroactively crafted to be so compatible. A cultural and interpretivist Weber commits to a relation to the world in which, in a *primary* sense, meaningful content is projected onto an otherwise "opaque" world of forces, naming it, giving it a point, constructing or "forming" it, and thus enabling the meaningful interpretation of action despite inherent chaos.[3] This assumption is a hefty one to build on, and as Weber himself recognized, it may commit one to an explanatory frame more suited to a game of chance than anything else, in which the world appears opaque and nothing we can do seems to augment, change, or redirect it in any way. This assumption also appears as a restriction on what can and cannot be meaningful by preempting any other meaning of "meaning" apart from those defined by recourse to a *theory* of meaning. That assumption is also what the anthropologist Clifford Geertz took from Weber in developing his influential approach to the "interpretation of cultures."

We have followed Geertz down that path for far too long.[4] Weber's sociology, and interpretation more generally, can be read more productively as being centered on something quite different than what the Geertzian picture portrays. Geertz reads Weber as subscribing to the dichotomy of culture versus chaos that undergirds Geertz's influential approach to culture. For Geertz, without "culture patterns" or "organized systems of significant symbols" our lives could unfold only as a "mere chaos of pointless acts and exploding emotions, [our] experience virtually shapeless."[5] Geertz grounds his claims here in the coevolution of culture and cognition, which had become popular by the early 1960s alongside a revival of Franz Boas's cultural particularism. Geertz's formulations were cutting-edge at the time, but they also set the study of culture on a course based on another dichotomy, this time between "culture and mind."[6] If culture plays an integral role in the development of human cognitive capabilities, those capabilities have no bearing on the nature of culture itself. In Geertz's view, the arrow does not go both ways. Such a strict separation means that culture provides for a unique kind of "learning" as it displaces states of the world that would otherwise be chaotic to us. Cognition plays no role in ordering chaos, and so we can safely disregard cognition when we set out to explain "how culture matters."[7]

It is through this lens that Geertz reads Weber and finds him to be a ready ally in the study of culture as the antithesis of meaningless chaos. When we read Weber as a *probabilist*, however, we can see that he did not commit to a metaphysics of meaningless chaos, which amounts to a considerable departure from Geertz's version of Weber. What we find in Weber's interpretive sociology is, rather, a sustained focus on the "existence of a (specifiable) *Chance*" as a point of orientation for social action. Such a focus leads us to ask two primary questions of Weber, which, it is worth noting, fly under Geertz's radar, and because they do, serve to further enhance the distinction between interpretation and probability in social science: How is objective probability generated? How is our subjective orientation looped into it?

In this chapter, we challenge the inherited interpretivist view of Weber's sociology by recasting it around probability and the concept of *Chance*. It is still possible to retain Weber's own understanding of sociology as interpretive, but not in a manner that sets the study of culture on its own—on an "island of understanding," as it were, where culture analysts can safely dwell without any knowledge of what Geertz calls the "vacuum" between "what our body tells us and what we have to know in order to function."[8] We will sketch Weber's novel and underutilized tool kit for probabilism, and his way of answering the two aforementioned questions, by engaging with his most famous concepts and proposals. A probabilist analytic tool kit does not depart from interpretation or diminish its appeal for the task of human science. Yet, when concentrated on the loop, interpretation here becomes distinguishable from interpretivism's concentration on coherent symbolic structures, cultural systems, and landscapes of meaning.

The Making of *Economy and Society*

We can see the construction of canonical versions of Weberian sociology in quite material terms if we examine the tumultuous history of his key programmatic text, *Economy and Society* (hereafter *E&S*). The text comprising the first part of *E&S* today constituted Weber's primary task for what remained the most productive and relatively least personally turbulent period of his life. Between 1908 and Weber's death in 1920, he helped organize and edit what was meant to be a "handbook on the structure of modern capitalism," which eventually bore the title *Grundriss der Sozialökonomik* and featured several contributors working on various topics. Weber's *Wirtschaft und Gesellschaft* was to be used as an "up-to-date reference work" targeting largely business and commerce students. Alas, such best-laid plans would change many times. While Weber helped organize the endeavor with publisher Paul Siebeck, it never came to full fruition.[9] Weber's single contribution remained what he had drafted as *Wirtschaft und Gesellschaft*: three almost finished chapters and a very fragmentary fourth.

With Weber's untimely death in June 1920, Marianne Weber's assistant, Melichor Palyi, took control of organizing the text from the written, re-written, old, and new manuscripts that Weber had left behind, with Marianne Weber deciding on the final ordering of the text.[10] As Keith Tribe explains, "this dilemma—how to marry three and a bit new chapters, composed in 1919–1920 according to a new plan in Weber's head but nowhere written down, with a mass of preparatory material dating back many years—did not end with the solution of 1921–22" or the solution that Palyi and Marianne Weber reached at that time.[11] The 1921–1922 edition was ultimately published in four installments, beginning in October 1921 and ending in September 1922. It is the first installment of this first edition that Tribe has recently translated, as it was "the only section of the work that had been revised by Weber and typeset before he died in June 1920."[12] As such, it will also be the focus of the subsequent discussion. This edition would be followed shortly after by the second edition in 1925 (featuring Weber's text on the sociology of music) and the third edition in 1947. After Marianne Weber died in 1954, editorial control passed to jurist and founder of the *Max-Weber-Archiv* Johannes Winckelmann, who would publish a reordered and expanded fourth edition in 1956.

These details are not without consequence because coinciding with the travails of the *E&S* text is Weber's growing international prominence, especially in sociology. Arguably, nothing helped secure this reputation more than the translation of the first installment of the 1921–1922 *E&S* edition by Parsons and Henderson in 1947 as *The Theory of Social and Economic Organization*. Their translation would be the basis for the first part of the 1968 two-volume English-language edition, published by the University of California Press, with a visually striking light-blue cover with yellow font, and edited by sociologist Guenther Roth and political economist Claus Wittich. This version would now bear an English translation of Weber's original title, *Economy and Society*. This text mirrored the fifth German-language edition, which was published under Winckelmann's supervision. It compiled many unpublished manuscripts and fragments that Weber had left behind, not initially included in the 1921–1922 edition, most of which had been translated and published separately by that time (e.g., *The City*, *The Sociology of Religion*, *Max Weber on Law in Economy and Society*).

The principal knowledge-political context for this translation history was the growing "Americanization" of sociology.[13] These circumstances are essential for the following reasons. Roth and Wittich's 1968 (reissued in 1978) two-volume English edition of *E&S* has effectively become *the* introduction (alongside the *Protestant Ethic*) to Weber *as a sociologist*. Such an introduction by this particular text leaves the reader with an impression of Weber as a historical dabbler or scattered dilettante rather than with Weber's vision of himself as a *systematic* sociologist—a vision he would identify with as he worked on the first and only partially finished part of *Wirtschaft und Gesellschaft*. Such a view of himself is also present, in embryonic form, in Weber's development as a probabilist, from his first use of Kries in 1906 to the systematic development of probabilistic principles (particularly the loop) in 1913, and finally to their fruition as interpretive sociology in the first edition of *E&S*.

In March 1920, just a few months before his death, Weber identified his ongoing work on the book as that of a "sociologist" in a letter written to economist Robert Liefmann. In the letter, Weber includes the following noteworthy sentence: "In sociological terms, the state is no more than the chance that particular kinds of specific *action* occur."[14] On the one hand, such a statement could easily be shrugged off as a weak probabilistic commitment that could presumably be strengthened with more data or better measurement; it could also be read as immaterial to or *less important than* Weber's better-known definition of the state as a territorial organization with a "monopoly on the use of force."[15] Neither of these perspectives is on the right track. Rather, Weber's sociology gives ample room to the probabilism evident in his letter to Liefmann.

We can find more evidence of Weber's probabilism toward the end of his life from students' notes jotted down during lectures Weber gave in Munich in May of 1920, less than a month before his death. One student records the following about Weber's recommendation for how to study the state sociologically: "The sociologist asks, of what are people thinking when they speak of the state: (1) school, chances to be beaten, (2) policeman: they wanted the policeman to come, (3) military service, (4) taxes, (5) court, laws. Also this constellation is only a *Chance*." The same student then records the following, more general points from Weber, which focus more closely on the connection of *Chance* to action: "They are always merely chances of a definite art of human activities. The sum of these chances is the state. They are those chances that count. One's action is oriented to these chances. When does the state exist; when there is a chance that it will be obeyed!" Another student writes down similar points from Weber's lectures, and suggests further the connection of sociology to the study of *Chance*: "Sociologically: what is a person thinking of 'the state'? Always merely chances of a certain type of action: the state. One's action is oriented to these. Sociology: a science of action. Existence of the state: chances of being obeyed."[16] The purpose of revisiting these little time capsules—fraught no doubt as the reader can surely attest, whether based on their own note-taking or, more pointedly, that of their students!—

is the special lucidity we can find in them about the connection Weber appears to draw, in a kind of last testament, between *Chance* and what are agreeably core elements of his sociological oeuvre: the state and action.

Similar premonitions, and what they meant for a sociology *status nascendi*, were apparent to Weber as early as the 1913 *Logos* essay, which he associated with a "comprehensive sociological theory and presentation." The essay first presents many of the central ideas on *Chance*, objective probability, and expectation that he flirted with in 1906 and would systematically develop in the first two chapters of *Wirtschaft und Gesellschaft* despite the text remaining incomplete. They were also clear (in part and thematically) in articles Weber published in the *Archiv für Sozialwissenschaft und Sozialpolitik* during the first decade of the 1900s, which were later collected posthumously as *Gesammelte Aufsätze zur Wissenschaftslehre* (1922)—the "Theory of Science" or the "Methodological Essays." Thus, the bulk of material known to English readers as *E&S* was sketched *before* Weber worked on his fundamental conceptual and methodological framework. Accordingly, none of this well-known historical and typological work had yet been reconceptualized according to the core concepts of what Weber understood to be *his* sociology.

Weber Discovers the Probabilistic Loop

Weber would be the first (to anyone's knowledge) to bring Kriesian probabilism to bear as part of an argument defending the prospects of the historical method. Weber laid out his argument against Eduard Meyer's exhortation that historians focus on free will and chance occurrences in order to preserve the strict particularity of the historical past. On the contrary, Weber argued, historians could make *adequately* causal arguments by making judgments of objective possibility. They made these judgments by drawing on the "rules of experience," treating what they learn as "nomological," to which they draw together "certain 'facts' of the 'historical situation,'" or what is "ontological knowledge." In fact, they must already do so, in Weber's view, if their narratives are to assign any causal significance to events and actions.[17] What happens next in Weber's remapping of Kries's ideas to the center of his sociology shifts from *Chance* as, in this case, a critique of knowledge, to *Chance* as what Kries himself understood by it in his recovery of probabilistic reasoning as a critique of frequentism: namely, *Chance* as a feature of the world.

However, taking the objectivity of *Chance* on board creates a certain paradox for Weber in trying to adopt these principles to develop an interpretive sociology. *Chance*, when illustrated in the examples Kries used, relies on initial conditions easily categorized as "natural" in the sense of being action- or mind-independent. While we can be subjectively oriented to them, our actions in these types of *Spielraum* do not depend on those orientations. Even if their probabilities are unexpected, they will occur regardless. In Weber's approach, this indifference to orientations does not apply to the topics of sociology unless we adopt a naturalistic approach to sociology dubiously focused on lawlike evolutions of a collective object independent of *any* subjective orientation—the type of collective object that would therefore be, in a strict sense, *meaningless*, at least in Weber's view.[18] We saw at the end of chapter 2 that Du Bois rightly rejected this approach.

To resolve the paradox, Weber discovers a *looping* perspective. Whatever factor might seem important for social life is important because of how it impacts the construction of *Chance*, in the creation of objective probability and the creation of subjective orientation. Like Du Bois in his own paradoxical combination of "Law and Chance," Weber accounts for order and unpredictability by giving the tendency for social order not over to values, or social networks, or a constraining collective object (like a "structure") but rather to *Chance* as what can both be objectively ordered as well as serve as a subjective orientation.

Weber does not claim (*pace* legal reasoners in his case) that the mere existence of rules is sufficient to generate social order—though we can observe rules as explicit attempts to specify *Chance*. Without taking the form of a *sanction*, rules will not matter for social action because, as limited "legal" mandates, they cannot create expectation. More generally, whatever we might statistically measure as probability will not matter for social action unless it assumes some—empirically documentable—form as a subjective orientation. A "judgment of objective possibility," once reserved for historians in Weber's earlier treatment, now takes form as the *actor's* expectation of the future in alignment with a specified *Chance*. Thus, while some factors (rules, agreement, promises, consensus, conceptions of order) construct objective probability as initial conditions for likely outcomes, other factors (sanctions, writing, shame, memory, even a probability calculation) create orientations in a manner that alienates people from their purest subjectivity as capable of *deciding* what to expect.

As Weber realized, *Chance* becomes significant sociologically for its ontological implications. Like Du Bois, he had found the answers given by past thinkers like Auguste Comte and particularly Herbert Spencer to be completely unworkable for their ontological implications (i.e., because they conceived of society as an organism). His rejection of Spencer and Comte does not mean Weber punted on ontology or settled for a vulgar empiricism (only individuals exist, just look around you!). He simply answered it differently, in a way we have not yet been able to recognize: "The objectively 'valid' consensus—in the sense of calculable probabilities—is naturally not to be confused with the individual actor's reliance that others will treat his expectations as valid. Similarly, the empirical validity of an agreed-upon order is not to be confused with the subjective expectation of compliance with its subjectively intended meaning. In both cases, however, there is a reciprocal relationship of intelligibly adequate causation between the average objective validity of the probability (logically a part of the category of Objective Possibility) and the currently average subjective expectations."[19]

Here, we encounter Weber's version of the *loop*: specific configurations of objective probability that capture subjective orientation within a repeating connection of *Chance* and expectation. Weber describes this loop as reciprocal and causal, in which objective probabilities are adequate cause of subjective expectation and vice versa. The relationship between objectively "average probability," which is statistically measurable, and subjectively average expectation is direct in this case, as an example of a way in which we can learn what is possible without needing quantified knowledge of probability. Via learning, people "loop into" objective probability, accessing, in the subjective form of expectations, the mechanisms specifying *Chance* as repeatable and recurrent.[20]

Probability learning counts when rules rigidly establish the *Spielraum* in the relevant case. The *range* of what is objectively possible constitutes essentially the totality of the play space available to the actor. Learning can occur when one grasps "rational principles," such as "equality of opportunity," when they effectively order *Chance* as the justification of a certain range of possibility, usually via organizational action, which can also include trial and error in more consensus-based contexts.[21] Where "agreed-upon order" allows for a wider range, people learn what can elicit consensus approval as a "convention," which more often takes form in simply *not* meeting with "tangible disapproval."[22]

In cases of specifically social action, expectation is no one's possession. It arises from learning that *reduces* subjective motivation and meaning. For Weber, probabilistic expectation is the subjective construct corresponding— via a causal process—to objective *Chance*:

> Specifically, for us an action is "adequately caused" when, according to the then-current *average probable assessment of facts*, the action is subjectively oriented in meaning toward those facts. Thereby the *objectively calculable probabilities* of the possible expectations also function as an adequate cognitive basis for the *probable* presence of those expectations in actors. That the terminology of the two converges almost unavoidably does not eliminate the logical chasm between them. Only in the first sense, by *a judgment of objective possibility*, we

obviously mean that those objective probabilities (Chancen) are suited on the average to serve as meaningful grounds for the subjective expectations of the actors, and therefore, that they actually (in a relevant measure) did so serve.[23]

Thus, the looping of objectivity into subjectivity, evident here as a "judgment of objective possibility," serves as the cognitive basis for whatever specific form *Chance* takes. Action can continue forward in time without finding an orientation to the "existence of a (specifiable) *Chance*," though it will, quite noticeably, not feature expectation.

Probabilistic loops enlist people via recurrent and reinforcing orientations, which save the need to maintain or even encourage a subjective orientation to meaning. There might be occasions to interpret *Chance*, perhaps in circumstances where it appears most alien; and yet, if we still loop in, we cannot easily control our expectation, regardless of our interpretations. Individuals do not need to be the sources of their expectation: "That an action is subjectively oriented in meaning to an established order can thereby initially mean that the actual action . . . objectively corresponds to the action they had subjectively intended."[24] That subjectively intended action loops into the established order and becomes objective should, for Weber, draw our attention squarely on expectation. We will expect something when we act, even if (following those like Tversky and Kahneman mentioned in the last chapter) the expectation will inevitably be wrong compared to a calculated prediction; for Weber that does not make it any less objective. If a "purely subjective expectation of compliance with . . . subjectively intended meaning" is diminished by expectation, then we have looped into *Chance* and our being is changed—it is *less* subjective.[25] Social orders like this do not require actors to constantly expend "effort" in maintaining their orientation.[26]

Probabilistic Rationalization

The *Chance*/expectation loop is a central element in Weber's probabilistic sociology, which is meant as a revised interpretive sociology. The looping effect Weber describes is, as we will see, common to all probabilistic reasoning. Though Weber's approach owes much to Kries, the loop is nowhere more explicitly stated than in Weber. On these grounds, a revised interpretive sociology can proceed further, in this case toward the decidedly most "macro" aspects of Weber's sociology.

According to Weber, the construction of general concepts by sociologists implies that people possess "an average measure of the capacities required to evaluate [the] probabilities, thus helping construct the collective order that

the concept describes."[27] The core assumption is that "objectively existing average probabilities are . . . subjectively taken into account by . . . actors." Objective probability is in no sense uniform; there is no implication that social
action must be oriented in the *exact* same way, even if expectation is shared.
The *Chance*/expectation loop suggests many sources of variation in this regard. Weber again invokes the spirit of the gambler. A card game, for example,
implies a subjective and objective coincidence in a loop, and because it does,
a possible orientation toward this order, perfectly in line with shared expectation, is that of the lawbreaker ("the cheat") who "orients his behavior to the
very rules whose meaning he subjectively consciously violates."[28] Whether an
actor has orientation to certain specifications of *Chance* and, if so, *how*, indicates to us the manner in which the action is *social*.

In large-scale constructed orders, a plurality of social actions—in terms of
their modality and substantive contents—can coincide with the same range
of objective *Chance*. Moreover, the very empirical existence and continuation of a given social order often depends on the specifiable *Chance* allowing
for a range of possible orientations, as opposed to demanding just one mode
of orientation—for instance, to *Chance* as specified entirely as a conception
of order. This dynamic is also not a matter of "either/or." The probability of
orientation can vary continuously, in Weber's view, but that continuum does
express more or less of an orientation: "The association exists so long and insofar as an action, oriented toward the rules in accordance with their average
intended meaning, still occurs within a practically *relevant* range."[29]

Arguably, the most drawn-out discussion of these points comes from Weber's theory of rationalization. While the general sketch of this idea, with its
big themes of the triumph of bureaucracy and the "disenchantment of the
world," is typically associated with Weber's famous lecture from 1917, "Science
as a Vocation," Weber actually presents a formal treatment of rationalization
in the final pages of the 1913 *Logos* essay.[30] In this account, knowledge and explicit understanding can both sustain and transform *Chance* via conceptions
of order and the making of rules. However, as Weber points out, rationalization presupposes a social differentiation between those who *make* rules, and
establish the "rational foundation of the rules," and those who are "practically affected by rational techniques and rules" but do not know or cannot
alter those foundations. Thus, rationalization "does not produce a universal
knowledge of . . . conditions and relationships, but rather usually brings about
precisely the opposite."[31]

Phenomenological social constructionism, in the tradition of sociologists
Peter Berger and Thomas Luckmann in their famous 1966 book, *The Social*

Construction of Reality, theorizes the difference between experience-near "intimate" interactions characterizing local orders and the experience-distant interactions of large-scale orders by appealing to the specificity versus abstractness of what Berger and Luckmann call "typifications."[32] Weber's probabilistic constructionism, in contrast, points to the range of orientations as the more theoretically relevant feature. When social construction occurs as rationalization, a range of different typical orientations applies to "organizational action at least partially regulated through rational rules."[33] Weber emphasizes how, for most, rules find no rational foundation and are not "agreed upon." Instead, they are "imposed from above. People who are, on whatever grounds, capable of influencing action according to their will, impose statues on this social action on the grounds of 'consensus expectations,'" suggestive of a movement *within* a range of possibility in the shift from statute to consensus. Different typical orientations vary socially, temporally, and spatially, and this variation becomes particularly evident in different types of actors we can retrieve from Weber's account of rationalization.

Rule creators are distinctive for their orientation toward specifications of *Chance*, principally taken to be a "conception of order." Their orientation is therefore "inward" (i.e., affective, ethical, or religious), or we might say that it is only valid for expectations within the socially differentiated space of others and is also oriented by conceptions.[34] Such orientations, then, are typical for the center, origin, or inside a rationalizing space, such that "rational rules of an association are . . . imposed or 'suggested' . . . for specific purposes."[35]

Carriers consist of those proximate to the rationalizing space, the center, or the origin but who are oriented to the same specification of *Chance* as a rule rather than as a conception. "The rules are—though not necessarily with awareness of those purposes of their creation—more or less evenhandedly subjectively interpreted and actively carried out."[36] Carriers often find themselves in spaces already configured by rule creators, thus generating a potential for social change in the introduction of new *Chancen*. They do so by bearing the threat of sanctions (either official or unofficial) of a "coercive apparatus."

Those with a *follower* orientation are also oriented to the center, origin, or rationalizing space. This orientation manifests in social action of a more strategic kind in seeking to realize subjectively defined self-interests. Followers "subjectively [know] the usual application of the rules . . . as far as is absolutely necessary for their private purposes."[37] Eventually, if an order is durable, followers' specifications of *Chance*, which were once envisioned using exclusively experience-distant conceptions, come to coincide with and become durably repeated and reinforced by larger social-action arrays strategically used in the pursuit of varied material and ideal interests combined with other orientations.

Finally, "the mass" displays orientations most typical at the furthest distance from the center, found more often in peripheries, far from the rationalizing space, and, temporally speaking, distant from the origins. What Weber says about this typical orientation indicates a decline in conception and its replacement by consensus at the edge of possible orientation: "An action approximately conforming to the average understood meaning is 'traditionally' practiced and usually observed without any knowledge of the purpose and meaning or even the existence of the rules. Thus, the empirical validity *particularly* of a rational order rests on the consensus of actors to conform to the habitual, the familiar, the taught and the oft-recurring."[38]

Significantly, we can notice a transition in rationalization by moving away from the original source of rules. Conceptions of order can loop into novel specifications of *Chance* at the site of rule creation, but this loop is less effective as we move further away from and beyond the rationalizing space. On the edges, at a distance, in peripheral spaces: here consensus holds instead. Social action reveals a specification of *Chance* not because it has an explicit meaning but simply because it is typical and normal ("what people do"). Objective probability can be durable because of the absence of reprimand for certain social actions, even if a rule does apply that ultimately draws on a conception of order.

Weber offers a particularly vivid discussion of moving between orientations—from conception to sanction to custom—in the context of learning. Though a probabilistic expectation may never take form as a clear conception, it can be found in a subjective orientation to the same *Chance*: "The multiplication table is imposed on us as children exactly as a rational directive of a despot is imposed on a subject. And indeed it is imposed in the most intrinsic sense, as something at first wholly incomprehensible to us in its foundation and even its purposes, but something nevertheless bindingly valid. The 'consensus' is initially therefore, plain submission to the customary because it is customary. This remains more or less the case. One learns not through rational deliberations but rather through applied (imposed) empirical cross-checks whether one has calculated in what consensus terms the 'correct' way."[39]

Thus, in learning multiplication, people learn "consensus expectations" for this particular use of rational numbers. For most, what is possible about these numbers are the rules and sanctions that dictate their proper use. They do not learn the "rational foundations" that make these possibilities objective and specify the *Chance* of using them. Subjective orientation tends toward custom rather than conceptions of order as we move away from the ("other-worldly") socially differentiated spaces in which conceptions alone can specify *Chance*. Suppose multiplication practice remained merely a conception of (mathematical) order and did not transform into sanction (backed by educational institutions). In that case, we should not expect that so many would know it (nor expect that they would expect it from us). If multiplication were simply a "consensus expectation" without a rational foundation or organizational sanction, then we should expect to find limits in such an orientation; rules maintained by the educational sanction prevent this outcome by facilitating a more durable looping effect.

The key point is that different types of orientation exist via which actors can be captured in a loop to engage in recurrent social action. Ranging closer to or farther from a rationalizing center or historical origin, we tend to find certain orientations: conceptions closer to the center, consensus farther away from it. But while these orientations are quite distinct in rationalized constructions, they are also *linked* together. Notably, Weber emphasizes "fluid transitions" between orientations: The same specified *Chance* need not be maintained by the same orientation to be part of social action that is equally constructive.[40]

The Protestant Ethic as the Construction of a Probability Order

We can illustrate the analytic potential of Weber's probabilism still further by attempting an unorthodox reading of his famous essay *The Protestant Ethic and the Spirit of Capitalism*.[41] Nearly every reading of this canonical text puts the onus on themes like the role of "ideas" in action, or more generally of "culture." It is also told as a story of the seemingly fatalistic unfolding of "rationalization." Weber is portrayed as the tortured soothsayer of inevitable doom—a somewhat warranted characterization. Nevertheless, even if we read Weber in all these ways, as many do, we would never see how he is portraying a probability order in which some elements (like "ideas") find a way, through *Chance* and the multiple orientations to it, of affecting the possibility of other elements more distant in time and space (e.g., the machine-like "economic cosmos" of capitalism). It is telling, in this regard, that we can find a similar architecture here as one we can see in Weber's *Logos* text from 1913, which we are arguing is a seminal work on his probabilism. In both the *Protestant Ethic* and the *Logos* essay, we can find a continuum or distribution of these different orientations (rule creators, followers, carriers, the mass) in the different persons and groups Weber calls our attention to.

Over the historical period of Weber's argument, the original "creations" by

John Calvin and Martin Luther are "conceptions of legitimate order." These conceptions consist of an orientation to novel possibilities.[42] Such a starting point does not seem uncommon in Weber's rationalization account. The construction of new orders of *Chance* often become available as conceptions first. Just consider Luther toiling away at his desk in Wittenberg when, late one night in 1520, a revelation occurs in his head: "justification by faith alone!" An otherwise obscure *Chance*, first apparent to Luther, the theology professor, will thereafter become integral to ascetic Protestantism via the pastoral care of more practical men like Richard Baxter and John Robinson.[43] The "organization of life" by Puritans like these reveal a different orientation at work than Luther's—namely, a *carrier* orientation.

Over a hundred years later, and after a transatlantic voyage, the same *Chance* is revealed again in Weber's story, only this time very differently. Eighteenth-century inventor and statesman Benjamin Franklin demonstrates the orientation of a *follower* rather than a carrier. As Weber puts it, "all virtues, according to Franklin, become virtues only to the extent that they are useful to the individual."[44] Some differences in conception are specified, as evidenced by the lessons contained in Franklin's *Poor Richard's Almanack*; but the possibilities of the "spirit of capitalism" mark not a new invention but a different appropriation of the *Chance* contained in the Protestant Ethic. Such a follower orientation matures into the "middle-class vocational ethos" evident a hundred years after Franklin, in which his homespun wisdom (e.g., "A penny saved is a penny earned") now carries a firmly entrenched material interest. The "middle-class employer . . . is now allowed to follow his interest in economic gain, and indeed should do so . . . [R]eligious asceticism gave to the employer the soothing assurance that the unequal distribution of the world's material goods resulted from the special design of God's providence."[45] Asceticism becomes *conventional*, followed as "absolutely necessary for private purposes," because the expectation to be ascetic now applies as a matter of course.

The same *Chance* is buried under all these varied appropriations and uses. For Weber, a whole universe of mechanisms now surpasses the initial religious conception. At this point in the narrative, Weber famously pivots and describes the polar opposite of subjective meaning—the "steel-hard casing"—as what, for our purposes, an orientation to *Chance* looks like when it completely "determines the style of life of those born into it." Social action resembles not the "conduct of a vocation" in this circumstance, but "economic coercion."[46] The orientation is quite distant from religious asceticism and does not rely on "rule creators" who theorize the steel-hard casing as

Continuum of Orientation

Conceptions of Order	Law	Convention	Custom
←			→
Center			*Periphery*
Original			*Derived*
"Rule Creators"	Carriers (with sanctions)	Followers (personal Interest)	"The Mass
"The Protestant Ethic"	The Puritans	Benjamin Franklin	"The Steel-hard Casing"

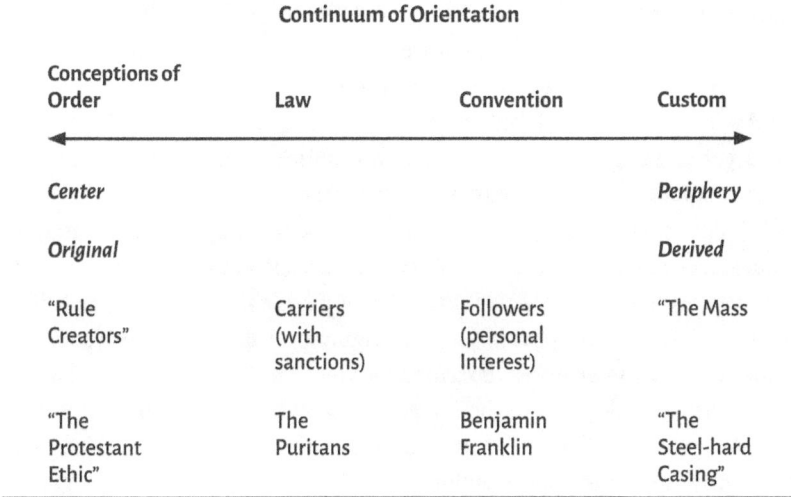

FIGURE 2. Mapping the Protestant Ethic as a probability order

legitimate order. As *Chance* becomes machine-like, instead, an interpretation of this sort (or any sort) becomes arbitrary and inconsequential; it does not really exist as part of the action.[47]

Throughout his narrative, and as exhibited in figure 2, Weber describes different orientations to *Chance*. He also suggests that orientations to "belief in legitimate order" are not necessary for a probability order to exist. This predicament applies to the majority of those involved in rationalization. Yet even in this case, it still matters that a "conception of order" (or "rules," "legal norms," "knowledge"), somewhere, "could be known," or in other words genealogically retrieved for "the resulting 'probabilities.'"[48]

Only religious actors, Weber implies, within a socially differentiated space, oriented toward an otherworldly *Chance*, could generate such a probability order. Richard Lachmann's observation seems telling in this regard: The "external ideological shock from a Protestant Ethic" is all that could interrupt the "chronic inelasticity" of feudal domination.[49] However, the typical orientation that appeared could not remain a "conception of order" for the Protestant Ethic to cause societal transformation (i.e., move "out of monastic cells into everyday life"). If these conceptions were to function as an adequate cause on such a large scale, they would have to become sanctions by rule makers (pastors) that removed certain expectations from the contingencies of subjective decision. "Work in a calling" became the practical orientation to the possibility of predestined eternal damnation or salvation, testifying to one's saved status. The effect was to create a highly motivating "psychological premium" for those who knew little about the "rational foundations" of the possibilities they so desperately feared. Ultimately in figures like Franklin, they lose the association with religion entirely.[50]

As "societalization" takes its course, we find that social relations form on larger and larger scales (from organization to society) on the grounds of shared expectation. Seemingly, everyone comes to occupy the same order. We should expect to find this continuum of orientation, particularly as it becomes skewed toward "custom" and away from "subjective meaning."[51] There is a distal element to the distribution that appears over both space and time, with a center and periphery, with an origin and subsequent derivations of it that take many forms, as described by Weber in 1913 as "rationalization." But in the later additions to the *Protestant Ethic*, Weber describes these roles as different orientations to *Chance*, and *Chance* understood in a seemingly substantive sense, as if social action—and the causal relationships that many credit to "ideas" or "culture"—is "moderated" by the existence of *Chance*.[52] Weber will flesh this point out more fully in *Economy and Society*.

As a general rule, then, the *wider* the range of orientations, the more objective (i.e., taken for granted, simply assumed) a given orientation will be, coinciding with more social action within a spatially larger and, we might assume, temporally longer "area of expectations."[53] When the Protestant Ethic was possible only as a conception by Puritan pastors, it was less objective, far more tenuous, and with a much smaller and shorter reach. It defied other orders of expectation, as evidenced by the ostracization of Puritans due to their "otherworldliness" and exhibited by their strange asceticism, ruthless religiosity, and extraordinary discipline. When a judgment of objective possibility persists all the way to the "steel-hard casing," salvation is still at issue, but it is salvation of a different kind, as it needs no conceptions or subjective meaning for the purposes of orientation, has seemingly no unpredictable distance from us social actors, and in this respect no longer *needs* to be a "legitimate order" for most.

Even here, constructions remain subject to adequate cause by expectation. If the loops break down, so too will the objective probability of whatever they construct, no matter how long a duration it appears to have. However, when what is expected is as objective as machine-rational capitalism, the contribution of this orientation fades from view. *Chance* can simply mean what will happen if one does not "show up at work on Monday morning." Nevertheless, depending on these orientations, even such a highly specified and seemingly predictable *Chance* as this is rooted in a once-very-tenuous process of social change in which the same objective probability first took the form of a conception of order, providing an entry point, then, for what are sure to appear as novel aspects of Weber's argument about social construction: particularly, the distance of a rationalizing center from a periphery; the range of applicable orientations and how they change across that range; and both the metaphoric and literal inclusion of space here, with the implication that it is possible to move into or create a space where even the objective probabilities of capitalism do not apply.

Distance, Range, and Orientation

Weber's probabilistic constructionism strongly suggests that something like the state is only as present as objective *Chance* within a certain geographical space that is not uniform.[54] From this perspective, the threat of physical violence aside, the subjective orientation to the state is not constant but features *variation*, one most accurately captured by Weber's theory of rationalization, which describes, in detail, differences in subjective orientation according to a measure of *distance* from a center.[55] Notably, this claim is a *formal* one with application to no particular case, despite the "model system" being what Weber described as the historical tendency of European rationalization based on the appearance of autonomous value spheres from an originally undifferentiated religious base. Despite the limitations of this account, the probabilistic application shows how *Chance* can become embedded in social action, action in which a *loop* creates expectations not necessarily relating to *local* objective probability (i.e., "custom" or "habit") but instead linking to explicit supra-local knowledge or "rules" produced by others at some *distance* from the actor, who retains an orientation to something like a center, even if the actor has no recognition of this fact, or more specifically, even if their orientation is necessarily different from what it would be at the center (or originating point, or source of rationalization).[56] The basis of the formal theory, which Weber articulates primarily in the 1913 *Logos* essay, bears a strong resemblance to his account in *The Protestant Ethic*.

In talking about rationalization, Weber specifically tries to capture a series of *level* distinctions (rather than historical stages) in the "cognitive basis" that emerges within the loop from a direct interface with objective probability and that indicates a difference in the *Chance* of orientation to rules and knowledge according to a measure of social distance.[57] The "rationalization of social action," via the enactment of explicit rules and statutes "governing" activity, as Weber claims, paradoxically "does not produce a universal knowledge of their conditions and relationships, but rather usually brings about precisely the opposite."[58] Explicit knowledge as to the rational bases or intent of the rules diminishes among the vast majority of people subject to them, even as it increases among a few who initially had the power to enact them and impose them on the masses. However, this diminishment could not occur unless a different cognitive basis for "subjective meaning" exists independently of explicitly rationalized meaning.

Weber here suggests that rationalization only occurs by essentially creating a *Chance*/expectation loop with the paradoxical effect of making explicit knowledge and meaning ("rules") both *more important* (as potentially explicable) though *less of a concern* for most. As Weber expands on these points in his classic lecture "Science as a Vocation," he refers to "rationalization" and "disenchantment" as reflecting a shift in orientation. The context is one in which "ultimate and most sublime values have withdrawn from the public sphere," in which "only in the smallest circles of the community, from one human being to another, pianissimo, that a pulse beats as a faint echo of that prophetic spirit which in former times went through the great congregations as a firestorm and welded them together,"[59] referring to the development of explicit knowledge and rules that are less important for their content than for the fact that, for most, they are produced *elsewhere*, in smaller, distal circles, to which most are therefore oriented primarily as a received "average understood meaning."

In such a rationalized setting, the *Chance* of social action being oriented in this manner enhances the *Chance* of a social order being "rational." According to Weber, the "generally established belief [is] that the conditions of . . . everyday life . . . are *in principle* rational, that is, are human artifacts accessible to rational knowledge, creation and control—a belief that has certain significant consequences for the character of the 'consensus.'"[60] Rational knowledge does not create this consensus, though it can heighten its *Chance* and relative frequency, which will deepen matching expectations in the loop. Nevertheless, social orders can be maintained without most participants ever needing an exact reason "why." This belief is added, then, as a product of "social differentiation and rationalization" of the sort that finds distinct groups relating to a given order in different ways: by rational rules, by the application of rules (whether selectively or generally), or by averagely understood meaning and habitual "consensus."

This formulation is arguably Weber's most fully articulated treatment of the rationalization process, one that cannot be fully understood outside the probabilistic standpoint. *Chance* applies, more generally, in that a given orientation to the rationalizing space is present. While academic or scientific spaces often serve in the role of "centers," they do not have to. Organizational, rationalizing spaces can exist; the state can serve in such a role; and religion in its literal otherworldly orientation and "process of abstraction" provides a prime example.[61] Whatever serves as the rationalizing space, the transmission of its novel objective probabilities can affect the subjective orientation of those distant from this originating space.

Thus, like social relationships and the state, social action here is the focus of a probabilistic accounting; sociologists identify the conditions necessary for more and more people to be captured (willingly, unwillingly, unknowingly) by a loop. But this kind of focus also implies that, in a historical sense, there can be more or less *range* to a loop. Differentiation is a process that generates *more* social action by creating different objective *potentials* for social action. If, in Weber's cryptic account of "value-spheres," he is concerned with the "most rational forms reality *can* assume," this account implies the construction of a center and a range that make "ethical action" possible beyond the unmediated potentiality of "brotherliness."[62] If this state of affairs is referred to as "rational," the label only means that it features the spatial dynamic of a center, resulting from some form of dispossession and contingent in some way on orientations to "conceptions of order." For most people, the *Chance* produced in this manner takes the form of a test that maintains one distribution as separate from another, for instance, "proving oneself" in the world (experiencing a "life-fate") via profit rather than for reasons of state.[63]

Probabilistic Power

We have seen that for Weber, rationalization occurs via probabilistic pathways that construct social order by specifying *Chance* as an orientation for action. Elsewhere, he uses a similar form of probabilistic reasoning to make distinctions between "communalization" and "sociation" as different ways of constructing social relations.[64] First, social relations produce a sense of belonging and cohesion by reducing the transparency of subjective orientation. Individuals cannot, alone, be adequate causes of what happens. Second, we find more subjectivity, with sociation featuring more "consciously chosen" adequate causes. The distinction mirrors that between an "objectively correct" orientation (carriers) and an instrumental orientation (followers). Noticeably, these orientations do not have to feature exclusively in social action. Where a central authority claims rules of "selection," sociation consists of an orientation to the expectations of others via rules in a competitive setting.[65] Selection that is not socially ordered, Weber contends, will otherwise consist of adequate cause in the form of biology or of one "elemental force" paired off with another: In neither case can our expectations change what happens.[66]

The implication is that social action requires an adequate cause to be rooted in a judgment, as indicating the parameters of a "reality known

through experience" and its delineation of what would quite literally *be* random should it arise in a situation not already shaped by its order. Arguably,
the clearest example of this point is found in Weber's analysis of power and
legitimate order, which might include examples of both sociation and communalization, in addition to conflict and selection, but in all cases, the order
in question revolves around the construction of *Chance*: subjective orientations looping into objective possibility, creating expectations of what should
or what will probably happen—judgments maintain the order. The same is
not true outside of probability orders.

But what does this argument mean for Weber's famous analysis of power?
According to Weber, "power can be defined as every *Chance*, within a social
relationship, of enforcing one's own will even against resistance, whatever the
basis of this *Chance* might be."[67] Two things deserve comment here. First, Weber's definition of power, like his definition of the state, has been broadly influential across all corners of social and political theory. Second, the fact that
this core concept is squarely defined in terms of *Chance* is analytically consequential, although a lot of secondary commentary has not focused on this
aspect.[68] One who did notice this aspect in Weber is, quite tellingly, political
theorist Carl Schmitt, who, as mentioned in the introduction above, sets off
on a diatribe against the "chance" created by the Weimar constitution and is
sure to mention that "'*Chance*' occurs frequently in Max Weber's Sociology."[69]

As a probabilistic phenomenon, power must be an adequate cause, which
in this case means that both conditions in Weber's definition must apply:
(1) There is the possibility of resistance in a relationship that involves the enforcement of will, but (2) resistance is not typically pursued. Most notably,
then, a probabilistic approach to power, like the one we claim Weber pursues,
involves mechanisms constructing (and maintaining) probabilities that oppose the *Chance* of its dissolution. When Weber defines the term "domination" in the 1913 *Logos* essay, he puts particular emphasis on a looping relation
giving a central role to expectation in which a "stronger elemental force . . .
somehow asserts itself." In domination, "the action of those giving the orders
is related in meaning to that of those obeying, and vice versa, in such a way
that both *can* ordinarily count on the realization of the expectations toward
which they have oriented their action."[70] In domination, the expectations of
one party (order givers) typically coincide with the expectations of another
(order takers). For Weber, likewise, "rulership is the *Chance* that a command
of a particular kind will be obeyed by given persons." Relatedly, "discipline
is the *Chance* that, because of a practiced disposition, a command will find
prompt, automatic, and schematic obedience."[71]

In Weber's famous observation, "no rulers will voluntarily rely merely on the material, affectual [*sic*] or value-rational motives for the *Chancen* of survival. Instead, they will seek to arouse and foster belief in their 'legitimacy.'"[72] A probabilistic translation of this statement goes something like this: No ruler can rely on "action" to maintain rule. Rulership must acquire an adequate cause, keyed to the fact that rulership is a type of social relation with those who are ruled. Because social relationships are probabilistic, consisting primarily of "the *Chance* that behavior corresponding to its meaning will recur," so is the ability to rule.[73] Thus, to rule requires the enrollment of others oriented by expectations. However, these expectations need not necessarily loop into a conception of order (e.g., "the divine right of kings," "*liberté, égalité, fraternité*"). In a probabilistic sense, legitimacy refers to sources of rule (often these are conceptions of order) as a specification of *Chance* that opens up the relationship to the possibility of resistance but also typically ensures that one party will *not* meet resistance in this relationship, creating the recurrence and repetition that constructs a ruling order.[74]

Part of the story of rationalization, for the time and place that Weber tells it, is a story of the replacement of *fortuna* with *Chance*, a cunning trick performed, in particular, by bureaucracy as perhaps the ultimate *Chance*-making institution in its capacity to reduce the expectation of randomness. Some things adequately cause other things. They might always have done so, but now we learn that we can expect these effects (and only *these* effects). A bureaucracy gives us expectation as nothing else does in Weber's account, and more generally, as steward of rationalization, bureaucracy exemplifies a probability order that makes us expect that there will be a "*reason* why" things happen, held quite generally. Arguably, without this *Chance*, and with the reign of *fortuna* by contrast, adequate cause had a much more limited presence. In a world shaped by *fortuna*, "things happen," and to attribute reasons to them is different, because accidental cause is far more typical and standard—and *everyone* knows it. Such a world corresponds with what the philosopher Ernst Cassirer calls "mythical consciousness." In that consciousness, we do not "represent" a phenomenon. In myth, we see "real identity. The 'image' does not represent the 'thing'; it *is* the thing."[75] Renaissance-era political theorist Niccolo Machiavelli demonstrates such a view in action in his perspective on *The Prince*.[76] A prince fits the very figure of mythical consciousness. In Machiavelli's portrait, by subduing what undoes planned order (*fortuna*), the prince *becomes* the order ("sovereignty").

Contrary to most readings and applications, it is only now, after having defined rulership and power in relation to *Chance*, that we are in a position to discuss Weber's definition of the state, which might appear to be quite the opposite brand of sovereignty from Machiavelli's *Prince*. Yet both have in common the capacity to create an indistinction between orderly existence and *them*. It seems that Weber would find some agreement with another book by Cassirer entitled *The Myth of the State*. But the bits of mythical consciousness we can find in a bureaucracy are different from those we can find in a prince—whose prowess comes down to us today in the phrase "making your own luck."

The state, according to Weber, is a subtype of ruling organization, which he referred to as *political organizations*. A political organization is characterized by the fact that "the existence and the validity of its orders can be continually guaranteed within a given geographical area by the application and threat of physical coercion by an administrative staff."[77] Political organizations are thus inherently *territorial* and built on objective probability, particularly via the authorized use of physical coercion in the exercise of rule over other people within that area. Whatever other adequate causes ("consciously chosen" or not) might apply in a territory, social actions coincide with the existence of the state. More bounded types of rulership lack "territoriality," such as when sovereignty moves as the prince moves through space, making an orientation to it subject to a spatial and temporal variability that does not apply to states.[78] States, meanwhile, become adequate causes for social actions at all distances from a territorially defined central authority (e.g., "the capital") and in all temporal periods after the moment of founding or constitution. More specifically, a state is an "institutionally organized political enterprise . . . [whose] administrative staff can lay claim to a monopoly of legitimate physical force in the execution of its orders."[79]

Thus, the state only exists insofar as there is a specific (and therefore non-negligible) *Chance* of its being an adequate cause for all the social action found in a territory. Yet, the sole focus on the state as a specific mechanism for monopolizing violence within a territory is misguided. The state emerges here as a recurrent and punctuated (rather than inevitable and constant) entry in a larger background of non-statist associational/consensual action. The existence of a state (like any other organization) is therefore fully probabilistic since it "ceases to 'exist' sociologically with the disappearance of the *Chance* that particular forms of meaningfully oriented social action occur. This *Chance* might be very great, or infinitely small . . . [t]here is no alternative and clearer meaning for the statement that, for instance, a particular 'state' 'exists,' or 'no longer exists.'"[80] Put differently, a state, or any probability order, exists as a *distribution* or *range* of possibility, in this case in a territorial sense, as this range concerns the *Chance* that *this* political organization (and no other) will be recognized (or not) as the sole bearer of the legitimate right to enforce their rule via the threat of physical violence.

Hence, the state, as Weber understands it, defines a continuous probabilistic field of potential actions and interactions distributed within a given territory that depends on action-oriented ruling relationships as objective sources of probabilistic expectations. As a form of *Chance*, power is not constant or deterministic, and neither is it episodic. Whatever factors are the source of power (discursive, material, performative) are also the source of this *Chance*, as constructed from a repeat "taming" of the possibility of resistance to the imposition of will only after having engaged that possibility. Without engaging the possibility of resistance, Weber implies, there will be no power, because there will be no *orientation* to it (whether it assumes the form of a state or not).

The Legitimacy of Legitimate Orders

Power, rule, and rationalization: As we have endeavored to show, these central Weberian concepts can all be redefined in probabilistic terms, specifically as they involve specifications of *Chance* and entail looping effects. Understanding these concepts as probabilistic entails a shift in explanation, not least because we cannot rely on subjective meaning alone. Subjective meaning must loop into conditions that create objective probabilities, at least outside circumstances where there are no such conditions to loop into and subjective meaning *alone* becomes an adequate cause of action.

Thus, the true test of the extent of probabilism in Weber's thought would seem to be its application to arguments that are typically reliant on subjective meaning or these cognate terms, which in our earlier discussion was a point of confusion for both Schutz and Parsons in their engagement with Weber. They could not break with an image of thought that posits subjective meaning as a bridge to the opaque world. For Weber, belief can itself be *Chance*; it can be subject to looping effects just as much as anything else. Such a claim stands opposed, however, to belief as a kind of meaningful (and hermeneutically available) content that constructs a tenuous relation with chaos. In Parsons's influential appropriation of Weber's argument, legitimate order is left at furthest remove from any connection to probability.[81] Specifically, Parsons associates legitimate order with the "*idea* of legitimate order" and, most influentially, with "common value *attitudes*."[82] However, this proposition omits a key mediator that cannot be accounted for other than as probabilistic: *belief* in legitimate order as a specifiable *Chance* of belief. As Weber puts it, the "*Chance* of orientation by a belief '*is*' 'the' valid order."[83]

For Weber, an "order" requires a particular meaning, as it becomes distinguishable from "regularity in the orientation of social action." As mentioned earlier, regularity is a critical component of "practice" in Weber's view, for which the *Chance* is strictly tied to "actual performance." But in the token example that Weber gives of "an official [who] routinely appears in his office at the same time each day," the regularity of his behavior is "not only the result of a familiar custom, nor only determined by his given interests . . . This happens as a rule generally because of the imperative 'validity' of an order . . . infringement of which would not only bring disadvantage but would normally be abhorrent to his 'sense of duty.'"[84] For the *Chance* of legitimate order, then, there are two preconditions: first, that there be "principles" to which action is "on average and approximately oriented," and second, that an "actual orientation to those principles is also in practice followed because [they] are in some way or another recognized as binding or exemplary for the action." As Weber adds, legitimate orders are "less volatile" than those that only arise "for purely purposively rational motives" or for orders in which "an orientation [is] based solely on custom."[85]

Significantly, then, the probabilistic component of Weber's argument comes through here as a kind of gradation or continuum, not to mention with a high degree of fluidity. It is possible, Weber contends, with the range of possibility that is a legitimate order, to break the rules. But if the order is "valid," rule-breaking will always come through some medium of concealment; *that* is in an indicator of an orientation by way of exemplary principles. It is also possible to be oriented to different, and inconsistent, legitimate orders at once as "simultaneously valid." What Weber portrays is a landscape not necessarily of formations of meaning but of self-contained orders all of which have the specific looping effect of creating a *Chance* of belief based on an exemplary or obligatory principle.

At this point, Weber makes a relevant distinction. Legitimate order is not *legal* order, because accounting for law cannot answer the empirically relevant, causal question that applies to inquiries into whether the adequate causes of legitimate order are those that are active. There simply is no "causal relationship between an empirical event and the normative validity of an order in the strict legal sense," as any consideration of the law can only answer the "question of whether the order properly interpreted in the legal sense 'applies' to the empirical event."[86] Weber allows for the law to be the "exemplary or obligatory principle" that draws the orientation of people, but the empirical validity of that principle is a different question than a legal analysis. The same could be said about what it means to claim that actors are "oriented" by meaning more generally. What a concentration on legal interpretation primarily forgets is what we might now call Weber's *relentless*[87] focus on action, which treats it as the main indicator of ontology.

The probabilistic approach Weber develops here finds many different sources of regularity. What is at stake, above all, are the sources of regularity in social life that create *Chance*, which can be diagnosed as the expectation of something—in that we perceive something to be *missing* when we are oriented by *Chance*. This perspective can apply equally to the perception that exemplary action mirrored in a principle is missing as it can to the perception that a custom or tradition (what it is typical to do) is missing. The "missing" aspect, in both cases, becomes apparent in perception. Meanwhile, action maintains *Chance* by correcting these errors.

We will examine that process more fully in part III below. At this point, suffice it to say that while a similar perspective on action has taken years to recover, Weber offers a prescient glimpse of it, because he draws from objective probability. The various factors that construct *Chance* in the first place, which in the case of legitimate order includes the devising of principles, provide a means for creating an orientation to them. A probabilistic reading of Weber's *Protestant Ethic* does not find an argument for the universal role of "ideas in action" as much as it finds an account of the construction of the *Chance* of orientation to a new legitimate order, and then the shift of that legitimate order into what, in its "averagely understood meaning," now resembles more of a practice—an order maintained by a judgment to minimize or make objectively impossible any alternative; only with some exteriorization (like in the form of a calculated probability) do they become apparent. In this case, social action creates its objective conditions, which are also presuppositions of the action. Interpretation, as envisioned by those in a theological field, can be a condition for free action, as interpretation can then be its presuppositions (because nothing else is). That, in a probabilistic sense, is the "contingency of interpretation."

Coda: Weber, the Probabilist

We can no longer typecast Max Weber's sociology as interpretive in the typical meaning of the term. The probabilistic reading we advance here pivots from this convention by making it clear that when Weber embraced sociology, particularly in work over the last decade of his life, he increasingly associated sociology with the study of *Chance*. Sociology is linked to a theory of action that emphasizes the role of probabilistic expectation *in* action. For Weber, a looping relation between subjective expectation and objective probability becomes an integral part of all collective orders in this regard, which allows him to avoid the kind of collective object problem he observed in sociology at the time. Looping effects blur distinctions between subjective and objective, making it less clear that action must be subjective and that "collective entities" must be objective.

For Weber-the-probabilist, the *Chance* of subjective meaning meets several hurdles, which makes it not impossible but exceptional. Judgments of probability, or orientations to *Chance*, are consequential for social action not as a reference to subjective meaning but rather to expectation, which can be broadly shared. In these ways, Weber draws time and motion into sociological reasoning, but he also draws them together with social construction, which is unusual. Probabilistic constructions can appear from initial visions of possibility found within narrow circles, in socially differentiated spaces where those possibilities remain conceptual, only to become social orders later on that we can refer to using a collectivist language, as general entities of long duration with apparent cycles and laws, built on shared orientations captured within ever-recurrent loops. Weber's *Protestant Ethic* contains lessons of this kind when we pair its narrative with proposals that Weber makes by envisioning sociology and social knowledge on probabilistic terms.

Yet our revisionism should not be understood in an entirely relative manner, as proposing yet *another* Weber, because it concerns a difference both formal and in kind. Weber-the-probabilist calls forth not a kind of stabilizing recognition but the potential of a completely different model, an essentially unrecognized *terra incognita*. In a sense, a difference such as this one can only begin from what has been established as common sense by making a distinction using a conceptual armamentarium of established value, even to the point of being unquestionable. As with any proposition, we can distinguish between its expression and its designation.[88] Weber's probabilism expresses a host of ideas that seem to lack objects to designate because it breaks with recognition and representation within the sociological field, as these concepts are understood in the protective mode of theorizing mentioned above, with the goal of maintaining the identity of concepts and resemblance with regard to objects. Yet, probabilistically understood, concepts only ever give rise to possibilities. They are themselves judgments of possibility; they do not create claws of necessity. What we have attempted to do is give reasons to think about Weber again.

Though we do not wish to get lost in the depths of Weberiana by claiming Weber as a probabilist, neither, for that matter, do we have to. A certain reading of Weber resides at the heart of what is typically understood as culture, as a resource rather than a topic, with implications for the recognition and representation of the term. By contrast, Weber-the-probabilist moves toward distinguishing what now appears as a post-cultural analysis by finding potential in sociological reasoning, and especially concept formation, beyond a common project of recognizing that culture or action need to have the same traits a priori, as opposed to effectively embracing all their *possible* traits. Probabilism proposes a divergent project, guided by new conceptions of what social order is (objective probability, *Chance*, loops) and a different way of making judgments and providing explanations of orders with generality and duration. But we do not have to stop with Weber. A line of influence arises with Weber's probabilistic approach, based on a different and still under-the-radar encounter. If Parsons and Schutz pivoted away from probabilism, and if contemporary sociology followed them, Pierre Bourdieu did not.

4

Pierre Bourdieu Rediscovers Probabilism

A worldview is a system of predictive schemas that, being shared by all, become true and validated. The system of prediction that you are using may seem crazy seen from a different forecasting system, but, within a universe where everyone shares the same system, you are in the right.

PIERRE BOURDIEU, *Principles of Classification*

In 1981, French sociologist Pierre Bourdieu was elected to the Collège de France, the first sociologist to join the institution since the retirement of Raymond Aron in 1978. Aron, in 1970, took up a chair position at the Collège with the title of "Sociology of Modern Civilization," himself the first sociologist to join the Collège since Maurice Halbwachs's tragic death at Buchenwald in 1945, whose chair was titled "Collective Psychology." Halbwachs, for his part, had succeeded Marcel Mauss (elected in 1932), whose chair had the title "Sociology." Following the tradition of the Collège, those with chairs can rename a chair when one becomes available upon death or retirement, including giving it to another discipline. Halbwachs's chair was not given to another sociologist, however, and the Collège lacked the presence of anything that looked like sociology until Claude Lévi-Strauss was elected to a chair in "Social Anthropology" in 1959. In Bourdieu's case, in 1981, the then-members of the Collège—among them Michel Foucault, Fernand Braudel, Roland Barthes, and the soon-to-be retiring Lévi-Strauss—simply renamed the available chair "Sociology."[1]

By this point, Bourdieu had published what would be his magnum opus, *Distinction*, in 1979, and, shortly after that, its theoretical companion, *Logic of Practice*, in 1980, a revised and expanded version of the earlier *Outline of a Theory of Practice*, which came out in 1972.[2] His coauthored work on photography and education had appeared earlier, in addition to a host of articles on rural marriage, the intellectual field, art, structuralism, and Max Weber's sociology of religion (among other topics). Sprinkled among the pages of this work are Bourdieu's well-known concepts and methodology: habitus, capital, symbolic power, fields, correspondence analysis, and classification.

In the revolutionary year 1968, more than a decade before his election to the chair, Bourdieu had also authored—with coauthors Jean-Claude Passeron and Jean-Claude Chamboredon—a kind of sociology textbook, which began its life as a mimeograph Bourdieu had prepared for a 1967 sociology seminar he gave to the top statisticians in France. Entitled *Le métier de sociologue: Préalables épistémologiques*, the book featured a long introductory chapter and conclusion along with a selection of canonical readings, including from Weber, Durkheim, and Marx, arranged in between.[3] The book emphasized *epistemological* preliminaries over methodology, as influenced by philosopher Gaston Bachelard's notion of "epistemological break."[4] According to Bourdieu and collaborators, sociology must take as its organizing theme the dictum that "the social fact is won, constructed, and confirmed," which the book resolved into a series of steps.[5] As they envisioned it at this time, Bourdieu and coauthors saw sociological explanation as a distinctive part of a coherent scientific community (*cité*), and the *métier* in this sense is based on mutual "epistemological vigilance," particularly against intrusions of "spontaneous" folk knowledge.[6]

In an important respect, however, it is difficult to reconcile *Le métier*'s proposals—aside from an aggressive anti-positivism—with the intellectual project Bourdieu would pursue in the years immediately following its publication, and particularly with what he would go on to propose as "General Sociology" in his first set of lectures at the Collège de France from 1980 to 1986. For example, "practice" is not a significant element in sociological explanation for Bourdieu in 1968, and neither, we will show, is "objective probability."[7] Given that Bourdieu would pursue these themes extensively in the coming years, it is not unfair to say that while he had positioned himself in sociology by this time, the kind of sociology Bourdieu would pursue was not yet fleshed out. Beyond this, sociology as a whole was in flux in France, with rival camps entered around competing journals. Bourdieu would in 1975 (along with frequent collaborators at the time like Luc Boltanski) found the journal *Actes de la recherche en sciences sociales* as a venue for research that did not fit favorably with, and could not, in fact, be published in, the more established *Archives européennes de sociologie* and *Revue française de sociologie*.[8]

Bourdieu had fallen somewhat backward into the field of sociology to begin with. His *agrégation* at the famed École Normale Supérieure was in philosophy. Sociology had a lowly reputation during this time, particularly among the far more prestigious philosophers, and Bourdieu was taught (not least by Louis Althusser) to have scorn for the Durkheimians in particular. He completed his *diplôme* at the École Normale Supérieure as a translation and commentary on Gottfried Leibniz's *Animadversions* under the directorship of Henri Gouhier. His first teaching post at a *lycée* in Moulins in 1953 was in philosophy. When he was conscripted into military service in 1955, Bourdieu had to abandon a planned dissertation with Georges Canguilhem (as Foucault had done before him), with the tentative title "The Temporal Structures of Affective Life" or "Emotion as a Temporal Structure: An Interpretive Essay on Physiological Data,"[9] which would presumably have dealt with "the somatization of the social . . . the origins of the language through which people express their various physiological disorders, their emotions and bodily experiences."[10] Instead, Bourdieu was sent to Algeria for compulsory military service. His work there, in close collaboration with Abdelmalek Sayad,[11] culminated in two reports that later formed the basis of his first scholarly book, *Sociologie de l'Algérie* (1958)—translated into English in 1962 as *The Algerians* by Alan Ross for Beacon Press—which, with the Service de Documentation et d'Information of the Gouvernement General, set him on a trajectory that would, somewhat miraculously, culminate with the Collège de France election a quarter-century later.

Yet, even throughout the intervening years, which would see Bourdieu—under Aron's sponsorship—become involved, starting in 1960, in what would later be called the Centre de Sociologie Européenne and, in 1964, be appointed to the sixth (social sciences) section of the École Pratique des Hautes Études (renamed the École des Hautes Études en Sciences Sociales in 1975), it was not clear in what sense Bourdieu could be considered a sociologist and in what respect his work should be read as part of that field, though Bourdieu certainly thought of his own work during this time as sociology. He knew enough about the (globally) dominant strains of American sociology (e.g., Harvard functionalism and Columbia-style middle-range theorizing and statistical analysis) at this point to know that he had not been doing *that*, nor did he want to.[12] Bourdieu was also not trained in the canon as it had come to be enshrined in American sociology; he had read Weber at least as early as the late 1950s in Algiers—Bourdieu uses the *Protestant Ethic* extensively in his first book on Algeria—and taught him at his first university teaching post at Lille in 1964. Bourdieu knew he was not pursuing Aron's version of Weber, which inclined more toward general history and political commentary, or the kind of sociology represented by Alain Touraine, Raymond Boudon, or Michel Crozier, all increasingly prominent by the late 1970s—with Bruno Latour just beginning to lurk along the edges. Touraine was much more well-known than Bourdieu publicly, and he was also considered for the available chair at the Collège.[13]

All this history makes what Bourdieu would say when he took the podium for his first public lecture as a member of the Collège in the midafternoon of April 28, 1982, that much more intriguing. He seems to have been encouraged to, as it were, "rise to the occasion" of the chair—something he somewhat mockingly acknowledged in his *"leçon inaugurale"* a week earlier—and define sociology. For the second time around, sociology had been elevated to this remarkable institutional recognition, following the stillborn iterations of Mauss and Halbwachs as representatives of a Durkheimian tradition a generation earlier. Hopefully, this time, it would stick around. Bourdieu would go on to dedicate the first five years of lectures at the Collège to "general sociology."[14]

With the full compendium of Bourdieu's lectures at the Collège de France now finding their way into English translation and publication, it seems warranted to take stock of exactly what these lectures say and what they imply for an increasingly fixed and canonized view of Bourdieu and "Bourdieusian sociology" in the American and global sociology fields. Our argument in this chapter—using this preamble as a way of setting the scene—is that what Bourdieu fashions as sociology in the first set of lectures has overarching and consistent themes that can only be faintly gleaned from familiarity with his other, better-known, work.[15] In the end, it all leads to a yet-to-be-acknowledged—but decisive—turn toward probabilism in his thinking and his association of sociology with the study of objective probability.

The Origins of Bourdieu's Probabilism

Throughout the development of his thinking on social action, Bourdieu retains a looping formula codifying the relation of expectation and *Chance*, or subjective expectations and objective probabilities. This constancy does not mean that there will be no shifts in emphasis or refinement of the position. Some of the earliest versions appear in *Travail et travailleurs en Algérie* (1963), a book to which Bourdieu contributed one-half ("Étude Sociologique") and statisticians from the Institut National de la Statistique et des Études Économiques Alain Darbel, Jean-Paul Rivet, and Claude Seibel contributed the other half ("Données Statistiques"). In Bourdieu's half, we can find statements like the following:

Everything happens as if the material conditions of existence exercised their influence on attitudes, and particularly on attitude towards time, that is to say on economic attitude, through the mediation of the perception that the subjects have of it. Indeed, because it is circumscribed by economic and social necessity, the field of possibilities varies as the *field of effective possibilities*. The economic attitude of each subject depends on his material conditions of existence through the mediation of the objective future of the group of which he is a part or, more precisely, through the mediation of the consciousness, implicit or explicit, that he takes from this objective future.[16]

This formulation is not yet a statement that is informed by Weberian "objective probability" but rather reflects the influence of philosopher and pioneering phenomenologist Edmund Husserl, who, alongside Martin Heidegger, was a familiar source from Bourdieu's "fieldwork in philosophy." Both thinkers, as we mentioned in chapter 2, have a connection to Johannes von Kries, particularly in the way Kries conceives of *Spielraum* and its connection to ontology.[17] Bourdieu appears to combine what he draws from Husserl and Heidegger with the notion of "effective possibility," which he elsewhere draws from Marx's *Outline of a Critique of Political Economy*, specifically the idea of "effective demand" as demand that reflects the possession of what would be required to obtain its object, versus "demand without effect, without being real, without an object" as being more like a fantasy or wish.[18]

A close reading of the essay also conveys aspects of what might have been Bourdieu's abandoned philosophy doctorate, with a noted emphasis on how temporal relations (*sens de l'avenir*) translate into affective experiences like hope, fatalism, paranoia, and the "wild" fantasies and plans that characterize those who have been violently displaced from a structured flow of time.[19] Bourdieu later states that what, in retrospect, his early work in Algeria addresses is how a "particular structure of objective probabilities—an *objective future*—generates determinate dispositions toward the future" (emphasis original). He then restates the formula for habitus proposed in *Outline of a Theory of Practice*, published during the intervening years: "These dispositions are structured structures which function as structuring structures, orienting and organizing the economic practices of daily life."[20]

What is significant about this explicit mention of "objective probability" is that it coincides with Bourdieu's move toward a clearer break with structuralism following 1968. In fact, Bourdieu's entire conception of what counts as "objective" shifts gradually from an understanding grounded in a structuralist conception of objectivity (i.e., as a subjectless *langue* separated from *parole* or a system of "objective relations" designed and uncovered by the third-person anthropological observer) to an increasingly *probabilistic* conception molded in line with Weber's application of Kries's notion of *Chance*. The 1968 English-language essay "Structuralism and the Theory of Sociological Knowledge" represents the clearest alignment of Bourdieu with structuralism, alongside his essay on the Kabyle house and the *Le métier* mentioned earlier.[21] However, the essay also previews Bourdieu's own (idiosyncratic) "post-structuralism," which he accounts for using nearly the same terminology that he will use to discuss objective probability later on, suggesting that the turn to probabilism helped resolve various epistemological and conceptual tensions Bourdieu had recognized in structuralism but did not yet have the tools to transcend.

According to Bourdieu, "[the anthropologist] obtains the means to discover how the relations objectively defining the differential *chances* of marriage are realized in and through the attitudes that directly condition the capacity to succeed in the competition for marriage."[22] This argument contains an early version of what Bourdieu would later refer to as "the relationship between expectations and chances." The link between the "system of objective relations" uncovered by the structuralist observer and the "attitudes" of actors, in this case, represents an important move *away* from what would otherwise be a satisfactory structural analysis. Still, it also introduces the paradox of how the two phenomena (i.e., chances to marry and attitudes toward marriage) could relate. Bourdieu follows this statement on chances/expectations with an argument that will remain (relatively unchanged) at the core of his resistance to appropriations of structuralism (anthropological, symbolic) that do not remain "methodological":[23]

> To give primacy to the study of the relations between objective relations rather than to the study of the relations between the agents and these relations, or to ignore the question of the relationship between these two types of relations, leads to the *realism of the structure* which, taking the place of the realism of the element, hypostatizes the systems of objective relations in already constructed totalities, outside the history of the individual or the group. Without falling back into a naive subjectivism or "personalism," one must remember that, ultimately, *objective relations do not exist* and do not really realize themselves except in and through the system of dispositions of the agents, produced by the internalization of objective conditions.[24]

Bourdieu uses these arguments to characterize the mediating role of habitus as a "geometrical locus of determinisms and of an individual determination, of *calculable probabilities* and of lived-through hopes, of objective futures and subjective plans."[25] The intriguing thing about this proposal, which is also evident in the 1979 preface to the collection of Bourdieu's writings in *Travail et travailleurs en Algérie* from 1963, is that habitus is directly connected to probability here (i.e., objective chance-expectation connection with habitus as a mediator), thus avoiding the tendency of structuralism to commit to a substantialist "realism of the structure," while also staying clear from a "subjectivist" counter-reaction that denies placing action within a system of objective possibilities. The counterpart to habitus, as the other element of the relation between "subjectivity" and "objectivity," is still murkily defined in terms of the "constructed" objectivity of the structuralist method.[26] "Field" (*champ*) is not yet found in these arguments. Neither is it present in the arguments found in Bourdieu's coauthored (with Passeron) research on education from this period, *The Inheritors* (1964) and *Reproduction in Education, Society and Culture* (1970).[27]

In this research, which will be (and in some sense remains) Bourdieu's most influential sociology from this pre-probabilistic period, we can find phrases that resonate directly with those found in "Structuralism" from 1968 and extending back to *Travailleurs* from 1963. Take, for instance, the claim that "the concept of subjective expectation, conceived as the product of the internalization of objective conditions through a process governed by the whole system of objective relations within which it takes place, has the theoretical function of designating the intersection of the different systems of relations . . . [This is] explanation in terms of the relationship between subjective expectation and objective probability, i.e., in terms of the system of the relations between two systems of relations."[28]

This rendering of probability combines its methodological meaning (statistically derived) with a somewhat shadowy and awkwardly phrased structuralism ("the system of relations between two systems of relations"). This formulation makes any reference to "objectivity" ambiguous because, as Bourdieu notes, it cannot carry ontological status without the danger of reifying the constructive operations of the sociologist. The contemporary popularity of these arguments in the sociology of education, meanwhile, has made terms like "habitus" inconsistent with Bourdieu's later (especially in *Pascalian Meditations*) probabilistic rendering of the same terms. As is particularly evident in the "Structuralism" essay and Bourdieu's development of the *field* concept,[29] the absence of an understanding of objective probability pre-1973 has resulted in an analytic overreliance on "systems of relations," something that remains overextended in Bourdieu-related scholarship to the present day.[30]

This discussion makes clear, however, that from the very start Bourdieu's conception of habitus has involved a deeper connection with probability than has been appreciated, specifically that habitus consists of something like the internalization of what exists objectively as probability.[31] Furthermore, Bourdieu had begun to theorize the origins of this internalized probability as linked to the connection between "agents and objective relations." He would refer to this last phenomenon as "objective" in the usual sense of nonsubjective but also to refer to an epistemic construction by the analyst. As Bourdieu's thinking develops in this regard, he gradually drops reference to "objective relations" (or "systems of relations") in the way structuralists in linguistics or social anthropology typically used the term at the time and moves toward a characterization of a probabilistic loop. The difference between "objective chances" referred to after the incorporation of Weber's probabilism (post-1973) and "objective relations" is that objective probability is unambiguously *ontological*, marking the end of Bourdieu's structuralist period.

Objective Probability After *Logos*

Bourdieu's arguments before 1973 remain uninfluenced by Weber's 1913 *Logos* essay and Weber's proposal (as analyzed in the last chapter), informed by Kries's probabilism, that "objective probability" should be at the core of any interpretive sociology. Bourdieu's proverbial "Letter of Paul," in this respect, is the 1973 English-language article "Three Forms of Theoretical Knowledge," rightfully acknowledged as a pivot point in his thinking.[32] The article condenses and further develops points from *Outline*, summarizing various developments that would make their way to *Logic* while also indicating a more thorough connection to Weber's "objective probability." While the 1973 article includes no citations of Weber, it does include a notable mention of the German sociologist: "Someone who accepts money as an instrument of exchange implicitly takes into account, as Weber shows, *the chances that other agents will agree to recognize its function*. Automatic and impersonal, significant without intending to signify, the ordinary conduct of life lends itself to a no less automatic and impersonal decoding: the *decoding of the objective intention* which they express in no way requires the 'reactivation' of the intention 'experienced' by the person who accomplishes this conduct."[33]

Revealingly, this statement features a more explicit critique of an interpretivist approach while leveraging a version of the expectation-chance connection as directly impacting the course of action. Accordingly, rather than interpreting what someone will do when given money by "reactivating" intentions (beliefs, desires), it is the "automatic and impersonal" recognition of objective probabilities, allowing for the "decoding of objective intention," that matters in this sequence. Compare this claim to the following assertion from Weber's 1913 *Logos* essay: "An important (though not indispensable) normal compo-

108   CHAPTER FOUR

nent of social action is its meaningful orientation to the expectations of certain behavior on the part of others and, in accordance with that, orientation
to the (subjectively) assessed probabilities (*Chancen*) for the success of one's
action. A most understandable and important basis for the explanation of action, therefore, is the *objective existence of these probabilities*, i.e., a greater or
lesser degree of probability as expressed in a '*judgment of objective possibility*,'
to the effect that these expectations are well-founded."[34]

It seems likely that when composing the earlier passage, Bourdieu had
this specific argument in mind, suggesting that he had, by this point, read the
1965 translation of Weber's essay in a volume of Weber's writings that the philosopher and sociologist Julien Freund had compiled.[35] Instead of decoding
intentions, Weber concentrates on the "judgment of objective possibility" and
the "objective existence of probabilities." In different terms, this idea is almost
directly comparable to the *relation* that, in 1968, Bourdieu used to make his
early proposal for habitus. He now begins to phrase that relation as a *loop*.

In the 1973 article, Bourdieu helps himself to the idea of "objective probability" when trying to differentiate the way he believes the habitus engages
in expectations from more "naive" models (later to be referred to as "rational choice") whereby people construct, consciously and strategically, "what
the habitus carries out in another manner, namely an estimate of the chances
based on the transformation of the past effect into anticipated future effect."[36]
In this connection, Bourdieu notes that "one regularly observes a very close
relationship between scientifically constructed objective probabilities (e.g.,
opportunities for access to higher education or to museums, etc.) and subjective aspirations,"[37] reiterating that a mutual adjustment does not happen via
conscious regulation or adaptation. Bourdieu does not mention Weber in this
context, yet the connection to Weber's *Logos* essay will become fully explicit
in Bourdieu's 1974 article "Avenir de classe et causalite du probable" ("Causality of the Probable and the Future of Class"):

> Consider the Weberian theory of "objective probabilities," which has the merit
> of bringing to light one of the most fundamental assumptions, although tacit,
> of the economy, namely the existence of a "relation of intelligible causality"
> between generic chances ("typical") "existing objectively on average" and "sub-
> jective expectations." By speaking of "average chances," that is to say, valuable
> for anyone, for an indeterminate and interchangeable agent, a "one," as Hei-
> degger would say, and by recalling that rational action, "carefully" orientated
> according to what is "objectively valuable," is that which "would have hap-
> pened if the actors had knowledge of all the circumstances and all the inten-
> tions of the participants," that is to say, what is "valuable in the eyes of the sci-
> entist," who is the only one capable of constructing by calculation the system

of objective chances to which an action accomplished in perfect knowledge
of its causes should adjust, Max Weber clearly showed that the pure model
of rational action cannot be considered as an anthropological description of
practice.[38]

Bourdieu includes a footnote here to Weber's 1913 *Logos* essay in Freund's edited volume.[39] This encounter is a crucial turning point because it appears
that having Weber's 1913 argument for objective probability firmly in hand allows him to restate the relation between expectations and chances in a much
more consistent and comprehensive way—a way that is clearly informed by
Weber's own analytic specification. For our purposes, this argument secures
the fact that integral to Bourdieu's sociology is a concern with probability,
albeit in such a heterodox form that it easily goes unrecognized and remains
essentially irrelevant to conversations on prediction and probability in sociology that are, by contrast, far narrower in their methodological focus.

Internalized and Objective Probability in *The Logic of Practice*

In *The Logic of Practice*, Bourdieu's incorporation of Weber's 1913 essay becomes even more explicit. Most pivotally, it becomes foundational to the
well-traveled theory of habitus. The argument here, however, is that habitus
connotes the internalized form (in people) of what exists (in the world) as
probabilities (or objective chances). *Logic* is a revision of the earlier *Outline*
and a development of points mentioned in the 1973 "Three Forms" piece and a
1976 *Actes* article entitled "Le sens pratique." Importantly, between *Logic* and
Outline, Bourdieu added an entirely new chapter—"Belief and the Body"—
which draws out and highlights points that were more scattered in *Outline*.
The revision also includes a discussion of Pascal's wager missing from both
Outline and "Le sens pratique." The more substantial incorporation of Weber's
"objective probability" and the novel engagement with Pascal indicate that,
arguably, at the pivotal moment of its mature conceptual formation, Bourdieu's concept of habitus becomes tightly linked with—even perhaps being
equivalent to—internalized probability.

In a curious string of references present in *Logic* but found nowhere in
either "Le sens pratique" or the earlier *Outline*, Bourdieu introduces an approach to *probability learning*, specifically by making the habitus a *product* of
probability learning:

> Dispositions durably inculcated by the objective conditions and by a peda-
> gogic action that is tendentially adjusted to these conditions, tend to gener-
> ate practices objectively compatible with these conditions and expectations

pre-adapted to their objective demands (*amor fati*) (for some psychologists' attempts at direct verification of this relationship, see Brunswik 1949; Preston and Barrata 1948; Attneave 1953). As a consequence, they tend, without any rational calculation or conscious estimation of the chances of success, to ensure immediate correspondence between the *a priori* or *ex ante* probability conferred on an event (whether or not accompanied by subjective experiences such as hopes, expectation, fears, etc.) and the *a posteriori* or *ex post* probability that can be established on the basis of past experience.[40]

Later on the same page, Bourdieu includes his most direct reference to Weber's *Logos* essay to date, with "1922" referring to a German-language collected volume in which the essay also appears: "They thus make it possible to understand why economic models based on the (tacit) premise of a 'relationship of intelligible causality,' as Max Weber (1922) calls it, between generic ('typical') chances 'objectively existing as an average' and 'subjective expectations,' or, for example, between investment or the propensity to invest and the rate of return expected or really obtained in the past, fairly exactly account for practices which do not arise from knowledge of the objective chances."[41]

Here, Bourdieu dissects, draws out, and emphasizes Weber's major points in the 1913 *Logos* essay (as incorporated into the first chapter of *E&S*), all revolving around the key idea of objective probability. Specifically, as we saw in the previous chapter, Weber emphasizes that knowledge of "average chances" can produce a kind of "objectively correct rationality" without any kind of explicit instruction or knowledge of "objective chances" such as would be produced by a sociologist or statistician.[42]

Probability learning can explain the kind of looping effect (i.e., "near-circular relationship") that Bourdieu wants to capture in his much-bemoaned definition of habitus given earlier in the chapter ("structured structures predisposed to function as structuring structures"). Bourdieu's earlier discussion in *Logic* of Pascal's wager thus becomes relevant in a way that has not been appreciated to date by suggesting that the breakthroughs on probabilism that Bourdieu makes during the 1970s and that culminate in *Logic* will continue to preoccupy him for the rest of his career and find their last statement in the appropriately titled *Pascalian Meditations*.[43] The somewhat-obscure citations in the first quote above—Brunswik 1949; Preston & Baratta 1948; Attneave 1953—at first seemingly odd for a French sociologist, are all to psychologists institutionally affiliated with mainstream departments in the US and working in the "neobehaviorist" line of research ("neo" because they accommodated such mentalistic constructs as "purpose" and "goals") developed by Edward Tolman and Egon Brunswik, who, as noted in chapter 2, went on to develop a distinctive version of psychological probabilism with attention to the probabilistic texture of the environment allows the animal to learn objective chances.[44]

Of particular interest for our argument is the Attneave study. In it, a hundred subjects were tested according to how they internalized letter frequencies from the English alphabet as present in natural language. The hypothesis that Attneave tests is whether, because these letters appear with stable relative frequencies in natural language, he can prove *"probability learning"* by adults as they "observe these proportions . . . throughout their entire lives."[45] As Bourdieu read this article, he would have come across lines like "Psychological probabilities [do seem to] correspond to their environmental counterparts," at least when "they are appreciated and utilized by the observer,"[46] evidently suggesting a connection between probability learning and practice. If the test subjects in Attneave's study had been asked to guess the frequency of a different alphabet, or something with which they had no practical experience, we should not expect such a psychological/environmental correspondence, and certainly not at such a high ratio.

Bourdieu's Journey to Probabilism

Attneave's long-lost study marks an early attempt at what has only more recently been documented in language acquisition as probability learning, which is a key demonstration of the influence of probabilism in contemporary linguistic theory.[47] It is also important for understanding Bourdieu's trajectory because it marks a kind of culmination of shifts in his thinking from 1973 forward. His shift toward probabilism coincided with the development of his own version of post-structuralism, as Bourdieu retooled structuralist principles in his development of what would become a distinct bank of sociological concepts, particularly habitus, capital, and field.

Central to Bourdieu's trajectory during this time is the renewed attention he would give to the field concept. Before the early 1970s, Bourdieu rendered fields along the lines of structuralist "systems of relations."[48] Yet between May 1972 and January 1975, Bourdieu would give a seminar series at the Maison des Sciences de l'Homme on the concept of field, to which he gave the indicative title "De la methode structural au concept de champ" ("From the structural method to the concept of field").[49] This (nearly verbatim) move toward post-structuralism occurs in tandem with what we claim is Bourdieu's seminal encounter with Weber's probabilism. The alignment of these influences would indicate that the field concept was revised by Bourdieu away from being comparable to a structure and to accommodate objective probability.

"Field" as a probabilistic concept also shows a departure from the authority associated with probability mentioned above, when it takes on a purely *epistemic* form. In Weber's probabilism, Bourdieu found a way to transform previously epistemic theoretical statements into formulations that hooked directly into reality, and which therefore must be accessible to people beyond sociologists. In his analysis of Pascal's wager, Bourdieu is critical of Pascal to the extent that he commits a rationalist fallacy—along the lines of "deciding to believe," a paradox made famous by the philosopher Bernard Williams—but he is praiseful of Pascal in concluding that beliefs are habits and are relative to the flow of time, thus coinciding closely with expectation.[50] This Pascalian formulation—along with the other arguments Bourdieu arrives at by the end of the 1970s—reveals a more significant turn in Bourdieu's thinking, with implications extending far beyond mere exegetical interest and Bourdieusian historical lore.

Across the 1970s, from the founding of *Actes* to his incorporation of probabilism, Bourdieu is fighting the epistemic authority he finds in structuralism that appreciates itself not as a method but as a statement of reality. He finds a similar problem in the frequentist probability described above in chapter 1, which had become established in the late nineteenth century and culminated in the professionalization of statistics around a distinct scientific capital.[51] Bourdieu comes later in this history, and he writes from a position outside of sociology in what had become its mainstream American version rooted in frequentist principles. Bourdieu's 1970s trajectory reveals a discomfort with having, by this point, unknowingly become a purveyor of a kind of authoritative mental labor in the form of structuralism—one that created and then imposed categories on those whom it studied, claiming that its complicated models represented a kind of knowledge that everyday people *could* know if they had as an authoritative grasp on reality as the anthropologist or sociologist does.[52] Bourdieu scholar Derek Robbins suggests that Bourdieu had by this point come to the realization that his earlier work, rooted as it was in structuralism, "[betrayed] the primary, domestic, or familial experiences of his upbringing in the Béarn and the primary experiences that he had observed among the Kabyle in Algeria."[53] Subsequently, Bourdieu would seek to avoid "simply [being] part of a process of consolidating the self-referentiality of an introspective and socially distinct sociological epistemic community."[54]

Such a turn away from authoritative knowledge is as integral to Bourdieu's turn to probabilism, as is his reading of Weber's *Logos* essay. We can thus arrive at a kind of recipe for probabilism in Bourdieu's case. The exhaustion of structuralism (which Bourdieu was not alone in sensing) by the late 1960s, combined with its authoritativeness, coincided with Bourdieu's encounter with Weber's probabilism. It is also worth remarking upon what was mentioned earlier, about the relative instability of French sociology at this time, which among other things allowed Bourdieu to read Weber without the threat of suffering professional costs by reading him *wrongly*. If any one of these elements were taken out of the equation, Bourdieu's key concepts of habitus, capital, and field might never have come to be. Our task now is to account for these concepts as part of a distinctively probabilistic version of sociology that we will flesh out in greater detail in what follows. Habitus, capital, and field mark the most thorough development of probabilism in sociology to date, building off Weber's own claims to the same effect, Weber's own novel categories drawn and adapted from Kries, and in particular the key idea of the looping effect. To this account we add other key probabilistic concepts like *illusio* (drawn from Christiaan Huygens), which, in addition to Bourdieu's engagement with Pascal, situates the French sociologist within an even longer arc of probabilistic thinking.[55]

Recasting Bourdieu's Key Concepts

What we seek to do now is to take the conventional meanings of habitus, capital, field, *illusio*, and power and recast them in probabilistic terms to show the *conceptual* difference objective probabilism makes when given broad application. We concentrate on Bourdieu's last two big "theory" works after *The Logic of Practice*: the *Cours de sociologie générale* (1981–1986), given as his initial years of lectures following his election to the Collège de France, and *Pascalian Meditations* (1997). The core concepts, with their usual definitions on the left and their probabilistically recast definitions on the right, are shown in table 1.

In a probabilistic mode, sociology consists of a form of mental labor that makes and uses classifications, and it does so amid other specialists competing to "establish the existence of groups."[56] Between classifications and objective probability is a relative match or mismatch related to their *mutually independent* effects on group-making, which Bourdieu describes as the relationship between the "theoretical and practical existence of groups."[57] The significance of "symbolic structures" for *prediction*-making is rarely acknowledged.[58] The creation of explicit and public (i.e., "group-making") classifications, in which sociology as mental labor is closely involved, generates "recognized distinctions" and provides a means with which to make predictions about the people fitted to them.[59]

In a lecture delivered at the University of Chicago in 1987 and addressing the analytic challenge of differentiating between the theoretically constructed groups (or classes) and actual (practically existing) groups in the world,

TABLE 1. A probabilistic recasting of the core concepts of Bourdieu's general sociology

Concept	Non-probabilistic meaning	Probabilistic recasting
Habitus	"Structured structures predisposed to function as structuring structures" for systematic production of thoughts, perceptions, and actions (Bourdieu, *Logic of Practice*, 53).	The learning of objective probabilities offered by a field and generative of practical anticipations that tend to adjust action in the present to the future objective *Chances* by the field.
Field	"Structured spaces of positions (or posts) whose properties depend on their position within these spaces and which can be analyzed independently of the characteristics of their occupants (which are partly determined by them)."[a] Position-taking in a field is indicative of a struggle over the monopoly of symbolic capital.	Delimited arenas of striving, characterized by a given (unique) distribution (a "play space") of objective *Chances*, partially determinative of individual trajectories and regulated temporal successions to which individuals adjust via an anticipatory habitus.
Capital	Resources at stake in a struggle between commonly oriented actors, with the capability of being transformed into other resources when transferred outside the field.	A set of unequally distributed (or, in an ideal case, monopolized) resources (cultural, social, economic, etc.), allowing individuals to better grasp the objective *Chances* distributed within a field via an anticipatory habitus. More consequentially, capital may be used to alter the structure of objective probabilities constitutive of a field, thus having an indirect influence on the anticipatory moves of other players.
Illusio	Interest or investment in the contest or "stakes" taking place in a field.	Subjective motivation to invest in a game defined by the objective probabilities constitutive of a field, fueled by the capacity to use practical expectations of the habitus to link to objective *Chances*, thus "buying into" the game.

Note: The table should not be read as a substantive claim that there is a left-to-right shift in Bourdieu's conceptualization of the relevant notions, or an early versus a late Bourdieu, although as we argue throughout, the specific conceptualizations on the right appear later in Bourdieu's larger body of work (and are layered on top of or next to the ones on the left), as he works out the implications of probabilism in the General Sociology lectures and one last time in *Pascalian Meditations*.

[a] Pierre Bourdieu, "The Field of Cultural Production," *Poetics* 12 (1983): 311–56; quote at 342.

Bourdieu goes on to define both the "classes on paper" and the structure of the social space generating their counterpart "groups in the world" in terms of probability:

> The theoreticist illusion which grants reality to abstractions hides a whole series of major problems, those which the very construction of well-founded

theoretical classes allows us to pose when it is epistemologically controlled: a theoretical class, or a "class on paper," might be considered as a *probable* real class, or as the probability of a real class, whose constituents are likely to be brought closer and mobilized (but are not actually mobilized) on the basis of their similarities (of interest and dispositions). *Likewise, the social space may be construed as a structure of probabilities* of drawing individuals together or apart, a structure of affinity and aversion between them.[60]

Here, Bourdieu differentiates an *epistemic* sense of probability as the "probable" classes constructed by the analyst—the probability that the class on paper is a "class in reality." This differentiation is easily understandable, because here Bourdieu invokes probability in its most familiar form. Yet he then adds something unusual and perhaps difficult to notice without the history we have recounted in this chapter. Bourdieu refers to "the social space" as a "structure of probabilities" capable of "drawing individuals together or apart." For our purposes, this reference is not an idle one, nor is it a confusion on Bourdieu's part, and neither is it an epistemic application of probability rooted ultimately in frequentism. Rather, it is a statement of objective probability. Social space is composed *of* probabilities "drawing individuals together or apart" and creating a "structure of affinity and aversion between them." If anything, Bourdieu implicitly invokes Bachelard's notion of the "causality of the probable," which as discussed above, is a concept that has a family resemblance with Kries's *Spielraum*.

Our argument is that Bourdieu treats probability as an *ontological* term here, a statement about how groups exist, and that to make sense of what this unusual application means, he understands he needs new concepts. Fortunately, by this time, Bourdieu has them. Potential groups in the world take the form of *habitus* (learned probability) and *capital* (capacity to shape objective probability) relative to *fields* (spaces of objective probability). There is a relevant contrast to draw between groups formed in fields, *apparatus* (spaces of determinism), and *games of chance* (spaces of randomness). Probability in action takes form as *illusio* as an investment in objectivity probability. Like Weber, Bourdieu believes sociology should be interpretive—sociologists should meet and recognize agents in the world rather than impose categories on them. The "gap" between analyst and agent is closed by focusing on their mutual relation to probability.[61]

Among the host of other influences on Bourdieu's conception of habitus, an important one is found in what was mentioned above: "learning probability."[62] Since at least the early 1970s, Bourdieu had been slowly unveiling the elements of his *gnoseologica inferior*, including a focus on temporal experience and the primacy of practice, and placing value on data and concepts that attempt to get as close as possible to qualitative immediacy. An "inferior" science of this kind is a science in which knowledge assumes a "reverse hierarchy." As Bourdieu puts it, it is a "science of knowledge that is inferior . . . because its object is inferior" and subject to contempt, with its closest cousins being phenomenology, ethnology, and aesthetics.[63] In this case, the inferior science promotes a knowledge of probability that, true to form, *reverses the hierarchy* that applies to the frequentist statistical version that draws its "objectivity" from a past successful attempt at establishing a form of authoritative knowledge.

For his part, Bourdieu uses internalized probability to redeem the kind of "rational/reasonable practice" that comes from learning probability *without* the technical tools inherited from Galton, Pearson, and Fisher. His orientation is toward remaking sociology in a mold that breaks down knowledge-political barriers rooted in epistemic authority, particularly in the generalizing effect of "representing" social groups and forming explanations about them while wielding unilateral control over a means to prediction as powerful as modern statistics. Bourdieu references Husserl's theme of "habituality" in the German philosopher's *Cartesian Meditations*,[64] specifically the section on "habituality as the substrate of ego" as "[developing] an analysis very close to the one I want to make." He then mentions Merleau-Ponty's *Phenomenology of Perception*[65] as marking the "natural prolongation of Husserl's thought" on habituality and resulting in a kind of "intentionality incarnate" that Bourdieu connects with "the habitus being that familiarity with the world of which Merleau-Ponty quite rightly said . . . is an intermediate term *between presence and absence*. This expression seems very apt to describe what I wanted to say, which is that the habitus is neither an ever-present consciousness constantly on the alert nor an absent automatism."[66]

Bourdieu suggests that it is misleading to make the habitus substantive—as equivalent to, say, a personality type—and equally misleading to make it deterministic. As this language would imply, the habitus is *probabilistic*; it joins the contradictory terms of *presence* and *absence*. Habitus is neither a fixed "variable" nor a "feature." The concept therefore introduces a question about the way sociologists tend to use probability to generate predictive knowledge—particularly with variables to engage in statistical model fitting. The classifications that sociologists produce appear independently of the epistemic practices they use to measure and define them; but the ontology of those classifications is probabilistic rather than substantive or static. So how can the variables that sociologists use have *predictive* value at all?

Bourdieu's two key concepts of habitus and field have mutually implicative definitions, and their mutual links come from recasting them in terms drawn ultimately from Weber's probabilism. Internalized probabilities can only exist if there are, quite simply, objective probabilities in the world. Fields are such localized distributions of objective probability. For Bourdieu, this insight is significant for the way in which objective probability is "translated into reality" as habitus. He describes this process in terms reflective of those mentioned above as "the tendency of aspirations to adjust to objective opportunity,"[67] conveying an engagement with a space of objective probability, in this case through a "quasi-experimental" process involving "progressive disinvestment."

Contrary to reproductionist readings of Bourdieu, however, nothing about this process is deterministic, and to focus on that fact is not even the main point. What Bourdieu describes here are relations within a given space of objective probability that appear mainly as a distribution of aspirations. Those aspirations are ways of translating probability into reality, though they are not the only possible ways of doing so. Here Bourdieu remains true to form, presenting sociology as *gnoseologica inferior*. For that reason, he cannot fix the distribution in advance by any commitment to broad theories of reproduction or even insinuate how aspirations *should* be distributed. Both choices would simply affirm an authoritative division of mental labor. Regardless of what Bourdieu says about social reproduction, the source of aspiration will remain *probabilistic*. If there are patterns in aspirations that do persist, their existence indicates some persistence in the mutually implicative counterpart to habitus—specifically, the objective probability localized as a field.

In the *Cours*, Bourdieu refers to *capital* as distinct from probabilistic social spaces, among other reasons because it "manipulates the propensity to invest . . . basically [manipulating] the *illusio*."[68] In both the *Cours* and *Pascalian Meditations*, Bourdieu uses Franz Kafka's *The Trial*—particularly the fortunes of its main character Josef K.—as an example.[69] In Bourdieu's eyes, Kafka's main character is desperate to be judged, regardless of the verdict, and if Kafka reveals a basic absurdity here, his story also makes clear the mechanisms that "manipulate [our] propensity to invest" or, more simply, to take things *seriously*. In *Pascalian Meditations*, Bourdieu ties this investment to the probabilistic propensities of *capital*.[70] In this instance, the stakes of "being *tried* by" (evaluated, judged by) a capital-leveraged field can encourage a high investment, with much sacrifice and anxiety. Yet the investment discloses the sheer tenuousness of what Bourdieu now refers to as the "justification for existing."

For those historically excluded from fields—those who are stigmatized, who lack capital as deemed by the fields they are now forced to enter under the auspices of being given an "opportunity"—they might find themselves in a position directly analogous to Kafka's K., awaiting the decision of an absolute and unpredictable judge.[71] Whatever the decision, it will appear arbitrary. The "temporal experience" of others is much different: "To be expected, solicited, overwhelmed with obligations and commitments is not only to be snatched from solitude or insignificance, but also to experience . . . a kind of continuous justification for existing." To have expectations set upon oneself by others is to pass a kind of "permanent plebiscite of testimonies of interest."[72] The point Bourdieu wants to make is that these two very different temporal experiences both reflect a "causality of the probable." They are both attributable to structures of probabilities in the world. Those structures, as fields, are arranged to make us invest in them—to make us care, whether that care appears, to us, primarily as a pragmatic need for success or a search for "recognition." Only because a field is a structure of probabilities can they elicit subjectivity in these ways. We *take an interest* and act with *illusio*, blind to the Kafkean absurdities. But something is always on the line as we stand at the mercy of a probabilistic world—at stake is our "reason for being," us humans being without one by nature. More simply, we will refer to it below as *fate*.

We cannot find the same justification available in a game of chance, because the structure of probabilities is very different. When those probabilities congeal into a field, participation will appear like a gamble, because the field (as objectively probabilistic) draws upon our will to prediction; but the gamble-like nature of participation in a field varies. To some, success and recognition always seems more of a guarantee. The same is not true for a game of chance. As a structure of probabilities, a game of chance cannot accumulate history; capital is not present. In fact, a physical mechanism like a roulette wheel is designed to be capital-negating; here, nothing is allowed to control the future, and neither does the past of only one play matter. All that matters is the mercurial present. And because there is no way to control the future (i.e., no "capital," in Bourdieu's terminology), there can be no socially distributed advantage, no hierarchy or privilege. Games of chance are the only place in the social world where "equality of opportunity" can ever truly apply.

Probabilistic Sociology in a Bourdieusian Mold

This chapter has engaged in a mimetic retracing of Bourdieu's steps from 1973 forward as he engages in novel concept formation. A well-known set of concepts—habitus, field, and capital—appears from the endeavor, which has made Bourdieu one of the most widely cited scholars across all social-scientific fields for the past several decades. Our contention has been that these concepts formed in connection with probabilism, or the idea that probability is *objective* as part of the world, placing Bourdieu in a tradition with Max Weber. Retrieving Bourdieu's probabilism as part of his concept formation (both narratively and analytically) makes it possible to relay new schemes and practical approaches for a general incorporation of probabilism into sociology. Note that insofar as sociologists have already been making (perhaps good, perhaps ritualistic) use of Bourdieu's core concepts, then they are already probabilists in practice. So perhaps this transition may not entail such a radical subjective dislocation.

Any such transition has three relevant points of conceptual focus, we believe, that are understandable in sequence, drawing from Bourdieu's novel concept formation. First, Bourdieu's early adoption of Weber took the form of a *looping relation* between probability in two forms, which over the course of the 1970s he would articulate as the linked concepts of habitus and field. Second, Bourdieu would use this probabilism to *reformulate the notion of structure* by introducing and revising concepts like capital as a way of explaining power, external force, and action-at-a-distance, which all come to fruition in the *Cours* without holism or organicism (a goal he shared with Weber). Third, he would revise this probabilistic vision further in his last theoretical book, *Pascalian Meditations*, to *theorize motivation* by deploying a new terminology—*illusio*, alongside *conatus* and *nomos*—that does not rigidly divide subjectivity from objective probability.

To these points we can add one more. Despite the multitude of forms of "capital" in the social science literature today, Bourdieu mentions one that gets very little attention: *informational capital*. It features in two of his *Cours* lectures, and in *Invitation to Reflexive Sociology*.[73] Bourdieu suggests that *all* forms of capital are constituted of informational capital, because they all indicate a kind of internalized probability: a reflection of a current structure of probability and thus of the objective contours of social space, in something that resembles a "kind of spontaneous statistical calculation that we all practice." Informational capital gives us the "sense of one's place," as Bourdieu puts it, a sense of "our 'right place' and situation in the world."[74] Elsewhere Bourdieu describes informational capital as referring to the "dispositions that compose a habitus."[75] To obtain it is to know what it would mean to act "in conflict with the world."[76]

We might read this description dismissively; after all, what do we find here but another form of "capital," stretching further its loose definition, and yet more terminology—it all appears quite scholastic, or the opposite of a mimetic reading? But it is striking how a concept like informational capital in particular becomes practical if we align it with the kind of inchoate social

sense presumably at the core of the corporate form of data-centricity. The
proprietarily most valuable kinds of data attempt to learn this habitus and
encode it, by *leading* it via digital practices like targeted advertising, product
funneling, and the anticipatory channeling that is the most visible application
of artificial intelligence today.[77]

Bourdieu connects informational capital in its explicit and objective form
to a "code," the most explicit form of which would be a codification of rules
in a legalistic or linguistic sense.[78] In probabilistic terms, codification constitutes an explicit rendering of objective chance and one of the clearest ways of
taming and ordering it. Codes generate a clear sense of probability. Bourdieu
mentions specialists like lawyers and grammarians as devising code through
their "objectifying activities." The contemporary iteration is the computer
programmers—"coders"—who now code for a living, with *coding* now a verb
as opposed to just a noun. The coder is the child of the lawyer and the grammarian; they encode information as both rule and structure. But the coder
is different from their parents. A grammarian cannot teach us how to speak,
nor a jurist how to act. A coder does not confront similar practical limits;
for them, the code is the tool not the outcome. And all the world is potential
code.

For Bourdieu, all the world is information, then, at least when the world
consists of probabilities. Informational capital is embodied in a human being,
most evidently, perhaps, in telling *just* the right joke to the right audience at
just the right time.[79] Kant thought highly enough of such displays to place
"wit" (somewhat tentatively) alongside understanding, judgment, and reason
as a higher faculty of cognition.[80] Today we might simply call it "having feel."
Bourdieu's point that information can be *made* into capital still holds even as
information takes a digitized form; in fact, information channeled through
computer code seems to be *more* likely to become informational capital.

When the information of professional coders becomes informational capital, the latter fragments and more rapidly shifts; the structures of probabilities "drawing individuals together or apart" is altered. Not all culture can
bear the distinctions of cultural capital; yet, as informational capital, even
the most common knowledge, seemingly able to bear no social distinction,
can become a marker of insider versus outsider. Bourdieu critiques "Bayesian
decision theory" for attributing "no lasting effect to 'conditionalization' (the
assimilation of new information in the structure of belief)."[81] Outside of a
codification, desire is understood to be fluid; the probabilities frozen in code
do not mediate it. We cannot act according to informational capital where
none is to be found; increasingly, the coders allow it to be found everywhere.

Probabilistic sociology in Bourdieu's mold would use these conceptual and meta-methodological arguments to propose and pursue significant changes to sociological practice (something we take up in part IV), not to mention providing a sociological basis from which to challenge an increasingly popular framework like Bayesianism on its own turf. Theoretically, this approach opens new avenues and perhaps a probabilistic recasting of other core notions of both Bourdieusian and non-Bourdieusian provenance. These include core notions in action theory, such as "belief" and "trust," and even traditionally "macro" concepts such as "institution" and "structure," as we saw earlier. Take, for instance, the idea of "hysteresis," which is featured prominently in Bourdieu's work.[82] This notion can naturally fit into the probabilistic framework, referring to instances of prediction in action from learned probabilities in previous experience that fail to match a novel configuration of objective chances offered by a dynamically changing environment. What we have sketched here is merely the potential relevance of these general points by using Bourdieu's probabilism as a demonstration (and far from the last word) of such concept formation.

PART III

Theory and Cognition

We have so far attempted to draw a throughline from classical probabilists like Pascal and Huygens, to nineteenth-century heterodox theorists in Peirce and Kries, to representatives from social theory—including classics like Du Bois and Weber—to someone more contemporary like Bourdieu. We are saying that, in distinct ways, they are all part of the same intellectual tradition. As we have suggested, Bourdieu seems to have recognized this shared history late in his career. It is not by accident that he engages with Pascal and acknowledges a debt to him (and Huygens) in his last theoretical testament.

The chapters that follow in the third part of the book move from genealogy and exegesis to analytical theory building, situating probabilism within contemporary debates in social theory and more specifically within what is generally called the theory of action. As mentioned above, the data analytics enterprise strikes some as grounds for a new unity across disciplinary boundaries, built this time not on substantive claims but on a methodological tool kit typically falling under the heading of "computation." Probabilism, we claim, provides the grounds for unification as well, but of a different sort. It is a unification rooted not in a method but in a question: *What is action for?* Disciplines from sociology to physics, from literary studies and history to organic chemistry and, yes, even data science—all must answer this question. How do they do it? Probabilism, as we will now show, provides an answer; though its answer is untypical. We can preview it by considering someone who thought deeply about action but is not generally considered a *theorist* of action.

For Erving Goffman, famed sociologist of the performance, chance was alive and well outside statistical formulations.[1] It existed in "extraordinary niches in social life"—Goffman mentions live entertainment, the criminal life, the soldier's call and the police officer's lot, dangerous construction work, well-capping, and sports including football, boxing, and bullfighting all as examples—where activity is both problematic and consequential.[2] To be in or to observe these niches is to orient ourselves toward "fatefulness." It is in Las Vegas, however, at the blackjack tables, that Goffman says we can find the epitome of what makes each of these niches extraordinary. There, and there alone, can we get in on, in a very direct sense, "a bit of the *action*."

For Goffman, action of this sort is simple; it consists of activities that are "consequential, problematic, and undertaken for what is felt to be their own sake."[3] Action must be challenging, and it must have stakes; but it cannot be a strictly utilitarian means to an end. There must be something about action that justifies it for its own sake, regardless of the outcome. Goffman would seek out action at the casinos, apprenticing himself as a blackjack dealer—as one who metes out action as he shuffles the cards.[4] For Goffman, to determine "where the action is" requires that we be attentive to such spaces and practices ("niches") like those we find in a concentrated state in Las Vegas casinos. Goffman gives us a theory of action, just of a different sort. He does what the ancient Greeks would call *Theoria*[5]—travels to a special place to observe a significant event only available at that spot.[6] The goal, historically, was then to report back to the people in one's city-state. For the Greeks, *theoria* were often visits to oracular centers. Goffman heads to Vegas but likewise understands that what he witnesses there, he can *only* witness there.

Goffman's instincts are not altogether different from those that guided Pascal in his endeavor to understand chance, in all its forms, by understanding a game of cards. Roughly three hundred years later, Goffman pursues a similar research design. While it can be possible for chance to lie "in the attitude of the individual himself—his creative capacity to redefine the world around him into its decisional possibilities," the casino is different because it is more *objective*. Its "physical and social organization is designed to facilitate the occurrence of action."[7] For Goffman, casinos make it clear that "where the action is" is a pretty good reflection of whether a given niche is organized around "chance-taking" or not, simply because it makes chance available *to* take. To take a chance, to seek out the action—this is to reveal character, because one is tested in these scenarios. Chances can be invented and tests fashioned at any time; for proof, you only need to act deliberately offensively. And that is the other thing about action, Goffman says: It can be avoided. So why do we seek it?

Goffman concludes from his study that sociology tends to adhere to an "optimistic" view of people: Once you get them "to desire socially delineated goals under the auspices of 'self-interest,' you need only convince them to regulate their pursuits in accordance with an elaborate array of ground rules." Such an arrangement renders them fully predictable—at least in principle.

We know that it never works out in that way. People keep deviating from this model; they are all too alive to the contingencies around them. They will break the rules for the sake of it; they will seek out action where self-interest is not easily discernible. For our purposes, Goffman's foray in the casinos provides us with a useful vocabulary—chance, chance-taking, niches of action, tests, expectation—because from a probabilist perspective, and in line with what we can also learn from Weber, Du Bois, and Bourdieu, Goffman's version of action can help us answer that great unanswered question: *What is action for?*

It is worth noting, on this point, that perhaps the distribution of action in the social world, the niches where we can find it, would not include Las Vegas casinos today as it did for Goffman in the 1960s. Anthropologist Natasha Dow Schüll followed Goffman into those same casinos forty years later; once there, she found far less of the action. What she found instead was that *machine* gambling had taken over the casino floor, having a dampening effect on the organization of these spaces around action. In fact, the appeal of casinos is, perhaps, quite the opposite. As Schüll puts it, "the continuity of machine gambling holds worldly contingencies in a kind of abeyance, granting . . . an otherwise elusive zone of certainty."[8]

Schüll's observation gets us thinking: If machines can reduce probability at its most heightened site, then could probability disappear from our patchwork world as it is rearranged by machines? We will revisit those points further below. In this part of the book, we recommend a different paradigm that might help us understand why this possibility might be a concern. If we want to get in on the action, we would do well to see what cognitive science is up to these days. There, the prime concern is how we brain-burdened creatures do that very vital thing—*predict with consequences*—that was at the heart of Pascal's concerns nearly four hundred years ago, and which Goffman found so deeply existential and appealing. Today, we can learn the most about predicting with consequences by studying how one neuron relates to another.

5

Probabilism and Social Theory

Chance can mean our conviction that it is impossible to give a causal explanation, or our faith that somewhere, someone could give an impersonal explanation if they cared enough, which they don't. Whether the world has millions of causes or not a one, "chance" is a polite way of ending the inquiry.

JOHN LEVI MARTIN, *The Explanation of Social Action*

Sociologists have long condemned intellectual tendencies in other fields, especially psychology or economics, dismissing them as individualistic, ahistorical, non-emergent, non-processual, and all-too-static—among other accusations.[1] More recently, this critical tendency has turned inward, focusing on the definition of what constitutes social reality and, by extension, how sociologists should explain it. If, during the postwar period, positivism served as a kind of half-fractured crutch for the justification of sociological knowledge,[2] its collapse over the last several decades has left a vacuum of sorts in sociology's sense of its project.[3]

While positivism is by no means a unified or homogeneous intellectual tradition, broadly speaking, it lent the sociological project a certain coherence based on interrelated themes and directions, including the following once-well-regarded tenets: (1) Explanations should be associated with generalizable covering laws or at least general propositions; (2) the only subject of scientific generalization is directly observable empirical data and phenomena; (3) sociology is a science in the same way as other sciences; and (4) a critical task for sociology is to create a "'natural science of society' which can hope to reproduce a system of laws and logically interlinked abstract generalizations similar to those (presumably) achieved in the natural sciences."[4]

All these claims are of disputed validity today, including the positivist characterization of the current state and history of the natural sciences themselves,[5] though, in the absence of anything of comparable impact and all-encompassing scope as positivism, it can be "much harder for young sociologists to do good work"; moreover, "when push comes to shove—when editorial boards and tenure committees weigh in, and final decisions are made about publications and positions—it is to the positivist standards that we must all still appeal."[6] So it has become imperative, at least for some, that a programmatic framework of comparable breadth may help fill the void its dwindling fortunes have left in our (purportedly) post-positivist time.

It is consequential that what these conversations about sociology's present and future in a context definitively beyond positivism have not yet discussed is *probability*. Despite its reputation, data science shares sociology's post-positivist enthusiasm, as it does not seek fixed "covering laws" or the settled codification of empirical regularities but instead recommends a kind of "permanent learning." If data science is indeed a "fourth approach to scientific discovery,"[7] it must also be rooted in its distinction from the other, older approaches, including whatever indebtedness they might have had to positivist aspirations. Among other reasons, this distinction does (and could further) fuel the appeal of data science in a field like sociology.

Fearing a kind of theoretical takeover, many of the boldest theoretical frameworks in post-positivist sociology proposed over the past half-century have overlooked and underestimated the potential of a data-driven takeover, one that could very well be in the offing. The general concepts that theory-oriented sociologists have waiting in their tool kit are decidedly nonprobabilistic, or at least they have been cleansed—as we saw with the Parsonian and Schutzian reception of Weber's ideas in chapter 2—of anything resembling probability as a conceptual tool for theorizing and thinking about the social world. Accordingly, existing theoretical frameworks in the social and human sciences are unable to accommodate the idea of ranges of possibility, held together by orientations, taking form in expectation and resulting in systematic bouts of probabilistic judgment. This blind spot presents a problem, we argue, for many of the inferences sociologists typically make, and particularly for how our conceptual and methodological tools for making inferences might leave us flat-footed in the face of data science's apparent capacity to enact a direct interface with what Weber and Kries call *Chance*, bypassing any form of conceptual or theoretical mediation.

Consider, as just one example, the categories for distinguishing various types of social and group identities, a theme Bourdieu also touched upon in the last chapter. Following the usual approach characteristic of standard quantitative methods in the social sciences, these must perforce take the predictable form of binary codes (sometimes appropriately called "dummy" variables) to enable statistical aggregation and linear model fitting. The same is true for those (biopolitical and nominalistic) "state categories" recorded by a census or other large-scale administrative surveys.[8] Data science, by way of contrast, presents us with something different. As one analysis puts it:

> Those aspects of identity once thought fixed or almost unchanging—gender, race, citizenship, nationality—become readable in this virtualized way. For instance, patterns of web browsing and other digital activities can be mined to determine whether one is likely to be a woman or a man. But these assessments (another set of algorithmically derived classification situations) are always flexible and provisional, depending on data flowing in and on the particular combination of classifiers. Consequently, the algorithmic inference of gender identity may change at any moment. Technology, then, builds on and feeds into a broader cultural shift by which gender identity may be increasingly experienced as multiple and fluid rather than binary and stable.[9]

The data science category of gender identifies a *range* that includes *any* of its specific manifestations, or what we can translate more simply as fluidity. Yet "fluidity" here only has a data science meaning as "datafied" behavioral traces on which an algorithm constantly learns and makes updated classificatory inferences. It does not translate into lived reality in this way; sociological probabilism would make that link in the form of what Ellis Monk calls "cues for categories" and what we in chapter 2 drew from Kries as a synchysis.[10]

As we have argued, data science is not unique for the reasons that its boosters might tell us, most of which pertain to its "performativity" and potential for impact, its practical and commercial value that has no apparent need for some elements of the scientific toolkit, among them pedagogical training in a discipline. Data science is unique, in our view, because it is *probabilistic*, a quality that has certain, definite virtues. Yet data science's implementation of probabilism comes with limitations, particularly its incapacity to translate probability into action, which leads it to favor the algorithmic black box over judgment. If data science breaks with naive substantialism, then it does not return us to lived reality, where probability alone can be concrete. To the degree that its promise rests in datafication alone, the promise is false, a fool's gold—data science invites back (albeit more covertly) the same problems of nominalism and abstraction as those it critiques.

In this chapter, we situate probabilism among other general orienting frameworks that have developed in sociology's post-positivist era. Two of these frameworks help showcase the distinctiveness of probabilism for sociology: *realism* and *interpretivism*.[11] Both have appeared during the post-positivist era as ways of defining what sociology should be like if it can no longer rely upon its past positivist commitments. Probabilism shares aspects with both frameworks yet pivots away from realism and interpretivism on several key fronts. Primarily, probabilism breaks with what is arguably the most significant holdover from the positivist era but which is rarely acknowledged as part of the interpretivist and realist renovations of the field. They have both attempted to reconcile significant movements in social theory with a method that, at least in its stance on probability, remains essentially unchanged from sociology's positivist past.

Beyond Realism and Interpretivism

Realism and interpretivism span a few academic generations now and have grown up in the post-positivist era.[12] They are also more than mere theories. In the present sociological field (both US-based and globally), they have operated as "scientific/intellectual movements," with institutional supports of various kinds, both inside and outside the academy, to help move their respective projects forward.[13] Adapting these tactics makes perfect sense—to overcome the positivist legacy requires more than challenging it on principle. And within these niches, realism and interpretivism have been subject to much rationalization. But as general tendencies, realism and interpretivism are far from limited to sociology. They extend across the manifold of social sciences, replicated in distinctions pertaining to relativism, universalism, the abstract and the concrete. Here we will sketch what we see as the broad arcs of both movements—what they mean as programmatic statements for what social scientists should do once they realize that positivism provides no way forward.

In presenting their salvo against positivism, realists focus on ontology in the form of real structures and mechanisms behind empirical observations and experiences. It is these real objects that the social sciences, and sociologists in particular, should pin their disciplinary identity to, though not to rehash the lawlike reality the positivists hunted so aggressively. Realism breaks primarily with the *empiricist* tenet of positivism. As real but typically unobservable structures and mechanisms enter into unique combinations, the emergent effects *cause* what we can record and measure as empirical or actual. Realism is generally defined by three fundamental commitments: (1) to the "mind-independent existence" of the objects that science studies; (2) to the literal interpretation of scientific claims, meaning that theoretical statements, even if they feature unobservables, are always either true or false (and never, for example, metaphorical); and (3) to the tenet that theoretical claims, given this literal interpretation, constitute knowledge of a mind-independent reality.[14] In a deep understanding of realism, what we call the empirical and actual (or "phenomenal") are essential aspects of knowledge, but they are by no means sufficient. As we return to below, realists insist above all that we cannot make a knowledge claim based only on the "constant conjunctions" of repeated empirical patterns. We must instead refer to unobservables as what the world is really made of.[15]

For some realists, this approach to scientific knowledge is best exemplified by careful study of the practice of experimentation. Influential in sociology is the argument put forth by philosopher Roy Bhaskar to this effect: "It is not necessary that science occurs. But given that it does, it is necessary that the world is a certain way."[16] Experimental activity, the key knowledge-producing practice of the most prevalent styles of reasoning in science, would not be intelligible, according to Bhaskar, if the world did not have the depth alluded to between the empirical and the real—with structures that are unapparent to us but that generate, if experimentally manipulated in the right way, what *is* apparent to us empirically.[17] In the experimental context, a scientific intervention is responsible for the actual regularities we perceive; but even in a "world without men [*sic*] the causal laws of science would continue to prevail."[18] For those who recommend this brand of realism, only with such an approach can sociology retain any commitment to causal explanation.

A different perspective in sociology takes a series of different stances on these issues. From this perspective, a post-positivist sociology should ground itself not in the reality of its objects but in the study of meaning through and through. For the *interpretivist*, the problem with realism is that there is no definitive way to call out and point to "reality" that is not already contained by an interpretation, and one that can claim no particular distinction for itself. Instead of seeking transcendental conditions, which are only accessible with specialized tools, the sociological task is anchored on a single plane, which the sociologist shares with everyone else. The interpretivist seeks a "consensual comprehension"[19] of society along with actors *in* society, placing the onus on finding a point of connection between analyst and actor. The interpretivist defines that point of connection as a "meaning structure."[20]

For interpretivists, the realist search for the equivalent in social science of the experiments we can observe in natural science is terribly fraught. In sociology, the "compensator" for such experimental interventions can only be what we can reflexively acknowledge as necessary conditions for the social practice and human experience that we can directly have or observe. In application, this solution takes the form of something like: "what[ever] must be the case for the experiences grasped by the phenomenal forms of capitalist life to be possible."[21] However, according to the interpretivist, the realist solution is *not* an effective block on an unsettling arbitrariness—moving "from any sort of knowledge to what it implies exists (from belief in witchcraft and its practice [spell-casting] to the existence of demons, for example)."[22] Once we have dropped positivist commitments, the social scientist and social theorist have nothing to prevent their realist best intentions from leading them into interminable debates about what is more real than the next thing—with no resolution in sight.

For the realist, however, the interpretivist essentially mistakes knowledge for meaning.[23] The two must be kept distinctive, as the former is always based on a kind of intervention into the world, whether we understand that intervention to be experimental or practical. Importantly, such interventions are how unobservable but real aspects of the world are rendered actual and thus empirical—available to measurement and phenomenal experience. Regardless of how it is interpreted, then, what presents itself as empirical to us is sourced in such a deep structure, rendering it mind- and meaning-independent.[24] The realist refers to as our point of access to reality as *retroduction*, or the "retroduction test," in which an extrapolation is made from a hypothesis (or phenomenal experience) to its properties and what those properties necessarily imply about reality.[25] Because we do not have access to structures in phenomenal experience, knowledge must involve a "break" with nonscientific (or folk) ways of knowing them.[26] Many realists would claim that if science, let alone social science, did *not* make such a break, then it would have no grounds for claiming any distinction at all for itself.

For the interpretivist, however, we get off on the wrong foot when we commit to such special preserve of knowledge as the way out of the hermeneutic circle—thus solving its riddle. The goal for the human scientist is therefore not to find something that only the scientist or analyst accesses. Our "epistemic mode" must be one where, when marshaling evidence for our claims as sociologists, our goal is *reconstruction*, namely of the "meaningful context of social action" in which the human actors we are studying live their lives.[27] If there is depth here it is "deep interpretation," not ontology, which means that while our reconstructions might surprise social actors in the world, those actors *can* find them just as meaningful as we do. The only real difference between us analysts and social actors is that those actors do not have as wide (or deep) a grasp of the "landscape of meaning" as our epistemic tools allow us to achieve.

The differences between realism and interpretivism are significant, but they can at least agree on one thing: that knowledge in the post-positivist era should be formed in *retrospect* based on things that have already happened—in other words, on *reconstruction* or *retroduction*. Post-positivist knowledge is first empirical, then subsequently filled out, whether this filling-out entails supplying it with a meaningful context or the ontologically real structures and mechanisms that cause it. Post-positivist knowledge is distinctively *not*, in this sense, predictive. We might speculate that this characteristic of post-positivism signals a pointed resistance to positivism's willingness to predict, though realists and interpretivists say little about that. What they do tell us is that theory is essential for any kind of non-positivism, though not because theory, as the positivists thought, is what allows us to predict.

For the realist, the best theory is instead a *metatheory*. It is theory that is capable of uniting our methods with our ontological commitments. Anything purporting to be a theory should be put to a series of tests (including retroduction), with "the metatheory test" found as the final and, in a sense, *ultimate* one.[28] Theory is therefore meant to challenge our own preconceptions (perhaps built into our methods) of what does and does not exist; it needs to provide us with an ontological picture of what exists and how. Thus, in answering the question "What is a person?" we must be thorough about what a personalist ontology entails in its full scope, as only such an approach will indicate to us what methods are suitable for knowledge of persons and what they are responsible for.[29] For the realist, a little bit of theory can go a long way, then, but that theory must be rich and elaborate, showing no fear of chastisement as metaphysical. Above all, a theory must offer comprehension of the large number of actual occurrences that a relatively small amount "powerful particulars" can cause.[30]

For the interpretivist, the best theory is a *lot* of theory. The interpretivist is an advocate of theory not measured by how encompassing and one-stop-shop it can be (including everything from metaphysics to method). The value of a theory is weighted instead by how well it contributes to the "plurality of abstract theoretical schemas." If, for the interpretivist, analysts and actors are oriented by the same thing on a single plane of existence, the analyst can only reveal it to be wider and deeper in its semiotic entailments and connections; they cannot "break" with it as the realist does with knowledge limited to the empirical and phenomenal. In this task, the social sciences need all the theory they can get, as social theory is the "meaning system" the social analyst alone has available.[31] Only in being conversant with lots of theory can the working researcher overcome doubts common in the post-positivist era, specifically "the existential near-impossibility of true understanding" and the sense that "interpretation is always flawed and in some sense a misrecognition."[32] Hence, *theoretical pluralism*—reading and applying theories broadly, even theories that contradict; not attempting for consistency or to stake out a single position; proliferating the concepts we have available about something (like power) rather than attempting to negate and reduce their number—

is what will best allow analysts to "reference the meaningful particularities" exhibited by people in context, which is what social science *can* do post-positivism.

In different ways, then, realism and interpretivism both argue for the merits of theory. Quite unlike positivism's hypothetico-deductivism, neither approach situates theory at the beginning of research—instead, it seems to come more toward the end. With such specific recommendations, we are led to wonder: How influential have these frameworks been in the post-positivist era? Even the most rabid interpretivist or realist would have to admit that the results have been mixed. Both frameworks enjoy a certain intellectual and institutional success, though that success is largely concentrated on handfuls of believers and their immediate offspring. Most sociologists appear to carry on with business as usual, unaware that these "revolutions in thought" (to borrow from Marx and Engels) might be happening in the office just next door. If post-positivism is observable anywhere in sociology these days, it might be in something quite different than rich frameworks like realism and interpretivism—in an emphasis on method, instead, and in the significance given to cases as sources of novel data, quite apart from any philosophy of science. The concentration on method has grown increasingly detailed over the years, and not only in sociology. Such attention can even appear sui generis in its orientation, and we should not blame new entrants to the field for believing method itself to be the primary element of the disciplinary identity they stand to gain in our post-positivist era.

Suppose we place ourselves in the position of a graduate student in sociology or related field, nearing the end of their time served. They have received significant methods training and have answers for all the tough questions. They've also gone through the school of hard knocks: data analysis and data gathering. They are accomplished, in other words, and are well on their way; but then they find themselves haunted (or perhaps pestered) by an inopportune question—*what is my case a case of?* They have thorough knowledge of their case and findings, but their research was not exactly "theoretically motivated" at the start; in fact, they always felt like their theory class was the least valuable to them. But theory must be invited in at this stage—here at the end of the research process with much on the line (like finishing a dissertation). What our graduate student does next would probably not impress the committed realist or interpretivist: They stroll the aisles of the "supermarket of theory" looking for some to *use*. The shelves are overstocked after years of accumulation and a little dusty, and much like shoppers in the bread aisle in an American grocery store, our graduate student finds themselves paralyzed by choice. In their desperation, the criteria they will use to decide on a theory would likely not pass muster from a realist or interpretivist perspective, if something like the search for deep ontology or deep interpretation are those frameworks' respective criteria of choice.

To call this scenario post-positivist is mainly to draw attention to the fact that, at the very least, positivism gave a theory a definite role to play in social research.[33] In fact, in many respects, it played the most important role in a straightforward deductive test.[34] If our account of the graduate student's plight is even remotely accurate, it would seem to reflect how the post-positivist era has settled into a standard practice and pedagogy in which the decline of theory in a field like sociology proceeds apace, despite realism and interpretivism providing philosophies of science that so strongly seek the contrary. A possible reason why we see this apparent shuffling in opposite directions has less to do with what realism and interpretivism actually argue and more to do with what they, and pretty much everyone else who ponders post-positivism, studiously avoid: the meaning of probability.

Both realists and interpretivists recognize that post-positivist research starts with a fact, not a theory, and that fact-finding not infrequently involves probability. If only by implication, and carried by methods, probability is frequency at the present moment. Thus, we can say that we have a fact because we have frequency (repeat observations, commonalities in interview responses, large-N, time in the field, etc.) on our side. The link of frequency to probability and then to empirical fact is carried forward more or less without question, as we seem to need it to answer a very important question: *What are we trying to explain?* A frequency is a great way of finding something to explain in the form of a pattern or trend, perhaps even a puzzle.[35] All of these examples reduce the sense that our explanations are *merely* a single case instead of something general, thus upping the ante.

The reach of the late nineteenth-century frequentists (Galton, Pearson, and Fisher) extends far, in this regard, even into research that we would never mistake as statistical. It is because frequentism defines probability that it can have such a long reach. As the Bayesians are only too quick to remind us: How you define probability will dictate how your research will unfold, and there is much more at stake in such a choice than whether you are qualitative or quantitative.

In committing to frequentism de facto, the recommendations of realism and interpretivism appear in a new, perhaps contradictory light. Both frameworks recommend that theory be used to translate a probabilistic phenomenon *away* from probability just to explain how probabilities can *themselves* be explanatory. Both realism and interpretivism avoid probability for the most part, because they both seek to avoid explanations that rely upon "con-

stant conjunctions," which positivism treats as the factual sine qua non. Both
frameworks strongly pivot from positivism on this point. In doing so, the
interpretation of the philosopher David Hume and his argument that we have
no right to claim any deeper causal knowledge beyond the directly observable
repeated succession of events becomes of material importance. Here, we can
return to points we mentioned in the introduction on the philosopher David
Lewis's "Humean mosaic" and what it means to think of the world in terms of
patches as opposed to grids.[36]

Hume's Wager

A key passage from Hume's *Enquiry Concerning Human Understanding* is
typically read as recommending the much-bemoaned correlational empiricism; yet we can read it differently as a claim about expectation. As we watch
a "billiard-ball rolling in a straight line towards another," Hume writes, "may
[we] not conceive that a hundred different events might as well follow from
that cause? May not both these balls remain at absolute rest? May not the first
ball return in a straight line, or leap off from the second in any line or direction? All these suppositions are consistent and conceivable."[37] Yet, we are still
bound by an expectation that something specific will happen. No matter what
we might imagine a priori, we cannot remove this expectation.[38]

If we push this idea a bit further, then the task of knowledge shifts toward
more probabilistic questions: less "Did this billiard ball *cause* that billiard ball
to move across the table?" and more "In what order of things is this sequence
probable? How, in Hume's case, does the smacking of one billiard ball into
another lead to these *expected* results? Why are these events not unrelated but
instead fall within a *range*?"

Hume's wager, if we are allowed to call it that, focuses here—on the
chance that probability has sociohistorical conditions, which would mean
that it cannot be epistemic, or delegated to a method, or applicable to anything about which we are condemned to a Laplacean ignorance (which for
Laplace meant *everything*). Is Hume's wager as drastic as Pascal's wager? Not
exactly, but it does come with its own stakes and a gamble to be won or lost.
If you wager, as Hume does, that probability is sociohistorical, then you allow
it to be learned inductively, but without frequency as a standard (as Peirce,
in particular, came to realize). If, on the other hand, you do *not* wager that
probability is sociohistorical, as frequentists and Bayesians and most others
do by default, then you render it epistemological. From our perspective, a
field like sociology has historically wagered on the second point, but not for
very good reasons—after all, if our above account of the reception of Weber is

right, then sociologists have had no idea there was even a wager to make. One result of this circumstance pertains to how oddly positioned sociology finds itself today—post-positivist in principle, quasi-positivist in practice, with a commitment to theory but a sense of theory that perhaps more easily lends itself to a "tack on" than a purposeful driving force.

In our view, Hume was right about one thing: How you wager on probability in large part decides what you will allow to *exist*. Here, we build on historian Lorraine Daston's claim mentioned earlier, to reassert how, we believe, Hume's wager forces us to pivot from a philosophical view like "the Humean mosaic." Here we come full circle, and for a purpose. To take Hume's wager, to gamble our discipline on probability as a sociohistorical construction, leads us into an interesting space, one that is definitively post-positivist simply by pointing out how enormously incompatible positivism is with the world—it cannot help but posit a "general linear reality." But to focus on the world, and on stuff like probability existing in it, does not mean making metaphysical commitments, if by that we mean claiming dominion over entities that can never become apparent in action—in Spinoza's view, all such an approach can do is render *all* action accidental. Rather, to be ontological is to claim that the actualities we encounter and measure, the phenomenal experiences we have, are constituted not of causal necessity or historical contingency but of probability, the modality of habit or "disposition"—what will unfold with predictability, if the world is right.

To take Hume's wager, then, requires a different vocabulary and approach, one focused on things like *pockets of predictability* or *probability orders* (e.g., Goffman's "niches"), *adequate causation* (from Spinoza), and Chance (Du Bois), *Chance* (Weber), and objective chance (Bourdieu), where we might otherwise posit structures, mechanisms, or landscapes of meaning. In this case, among the contributing factors for what transpires with measurable regularity, expectations must always be found, as the Bayesians insist; but they are not simply infinitely revisable bits of information or subjective states—they are the product of *looping* into the world, and they help us reveal what exists in it. Any sort of concentration here, however, requires a change in theory as it has come to be in sociology over the last several decades and is reflected in the recommendations of why a field like sociology should, even now, be *for* theory for any reason at all.

From Central Problems to Basic Questions

One legacy of the collapse of the positivist hegemony in sociology concerns theory, its meaning and use, and what exactly it should be in an empirical field like sociology. For better or worse, theory is given an essential role to play in a positivist understanding of knowledge; it constitutes the starting point and the prime mover. It is from positivism that sociologists seem to inherit the phrase "making a *theoretical* contribution," which still haunts publication decisions like a specter. It is indicative, then, that post-positivist efforts like interpretivism and realism place so much onus on theory, lending it a new purpose as a way of moving sociology beyond positivism. As we have claimed, however, their efforts do not seem to have stemmed the tide of the decline of theory—specifically, the reasons for theory to have any essential status for the sociological enterprise—that unsurprisingly coincides with the demise of positivism.

In part at least, realism and interpretivism are not entirely innovators in their efforts; in part, at least, they stand as inheritors of a general mode of theorizing that grew up in the wake of positivism, was not fully expressed as a general approach to sociology but instead has stood more as a reason to "do theory" as a sociologist. We can call this approach to theory in sociology the *central problems* approach. If we were to date central problems' official coronation, 1979 can serve as good as any, though the preceding several years find the fleshing-out of the approach and the publication of core contributions. This year sees the publication of the book from which we borrow the phrase: specifically, Anthony Giddens's *Central Problems in Social Theory*.[39] The quasi-pragmatist "problems" focus, well-represented by Giddens, guided general theory out of the post-functionalist, anomic, warring schools of the sixties, particularly around the classics, by engaging in a then-risky position-taking, but one that in hindsight appears perfectly adapted to an era marked by coexistence, synthesis, and fluid adoption of concepts across formerly hard lines.[40]

We can characterize a central problems approach to theorizing as follows. In the dualism of structure versus agency, a theorist is tasked with solving it in a "single conceptual move." They must phrase their answer in a way that gives it bearing and accessibility on the topic for sociologists knee-deep in the muck of the empirical world; the task at hand can seem to rival analytic philosophy in the subtlety of discrimination and distinction-making required. Thus, as Giddens puts it: The solution to the structure-versus-agency debate lies in the "essential recursiveness of social life, as constituted in social practices. Structure enters simultaneously into the constitution of the agent and social practices, and 'exists' in the generating moments of this constitution."[41] Such a complicated spate of claims is then condensed into a nice, crisp phrase—"structuration"—this is an argument primed to be *used* by any sociologist at loggerheads.

PROBABILISM AND SOCIAL THEORY

Giddens himself appreciated such traits as giving theory a raison d'être in the destabilizing circumstances both *"après la lutte"*[42] of functionalism and of the warring schools from the sixties. Sociology could find a united front in the usefulness of the big four concepts—structure, agency, culture, power— and a general focus on social inequality as opposed to a prior one, more suited to functionalism, like social order. Yet—as a potential source of knowledge capital, promising some hold over an uncertain disciplinary future—has central problems theorizing and its extensive archive run out of steam? Mastery of central problems seems to carry less disciplinary cachet today than ever, and with each passing year the theory appears to drift further into the history of sociology, coinciding with the extinction of the occupational niche of the "theorist" allied principally to theory rather than to a topical subfield.

Still, the concepts and frameworks inherited, whether directly or indirectly, from central problems theorizing has given sociologists a conceptual armamentarium for generalizing beyond specific cases (and thus "casing them") in ways that offer recourse and rebuttal to what might otherwise appear as a singular reliance on data and method alone. The situation is a contradictory one, however, as evident in the torment of our ideal-typical graduate student, though the contradiction is also not simply a byproduct of the fact that all-too-human theoretical learning simply pales by comparison to what machine-enhanced algorithmic learning can do. There is something particular about the central problems era that appears to operate today more as an Achilles' heel for sociologists.

In the parlance of the Bayesian cognitive science we will meet in the next chapter, central problems have come to serve in the role of "hyper-priors" for sociology: an obdurate knowledge base maintaining itself via "self-evidencing" error-reduction mechanisms. In slightly more palatable terms, central problems smooth over the theoretical landscape by restricting "large swaths of possible hypothesis spaces."[43] They are general enough to draw in as the grounds for making a judgment, effective enough to absorb uncertainties and cast aside the residual in whatever stands as "particular" in relation to them, but the fundamental way they do so, as we will expand on below, is by taming chance—that is, *Chance* as an objective state of the world—as opposed to explaining it.[44]

For an example, take the following two arguments, published nearly forty years apart, and which bear a definite similarity, though for various reasons that should surprise us. First from Giddens: "Marx says that workers 'must sell themselves'—or, more accurately, their labour power—to employers. The 'must' in the phrase expresses a constraint which derives from the institutional order of modern capitalist enterprise that the worker faces. There is only one course of action open to the worker who has been rendered propertyless—to sell his or her labour power to the capitalist. That is to say, there is only one feasible option, given that the worker has the motivation to wish to survive."[45]

Giddens makes no mention of agency and structure here; technically, he only presents a reading of Marx. But he condenses the Marxian portrayal of the situation of the worker under capitalism into a central problem formulation—here is structure, there is agency; here is how one reproduces the other in an easy recursion. Next from Vivek Chibber, who in a more recent argument makes no mention of Giddens and would certainly oppose him on several fronts, but who appears to inherit the same paradigm as the British theorist:

> A structural theory does not have to suppress the role of social agency. The challenge is to show how structures are involved in generating reasons for the actions in question. In other words, structures can be causally relevant, not because they turn actors into automatons but because they have an impact on the actors' reasoning about *how* to intervene in the world. They can perform this function because they are part of the constraints actors have to account for as they engage the world around them. Those constraints make it attractive to pursue one course of action rather than another because of the consequences they are able to impose on the individuals embedded within the structure.[46]

These are two examples of sociologists doing what we would, in the central problems mold, call "theory." The more recent claim from Chibber adopts the concepts more explicitly, which in part is indicative of their pull more than forty years after their official birth. Agency and structure are imported into the situation of the worker, remaking it into a situation that carries the central problem: namely, how can agency, which involves the apparent contingency of the actor, reproduce structure, which is predictable and thus the opposite of that contingency? The importation of concepts clarifies and targets the central problem, putting it into interpretable terms, specifically by focusing on the agency that appears by contrasting choice against constraint. We are thereby put into the worker's shoes. They have agency; they are not ideological dupes. And the choice they face is a stark one, which we can understand perfectly using a vocabulary of folk psychology.

On the surface, such an account makes good sense, and there is little call for dispute. Yet, a probabilist will interject at this point with a basic question: What does this worker *orient* to? The situation of the worker is composed of an orientation to limited choices and many constraints. The space that Chibber and Giddens tell us about appears to be as solidly fixed as an iron cage—but for Weber, the construct ("*stahlhartes Gehäuse*") in question references the highly predictable *Chance* that arises when subjective meaning almost entirely disappears relative to expectation in one's orientation. There is no room for interpretation in that situation, and so to place the worker at the crux of structure and agency, as Chibber and Giddens do, lends the worker a unique capability: They can make *extremely good predictions*, as there is no apparent obscurity between them (the worker), their action, and the outcomes of those actions. But this point raises another basic question: How can they do that predicting? How have they learned their *Chances* so well?

Central problems theorizing is useful for providing specific answers to tough, seemingly intractable questions; it had to be useful in this way if it was to be successful in the anomic world of post-functionalist sociology. Theory becomes a source of limitation in scope and focus—in this case, to limit agency to a fixed option, using concepts to distinguish, with precision, where the *agency* is and where it is not. But the advantages of this limitation come with a cost—in this case, to catalog the other options in the situation of the worker not as agency but constraint is to ignore the contribution the agent makes *to* the agency they do have. To put the same point more simply, there *is* an opening between the worker and the world, and without sounding badly idealistic, the situation of the worker under capitalism is not as *closed* as the central problems terminology denotes. The worker in question knows perfectly well what will follow should they take certain *Chances* as opposed to others. They have a clear sense of their own adequate causation in this case— they know, for example, that there will be hell to pay should they sleep until ten tomorrow morning instead of waking at six and heading to work at seven. If that is not agency, is it the accidental result of a structure? And, further, why is there no *Chance* of something still different? Like collective agency? A strike? What does this worker expect in relation to those *Chances*?

For a probabilist, each of these *Chances* is found within the same range of possibility, within the same continuum, which means they all feature some continuity with the situation of the worker—they all overlap with the position of "worker" as it stands now, but they do not completely overlap with each other. Chibber and Giddens signify the situation of the worker as a central problem of structure and agency; for a probabilist, the choice/constraint dynamic they favor conveys a *Chance*/expectation loop just as much as if Chibber and Giddens diagnosed the situation of a worker as "all in their head" and asserted that for a worker to no longer be in the situation simply requires them to change their mind. What becomes evident in the probabilistic retelling of structure and agency, then, is something more like a "causality of the probable" that scrambles the logic of operating under structural constraint, though not by eliminating the objectivity that applies to the situation. While these *Chances* might all be possible, they do not all carry the same probability in an objective sense: They indicate not a number but a connection to the present situation of the worker, their sense of the "average probable assessment of facts," to borrow from Weber.

If central problems cannot help us account for this, where else can we turn? To sketch an answer, we must take a detour. For we are far from the first to sense problems in the central problems mode of theorizing, and nor are we the first to pose questions of the kind that we do above—*basic questions*, as we will now call them.

Bruno Latour's Clean Slate

A basic question is, on the face of it, simply a *dumb* question—dumb relative to the clean and elegant designs of central problems theorizing. By "basic" questions, we do not mean to endorse a kind of "great chain of being" searching for the supreme form of reality in what is basic to all.[47] Rather, basic questions are questions to which answers are assumed; because nobody knew how they could be *important* before. Switching from central problems to basic questions entails trying to theorize outside the bounds of familiar hyper-priors like structure and agency, then, or relying on the central problems language. It also changes the meaning and purpose of theory when it is no longer a statement of law (as in positivism) nor a "supermarket" product nor the resolution of a central problem that the research will in fact confront. So what, then, does theory *do* when we ask a basic question? It is helpful to start with what we believe is an example of it at work, which seems to have been written for the purpose of removing all general, central problems–esque concepts and questions from sociologists' view and creating a clean slate.

Bruno Latour, in one of his early articles, admits that as a novice in the sociological field, having a limited orientation to its possibilities (and central problems), perhaps he is misunderstanding the stock put into certain ideas. He appears to state the obvious as a result, though his naive musings can come across, at least to some, as revelatory:

> Sociology had become a positive science only once it stopped bickering about the origins of society and instead *started with* the notion of an all-embracing society that could then be used to explain various phenomena of interest . . . There is always enough already accumulated energy to explain, say, the spread of multinationals, Pinochet's dictatorship, male domination in Black ghettos, the division of labor in factories, and so on. You start with so many inequalities that their origins seem to be irrelevant. It thus seems unproblematic to say

that Reagan, Napoleon, the City of London, or capitalism "have got power"—
unproblematic, that is, so long as you are able to draw on the big reservoir of
energy provided by an ever present and overarching society. If you apply the
translation model, this reservoir dries up immediately. You no longer have any
stored-up energy to explain why a President is obeyed and a multinational
grows since these effects are a consequence of the actions of multitudes. You
are thus faced with multitudes that wonder how to act as one.[48]

Nothing is central here. No established categories ("power") with their
"stored-up energy"; no explanatory privilege. Nothing *has* power; rather,
power exists instead as the *possibility* "of enrolling many actors in a given
political and social scheme." Latour does not know what society is, and more
tellingly, he believes that should he try to answer that question, the only possible effect will be "holding society together and enrolling enough people
to constitute power."[49] If we refuse to do so, and bracket or (or abolish) the
hyper-priors that are capable of doing so, we perforce change our frame of
reference. In Latour's case, such a shift leaves him "to wonder" at the basic
mystery of it all—more specifically, the mystery of why sociology, under the
guise of being modern, would prefer the big reservoir of energy required for
central concepts and ignore the mere "actual" face of the world. On these
grounds, Latour argues that we should collectively reorient sociology from
the study of society to *the study of associations*.

Thus, the first rule in having a clean slate is that a sociologist should study
all associations as having equal potential. To read Latour recount his realization of this rule is to read a man amid revelation (or on the brink of nervous
breakdown).[50] All else will follow from it. By focusing on "all the forces that
have been mobilized in our human world to explain why it is that we are
linked together and that some orders are faithfully obeyed while others are
not," we must admit that the "forces are heterogeneous in character: they may
include atoms, words, lianas, or tattoos."[51] We will find no mention of these
kinds of things anywhere in central problems theory; it makes a very different
commitment than treating all associations as of equal potential, as it gives
preference to some over others. For a sociology swept clean, however, there
are no central problems, nor any depth, whether ontological or interpretive.
A sociologist is successful by how well they describe what is very likely a heterogeneous assemblage of parts, including both humans and nonhumans,
that probably zigzags everywhere, and while it comes in a cohesive form, that
form is not conducive to a concept like structure or culture that can be cleanly
delineated by the work of a theorist prior to the start of research.

There is good reason for the mainstream appeal of Latour's clean slate.
From its controversial beginnings—which left it relegated (in some cases,

physically and institutionally) to science studies separate from sociology—these ideas have become mainstream. We could point to many examples of research in sociology that either directly or indirectly derives from Latour's clean slate, even if Latour himself is never mentioned in the research. This is not to sing his praises, per se, nor even to really credit him with saying anything original; it is only to convey that Latour asks his basic questions at just the right time. We can also see this in the appeal of Latour beyond the social sciences where he initially made his home base. "Post-critique" in literary studies and object-oriented ontology in philosophy have found Latour appealing for similar reasons as sociologists have—to get away, say, from suspicious readings of a text or from undermining (or overmining) the ontology of objects.[52]

From the Study of Associations to the Study of Chances

Latour plays a large role in one of the first key works of social theory published after the central problems era.[53] Isaac Reed channels Latour into a new conception of social formation based on power and hierarchy, but without a reliance on concepts of power, structure, or agency familiar from the past half-century. Reed asks basic questions too, like: How can we be certain that *we* are the "authors of our action"? For Reed, associations are turned into lengthy rector-actor chains that can together comprise a social formation as spatially large as an empire. Reed acknowledges the significance of Latour but adds an important critique.

While Latour points out that the "spread in time and space of anything—claims, orders, artifacts, goods—is in the hands of people," the study of associations has no way of giving those people a world of their own. It can only observe them as they "act in many different ways, letting the token drop, or modifying it, or deflecting it, or betraying it, or adding to it, or appropriating it."[54] Any of these actions will appear arbitrary for the sociologist who takes Latour's lead, because we can find nothing interior to those who do them, only what is exterior. We therefore cannot explain an orientation to the set of associations (what Latour sometimes would occasionally call an "actor-network") other than treating it as our (the analyst's) own limit concept—what we *could* know if we knew everything, which we do not.

For Reed, the weakness of Latour's basic framework lies here. The associations we are in do not have to be restricted to humans. Latour is right: They can, and typically do, include nonhumans. Moreover, those associations can be strung out in long connections, far surpassing the small alliances that Latour seemed to favor, and they can also have an internal heterogeneity—

mimicking what a more structure-based thinking would call "positions" or "roles," and which Reed condenses into actor and rector. Latour is also right that to be situated in associations is to be affected by them, principally in terms of agency, which is here more a function of accumulation than position and is not a term introduced to solve a central problem. As Reed puts it, "to accrue agency is to accrue, through *agents*, a distinct increase in the probability of achieving one's projects . . . The reification of action-reaction flows and the habits that accompany them into networks solid enough to be traced as hierarchical in both position and interpretation is a notification to us that we are dealing with power as a peculiarly important subset of the guide rails for actions and reactions in the world. But this solidity—what sociologists debate as 'power structure'—is itself subject to certain rhymes and rhythms and allows for the possibility of redescription by performance. This is because the navigation of the world requires its signification, which introduces contingencies of interpretation."[55]

Reed's formulation demonstrates the appeal of a basic questions approach, as it dissects a composite formation (like an empire) into associations as opposed to rendering them into the fixed form of a structure, which in turn will introduce a central problem. For Reed, on the contrary, we act "for a project," within these associations, "and even interpret the individuals and groups of humans who serve as our rectors as themselves allies in, and thus the 'means to,' the accomplishment of a project we value highly and of which we believe we have the best interpretation."[56] Thus, chains of association are not static; each moving piece constitutes a moving body. This approach is not a limit concept, and relatedly, it does not allow us to assume that *every* action we take is a *social* action—or, for that matter, that we are always in associations (and thus, in a sense, always *in* society). As Reed uses it, the word "project" applies to what is both collective and individual without inconsistency within associations. How does a project reconcile these seeming opposites? By accounting for the *interpretation* of the associations that give them a tenuous permanence, exhibited by the agency of all those who are now the "authors" of the collective body (though, importantly, not their *own* authors).

The conceptual move here is an important one in the wake of central problems, because it can allow sociologists to account for large-scale social formations without needing a concept of structure. For Reed, the chain of associations is, in fact, a "chain of representations," which are as real as our interpretations make them, and those interpretations are far more contingent than Latour, who pays very little attention to what it means to be situated *in* associations, will allow. For our purposes, however, something more needs to be said about interpretation serving as the glue for a kind of "transcendental social"[57] that receives its heartbeat from the meanings we give it; how it carries its own basic questions, most of which pertain directly to probability.

When Reed defines "interpretation" as playing this kind of significant role, the notion quickly assumes a probabilistic cast: "We can see discursive power in the naturalization, via various processes of typification and invention, of a set of interpretive tendencies concerning who is a *likely* rector, *likely* actor, or *likely* other given a problem situation, an established process, or a series of linked interactions. Here we find sense and reference, the comprehension of the world as significant by the human subjects who engage each other and form meaningful hierarchies that are both created and justified via signification."[58]

Here, Reed draws from an earlier engagement by Jeffrey Alexander with interpretation on similar grounds. Alexander associates interpretation with having the unique potential to typify the world and give us "expectation." To become a member of a "collectivity" is to experience a reduction in "surprise."[59] For us, the connotations here are important. When interpretation is brought into associations to bring them to life—when interpretation is given a basic social significance as opposed to one that might be more strictly hermeneutic—probability is not far off. Perhaps, then, the basic unit of analysis is not associations; perhaps it is something more like *objective probability*.

If so, then the consequences are significant. Namely, probability cannot be safely left to the statisticians if theorists want to devise some new set of concepts for sociology following the demise of central problems. Such an approach also suggests a different purpose for theory. As we can tell, Reed's revision of Latour draws on interpretivism, for obvious reasons. Reed has arguably done the most to formulate interpretivism, and we can see here a clear role that theory, in the pluralistic interpretivist sense, can play in figuring out the interpretations that are of material importance to associations. But what would it mean to say that associations themselves simply demonstrate the active existence of probability? Or, more cleanly stated: To the extent that associations make for a collective object (an actor-network, a "chain of power"), that collective object comprises a *probability order* (a pocket of predictability) in which the order we see (of rector and actor, of "actants," of positions) consists of patches of connected initial states with outcomes that can be stabilized by interpretation but not always and, more importantly, not *only*. Our purpose in the rest of this chapter is to sketch a framework for engaging with probability in this form, as the study of *Chance* or objective chances or Chance, as the theme is differently interpreted from Weber to Bourdieu to Du Bois, and to suggest a role for social theory in knowing it.

Investigating Probability Orders via Distributions

What is a probability order? Simply defined, it is an order that holds together because of probability—because of patches of maximally connected initial states that partially overlap with a range of outcomes, extending further and further until the order evaporates. To understand probability order requires not only something that can generate and create probability, it also requires a means of orienting to probability. Consider, then, a basic example of what we would consider to be a probability order. Philosopher Alan Garfinkel gives us a scenario in which a professor grades their class on a curve: "Suppose that, in a class I am teaching, I announce that the course will be 'graded on a curve,' that is, that I have decided beforehand what the overall distribution of grades is going to be. Let us say, for the sake of the example, that I decide that there will be one A, 24 B's, and 25 C's. The finals come in, and let us say Mary gets the A. She wrote an original and thoughtful final."[60]

In this case, we can find a distribution of grades (one A, 24 B's, 25 C's, and corresponding percentages) and a rough designation of how a given student will be situated in it. The order, here, is a closed range of possibility. There is no other grade, nor is a different distribution possible. As Garfinkel notes, the distribution begs a question about who gets the A and why. Here the explanation is that Mary, the student who received the single possible A, "wrote an original and thoughtful final."

The probabilities here are an objective feature of the world, and if we want to give them an epistemic formulation, we easily can simply by taking the ratio of possible grades versus total number of students. But that is the least important aspect of this order. Probabilistically, the relevant features of an order, then, are the available positions before the papers are ever graded that indicate the *range of possibility*. Combined with this range is the nature of the *test* that will have an effect shaping what matters in filling out the distribution that we will ultimately see as an *outcome*. Within this order, certain actions are made relevant for how they connect to that outcome, others are disregarded or prevented from mattering, and the actors in question can know those actions to be important in this way. Within the order, then, a clear sense of *adequate cause* arises. At least in principle, it does not matter who Mary is—that Mary is a "Mary," or was born to a certain family, or is Black, or that she is a "she." What matter is, on the terms of the test, Mary did the relevant action that situates her in the distribution, in this case at the top of it. The rest of Mary's traits, should they have any bearing on the outcome, are "inessential perturbations" or accidents.[61]

Garfinkel's example has several limitations. The first is the most obvious: This probability order is completely by design. In other words, its distribution and range of possibility are decided in advance, as is the adequate cause that will be applicable—what will make action non-accidental. A different probability order that is not made by design does not have these features decided in advance. The distribution and the range of possibility are not decided in advance, but rather are themselves outcomes of the action that unfolds. That action has an adequate cause that can symbolically be determined, but that cause is also not decided in advance; it is, rather, a form of power. The positions that appear in such a field become apparent only in being somehow irreducible to the others. This state of affairs might suggest an incredibly fluid order, which would be very difficult to call an order; but such fluidity is not always the case. As Weber understood well, the best way to create probability is to create rules or laws.[62] Garfinkel's case seems to vouch for this claim. But in a non-designed probability order, too, rules and laws can appear that make the range of possibility, distribution, and adequate cause more established by doing what rules and laws always do: solidify shared expectation.

The question that arises here—and in Reed's revision of Latour's focus on associations—is: What role do nonhumans (technologies, materiality, climate) play? The fact that Latour's basic questions give such attention to nonhumans is a considerable part of his approach's appeal. For Reed, interpretation allows for the association between humans and nonhumans, but not directly. Whatever effect they have is persistently mediated by their meaning, which is a contingent product. For the probabilist, interpretation can mediate how nonhumans affect a probability order, but something more fundamental is at stake; what "nonhuman" signifies is a distinct form of *test*, which becomes very noticeable when we become primarily subject to it.

Off the Port, Out to Sea

Consider philosopher Michel Serres's vivid portrait:

> At the slightest mistake you will fall . . . Minor causes, great effects. In one's bedchamber, everything is forgiving, the bed and the pillow, the armchair and the rug, supple and soft. A thousand causes with nonexistent effects. Walls, cities, and ports, havens from which death keeps its distance. Beyond, death roves through space, prowling. Never sated, it nests in low, black caverns; everywhere it lies in wait and yawns. Once you cast off, everything you do can be held against you . . . Here the causal space of cases is open, with no apologies or forgiveness. Every act counts, every word and even intention, down to the slightest detail . . . Reality clings to it: no sooner is an act begun than it is subject to sanction. You no longer have the right to fall. You begin to live in another way.[63]

Serres describes here a somewhat subtle, somewhat morbid distinction between two very different spaces in the world. For ease of reference let us call
them "the port" and "the sea." His point seems to be that, while there is something personal about the classification (one person's port is another person's
sea),[64] there is also something absolute about the distinction, an objective
dividing line—*we* change when we move between them, as we do when we
put on our coat before walking out the door.

When we remain in "the port," we can be sure of what to expect. The order
of things is forgiving of our mistakes, not least because this little-engineered
world largely anticipates those mistakes.[65] We can even say that certain outcomes "don't count" and demand a "redo." Events never seen before may exhibit an admirable competence or achievement rather than being a complete
shock; regardless of what happens, we can believe why it happened. In practical terms, to be on a port means knowing what you need to know in order
not to make the mistake—such things are discernible. What is and is not an
action, and therefore what is adequate versus accidental, can be understood
and anticipated, as can futures and consequences.[66] We can invest so fully in
the port because it is capable of provoking in us a sense of clarity. While we
can still be surprised, how we are tested in these places leaves us with a certain
doxic blindness as we grow accustomed; after all, what else does falling asleep
require but faith in the future?

"At sea," things are different. What we are tested by has not been prepared by our proxies or representations; the reality that clings to them affects us differently. We can "perk up" at the challenge or be awakened from a
slumber—we can "feel alive" in this relative sense as a result of the constant
surprise, the unpredictability, and the sense that every action carries stakes
we cannot be entirely sure of. Nothing, then, appears arbitrary. At sea, our
physiology is always tested; the port tries to keep those tests at bay through
climate control. It is up to us whether we want to appreciate tests of this kind
as ones of honor, strength, or status among peers; our interpretation of them
does not matter to the tests themselves, though it can motivate and inspire
us in dealing with them. What we encounter teems with chance mechanisms
that will always, to some degree, come across as accidental. When we press
the limits of tests that provide the safety of "the port," moving outside its
repetition and predictability, our subjectivity will again become prominent.
Even as we adapt, we know that one false step could mean disaster. In Serres's
words, "the sea" makes us "very supple, very intelligent; [it] keeps [us] awake.
Diligence against negligence."[67] Put differently, we notice *more* when our experience is not something we could have ever expected.

The contrast that Serres draws here is significant for what we recommend in the next chapter as an engagement point between social theory and cog-nitive science.[68] But consider first that, as opposed to reasserting a kind of nature-versus-culture distinction, to phrase both as different kinds of test cre-ates a kind of symmetry between them: They are *sources of objective probabil-ity* or *Chance* that command our orientation, though in very different ways. It is possible to know the tests at sea, and the very presence of a port, or a mode of production, is contingent on that knowledge. But something will constantly elude us about "the sea" as it stands in relation to us—not as a cha-otic mess to which we alone can bring order, but obeying a probability order all its own, effectively indifferent to our presence.

A test always involves, on one level, what Peirce calls "potential." It con-sists of what is *"indeterminate yet capable of determination in any special case."*[69] Thus, a test opens a potential or a space of indetermination; that space is one of equal chance and a range of possibility. The potential is then resolved into a certain determination, or an outcome that manifests the range as a dis-tribution. In between the indetermination and the determined outcome is what we can call action. "At sea," the range of possibility reveals probability orders that are not our own; they can therefore prove to be a constant source of indetermination as, in Peirce's words, their "determinations" surprise us. Thus, a simple walk outside can change our state of mind. On "the port," by contrast, a controlled test creates a "proxy" whenever specific conditions are replicated. What is indeterminate yet capable of being determined can be es-tablished in advance; if this means standing on an actual port and not falling through the wooden planks into the sea, the effect is to reduce our subjectiv-ity as we come to expect what anyone else can. Latour offers a critical insight here: We must have been *through* tests and then out of them to be anything at all; only through tests can we even know who (or what) is capable of action—including ourselves.[70] For our purposes, the dynamic involved here casts our attention more squarely onto tests and testing as of potentially enormous consequence for what theory can be in the present post-positivist era.

Toward a Theory of the Test

Even "the stablest thing" is an event, according to John Dewey, because it is "not free from conditions set to it by other things." Thus, "every idea and human act [is] an experiment in fact, even though not in design."[71] Jumping off the port and into the sea would seem to prove as much, in a perhaps ex-treme way. We are tested so differently by the two; the sea is a world apart. We ourselves change when we venture into it just in order to maintain *be-ing* ourselves. For his part, Dewey echoes Peirce's point, mentioned above, about tests and potential. He believes we can consider the notion of a "test" as generalizable in principle, so much so that every moment we exist as a semi-coherent entity can be framed as an outcome of a test—that is, what exists is the realization of a potential after it has been made indeterminate (by something). Our idea is that, in ontological terms and referencing here the general nature of interpretation and meaning-making, what is really at stake is a test—how well can our interpretations typify what we interpret so that we have no "no surprises"? How successfully can we *guess* the world by making it meaningful to us? In all cases, the task of anything organically coherent, or anything attempting to be coherent in that way, is to maintain itself against chance mechanisms (fully at work in "the sea"). As it does so, it (whatever it is) maintains itself in the state of being that can withstand tests. For Dewey, such a state of being refers to us humans just as much as it does a blade of grass or a nation-state. We agree with him, but the implications of test and testing get more interesting when we consider them in connection with a concept that comes from the Kriesian wing of objective probability, like *Chance*.

Heterodox probability theorist George Spencer-Brown offers a useful idea here in what he calls the "chance-machine." For Spencer-Brown, a chance-machine is what we are trying to prove the *absence* of whenever we believe we have found probability in the world; as he puts it, "a chance-machine is allowed by the properties we ascribe to it to give results which fall only within a certain range. If they fall outside this range, we at once cease to call it a chance-machine."[72] The logic here is a kind of retrospective one not unlike the probabilistic logic defended by Dewey. We find probability, or so we believe, and so we keep testing it until we have an expectation. A chance-machine will allow for *no* expectation, however, and thus it stands as a null hypothesis. How exportable are these principles? For Dewey, they are very basic, as the tendency of human and nonhuman alike is fall into habit by sooner or later arriving at probability. To conclude the chapter, we will sketch an outline for a theory of tests or testing on these grounds and argue that integral to the study of *Chance* in a social science *after* post-positivism is the concept of probability order.

An attempt at a theory of the test can be found in sociologists Luc Boltanski, Laurent Thevenot, and Eve Chiapello's prior work on worlds and on the "spirit of capitalism."[73] The approach here is influenced by Latour's basic questions; distinguishable worlds of worth (fame, industrial, domestic) and spirits of capitalism are contingent on tests, which give worth to different objects, and on different objects in association with people. Within a world or spirit, everything seems different and distinct: Different action is consequential, different traits are exhibited by who and what carries the most worth, and indeed different things exist that exist in no other world. In their collaborative work, Boltanski and Thevenot offer details about the nature of tests that are capable of "sublimation," or creating a desire among those not favored by the test for its unequal outcome.[74] In this case, the goal of the tests that Boltanski and Thevenot mention and of the worlds they describe is to disprove that an order of worth is really a chance-machine—in other words, to prove that a person or a thing is in a "worthy" state for the right reasons, thus generating *agreement*. For Boltanski and Thevenot, the right reasons include a fairly precise set of criteria: Worth must signal of (1) some element of sacrifice, (2) a benefit to the least worthy, (3) demonstrations that follow the right recipe (i.e., meet expectations) within the world in question, and finally (4) a "higher common principle" that provides symbolic formulation and running narrative of what the entire ordeal is about and is particularly useful for containing disputes when they arise.[75] For Boltanski and Thevenot, orders of worth must have these characteristics; for them, the mechanics here that group "diverse beings" into association with each other are most fundamentally a *model for justice*.

For our purposes, what Boltanski, Thevenot, and Chiapello describe is essential. It offers a purpose to social theory not distant from what is conventionally described as "practice." But it also falters in drawing a connection between tests and "agreement." Tests do not generate agreement primarily; what they generate is *Chance* that in turn creates expectation. Only because expectations are shared is agreement possible.

What Boltanski, Thevenot, and Chiapello document is a basic protocol for conjuring *Chance* of out thin air, just by setting up a test. We loop into that *Chance* by having a sense of justice. Thus, tests, like the randomized trials of modern statistical frequentism, have the equivalent ontological effect of holding together worlds of "diverse beings," establishing them in an order that a chance-machine never could. Much of the documentation that Boltanski and Thevenot provide in their collaborative work can be read as descriptions of typical expectations (about celebrities, say, or the wealthy, even good parents). But where do those expectations come from? In our terms, any expectation that sticks around long enough and is shared broadly enough is an orientation to *Chance*. For Boltanski and Thevenot, the equivalent would be knowing how to distinguish between who is real and who is a poseur, in addition to knowing that others know and will probably agree. Their proposal is significant, but for reasons they do not fully reconcile. For us, tests do one thing above all: They tame the "chance" of chance-machines and generate pockets of *Chance*—probability order—and their range of extension in the world.

Boltanski and Thevenot observe that the results of a single sports game could easily create its own "polity" and shape the distribution of objective probabilities in politics and economics, if not for certain safeguards that stop them.[76] That sports create *Chance* seems undoubted. What else could be the source of their appeal but a recipe for equal chance, a range possibility, and a clear outcome? The potential for the transposability of sports would seem to arise because of the apparent clarity of the sports test and the enviable way it "purges ambiguity" from *Chance*. Sports can make a talent or skill readily apparent, thus allowing for predictability and preparation among players, even a sense of fate in greatness or futures that were never meant to be. The strict policing of rules and violations indicates a preoccupation with adequate cause, which makes possible (perhaps remarkably so) the sublimation of desire in losing players and fans. That effect is not because the winning and losing side can agree on the result necessarily, as Boltanski and Thevenot contend, but because the losing side could have *expected* to lose as they did, having been given a fair shot—though those same expectations could send them into a furor on the perception of cheating or bias.[77] In all these ways, we can treat sports as a prime venue for *Chance*, demonstrating the apparent ease with which it can find its way into creation and the consequence it can have when it does. The popular appeal of sports—in some sense broadly cross-cultural[78]—seems an additional reason why the subtleties of *Chance* can be most easily understood here, in this domain, serving as the root for its analogues elsewhere. We can briefly mention other test situations that generate and apply *Chance* for different purposes, some none too subtle, ranging from justice to truth to faith.

Michel Foucault describes tests as being of integral importance to the administration of justice. Foucault traces a genealogical shift in the late medieval period in Europe, not toward testing—it was already present—but from one format of testing to another: from "ordeals" to "inquiries."[79] As modes of justice, the two differ significantly: from walking across hot coals to prove one's innocence to pleading before a tribunal. What remains the same between them is a recipe for generating *Chance*: (1) the creation of uncertainty about a crime, (2) the equal chance of innocence, and (3) the resolution of the chance of innocence into probability (or the certainty of God's divination) through means that relate to us objectively—what we could have expected after the fact, now that we know the outcome. Observers of science, from Steven Shapin and Simon Schaffer to Karl Popper, remark upon the changes to knowledge that occur with the arrival of scientific experimentation. In Popper's words, a "test" is all that can resolve the "probability" of a theory. It works by giving theory an equal chance of truth or falsity. *Chance* is activated as scientists try "to assess what tests . . . [the theory] has withstood."[80] In Shapin and Schaffer's famous history, the experimental test of Robert Boyle's air-pump in seventeenth-century England, appearing amid the English Civil War, could produce a seemingly miraculous outcome on command, drawing into question the metaphysical order of the world.[81] Thomas Hobbes feared it not as a revelation of the natural world but as a disruptor of political cohesion; the test brought into being a *Chance* that might very well displace Leviathan. Thus, Hobbes challenged Boyle's experimental principles as marking not a window onto the mysteries of nature but a power grab by a specialized guild wielding a test for its own purposes.

In each of these cases, and among them we can also place Latour's own work on Louis Pasteur and "the pasteurization of France," a test is generative of *Chance* as an objective probability order, which can be the source of expectation.[82] Even in a less designed or formalized sense, we can still observe tests creating *Chance*. Religious tests, for instance, can be initiated without the apparatus seemingly required for a test in science or law. When, in the Judaic tradition, God "tests the faith" of Abraham by ordering him to sacrifice his child Isaac, a range of possibility is opened, and Abraham's sacral state is suspended in equal chance. Depending on the result, something about him will become definitive—most of all what he can expect of his own divine fate. Abraham does not end up sacrificing his child in the story, but he was prepared to do so. The *Chance* to make the ultimate sacrifice, which could have arisen in no other way, "proves" his faith.[83]

Examples like these carry a distinct sociological importance, because what is social about them is not limited to whatever associations might teach us, let alone to central problems. *Chance* is an objectively existing probability order, and it appears here as a new object of sociological analysis. Because of its capacity to generate *Chance*, a test makes it possible to change associations in an instant. A test can still do this even if it generates *Chance* only within a limited range. Some tests, however, particularly those entangled with physiological tests that Dewey and Serres indicate, can—like the tests of a mode of production—extend far and wide in relative uniformity.[84] It is as probability orders that collective objects exist in such a real but unknowable state—that we can identify through their range of possibility (*Spielraum*, continuum), the particular things (people, objects, machines, even a religious deity) they gather together in association, with the *Chance* so constituted that we and others loop into it as expectation. *Chance* can also be interpreted from all the things gathered in the order: from belief and desire in human actors, to affordances in machines and objects, to divination and sacredness, even the presence of something as apparently transcendent as justice.

The settled nature of *Chance* can make it seem as if the order is given. But here probabilism subscribes to the so-called *myth* of the given, as no probability order is entirely closed. It can always itself be presented with a test, a moment of equal chance and uncertainty that suspends the present order of things, which at least makes it possible to find a different order or even none at all.[85] Associations between entities ("actants" in Latour's language) in a probability order carry a constant potential of uncertainty for every other entity in the order; the nature of that association can be highly dynamic and fluid. We could not see these orders if we relied on frequency counts. Probability can apply to associations or relations of dependence, exploitation, and oppression commonly associated with a social structure or "structured social system." Rather than a central problems term, structure here becomes a potential way of modeling a probability order that demonstrates certain very stable characteristics. But for a structure to be a probability order requires that certain *Chances* always be taken in lieu of others. A probability order can appear open—comprised of equal chances—but, in the contrast of the equal to the unequal, it is mediated by *Chance*, and such a view of equal order is negated by a distribution of probability. That contrast can tell us that to act unexpectedly is indeed a gamble, though the appraisal itself is not subjective; it is relative to the predispositions of actors who understand those probabilities from their own, ontologically very real, lives. Still, it is *Chance* we are speaking of—from the structural model to the lived experience—and we can understand it best when we get a sense of how the range of possibility is severely truncated, allowing probability to become visible only as a "structural effect" for which the term "constraint" naturally comes to mind.

For probabilism, a kind of duality applies to a probability order, combining the content of that order (what it orders) and objective probability (how it is ordered). There can be a one-to-one relation between these two sides when what it orders cannot conceivably be ordered in any other way. With such a close connection between the two, the order can seem closed and settled—the very opposite of being merely probable, and predictions can be easily made. It is also possible to draw "the what" and "the how" of a probability order apart in questions like, "Should this (X) be ordered in this (Y) way?" or argumentative claims like, "It is not right that (X) is ordered in (Y) way." Questions like these test a probability order, but with limited capacity to more fully pry open its range, we can assume that, if not paired with some other grounds for the *Chance* of its dissolution, they might prove merely academic.[86] Because there is the tendency for expectations to match *Chances*, action—as we will examine in the next chapter—can become caught in the loop, or what in a pragmatist sense is the tendency to fall into habit. In a probabilist sense, habit is like Hume's "opinion" that serves as inspiration for our view of expectation; likewise, habit is active and anticipatory as opposed to reactive and problem oriented. The effect of probability order on habit-formation can reinforce the loop and make it seem like there is *no* moment of equal chance, no range of possibility, and perhaps only a single *Chance* for our orientation. Theory can always separate probability from what it orders, if only in principle, by identifying new possibilities and *Chances* for resistance, which is here conceived as breaking habit and expectation while remaining situated in the present rather than in denial of probability order altogether.[87]

Such a framework, we believe, sketches a way to reorient social theory in its post-positivist moment, centering it around objective probability. We will conclude by drawing these several threads together. The most crucial step to take at present is to resist the positivist holdover, which remains largely unchanged, that interprets probability as frequency. We will more fully examine the difference that objective probability makes for social science in chapters 7 and 8. For now, we can say that probabilism gives social theory new tasks: (1) translating observations, including those gathered using frequentist statistical techniques as in a regression equation, into probability order (range of possibility, equal chance, test); (2) envisioning how a range of possibility, with varied distributions of probabilities, is created and maintained and does not devolve into a chance-machine; (3) drawing out those possibilities and new potential *Chances* by proposing and designing new tests; (4) revealing the aspects of a test that promote a certain result or disposition; and (5) constructing models of collective objects or systems as probability orders observable both in aggregates and single cases.

In each of these tasks, theory is less a description and more a redescription, less an interpretation and more an *objectivation*. Social theory is not substantive; it does not give us content (e.g., a "theory of"). Its main job is to help us reason through our explanations to reveal the effects of objective probability. In this regard, theory is most distinguishable when it is the *least* ontological; and it is the least ontological the further removed it becomes from action. The ultimate translation that theory, of all kinds, can perform on ontology is to shift events onto the plane of probability order and its formations of *Chance*. Such formations are real but unknowable in their entirety, and to take them as our principal object will take us beyond the available post-positivist fare in realism and interpretivism by demanding changes to both data and theory. Data science is one front in these changes. To signal the possible presence of objective probability is the chief virtue of the explorations of the data scientist; yet data alone cannot reveal a loop or a range of possibility—all are necessary elements of a patchwork world. As we will expand upon below, such a rubric gives theory a role to play, aligning sociology with data science without simply allowing it to be absorbed by data-centric methods. Probabilism of this kind also does not require that social theorists ascribe implausible cognitive mechanisms to those who do the action; rather, social theorists can make sociologically satisfying contributions and remain naturalistic. We demonstrate how in the next chapter. First, a brief return to Giddens.

At the end of his *Central Problems in Social Theory*, Giddens offers some context and a few prescriptions. In the "current phase of social theory," he writes, "we are involved in two axes simultaneously: that of our understanding the character of human social activity, and that of the logical form of natural science."[88] Giddens stresses that "these are not entirely separate endeavors." He remarks upon the centrality of hermeneutic questions for social science. Social science that avoids causality, however, is of necessarily limited appeal. Giddens does not believe we can treat natural and social science as "independently constituted forms of intellectual endeavor." We would agree on all fronts with Giddens. The difference is that the logical form of natural science is not positivist, and neither is it post-positivist. Some might go so far as to call it data-centric—if not now, then soon. For us, the links between human social activity and the logic of natural science, between natural and social science more generally, can be found in something that Giddens does not mention: the meaning of probability.

Both axes that Giddens mentions in 1979—human social activity and the logical form of natural science—remain live issues. Data scientists dare not touch them. Social theorists can and should. To do so, however, and not find ourselves at the horns of central problems, we must acknowledge probabilism as grounds for unification, allowing both axes to converge rather than veer off to infinity. In fact, the principles for studying objective probability are already largely available to us in natural science. We can find them in the cognitive-science paradigm known as *predictive processing*.

6

Probability in Cognition

Dynamically speaking, the whole embodied, active system self-organizes around the organismically-computable quantity: "prediction error." This is what delivers that multi-level, multi-area grip on the evolving sensory barrage—a grip that must span multiple spatial and temporal scales . . . That grip, in the somewhat special case of the human mind, is further enriched and transformed by layer upon layer of sociocultural structures and practices. Steeped in such practices, our predictive brains are empowered to deploy their basic skills in new and transformative ways. Understanding the resulting interplay between culture, technology, action and cascading neural prediction is surely one of the major tasks confronting twenty-first century cognitive science.

ANDY CLARK, *Surfing Uncertainty*

When people talk about the possibility of foreknowledge of the future, they always forget the fact of the prediction of one's own voluntary movements.

LUDWIG WITTGENSTEIN, *Philosophical Investigations*

Proposals for sociology to forge a relationship with cognitive science are long-standing by this point.[1] If the terminological, analytic, and conceptual shift required leads some to resist the prospect of a "cognitive social science," an overlapping and shared probabilism provides a preestablished link between these two communities of inquiry that might make a relationship more palatable. In this chapter, we show a surprising point of commonality, on these terms, between probabilistic sociology and cognitive science in their mutual concern with action, looping effects, social construction, and probability. Capitalizing on this fortuitous link requires that we move beyond the frequentist understanding of probability in sociology by incorporating the heterodox tradition of probabilism we have documented in the previous chapters. Such an approach will require drawing probability and action into direct contact, just as predictive processing in contemporary cognitive science does.

Much is at stake. Since its inception, predictive processing has forced cognitive scientists to account for the outside-the-brain implications of socio-cultural practices in nontrivial ways.[2] Yet, sociology appears to fly under their radar; the cognitive scientists act on their own as they recognize the need to account for social construction in order to explain what the neurons are doing. For our sake, what they call for in blending such distantly related elements is a probability order of the kind fleshed out in the last chapter. It can therefore provide a tool to break the barriers that stand between cognitive science and sociology by fleshing out a link between probability, action, and cognition.

Continuism and the Predictive Brain

Predictive processing (hereafter, PP) marks a paradigm shift in cognitive science seeking to provide a unified theory of perception, cognition, and action. Our review in this chapter is necessarily schematic and incomplete, as PP is now composed of a sprawling literature ranging across several disciplines.[3] We also remain agnostic as to whether PP is a "grand unified theory" of cognition capable of synthesizing the entire field.[4] Instead, our purpose here is twofold: First, we aim to whet the sociological appetite with what we see as a promising approach to accounting for the roots of such high-level phenomena as motivation, enculturation, and action.[5] Second, we aim to show that PP, as it currently exists, presents a prima facie case that the approach to probability found in Weber, Du Bois, and Bourdieu in sociology is one currently being realized across multiple research programs in the biological, cognitive, psychological, and neurosciences.

As a theoretical framework, PP proposes unifying, or *continuist*, principles designed to describe brain structure and organismic action at multiple levels, in a way that appeals to the great challenge set forth by Spinoza. Of most importance for our purposes is the fact that PP uses similar principles to describe the operation of *subpersonal* mechanisms involved at the level of the neuron *and* descriptions couched in *personal* terms, like the language of expectation, anticipation, and orientation.[6] The basic principles of PP are applicable to phenomena at multiple levels. PP is one of the few paradigms across human science writ large to deal with the interface problem between personal and subpersonal explanations within an overall naturalistic framework.

PP focuses primarily on the relationship between actors and structures of predictive orderliness—that is, probability orders—and presents a resolutely continuist position across levels, using the same explanatory principles to account for neurons as for social institutions.[7] Drawing a theory of action in particular from PP can provide sociologists with conceptual tools capable of avoiding the bracketing usual in the severing of probability from interpretation. This move would further help reposition sociology with respect to the data-centric claim that "prediction matters" as a statement now funded by the experiential fact that *actors* themselves predict the existing probabilities that make up their action environments.[8] On this note, a larger point becomes visible to us should we peer into at least one of the recognized origins of PP.

Helmholtz Discovers Prediction

For German physiologist and physicist Hermann von Helmholtz, physiology could use studies of the tissues of the body to answer questions across the divide of natural (*Naturwissenschaften*) and human sciences (*Geisteswissenschaften*). Helmholtz did not envision a similar separation as necessary to preserve the cultural or "the human."[9] Even aesthetic responses to art and music were conducive to the "fully physiological human," as the core engagement with the aesthetic remained "perception itself or, even more fundamentally, *sensation*," which could only be "discovered and manufactured, altered and prolonged, regimented and liberated (all of these) in the context of a broad experimentalization of hearing."[10] Such an orientation is reflected in the unified approach of PP, which allows for inferences about neurons as much as addiction, cellular mitosis as much as linguistic meaning, and neural nets as much as narrative symbolism.

Helmholtz, for his part, differentiated his approach to optics from both "projection theory," which finds perceptual objects as the product of "psychic processes" projected into space, and "intuition theory," which assumed "that certain perceptual images . . . would be produced directly by an innate mechanism."[11] Helmholtz, by contrast, shows that "we are not simply passive to the impressions that are urged on us, but we *observe*, that is, we adjust our organs in those conditions that enable them to distinguish the impressions more adequately."[12] Helmholtz's concern is the nature of that adjustment. For instance, if we perceive an object (a bicycle) we are familiar with from a radically different angle—for instance: upside down, looking between our legs—this physiological act of generation will be *chased* by recognition. We will be unsure what the object is, and so we guess; but our guessing will be more like chasing as we attempt to catch up with the flow of sensory information. In this case, it takes a fraction of the time for recognition to happen, and when it does happen, the equivalent of "adjusting our organs" will *have* happened.

In such cases, there might be "more scope for interpretation," but even here, we continue generating sense information until we are "obliged to assign [the object] to some definite place in space."[13] Should we *believe* we recognize something familiar (a bird) but be unable to quite feel confidence, our sense information will chase the hypothetical, proving the initial recognition wrong perhaps (that "bird" is really a rock).[14] Physiologically understood, objects involve generation and recognition as a two-part product. The "mental process active in sense-perceptions" is top-down and synthesizes percepts by dictating how we "adjust our organs" to them.[15] Thus, the sensible emerges sui generis from these physiological adjustments and their "unconscious conclusions or inferences," which implies a "normal state" and training—how something should be sensed, right-side up rather than upside down—analogous to the role of expectation in the finite, "fully physiological human."[16]

While Helmholtz's influence within various strains of psychology is vast, it was not until recently that the core dynamic of his physiological and perceptual approach—that is, recognition chasing generation—has been formalized experimentally and conceptually. In one of the seminal publications of contemporary PP, however, Helmholtz's points are given their due. Karl Friston and Klass Stephen argue that "if one formulates Helmholtz's ideas about perception in terms of modern-day theories one arrives at a model of perceptual inference and learning that can explain a remarkable range of neurobiological facts."[17] In particular, "inference," as Helmholtz understands it, is combined with his later notion of "free energy" to yield the basic PP framework. In a technical sense, free energy is both non-kinetic and nonmechanical energy independent of heat or entropy but still threatens the potential dissolution of a complex system. It only has an *intensive* rather than a quantitative meaning. In probabilistic language, free energy is "the difference between the probability distribution of environmental quantities that act on [a] system and an arbitrary distribution encoded by its configuration."[18] The two distributions maintain a constant dynamic between generation (sense input) and recognition (predictive coding). Here we can observe a naturalistic portrayal of objective probability (*Chance*) as it turns into an embodied probabilistic configuration (expectation).

The Unbearable Lightness of Predicting

The core insights of contemporary PP thus build on Helmholtz's foundation but push the two-part chasing or looping dynamic at its heart toward probabilism, introducing this theory as a missing ingredient to Helmholtz's compatible approach. The brain, its subpersonal components (neurons, neural networks, cortical and subcortical layers), the whole person, and—perhaps—people in concert, are in one primary business, and that business is *prediction*. More specifically, across all levels of biological organization, prediction is the very "purpose" of the brain; or, more accurately, brain structures have been evolutionarily selected to engage in prediction to facilitate organismic survival and genetic reproduction via the control of action.[19] In its essence, prediction is a best guess about the causes of an incoming signal. The prediction itself is produced by a preexisting *generative model*—itself the product of previous experience.

The difference between model-generated expectation and what is experienced is what PP calls *prediction error*. The best and most effectively adapted generative model of the environment's probabilistic structure is the one that produces the *smallest* prediction error. Thus, the brain can be thought of as a dynamic system continually adjusting its generative models of the environment across multiple hierarchical levels and associated timescales so that they (in the medium and long run) *minimize* deviations from the predictions it makes. The goal is always to minimize the difference or error between the generative model's expectations and the incoming sensory information. According to PP, then, our brain and body adhere in their very basic workings to the goal of *prediction error minimization* (PEM).

As a form of continuism, PEM holds across *all* levels of explanation—from the most elementary subpersonal structures to the acting person in a lifeworld—which means that brain networks, subcortical regions, and the body embedded in an environment are all engaged in PEM.[20] PP makes probability extend equally to "subpersonal" components (like neurons predicting other neurons in association with them) and "personal" components (like action oriented to *Chance*) as mutually active, pattern-maintaining, surprisal-reducing systems working together across multiple time scales. Accordingly, from the PP perspective, prediction is an activity and a predicate applicable across our biological organization, from neurons to neuronal populations, structural and functional brain networks, organisms, and even populations of agents.

Even if people do not adhere to (or even know about) a normative statistical theory, they still perform a "predictive inference." Of all the attributes that might be cataloged as cognitive or mental predicates (e.g., perception, desire, belief, and the like), prediction is one of the few to have this "vertical cross-applicability" property in a way that goes beyond simile or the sort of category mistakes Wittgensteinian philosophers like to pounce on (e.g., a neuron that "believes" or a brain that "sees").[21] At all levels, then, the brain traffics not in sensory information about the world around it, finding its purpose in processing that information to *represent* it; rather, the brain actively attempts to *anticipate* information flows in the environment around it: "attempting to *guess* the present," in a manner akin to "adjustment" in Helmholtz's basic sense, to reduce the potential of free energy.[22]

Such a framework puts PP at the forefront of probabilistic reasoning in science. In the PP framework, "generative models" preserve the probabilistic structure of the world and preemptively send top-down signals that attempt to match the incoming bottom-up ones. From the activated neuron to the sense impression, what we find is an orchestrated attunement to a probabilistic environment aimed at an active cancelation, reconciliation, and resonance between the predictions generated by the internalized model and what is received from the senses.[23] Thus, generative models cancel out "raw" stimulation from the environment in the neural layers by immediately coding for environmental contingencies. Much of the reasoning here is Bayesian. The intensity of a given perception is a function of its surprisal—in other words, its relation to what we have learned to expect as average. Yet, in the next principle of PP, we can see why the brain consists of its generative models rather simply serving as a holding room for every new bit of information and thus engaged in a permanent revision.

The Principle of Active Inference

At the heart of PP account of the predictive error minimization is what PP theorists call *active inference*. The basic idea is that, when faced with prediction error across multiple hierarchical levels, we have two choices to minimize the error: (1) We reconfigure the probabilistic structure of the stored generative model, at the cost of discarding a profitable history of experience in the face of what could be merely temporary environmental disturbances; or (2) we engage in activities aimed at selectively sampling incoming sensory information that conforms with the hierarchically organized generative model. Some cognitive scientists refer to this pair of choices as "revision-PEM" versus "action-PEM."[24] We prefer these terms rather than something like "passive versus active" because among PP's breakthrough discoveries is that there is simply no such thing as passivity. Action is *constant*. The only difference is whether we are actively coping with the world by canceling errors via an active updating of a generative model or by self-fulfilling the selective sampling of the world that we receive as the sensory input that we can predict.[25]

Importantly, not all discrepancies (prediction errors) between generated likelihoods and experience are created equal in a PP framework. At both personal and subpersonal levels, prediction errors that are inconsistent and less structured than those with large variance are more often discounted and are less likely to generate model updates or motivate us to engage in active inference to cancel them out. Repetitive and consistent errors, or error signals with low variance indicating high-precision deviations from what is expected, are most likely to attract attention and motivate action to cancel them out. They cry out, "Listen to me!" This tendency is what gives action its predictable and regular character.[26]

Note that the sociological notion of "hysteresis," central to Pierre Bourdieu's account of the dynamic of action in changing fields,[27] can thus easily be conceptualized in terms compatible with PP, as a recalcitrance against updating internalized generative models of the environment produced by consistent experience in the face of disconfirmation (i.e., high-precision-weighted prediction error) by novel environmental circumstance that the probabilistic structure of the current model cannot accommodate. The prediction is that agents will try to use active inference to attempt to subsume the novel experiential set into the previous model (cancel the error), but this attempt will show up at the personal and institutional level as a form of "hysteresis" where old practices misfire (failed active inference).

Thus, to put the principle of active inference in a manner that can be transposed directly into what probabilistic reasoning can mean for sociological explanation, *we attend only to what we cannot consistently predict.* That is what we perceive, and it is always involved in our action. Because prediction is in the service of canceling prediction error as we engage with the surrounding objective probabilities, attention is necessarily a scarce resource to be mobilized only in the face of recalcitrant, precise, and insistent error. Hence, only when faced with reliable, stubborn evidence that extant generative models are not up to the predictive task does a "percept" become explicit and information-bearing, even if a generative model can never adapt to the probability that it will appear again in the active inferential loop.

In line with this loop, the PP framework generally rests on a two-step process modeled on Helmholtz's recognition/generation dynamic. The environment's probabilistic structure is encoded by persons as generative models. People then use and fine-tune those models to cancel the error produced as the ("free-energy") difference between the model's predictions and the information provided by dynamically evolving experiential manifolds. In this way, PP breaks with passive conceptions of the link between perception, cognition, and action, in which we only have a one-directional arrow *from* environmental stimuli *to* cognitive representation and then to action control. Rather, since action is constant, it is involved in the generation, adaptation and implementation of generative models to *guess* probabilistic environments.[28]

The idea that perception is not purely bottom-up or stimulus-driven but is instead subject to top-down influences based on attention, selection, and construal of stored constructs is not new or particularly groundbreaking. Some have argued for the resemblance of PP to the Hegelian dialectic.[29] The idea of top-down influences on perception is far from new to culture and cognition scholars in sociology. The "filtering" of perceptual streams by larger cultural schemas and categories is a fundamental premise emanating from the "sociological Kantianism" that animates the field.[30] The radical difference PP presents is that organisms cope with the environment by *anticipating* rather than representing it. Actors use generative models produced by experience to encode the probabilistic texture of previous states of the environment. It is in this respect that "predictive processing *inverts* conventional assumptions about the flow of information in the brain."[31] For PP, prediction is a *continuous* and *constitutive* feature of all action and cognition. Or, more simply, there is *no perception without prediction* and *no prediction without action.*

Building a Probabilistic Sociology via Predictive Processing

The preceding discussion of predictive processing provides a model of how to engage in probabilistic reasoning, showing how prediction can play a substantial role in the explanation of action distinct from present approaches found in sociology and data science. Along the way, we have seen that probabilistic reasoning implies various substantive theses. First, rather than epistemic statements *about* the world made by a third-person analyst, probabilities constitute the objective orders of the world. Second, everyone has cognitive and experiential access to these world-constituting probabilities, as they become available via mundane openness and attunement to the world, not via specialist probabilistic techniques only accessible to third-person analysts after a lot of training. Any cognitive system that engages with a probabilistic world via learning and action also has access to them, and only the form differs.[32] Third, action becomes a primary venue of empirical investigation and general theory because action is defined as continuous engagement and attunement with the probabilistic structure of the world.

While we have so far told the predictive-processing story at the "subpersonal" level of brain networks and cortical and subcortical structures—all of which seem to be neuro-architectonically arranged in the hierarchical manner predicted by the PP story—the same account transfers to the personal level with which sociologists interested in interpretation and explanation are typically concerned, involving believing and desiring actors, social identity and social structure, and the forms of social order and social change that generally fuel the sociological imagination. From this perspective, there is inherent *continuity* between the subpersonal and the personal, with both accounts commingling in action explanation.[33] On this basis, prediction in the PP framework provides a way to translate between levels of inquiry into a sociologically substantive form. At the level of action, perception, and cognition, people are not in the business of passive environmental representation but of using generative models of the probabilistic structure of environmental contingencies to minimize the expectations generated from these models as they attempt to guess the causes of current perceptions and feelings.

A probabilistic sociological imagination will focus on the means of prediction deployed in action to understand the objective probabilities comprising the social world, how people learn and are oriented to those probabilities, and how prediction in action maintains or changes our generative models of them. While this demonstration of probabilistic reasoning might seem unusual, we have seen in previous chapters how our probabilistic sociological precursors arrived at similar points as those we now retrieve from predictive processing. The principle of active inference proposes a *duality* between a structure of probabilities of past environmental contingencies and trajectories and the structure of predicted probabilities produced by the internalized generative models. That duality provides a precise analogue to what Weber and Bourdieu propose as the looping relation between *Chance* and expectation or, in Bourdieu's terms, "the universal tendency of expectations to match chances," which we explored in chapters 2 and 3. Similarly, the brain's main task is to use hard-won generative models acquired from experience to generate contemporaneous predictions as to the most likely causes of experience.

For the probabilistic sociologist, people are innately "open to the world" even if they may appear closed off from it in their habits.[34] This openness goes beyond the "narrow bandwidth" version in traditional socialization theory, in which only high-level constructs couched in the personal language of beliefs, attitudes, or "values" are allowed to durably modify people.[35] If the predictive-processing story is on the right track, then people are open to the *entire manifold of statistical regularities* in the physical, social, cultural, and psychological environments they occupy, across multiple hierarchical and temporal levels, from the perception and recording of the most minute "micro-features" of experience to the more spatially and temporally extended "features" of the social environment.[36] Such an openness to probabilistic regularities in the cultural environment, for instance, provides our best available computational model of how the culture "out there" gets "in here."[37]

More specifically, a probabilistic sociology will infer that for every synchronic or diachronic regularity we might observe in the social world—every A preceding B, X "going with" Y, or P following Q—there is a predictive *hypothesis*: $P(B|A) > \{P(B|C), P(B|D) \ldots\}$. As PP conclusively demonstrates, this internalization is hardly a passive process, which we can summarize with an additional principle: *Internalization is for prediction*, and *prediction is for action*.[38] The "recording" of an association between A and B via learning becomes a *resource* to predict B using A. Accordingly, even at the earliest stages of such "internalization," which, at the subpersonal level, consists of the tuning, strengthening, and weakening of direct synaptic connections and indirect temporal coordination of spiking activity in neuronal populations, people begin to use nascent "hypotheses" to generate top-down anticipations as to what the environment will bring next.[39]

The most significant theoretical implication this kind of probabilism has for sociology can be found in the kind of vocabulary that sociologists typically use to understand action or to make action a part of sociological analysis. The post-functionalist assault against the remnants of Parsons was mainly conducted by emphasizing continuity in one form or another. Many of these efforts have shaped how sociologists make action a part of their explanations. These approaches include the "temporal flow" of action, between "analytic" dimensions (such as "interpretation" versus "strategy"),[40] across temporally specified phases or elements (such as iteration versus projection versus practical evaluation),[41] or continuity across the "elements" of the action scheme itself (such as means and ends,[42] modes of action like creativity and habit,[43] or effort versus moodiness).[44] Importantly, these are all non-probabilistic approaches to action that subscribe to the severance between action and prediction. To avoid that, as we recommend sociologists should, requires that we define and name "action" in ways conducive to what a probabilistic approach like PP draws our attention to: using probability to theorize vertical and horizontal continuities.

Sense and Segmentation: Horizontal and Vertical Crossings

Continuism, as we have outlined it, centers on questions crossing familiar explanatory boundaries. For example, is accounting for the physical vibrations of eardrums adequate for grasping musical tonality, as Helmholtz once argued?[45] Today, we would be hard-pressed to deny that he had a point. Yet, "the physicality of the tone" is typically segmented from what is otherwise judged to be adequate for explaining why music sounds the way that it does or why we like it. Rules of tonality, musical genres, or ethnomusical conventions are taken as adequate to explain the sound in question. While these rules certainly depend on tonal physiology, what that physiology actually entails is typically regarded as irrelevant from the perspective of what really constitutes the objective potential of "music." For Helmholtz, the question was not whether rules of tonality had a physiology; *physiology* is fundamentally what those rules *are*. How can we make such a claim without at the same time being reductionist?

Continuism raises this question because it pushes the boundary between what we follow philosophers in calling "personal explanation" versus "subpersonal explanation."[46] A personal explanation is one that resonates with conscious experience and our own accounts of it; thus, it is consistent with a locus of control that centers around folk psychology. A subpersonal explanation references processes that are unavailable to our conscious experience and cannot directly resonate with folk psychology. A continuist will argue that the difference between the two is a reification that creates more trouble than it is worth. They try to do without the segments that allow for such accusations of reductionism or top-down domestication of the subpersonal. A continuist tries to use the same language to explain what is small as they do what is large, even while appreciating their differences of range. Rather than segment tonality from physiology, for example, and create explanatory rifts of one form or another, continuism instead asks what physiology and tonality both do in common as grounds for dialectically eroding their distinction.

On these terms, PP is strongly continuist, as there is nothing about the personal or subpersonal that can be explained without the other. Prediction error is the fundamental recipe for any kind of ordered pattern; but to even recognize that a pattern is ordered in conscious experience requires a combination of sense input and a generative or predictive model. As we reduce prediction error through active inference, either by acting to change the world or by adopting our model to it, the generation of information with minimal free energy is essentially segmentless. A persistent segment indicates, if anything, stubborn prediction errors that we persistently fail to predict. These prediction errors are reflected by the form in which we cast what we might otherwise call unknowable "singularities." If we consider these kinds of prediction error to be "uninterpretable," we do not do so because they are unique or important in any way. The label only indicates how much trouble we have predicting them—they always, in other words, *surprise* us.

For a field like sociology, the questions posed by continuism are particularly pressing because sociologists routinely engage with phenomena that extend across levels, raising significant questions about what is adequate and expectable versus what is random and chancy. Importantly, sociology tells us that "subpersonal" does not mean "small" or "micro." Subpersonal processes are in no sense limited to each individual's skull-sized kingdom. In their explanations of action, sociologists today may point to the interplay of people's intentions, desires, goals, beliefs, and plans.[47] Meanwhile, explanations using more hallowed constructs like "norms" or "values," popular when positivism was commonplace, have become mediated in post-positivist times by a personal vocabulary. When put into action, they are often translated into some combinatory variation of belief and desire.[48] For sociologists, a vocabulary of belief and desire is typically considered to be the grounds of *adequacy*, because it is presumed that actors have mastered that vocabulary and its attendant concepts. They will understand, therefore, what we sociologists are saying when we couch our explanations in folk psychology. Thus, something like values can be defined as the *desirable*—and thus as ways of having everyone strive for the right things[49]—and something like norms as *beliefs* in what should be done.[50] Once we have this mediation by desire and belief, we can add the *oomph* of intention or "effort" to (voilà!) generate action.[51] Even further, when tying explanations like these to certain normative ideal types dictating how people *should* behave, the personal vocabulary still suffices as an explanation of action even when it deviates from the ideal-typical normative case. One of the strongest warrants for the pervasive use of personal vocabulary to explain action is that it has the seemingly indisputable advantage of being subjectively meaningful.[52] As an explanatory practice, the personal vocabulary seems exceptionally well-designed to answer *"why"* questions.[53]

To introduce any kind of subpersonal explanatory construct, however, especially one harking back to a "psychological" (today neurophysiological) or otherwise nonmeaningful (in this autonomous sense) mechanical cause of action, seems to be a step in the wrong direction. Worse, the use of such "subpersonal" constructs in explaining action could commit what philosophers call a category mistake, since action is, by definition, that which can only be explained by the causal interplay of personal states like beliefs and desires, perhaps adding an understanding of "intention" as their combination.[54] Yet the problem with achieving continuity based on a personal vocabulary is that it must be protected *against* the subpersonal simply in order to work. Thus, we can find arguments that to be concerned with cognition as a sociologist is to adopt an analytically "small" or reductive focus.[55] To make these associations with cognition, however, might demonstrate more an attempt to maintain the segmentation of an autonomous "personal" explanation than citing processes about what "cognition" might, in fact, be.[56]

Apart from any explicit mention of prediction, anticipation, or expectation, there might be no way to make probability directly relevant for action without simply reaffirming a framework that centers "belief" and "desire." On these grounds, we can see why the desire-belief-opportunity (DBO) approach has been so appealing, but we can also see why it generates controversy.[57]

DBO can translate probability into action because it consists of a recipe for fitting pretty much any phenomena into the analytic frame of desire, belief, and the situational variable of opportunity. But because they extrapolate this framework so effectively, however, DBO theorists can also elicit an uncomfortable nominalism ("in name only") that arises essentially because of DBO's seeming universal applicability and translatability. Such worries leave an imprint on present theories of action. The data science critique seizes upon these traces as evidence of sociological accounts as *mere* common sense masquerading as explanation.[58]

If we persist in using the two terms ("belief" and "desire") so essential for personal explanation and also wish to remain cognizant of predictive processing, then we must stop belief and desire from being so strictly disassociated from the subpersonal. Rather, in a probabilistic framework, they both become interlinked expressions of expectation that we acquired by looping into *Chance* via PP processes like active inference. Yet, as we emphasize further below, while suspicion of personal explanations of action can run deep, frameworks like psychoanalysis that so heavily rely on subpersonal processes enjoy popularity largely because of how they can be translated into belief and desire terminology.[59] Contemporary cognitive science, however, is rooted in the idea that there are efficient and regular causes of action that cannot be accounted for by a personal vocabulary.[60] These causes are typically referred to as *subpersonal*. Thus, somebody "feeling" pain is a personal-level event that people can report in a manner that directly affects their actions. That is all we have as personal-level data. Any further "why" questioning must lead us to the "mechanical" world of the nervous system and its activities. We can explain the action by pointing to an organized sequence of neurophysiological processes, but we would no longer be engaging in personal explanation; instead, we would be producing a *subpersonal explanation of action*.[61]

Even when we *drop* from the personal to the level of "brains and events in the nervous system" and point to a series of events over time (nociceptor activation, a signal traveling via neural fibers, etc.), we are still engaging in a *horizontal* explanation of the action in question (e.g., withdrawing our hand from a hot stove after touching it and not anticipating that it was hot) that deals with a causal sequence in time.[62] In this respect, the "subpersonal" explanation seems very much like the "personal" explanation that sociologists use to explain, for instance, why middle-class conservative white people vote the way they do—for example, they believe that favored minorities were allowed to "cut in line" by liberal political elites, which alienated them from those elites and made them susceptible to an anti-elite populist message and persona.[63] As this kind of account might imply, the belief in question is treated as a *wrong* belief, and so is less personal, because the person in question believes only because of the influence of what is outside of their control. As we might be able to tell in this case, the strict distinction between the personal and the subpersonal is not irrelevant to the account the sociologist provides.

A further explanatory segmentation can be found cross-cutting the personal-versus-subpersonal distinction, namely, the difference between horizontal and *vertical* explanations. We are "explaining" someone's actions when we *drop* from the personal vocabulary and make recourse to subpersonal processes that are analytically distinct. But we also do so when we, say, *move up* and link subpersonal processes like prediction error minimization to the "layer upon layer of sociocultural structures and practices" that constitute the probabilistic landscapes in which we act.[64] "Dropping-down" or "moving up" refers to a vertical explanation, while a temporal causal series refers to a horizontal explanation. More specifically, horizontal explanations proceed from past to future, representing events as they fit on a diachronic line of temporality. They are "the explanation of a particular event or state in terms of distinct (and usually temporally antecedent) events or states."[65] Vertical explanations, by contrast, move *between* levels, "explaining the abilities or dispositions an organism has in terms of its parts and their causal relations."[66] Hence, we must distinguish *horizontal continuity* in the temporal flow of events from *vertical continuity* cutting across different levels and kinds of formations and distributions of probability.

When it comes to action, the vertical/horizontal distinction can crosscut the personal/subpersonal one. The usual interpretive explanation of action is both *personal and horizontal*: "When we explain a person's behavior, we cite the sequence of mental events that preceded the behavior, primarily in terms of propositional attitudes such as the person's beliefs and desires."[67] Philosopher Daniel Dennett, meanwhile, argues that in being forced to drop down to the subpersonal level to explain, say, the way our hand withdraws from a hot stove, we come up with an explanation of action that is both *subpersonal and horizontal*.[68] Here, a sequence of events in the nervous system accounts for the behavior. We can also imagine an explanation of action that is both personal and vertical. For instance, sociologists influenced by Alfred Schutz can take action within a temporal horizon ("projects") and see that action as being composed of shorter stretches of action.[69] Both the longer and shorter stretches can be rendered in personal vocabulary. The "vertical levels" of decomposition are defined in terms of nested timescales, thus incorporating a horizontal component at each level. In the same way, subpersonal explanations can be arranged in successive "vertical" mereological levels to explain a given subpersonal mechanism (e.g., the visual cortex) as composed of lower-level structural and functional brain networks, synapses, and the like.[70] These types of explanations are, therefore, both subpersonal and vertical.

Table 2 depicts these relations schematically, according to the combinations of vertical versus horizontal and personal versus subpersonal. Rendered this way, the segments are maintained; even as explanations attempt these combinations, they are not continuist. Reductionism is subpersonal and vertical relative to a "project" focus as personal in orientation but sharing the same concerns with arrangements across levels of analysis.[71] Behaviorism is the non-continuist version of a subpersonal-horizontal explanatory approach. Folk psychology appears as the diametric opposite of reductionism here.[72] The sequential relations of stimulus and response can be explicable in horizontal terms as behaviorism; in most cases, however, this approach presupposes vertical linkages, which will not be immediately apparent.

The crucial fact remains: Maintaining these segmentations without vertical and horizontal linkages will lead any explanation into traps. Predictive processing recognizes this fact, at least in its gesture toward a subpersonal/vertical link, by explaining active inference as a sociocultural practice. Figure 3 depicts a different kind of explanatory schema in which these links are emphasized as opposed to being segmented. Such an emphasis is not as

TABLE 2. Non-continuist segmentations in theories of action

	Vertical	Horizontal
Personal	Projects	Folk psychology
Subpersonal	Reductionism	Behaviorism

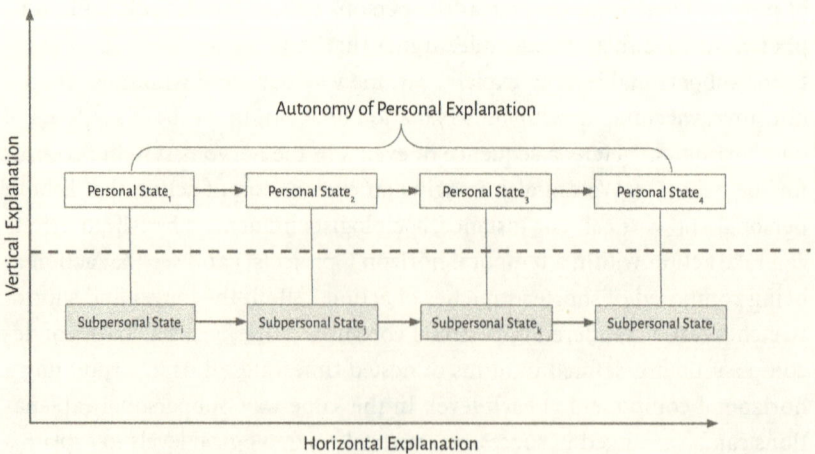

FIGURE 3. A continuist model of the explanation of action

unusual as it might appear at first; as we have suggested, engaging in subpersonal accounting is fairly typical in sociology. Yet, if the subpersonal process is not translated into beliefs and desires, such accounting cannot be considered action without being uninterpretable. Accordingly, sociologists maintain certain central problems, like how to pick out some action as "agency" and make it different from the rest.

Here is what we suggest. A probabilistic sociology calls for a radical continuity both *vertically and horizontally* and *personally and subpersonally*. To a reference a collective object (groups, structures, cultures) is a common way that sociologists give their accounts verticality. This vertical move is often the most problematic, however, because of the segmentation that often goes along with it. Paradoxically, the more verticality sociologists give their explanations, the more subpersonal those explanations get. Such a paradoxical maneuver is the only way to bring those collective objects into action, which means making our account both horizontal and vertical. While this point is not entirely original, its implications become clearer once we consider the following addendum: If they are to have any horizontal presence in action, then collective objects, or the concepts that sociologists often use to give their accounts verticality (structure, culture, groups), must refer to a *prediction error resolution pattern*, aimed here at error or contingency minimization, which can be collective, shared, and derive from the objective situation of social groups in a probability order. Probability becomes a linkage mechanism, then, as we can register descriptions of it both personally and vertically ("beliefs," "constraint," "social identity") as well as subpersonally and horizontally ("prediction error").[73]

With a strictly horizontal focus, the boundaries are rigidly maintained because there is only one *right* way of relating to the future—only one way that will be functional. The primary boundaries maintained are vertical boundaries. Eliminating these boundaries leads to new connections, and thus the task is to find the relevant levels that have become vertically integrated. The effect of this approach can be to dissolve collective objects we thought were there, or make new ones appear—ones with similar tendencies, involving interlevel capture, whether of lower levels traditionally associated with neurons, synapses, and cortical structures, or higher levels traditionally associated with states and economies. The result of a vertical arrangement is "emergent" but not in the typical sense of transforming lower-level properties into higher-level properties through a combination of independently existing objects. A vertical arrangement is emergent, rather, in its construction of higher-level or collective properties through a common orientation among lower-level properties to *Chance*.

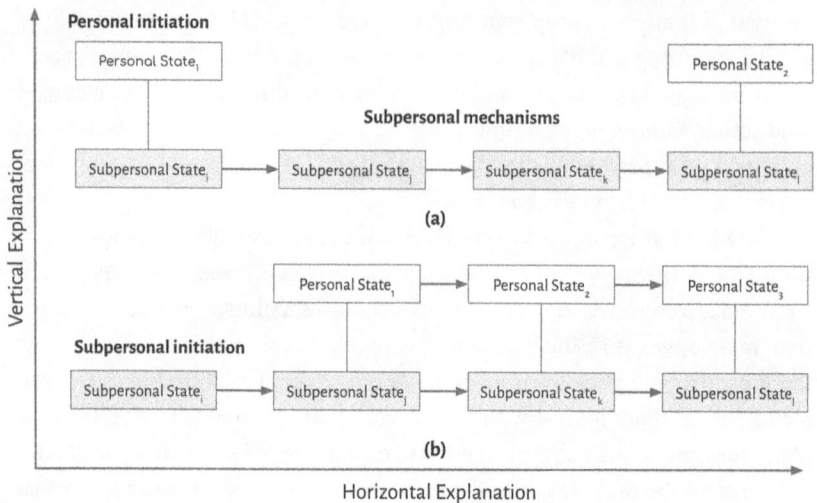

FIGURE 4. Two different types of continuist linkage in the explanation of action

In figure 4, the continuist linkages are shown through two different initiation sequences: one starting at the personal level, the other at the subpersonal level. These are two different ways of initiating a loop via the original orientation to *Chance*, whether this looping is made possible through a horizontal project or a vertical capture. A horizontal project starts with a personal initiation in the explicit positing of *beliefs-about* and *desires-for*, which could take the form of, saying, looking for a job, having a child, getting married, or joining a social movement. Whatever form a project takes, if it is to not remain artificially segmented, it must find a subpersonal linkage (or vertical capture) to be sustained horizontally through error reduction.

A vertical capture of subpersonal mechanisms by an explicit project can be the result of a process that resonates with a personally autonomous vocabulary (e.g., by talking yourself into it).[74] Yet typically, for sociology, such a focus demands a break from personal autonomy, by taking account of social structures, institutional logics, landscapes of meaning, and the like, all vertically arrayed and affording predictability between many individuals in *spite* of their personal autonomy. A vertical capture is not a singular intervention, however, and therefore implies a latent determinism if we do not translate collective objects into probability orders. As we have suggested, orders typically analyzed as macro only have predictable duration through action that loops back into them, rather than drifting off into other orientations.[75] As probability orders, vertical arrangements can be maintained subpersonally through PP mechanisms that make them probabilistic, like active inference and PEM, or acting forward in time by constantly looping back into an original capture. Our action becomes a form of maintenance, of error minimization, then, with the effect of leaving us blind to some precepts just as we take a particular or "precision" notice of others. Personally, we might register this phenomenon as having an interest, a passion, a duty, or an addiction—all of which refer, in some sense, to *motivation*.

In a probabilistic environment, then, any living being must act in ways well-attuned but adaptable. Such a being must "modulate the precision assigned to affordances in response to such volatility," allowing for flexibility within a potentially wide range, but the tendency is toward what is objectively probable. We come to follow a train of confidence in our current sensory state as indicators of future ones, rather than having to guess those future ones, an effort that lacks confidence. In subpersonal terms, dopamine signals indicate that the degree of "confidence (or lack thereof) [in] . . . current sensory states will lead to expected future sensory states."[76] This signal, and our precision-weighted expectations, "are attuned to [our] changing circumstances based on bodily feelings."[77] Those feelings serve as indicators of how we fit with an environment. "Feedback from the body alters the dynamics within the organism as a whole to ensure that the organism remains well adapted to a dynamically changing environment," based on the "circular causal relationship" people typically enter into in their everyday dealings.

For PP, the dynamic described here is in a constant state, which means that action too is constant. None of our perceptions are passive; all are the product of active inference. We are constantly engaged in action to bring the world closer to our predictions. Action, then, is our sole means for maintaining a homeostatic integrity against persistent errors that the world dispenses our way. The task is Sisyphean. But to hold to such an account would make sociologists strong believers in nominalism, for otherwise the only place we will allow action to be social agency is in our definition. As mentioned in chapter 5, a concept like "agency" fine-tunes our attention to what matters when we wade into the mangle of practice. PP, on the other hand, says that the mangle is all of the same kind. To test the PP view that all action is alike in its essentials, given that the cognitive need for action is always the same, we can see whether it can encompass as "action" on its terms something that seems quite the opposite, given its destructive rather than functional outcomes.

Addiction as Action

A challenge of this sort presents itself in the case of addiction. To even call addiction an *action* may tempt incredulity, because addiction appears so starkly absent of subjective meaning. Yet, to take addiction seriously as action can yield particular insight into a topic like motivation, as addiction reveals what it means to be so singularly oriented to a *Chance* that action becomes destructive of the integrity of a living being.[78] To "have" an addiction or to "be" addicted is conceptualized by PP to be a way of remodeling the world to fulfill singular expectations at the expense of expectations that adapt to the world in socially and physiologically normative ways. Addiction hijacks active inference and the *Chance*/expectation loop via error minimization that is almost completely uniform. As one argument puts it, addiction alters how "the organism and the structuring of the environment continuously co-arise together"[79]: "The life of many (but not all) addicts becomes increasingly chaotic in other regards. As soon as the drug's effect wears off, what they return to is a world offering all of the uncertainty that never really went away. So long as the addict is high, it seems to them as if they are succeeding at maintaining a grip on what matters to them. Once the drug wears off, they find reality is very different."[80]

As this argument would suggest, addiction creates a mismatch with the environment that puts bodily integrity at stake by leading addicts to so intensely concentrate on errors related to the source of addiction as opposed to those that pertain to food, hydration, sleep, and the like. They do not follow current sensory states that would lead them to expect future states in which such organic expectations are met. In sociologically resonant terms, we could refer to addiction as the extreme version of *having an interest* and the forward momentum of current to expected sensory states as the extreme version of *being motivated*. The intensity of addiction reveals them both in a nearly unfiltered state. To be addicted is to be motivated, and it is to embody an interest so powerful that it comes to be the central orientation to the world. Yet the consequences of this particular interest come at the extreme cost of not having any others.

The framework we can observe here does not change between addictive interests and motivations and non-pathological interests and motivations; the main difference between them is that the latter do not typically threaten bodily integrity by forbidding responsiveness to volatile environments.[81] In the same manner as addiction, we have interests and motivations when those environments co-arise with zones of potential *on the body*, which likewise become oriented toward confidence cues (biochemical or otherwise), a responsiveness to being interested and motivated, sometimes by urgent recognition of *needs* and of what must be done. These are errors that must be corrected and worldly arrangements that must be brought into place. The most fundamental form they take is probabilistic: Specifically, as expectation creates mismatch, that mismatch appears as perception, and in turn, expectation and *Chance* find partial restoration through action. Since the key dynamic to all action is error minimization, what sociologists typically refer to as "social action" tells a story of vertical capture—the role of probability order in organizing our state of being up and down. The formative moment comes when minimizing the specific errors of this order, our integrity being tested by them, becomes a prerogative—thus organizing our state of being horizontally between a past and a future. What we see here, in nuce, is the birth of repetition or, more precisely, the genetic history of a movement in time that will construct and maintain a probability order, or a pocket of predictability, in the continued existence of a living being like us.

The Study of Action Is the Study of Probability

To link cognition, perception, and action as predictive processing helps us to articulate the same basic process that, for Weber as for Bourdieu (see chapters 4 and 5), marks sociology's approach to explanations of social action. What we propose, then, is an integration between two probabilistic perspectives. If cognitive science, under the auspices of PP, recognizes the need to incorporate sociocultural practices, this recognition provides a desirable window of opportunity for transdisciplinary dialogue.[82] As we have shown, it is difficult for sociologists to avoid making subpersonal, vertically arrayed claims, even if this move does not align easily with the usual boundary work around the personal level and its autonomy. The typical result is that action explanation becomes a special preserve, maintained by careful segmentation, even while sociologists credit subpersonal processes that, for those on the ground, are lived and understood entirely personally.[83] Weber (by way of Spinoza) had already anticipated the predictable difficulties: Only by explaining action can sociological explanations find adequate causation; otherwise whatever we come up with will come across as accidental to whomever we tell it.

Predictive processing, as we have suggested, offers a compatible tool for meeting these difficulties without falling back into the segmentation-driven "central problems" of an earlier era. For integrating action at multiple levels, across segments, in a continuist sense, PP provides us with a glimpse of a constant, dynamic process, closely integrated with cognition and perception. Our recommendation is that, in reformulating sociological explanation after even post-positivism has been exhausted, sociologists can learn from the PP effort to theorize action—but to take this recommendation on board demands that sociologists break habits that, above all, keep interpretation and probability as separate analytic concerns. What would it mean to bring to bear on this conversation the well-established sociological expertise (to which the PP scientific community increasingly refers) in the in situ analysis of "sociocultural practices"? The work of synthesis would demand a continuist perspective on the side of both parties, one that would ask that we account for a sociocultural practice on probabilistic terms. But to do so demands something that reads likely as absurd to most sociologists: that we admit that the study of action is, in fact, the study of probability (and vice versa).

To build a bridge, let us take an example from a prominent PP theorist, the philosopher Andy Clark. Clark, true to his professional creed, uses the following example to demonstrate the basic principles of predictive processing and how they can apply to even the most personal-level situations: "The coffee cup sitting on the table is a prediction error that is rectified by bringing it to our lips."[84] As Clark unpacks this assertions, he explains that when we fill the coffee cup and put it on the table, we engage ourselves in a predictive process in which we will continually predict drinking from it until the coffee cup is empty, or until we forget about it by attending to other prediction errors. Still, simply by pouring the cup of coffee we encode an expectation of caffeine intake (or at least the taste of coffee) that we will actively infer until we no longer notice its absence.

For Clark, the situation is that basic. If we want to complicate the action and—say—describe the capitalist mode of production, we do not need to trade the terminology or the format; all we need to do is account for the way that "sociocultural practice" inserts its way into our predictive error minimization. Of course, an explanation would seem to commit a couple of theoretical faux pas from a sociological lens, which some take as confirming that an interfield like cognitive social science is simply a nonstarter. Clark's explanation is *reductive* in using subpersonal explanatory terms (prediction error, active inference) to describe a horizontal process (drinking coffee) more amenable to personal language (belief, desire, project). Furthermore, the explanation lends subpersonal processes *personal* characteristics—committing, as mentioned above, the silly category mistakes of attaching wants and beliefs to neurons.[85] What Clark most obviously does not specify for the sociological imagination is how this simple action intersects with history in a society. What remains unstated are the aspects of coffee drinking as a social action. For example, the absence of caffeine is not typically as noticeable at 2:30 a.m. as it is at 7:00 a.m., but this point is true only because of social and cultural constructions.[86] More generally, coffee is a commodity today and, as all commodities are, comprised of a long and extensive set of social relations configured around extraction and exploitation. Yet the goal, in correcting these problems, is to avoid shattering the *Chance* of "adequacy at the level of meaning" (in Weber's words) with arguments to the effect that "industrial capitalism causes coffee drinking." Without considering how coffee drinking arises from the perceptual fluency of habituation, however, in which the generation of free energy is chased by predictive coding, we will read this proposal as a top-down one in which tack-on categorization (emblematic of the supermarket of theory mentioned in the last chapter), rather than objective probability, comes *first*.

Our proposed integration of probabilistic sociology and predictive processing would imply what adequate causation is in this case. It would need to capture associations between coffee drinking and morning awakening as a unitary, durable experiential pattern, the embodied expectation of caffeine (we are assuming non-decaf as Clark does) as part of other rhythms and orders of succession for which it becomes a precondition, and thus our looping into *Chances* as we try to keep pace with them—our expectation being captured, in this regard, in ways that cannot forget or deny, which certainly implies configurations of cells. Sociocultural practices become necessary for the account, as the habit observed is more than contingently connected to loops (perhaps several) for which meeting the expectation of drinking coffee loops us back in until the *Chance* disrupts us again. Caffeination *is* contingent in the historical sense: it is a sociocultural practice constructed by unpredictably converging factors and unintended consequences. For one guided by PP, however, it is also astonishingly *predictable* as a sociocultural practice.[87]

As we have stressed, what people notice and perceive does not arrive from a top-down categorization, at least not typically. There are circumstances— perhaps ones that most meet the definition of "the sea" mentioned in the last chapter—that find no objective probabilities to loop into and in which we must therefore cast a net over what, from the perspective of action, are abyss and chaos. In PP terms, to be in such a situation would be to be overwhelmed by free energy, such that predictive coding would prove unable to cancel out sense information beyond a limited threshold. Accounting for the subpersonal, then, is significant for what it tells us specifically about the loop of *Chance* and expectation. Weber and Bourdieu both put stock in this account in ways that did not respect clean segmentations of personal from subpersonal. In this sense, they recommend a sociology that would align with predictive processing in drawing attention to probability looping as implied by any kind of social order we might care to document.[88] Accounting for such a loop, as we will argue more fully in the next chapter, means providing a genealogy documentable both collectively and individually, making evident socially and historically constructed habits that fulfill certain parameters of looping in, observable even in subjective traits of interest and motivation.

In proposing such vertical and horizontal links, a probabilistic sociology

Vertical Capture

Looping Effect

Horizontality

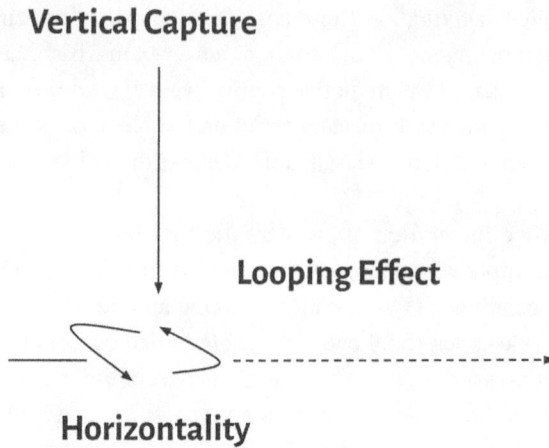

FIGURE 5. The looping effect and vertical capture

of this kind finds an ally in medical sociology and what that field has long insisted upon as the social determinants of health. This framework similarly eliminates the vertical boundary that makes a strictly individual orientation to health a meaningful point of focus on its own.[89] Horizontally, we can always point to health causes that draw in a personal level that might be framed by a term like "choices." Yet, when acknowledging the vertical dimension, sociologists working in this area typically identify a capture of individual health by what we would call a probability order, eroding the applicability of "choice" as a key source of variation and making expectations for health match what we can statistically record as a probability distribution. The idea is not that actors have those statistical chances in mind, however; their action is, rather, oriented to *Chance* that can become visible in that distribution, as differences in health and well-being based on college education, race, authority or autonomy at the workplace, and so forth.[90] Because there are such clear statistical patterns, this scenario would suggest a highly ordered phenomenon in which expectation is a key factor—the point where the personal and subpersonal are highly vertical and integrated and where stated "reasons" provide insight into action, though it might strike the sociologist as completely banal.

Relative to what can be accounted for in horizontal terms, the vertical effect of a probability order can come as a surprise to analysts like us. We will not be the first to notice it. When such an order appears, PP tells us that living beings will orient to it by acting in ways that minimize the prediction errors that would otherwise dissolve the order into randomness. This specific argument, we claim, holds the key to any future relationship between sociology and cognitive science; both fields need the other to account for it. The looping effect so described is a subpersonal process that achieves this horizontality or, in other words, the maintenance of probability order in time.[91]

To be oriented to worldly probability means to have expectations that find a counterpart in something objectively probable about the world. Probabilistic sociology reveals that whatever systematic patterning we find in the aggregate must be reflected in probability at lower levels of organization and order, which generally means finding *probability in action*, as the process of engaging with preexisting potential that is then made actual in some distinctive way but that is itself probable. In PP terms, this process is the minimization of prediction error or free energy by adapting models or changing the world. Generative models for social action, identified at a granular, more molecular level, are only possible because they are general, collective, shared, and found in a predictive loop, dictating the nature of inputs from an objective, probabilistic landscape. This statement, composed with probabilistic reasoning in mind, is the secret formula for the construction of probability orders. This formulation suggests that when people are in social environments, they acquire a sense of normativity before long—of what they and others *should* be doing. They have little choice in the matter. The sense of "should," "normal," or "can" they obtain is subpersonal, which means it need not align with what we (the analyst) might have devised as their (the actor's) best interest—that is as good a starting point as any for the overdue marriage of sociology and cognitive science.

PART IV

Implications

What does probabilism mean for the practice of research in social science, even more specifically in sociology? This final part of the book focuses on method and then on more general implications for what it means to approach the social world probabilistically. As we emphasized in parts I and II, probabilism scrambles the conventional distinction between the calculus of chances and interpretation of meaning that finds itself mirrored in many of the disciplinary distinctions—quantitative versus qualitative, hard versus soft science, STEM versus non-STEM, natural versus social, or even "two cultures"—that still pervades the conflict of the faculties. Evidence for this scrambling, as both will and representation, comes by way of data-centricity and the challenges it presents to epistemic cultures, many of which still carry a positivist taint. We can learn a lot about a field from the kind of response the specter of data science elicits from it.

A probabilistic sociology, contrary to what the name might imply, does not recommend implementing (perforce) a common mode of measurement in the field, not least of the kind that had been the great dream of the "becoming a science" project of midcentury sociology. That dream never took—sociology still recognizes a range of methods and measurements that distinguishes it from even close disciplinary cousins like anthropology.[1] Sociology is becoming more data-centric, nevertheless, and while the tendency might, thus far, appear to consist of a more or less tariffless importation of new methods into sociology's domain, that readiness of adoption signals a deeper tendency in sociology's disciplinary unconscious. Consider the call for a break with Eurocentrism in historical case studies or the search for epistemic surprises—these moves, which seem *far* removed from data-centricity, actually share something in common with it. What the postcolonial critique and abductive surprise both share with data-centricity is a rejection of the representational view of data, which has been all but de facto in sociology and most other fields since at least World War II.

Probabilism can draw a lineage all the way back to Spinoza and his insistence on adequacy and intuition. We can find a more contemporary parallel in what philosopher Nancy Cartwright calls "phenomenological science."[2] For Cartwright, the problem with a "theoretical science," of which physics is for her the prime example, is that it *lies*, all the time, and that it does so by necessity. If physicists' general theories allow predictiveness and elegance, nothing actually works in the way those theories imply. "The content" of those theories is necessarily phenomenological; their inner workings can only be fleshed out inductively. What Cartwright proposes here is something akin to the value of studying a *single case*. It is not altogether different from Kries's distinction between the nomological and the ontological, as discussed in chapter 2. Probabilism has been a way of bringing similar ontological concerns into sociology, largely in the work of Max Weber, but there is more to say for it, particularly if we account for predictive processing's need for sociology to join in collaboration, embarking on a study of the world as probability order. In the two previous chapters, probabilism has served as a guiding light—a way to move sociology beyond the post-positivist reckoning that has, arguably, not yet yielded a viable way out. Du Bois's statement would still seem to apply just as much as it did at the turn of the twentieth century: Sociologists favor the documentation of general patterns ("Laws") over the documentation of "Chance," but they have none of the faith that positivism gave to the discovery of Laws. If we are still intimidated by the physicists, Du Bois thought we had no reason to be; sociologists could find grounds of commonality by letting a little Chance in. Cartwright would, it seems, make a similar recommendation.

In the following, it is Peirce from whom we draw the most, not because the cantankerous polymath is attentive to the problems of sociology (he seems to have known nothing of the discipline) but because, far more than Kries, it is Peirce who offers us a tool kit for probabilism as a "style of reasoning."[3] He does so in a way that aligns with Cartwright's phenomenological science, with Kries's ontology, with Du Bois's focus the unification of Law and Chance, and with Weber and Bourdieu's shared effort at producing *adequate* ideas.

Our question in the next two chapters will therefore be: What would it mean for probabilism to remake sociology as an *intuitive science*? Among other things, it would require that sociology abandon the type of nominalism that has proven to be its post-positivist succor in lieu of anything else. If we can do that successfully, we might provide ourselves with a citadel in the stand against the machines.

An Outline of Probabilist Method

Physical intuition: the ability of scientists and ordinary people to look at a physical scenario—or a biological scenario, or a sociological scenario—and to "see" the *physical probabilities* of things and, more generally, to "see" what properties a physical probability distribution over the outcomes of the scenario would have, without experimentation or the gathering of statistical information.

MICHAEL STREVENS, *Tychomancy*

When probabilities became a matter of frequencies in the early twentieth century, objective probability went to philosophy; there was really no other place it could go. Frequentism papered over many issues it thought it best to leave unresolved. As the Bayesians learned firsthand, to engage the questions that the frequentists had black-boxed as method was to invite ridicule and professional purgatory. The stakes were high. Persistent questioning might undermine the capacity of frequentist methods to convince people (especially powerful people) of statistical claims about the world. As Ian Hacking tells us, probability has remained torn between a "degree of belief" and "aleatory" divide ever since.[1] Whether probability pertains to our state of mind and knowledge or whether it indicates some sort of indeterminism in the setup of the world leaves open a host of additional questions. Are probabilities frequencies? Are they indicators of our degree of belief? Can they be used that way? Is statistical variability in a sample population an indicator of the world or does it reflect present limits in our ability to know it? What about subjective probability, like a sense of risk or willingness to bet? What does it mean to call such things "subjective"?

Statistical methods are not often presented as answers to questions like these, as they generally rest on an answer to the first question that makes all the rest moot. Objective probability largely unfolds on the converse of that question, asking instead, "Are frequencies *probabilities*?" The answer is, generally, *no*, leading many to take the aleatory part of probability very seriously. In denying that probabilities are frequencies, however, objective probability opens a further question, perhaps more beguiling than all the rest—of what use is frequency?

In this chapter, we envision what a sociological research method might be like if probability was extricated from frequency and treated on its own, as objective. As mentioned in chapter 5, the most visible aspect of post-positivism in sociology today is, arguably, the seemingly sui generis importance lent to methods. That importance has become closely tied with a kind of de facto frequentism. Above all, it seems, a good post-positivist sociologist is firmly aware of the benefits that come from having an *n* of a certain size—number of interviews done, hours and months of observation, how many cases in a dataset. These all take up prominent real estate in their methods sections and abstracts. Outlining a probabilist method begins from the stance that such an emphasis might actually *prevent* sociologists from producing probabilistic knowledge. Our argument is guided by an insight from philosopher and historian of science Gaston Bachelard, himself a keen observer of probabilism.

Bachelard once observed that method in science entails a persistent "monitoring" (*surveillance*) in three different degrees.[2] We monitor at a first degree when we gather data, taking note of what can count as data (what an interview subject said in response to a question) and what cannot (they had really bad breath when they said it). We monitor at a second degree when analyzing the data to find what is important. Typically, patterns are important, though Bachelard also draws our attention to how pattern recognition is contingent on monitoring for "surprise." The first two degrees of monitoring have become routine across all contemporary epistemic cultures. They typically go by the common label "methods." Training in methods—and thus training in making distinctions between what is data and what is not, what is *usable* data and what is not—is essential to the pedagogy of all empirical fields. Far less common is to make the move to third-degree monitoring. That refers to monitoring about method itself—"the monitoring of monitoring of monitoring" in Bachelard's words. It requires "one to put *method* to the test."[3] Third-degree monitoring seeks to "[destroy] the absolute of method" and suspend the weight of history that accumulates *in* methods.[4]

Despite its post-positivism, sociology remains a thoroughly frequentist field. Sociologists typically infer probability from outcome frequencies, with the initial states provided by our independent variables, or our interview questions, the historical documents we examine, the circumstances in which we do observations. In our view, data science—at its best—exercises a third-degree monitoring on frequentism, because it questions not only the seeming sui generis validity of large numbers (of cases, data points, interviews, documents analyzed, hours of observation), but the sequential logic that frequentism facilitates, which at this point is mostly habitual. That logic tends to be highly categorical, asking for clearly delimited concepts, categories, and classifications to be defined at the start. Clarity and definition are necessary if concepts are to become variables. These demands are created by frequentism, but they are vulnerable to nominalism, or a version of collective existence that persists primarily *in name only*. The logic that we can find in Kries and Peirce is different from this logic and much more in line with principles (like connectionism) that make data science different. To appreciate how that is the case and why it matters, we first need to start another dialogue with the philosophers. This time, probability itself is at stake.

A Dialogue Between *Sociologicus* and *Philosophicus*

To see how frequentist assumptions could limit our capacity to think probabilistically, consider an unconventional presentation of points: a Galileo-style, hypothetical *dialogue* between representatives of two positions and two fields, featuring a philosopher (*philosophicus*) intrigued by objective probability and its third-degree monitoring, and a sociologist (*sociologicus*) who adheres to a frequentist creed de facto, mostly as a form of methodological knowledge.[5]

Imagine a cool autumnal day on a university campus in the northeastern US. *Philosophicus* has been reading up on the literature in the philosophy of probability. She is shocked by the challenge it seems to present to what she remembers as the basics of probability theory from a statistics class she took as an undergraduate. She wonders if the philosophical conversation has had any influence on a field that relies on statistical methods. As she walks toward her office, *philosophicus* notices an acquaintance approaching in the opposite direction—*sociologicus*. While *philosophicus* is much older, she was excited when *sociologicus* was hired several years ago. The two used to engage in animated and wide-ranging discussion, filled with possibility, but they've since grown distant. For her part, *sociologicus* looks tired and disappointed. Her introduction to sociology class went as predictably as ever—lots of head nodding at the various points she was making—but the students don't seem to have yet gathered the *imagination* aspect of "the sociological imagination." She wonders if they ever will. She keeps hearing that a significant portion of the students characterize sociology along the lines of an "easy major" and "basically psychology but without the math."

Philosophicus does not feel bashful. She is eager to ask her old friend questions, knowing that sociology is a field that uses statistical methods.

After some pleasantries, she jumps right in: "Something has been puzzling me, though, if you don't mind my asking. You sociologists seem to 'assume that frequencies of certain properties in populations are *stable*, which is to say that frequencies don't fluctuate wildly, but remain roughly the same over moderately short periods, and change only gradually over long periods.' The data, you say, appears to 'support such assumptions.' But in that case, I have a question for you: 'Why should frequencies of outcomes for members of social categories be stable? What explains that fact?'"[6]

The sociologist our philosopher is addressing already has a response in mind, invoking a trusted central problems concept: "It is simple, my old friend. We sociologists understand the stability of frequencies to be a signal of a social structure."

Our philosopher nods her head and then adds bemusedly: "Right, I understand. But what you sociologists tell us about social structure, as far as I understand it, appears to assume an *absolute* connection between probability and frequency. But would such a connection not contradict a further assumption that your statistics need to make in order to work: specifically, the whole notion of a 'random experiment?'"[7]

Our sociologist, taken slightly aback, and feeling a little annoyed, anxiously rebukes: "Don't be so hasty. Do you philosophers know what 'random experiment' means to us? Say, for example, that you want to know the probability that working-class males in the United States will attend college. We might point to the proportion of individuals in that group who actually *do* attend college. You would be right, then: To interpret a relative frequency in that way would rely on such an 'absolute connection,' as you call it. Of course, we sociologists know better than that. We are dealing with a dataset to make such an assessment, and if we want to be able to reach a conclusion about probability using it, we need to have the confidence that the data were generated by a known probability procedure. Sociologists are very willing to capitalize on what you call 'stable frequency,' if by that you mean 'what would happen if numerous samples were generated independently by the same process.' Thus, we can quantitatively 'represent the uncertainty in our parameter estimates' of the significance of class background for college attendance as a sampling distribution produced by 'a very large number of identical, hypothetical, trials.'[8] Confidence intervals and significance tests can then follow."

The philosopher again nods and puts a finger to her mouth; then she points it at the sociologist: "But you still haven't answered my question. How can you assume that the frequencies found in your dataset will be stable across numerous independent samples? Don't you need to make that assumption about the world to call such frequencies *probable*? And isn't that assumption

one of the more critical aspects of your conclusion? By making it, you are saying that something in the world is the source of a lot of homogeneity between
individuals. Is 'trial' simply a methods term for you? Is it something more?
Some of us philosophers say it is possible for the world to contain its own
'chancemakers.'[9] The problem is that they entail little more than frequencies."

The sociologist rolls her eyes: "'Chancemakers?' Interesting idea, but it
sounds metaphysical to me. Besides, how can we know what is happening out
in the world or build trust in what we *think* is happening without frequencies,
or what we in sociology often call our '*n*'? Sociologists try not to draw conclusions based on trends that are not observed often enough. We typically call
infrequent counts 'random error.' It seems you might not know much about
how we use data to draw conclusions. I don't blame you. You philosophers
aren't really taught how to do that."

Sensing loggerheads, *philosophicus* and *sociologicus* part ways, agreeing
to disagree. The former decides she'll go to the library and read up on social
structure (maybe she misunderstands it?), while the latter returns to her office
and her regression equation. Soon she will forget the conversation entirely.

A New Scientific Image

The reflexive goal of such a dialogue is twofold: (1) to draw attention to how
an underlying interpretation of probability—an answer to the question
"What *is* probability?"—matters as a kind of limiting assumption for the kind
of research sociologists *can* do; and (2) to engage with the claim that sociologists make the assumptions the philosopher suggests. Not mistakenly, it is a
philosopher who serves as gadfly here, asking annoying questions. In recent
years, philosophers have proposed a host of concepts for probability mindful
of the limits of frequencies: "microconstancy," "far-flung frequencies," "epistemic chance," and "the range conception."[10]

In the image of these concepts, probability exists in space and time; it extends out into the world in the form of "bubbles," "patches," and "ranges."
Much as we described in the introduction, the probabilistic world available in
this image is a patchwork rather than a Humean mosaic, as described above
in the introduction from the philosopher David Lewis. One philosopher describes the pivot from the Humean mosaic as follows. According to the mosaic, "information from the past is generally admissible" for inductive and
predictive purposes.[11] If the "best system" to understand the world consists of
the most particularized elements we can measure, then on that plane everything is (ideally) equidistant from everything else, and our probability estimates become a data problem, not an ontological one. In a patchwork world,

on the contrary, "admissible information" cannot just be "from the past" to be admissible. For the purposes of induction and prediction, information must come in the form of "sufficiently coarse-grained descriptions."[12] Knowledge of the coarseness is knowledge of what makes otherwise *fine*-grained points of data (events, actions) exist only within an "*n*-dimensional space." The more local and particular information can, in this sense, only indicate "patches" on a higher plane that *diminish* locality and particularity.

Philosophicus comes up with a unique phrase to refer to knowledge of probability that takes this form: "probability coordination."[13] Objective chances *are* out there in the world to coordinate with, but frequencies might not help us. "If the *physical* probability of a hurricane is high, you should . . . expect a hurricane strike." Probability would, in this statement, be constitutive of the hurricane itself. To coordinate with it would be to *expect* it, which would require knowing the physical probability. Notably, the physical probability of a hurricane here pertains to probability as a *single event*. So how, in this case, can we know and coordinate with it, if we cannot test our expectation across multiple trials?

We might wonder, as skeptics do, whether the image found in these arguments reduces probability to something like an indeterminate physical mechanism. Does probability carry any characteristics of its own? There are a few stipulations that *philosophicus* insists upon. The mathematical properties that Soviet mathematician Andrey Kolmogorov devised in 1933 to refer to "a field of probabilities" still largely obtain.[14] They can be roughly summarized as follows: (1) Any field of probabilities features elementary events (*E*), (2) these events are distributed in subsets (*A*, *B*), (3) each subset can be assigned a nonnegative real number (*P*) that is called the probability of the subset $P(A)$, (4) the total probabilities of each subset equals 1, and finally (5) if subsets *A* and *B* are independent but within the same field, then the following must hold: $P(A + B) = P(A) + P(B)$. *Philosophicus* reads these axioms as statements about a unique kind of space (a "vector space"). The philosophers often start by considering fields of probabilities as coarse-grained, featuring wholes and parts—though wholes that do not emerge through combination of those parts. Those parts ("elementary events") do not come in an entirely local and particularized form; they overlap and partially mirror each other. They exist coarsely, then, but also as "subsets," subregions, or segments, all of which add up to 1 if we put them together. The image, perhaps, is of the Russian doll, a container of containers (of containers), with some "original" the *deeper* we go, and all important to encounter for each in their own separate world of worlds.

Probability must be translatable into what we can designate as initial states and what we can designate as outcomes. Something sequential is at stake:

Initial states are present, and outcomes follow in time. The image does not suggest, however, that initial states and outcomes are necessarily different, as is typically the case in examining independent and dependent variability. The former could persist in the latter, though not all initial states can persist in all outcomes, or we would have no probability to speak of.

For *philosophicus*, we can think of initial states and outcomes as linked compositionally within "patches." Each patch is a "connected set of maximum size initial states [that] lead to one and the same outcome." Thus, a relatively coherent ratio of initial states creates a distribution over the possible outcomes: "For each outcome, the proportion of initial states leading to it is the same in any not-too-small segment of the space, which explains why there are stable characteristic relative frequencies with which the different outcomes appear upon repetition."[15] Patches will be smaller, and there will be more of them, the more unstable the field is—in this case, lots of different combinations of initial states are maximally connected to more outcomes. For *philosophicus*, the image of probability focuses on what holds *constant* across initial states and outcomes in many individual cases, and thus constant across the trials that make their linkages observable. How much, in other words, of the initial states remain *in* the outcomes? And as those outcomes become initial states for further outcomes, how much remains constant? Something must remain constant—there must be maximal links—otherwise they would not constitute a "patch," a "small, contiguous set," or a "range." For some ranges, the initial states only appear in conjunction with a small range of outcomes (i.e., stable frequencies). For others, the initial states might themselves be small, and nearly always co-occurring, but produce a broad range of outcomes (i.e., unstable frequencies).

Most of these principles are formed with physical systems in mind. *Philosophicus* often associates the image of probability with "deterministic chance" that applies best to a "deterministic contexts."[16] Nothing important can, in that sense, be found *between* initial states and the outcomes—no space or time. Objective probability, in this form, appears immune from "arbitrary functions."[17] Thus, regardless of how we toss a six-sided die, the probability of it turning up any given number upon landing is approximately equal, at least should its physical properties be balanced. How we toss it, at what angle or speed, does not matter. That should, of course, draw our attention to the die and its remarkable symmetry. In this case, it alone is the source of objective probability. But how can it be so effective at reducing arbitrariness, for instance in the shake and rattle of our hand, that would produce an asymmetrical distribution over the outcomes or even an entirely *new* outcome? This lack of arbitrariness is what yields probability and is the function of a physical mechanism. It is that physical mechanism that we coordinate with, and because that mechanism is real but unknowable in its entirety, our knowledge of it can only be probabilistic—we can only know its outcomes relative to our expectations. Just as there are no "bare particulars," then, that can be known absolutely, objective knowledge is conditional on knowledge of a range, which in most cases will almost never strike us as presenting outcomes that are all equally possible.

Rather than independent and dependent variables, *philosophicus* proposes patches of initial states and outcomes maximally linked to each other that, in turn, make the patches stand out as distinctive in the world. Theirs is a patchwork world that retains constants across particular cases and individual experiences, thus reducing particularity and locality. A regression equation, in this regard, attempts to serve as the description of a vector space the effects of which exist in space and time. Rather than frequencies, however, *philosophicus* recommends that anyone concerned with probability set themselves to describing what objectively *produces* probability by limiting arbitrariness and generating a range of possibility with more or less fuzzy borders.

Fields, Spaces, and Probability

The spatiotemporal, even cartographic, nature of this new image of probability has certain parallels with concepts in sociology, particularly as they have also been devised using a heterodox probabilism. As discussed in chapter 4, the concept of "field" (*champ*) associated with Pierre Bourdieu is understood to be deeply probabilistic. In its most basic form, it draws our attention to distinct spaces of connection between "positions and available position-takings."[18] There is an equivalence in this terminology with initial states and outcomes. The former, in both cases, have symmetry and alignment with the latter—though (in both cases) that alignment is not total but features partiality and mismatches. In the terms of the philosophers, a "ratio" of initial states leads to outcomes with varying probability. Likewise for a field, we can observe inequalities between certain positions in their links to certain position-takings; the difference here is also expressed as an "objective probability."

Fields, in this regard, consist of pockets of tightly arranged links that work to forbid accidents and arbitrariness.[19] In a field, the initial-state space is more defined than elsewhere, and it has unique symmetry with outcomes allowing for a relatively high degree of predictability among actors ensconced in it. In that case, it makes sense why we can expect *some* things (art, science, law) to be produced by a field, even if we cannot exactly predict the precise form they will take. The tight arrangement of links between the initial-state space of a field and its range of outcomes is maintained by forms of capital—a control on the future, as we mentioned in chapter 4—which is the major point of dispute in a field, just as we would expect if we follow *philosophicus*. Those acting under the auspices of a field most certainly coordinate their action with its probability. They must make their ways of creating outcomes from initial states obtain at least *some* probability, ideally the *highest* probability.

Beyond a field, however, the cartographic image of probability that *philosophicus* offers can also provide insight into social space more generally. One concept is "far-flung frequency," which seeks to account for another distinct type of coherence that has great range and large diffusion in space and time. Fling an individual with certain traits anywhere within a certain range and we can expect them to exhibit similar outcomes. A far-flung frequency refers to membership in some social categories, and typically only a few, that matter a lot for a broad range of outcomes. Stable frequencies like these do not change much over time and space, though if we move out of the space where they seem to apply, they might disappear, and we can find periods in history where they never applied.[20] They displace a unique kind of constancy across a very large number of individual cases spread out geographically, yielding the tightness of connection that maintains one shared initial state across the distribution of certain outcomes to such a large extent that it becomes predictive.

In this case, we are using frequency to learn about objective probability. But as *philosophicus* tells us, frequencies are only ever a "methodological probability" that arise from "sources other than facts about social systems." Hence, they can only signal that probability might be found.[21] They do not, by themselves allow us to refer to "probabilities" and attach them to individuals in any meaningful sense. Even with these far-flung frequencies, we must be able to tell a story of how their initial states and outcomes persist with such symmetry, such lack of arbitrariness and accident, and how they are able to do that within a bounded cartography of the world. On these terms, it becomes evident that probability is what *occurs* when individual cases become indistinguishable in some respect, and to know those individual cases probabilistically is to know how they *lack* particularity and locality.

At this point, however, a question presses in upon us, which again relates to the physical systems that anchor *philosophicus*'s imagination. Does it make a difference that when we go looking for objective probability in a human context, what we are calling "initial states" and what we are calling "outcomes" are only linked by the action of creatures (humans) oriented to and invested in what we are calling "patches" (or "bubbles" or "ranges")? The roll of the die is arbitrary if the die is fair. Our human action seems to make no apparent difference in changing the probability distribution over the outcomes if we throw it quickly or slowly. If a similar principle applies in a human context, if our action remains similarly arbitrary in the face of the production of outcomes, and if what we do (what anybody does) *does not* seem to alter the links we can observe from afar between initial states and outcomes, we might have grounds enough to refer to a "social structure." In part, *philosophicus* anticipates this conclusion—the image that the philosophers provide intends to help *scientists* with their probability coordination. In this case, it recommends that scientists not engage in an experimental design that does the equivalent of rolling a die a large number of times. Frequency will teach us nothing about probability that we could not have known from the start of such trials if we knew where and how to look. But does it matter that "ordinary people" also coordinate with probability? We can understand what this means most fully, perhaps, by reminding ourselves of our sheer bafflement at the outcomes of a game of chance. In other spaces, in other fields of probability, however, our action does appear to *reduce* the independence of probability over a range of outcomes, but not everything we do is equally as likely to have that effect—only certain actions seem to matter. The notions of "singularity" and "adequacy" that bubble up here invite a further point, which links to another core issue for *sociologicus*.

Single-Case Probability

Philosophicus is clear that objective probability, and more generally its image of probability, makes single-case probability difficult to fathom. Objective probability maps out what the ontology of probability must be if certain mathematical axioms are to apply. That means, however, that what occurs in a single case is essentially deterministic; nothing is probabilistic about its operation. It is probabilistic because of arbitrary functions that become active in the single case and which entail that the same set of initial states simply do not always produce the same outcome. The only way for probability to be active in the single case would be if someone (or something) could orient to it in situ and perhaps even be shaped by it to act in a given way.

At this point, *sociologicus* can again raise her voice. She can say to *philosophicus*, "We have just the creature in mind," namely, *homo socius*—in our view, they orient to *Chance* in the single case all the time. But what does that mean? Does it mean that *Chance*, as in objective probability, also upholds Kolmogorov's mathematical axioms? In a certain definite sense, "yes" would be the answer.

To return to Kries for a moment, we do not even need the human creature for single-case probability to have some validity. Kries's most famous example of objective probability concerns something quite non-anthropogenic indeed—a meteor collision with Earth.[22] What chance does it have of hitting Berlin versus Dar es Salaam, or one of the islands of Vanuatu? Or any of the seven continents? We could make a calculation in this way, though it would take no account of a single case. And for that reason, it would be meaningless, arbitrary, or "groundless" in Kries's words. The meteor does not recognize geopolitical divisions as possible outcomes, though it might respect different partitions, like how fast it is approaching relative to the current (and future) position and rotation of the Earth. That information could give us a non-arbitrary range, and one that would not include the entire planet, because it is one that applies only in the *single case* of this particular meteor. For Kries, that scenario could provide us with a differentiated space with subspaces (subsets, subregions) of equal chance. What happens in one subspace is independent of the other, though they both share the same *Spielraum* of initial states inclusive of all that applies to this meteor as it heads toward Earth (its speed, composition, rotation, etc.).

If we flip a coin and an outcome is produced (heads), how can we know how probable turning up heads was in that single case? What are we to do with no frequencies to count, no repeat trials, no reference classes to build, and, therefore, seemingly no way to make outcomes probabilistic? These questions are entirely epistemic. We should be asking a different one. Take Peirce's example: "If a man had to choose between drawing a card from a pack containing twenty-five red cards and a black one, or from a pack containing twenty-five black cards and a red one, and if the drawing of a red card were destined to transport him to eternal felicity, and that of a black one to consign him to everlasting woe, it would be folly to deny that he ought to prefer the pack containing the larger proportion of red cards, although, from the nature of the risk, it could not be repeated. It is not easy to reconcile this with our analysis of the conception of chance."[23]

Here, he is telling us what is, quite literally, *making* the probability. By knowing the distribution of the cards and the outcome they are connected to, we can know probability in the single case. But notice a further set of presumptions: that probability only means anything because we are oriented to an outcome, and that to bring it about requires our action. Reliance on action would suggest a connection between initial state and outcome that is different from an arbitrary function. What is capable of action here—a mortal human person—is capable of it because they can orient to and *activate* the probability present in their single case. Without them, there is nothing.

Contrary to *philosophicus*'s stance, then, single-case probability is possible. We just need to find out "where the action is" to find that probability.[24]

Notably, to put the emphasis here does not mean that a single-case probability entails simply a backdoor agreement with Lewis, a *philosophicus* of a different stripe. That agreement is avoided because even if the single-case probability appears to the *sociologicus* as possible, its appeal is not to data that is local and particular.

Peirce asks us to imagine a pendulum swinging smoothly back and forth. We can dissect its movement into a fully original sequence of parts. In that case, "there certainly is something in a moment altogether independent of past and future."[25] Yet we might be surprised to learn that "examining the moment under a microscope we find this independent element divided up into portions, less independent of one another." If we "divide the day into hours, we find that much that was unexpected on the whole is no more than might have been anticipated from a part." For Peirce, such a statement of perfect continuity means "the peculiar element of the present . . . is something that accumulates in time." It only "dissipates the more minutely the course of time is scrutinized."[26]

What appears single might only be an arbitrary division, the difference between 1:00 p.m. as number on a clock versus 1:00 p.m. as a possibility for certain kinds of action. What really *is* single is what contains all possibilities in single moments of a continuum. Peirce undoubtedly pulls lessons from his own research into observation (see above, chapter 3). Just as there and in alignment with Kries around the exact same time, we can make the most minute observations imaginable, but if we appreciate that data do not stand as the representation of the phenomenon—like a probability—but *are* the phenomenon, the most minute observations (local and particularized facts) will no longer be the best we can obtain.

Adequate Cause and the Limits of Interpretation

Single cases are where cultural and historicist approaches, in sociology and in other fields, are often presumed to make their living. Because single cases are believed to be unavailable to probabilistic analysis, interpretivism can thrive here—single cases become a primary venue to observe the "contingencies of interpretation."[27] A similar logic can be found across the humanities. To know Shakespeare is to be as much a historian of Shakespeare as a literary scholar trying to find meaning by reading his words, even if one is, in fact, a literary scholar by trade.[28] The goal is to ward off our (the analysts') imposition on a historical subject by figuring out what *their* interpretations are rather than our own. What *philosophicus* tells us about initial states and outcomes, however, suggests a limit on interpretation in this respect, by challenging the idea that interpretation is a point of access to the particular and local, on the assumption that it is ontologically reliable—it always occurs.

But suppose there might be variability in the *need* (or will) to interpret. When would that arise? In this case, all outcomes might not necessarily culminate in interpretation, as an initial state—found in all outcomes within a given patch, and beyond which we can find others—does have a link to chaos. Much as Clifford Geertz noticed, interpretation will serve as the initial state for outcomes when there is very little symmetry between the two—when, that is, the distribution over potential initial states does not match a distribution over potential outcomes, and no one is quite sure what *means* what, what will *lead* to what, and what is *capable* of what. In probabilistic terms, chaos refers to a patch that might persist very briefly in which seemingly all information is fragmented and all signs are partial and thus need to be filled in anew. In that situation, interpretation does define the range of what can adequately cause what and what remains accidental. Outside chaos, however, the tendency to fall into expectation will ground interpretation, and if not make it less contingent, render the links it draws between initial states and outcomes, as an intervention into partial signs and fragmented information, more accidental and arbitrary—and thus far less apt to stick. To draw attention to the single case, then, does not necessarily mean to recognize what is "single" as a reflection of contingent interpretation and thus a marker of discontinuity. It is possible to characterize a single case differently, as the *continuous* extension of the past into the present when ontological aspects of events come to be governed by certain ranges and allow for a very specific, though preprepared, potential to be realized—when, in other words, a situation arises that surprises us (the analysts) because of what has adequate cause in the situation but not outside it. Consider, on this note, two of the more famous examples of single-case analysis in historical social science.

In anthropologist Marshall Sahlins's narrative of Captain James Cook's arrival to the Hawai'ian Islands, the dramatic sequence of events that unfolded appears to hinge on an interpretation.[29] As Sahlins tells the story, the arrival of Cook and his ships, the *Resolution* and the *Discovery*, in Maui in November 1778 coincided exactly with Makahiki,[30] a Hawai'ian harvest festival when the Ku cult associated with the ruling chief is put into abeyance, allowing for the temporary ascendance of Lono, an *akua* (translated into English as "god") associated with fertility and agriculture. The procession of Lono lasts about twenty-three days, after which "Lono himself suffers a ritual death." What is most interesting for Sahlins about the case in question is the "sufficiently remarkable . . . correlation between the ritual movements of the Makahiki image of Lono and the historical movements of Captain Cook in 1778–79."[31]

Cook arrives at the islands when expected according to the lore associated with Lono's ascendency, and he stays as long as expected as he circumnavigates the islands. He also leaves the islands when expected, disappearing quietly over the horizon. In Sahlins's words, everything proceeded "right on ritual schedule."

Then something unexpected happens. The mainmast of the sloop *Resolution* is badly damaged by high winds, and Cook and crew have to return to Kealakekua Bay for repairs just a few days after their departure. In Sahlins's terms, such unscripted surprise renders Cook an "*hors categorie* . . . The abrupt reappearance of the ships was a contradiction to all that had gone before."[32] A series of unfortunate events ensues, and Cook ends up being killed. But "the killing of Captain Cook," Sahlins insists, "was not premeditated . . . neither was it an accident."[33] On the first encounter, we find a situation prepared by *Chance* in the careful construction of a patch of initial states and outcomes by the priests of Lono. The moment of Cook's first arrival is a "mythical reality," something that could "annul the possible effects of historical factors."[34] Cook follows the script, and his treatment, as Sahlins describes it, is completely different from the treatment he and his crew receive upon their unexpected return. It is the scripted version of Cook that sticks. As Sahlins tells us, native Hawaiians asked "when Lono 'would come again'" for many years after Cook's death. They even asked it when the dead Cook's bones were returned to his crew.

On these terms, the single case of Cook in Hawai'i was non-chaotic at first. When Cook initially appears, the "objective gamble" by the native Hawaiians of a particular "dialogue of sense and reference," to use Sahlins's probabilistic words, was not much of a gamble at all. Probability had come to mark this single case, and as completely contingent as it may seem, the outcome followed expectations.[35] Cook's return was different, and it was presumably filled with interpretation, judging by the immense and utter confusion on both sides. There was no preexisting patch, no symmetry, linking initial states and outcomes. Interpretation could have been an adequate cause in that instance; in the first instance, expectation played that role. The apotheosis of Cook was not unexpected to the native Hawaiians.

Consider another example. W. E. B. Du Bois's *Black Reconstruction* also features the analysis of single-case probability in what Du Bois calls "the General Strike."[36] The event in question refers to the enslaved peoples of the American south leaving the plantations in mass numbers during the Civil War, particularly as the Union armies, led by William Tecumseh Sherman, marched through the South in late 1864. As Du Bois presents it, no one could have predicted that the strike would happen—not Sherman, not the Union army troops, not US President Abraham Lincoln. Thus, we can find Sherman himself trying to interpret the General Strike as it unfolded, passing emergency measures attempting to stabilize the situation, many of which granted remarkable rights and benefits, which would later be subject to retraction even as they laid the groundwork for "abolition-democracy."

As Du Bois tells it, the General Strike was only expected by the very group who initiated it. It alone fell within their range as a possible event, and while it is singular in its occurrence and in the turning-point impact it has, as Du Bois tells us, it also demonstrates perfect continuity with the past as a potential constructed then and enacted now: "As the war went on and the invading armies came on, the way suddenly cleared for the onlooking Negro, for his spokesmen in the North, and for his silent listeners in the South. Each step, thereafter, came with curious, logical and inevitable fate. First there were the fugitive slaves. Slaves had always been running away to the North, and when the North grew hostile, on to Canada. It was the safety valve that kept down the chance of insurrection in the South to the lowest point. Suddenly, now, the chance to run away not only increased, but after preliminary repulse and hesitation, there was actual encouragement."[37] As Du Bois makes clear, the Union government "did not plan for this eventuality, on the contrary, having repeatedly declared the object of the war was the preservation of the Union and that it did not propose to fight for slaves or touch slavery." Now it faced a "stampede of fugitive slaves."[38]

In the terms adapted so far, *only* the enslaved Black laborer could make the Civil War about the end of enslavement because their enslavement was the only initial state extending across all outcomes directly or indirectly tied to the plantation system. Like Sahlins, then, Du Bois anchors his account in those expectations and the group who could possibly have had them. In both cases, the accounts they provide are of a single case, but the singularity of the case becomes clear in the ontological aspects of the events, which means the unique ranges in which the events become possible, why they become possible only there, and the distinct group who could orient to them. For his part, Du Bois makes the *improbability* of the General Strike his point of focus; that is how he prepares his discussion of it, not least by describing the plantation system in its seemingly static configuration. His explanation then accounts for why the enslaved peoples' instigation the end of the slave-based plantation system could be expected, as that event fell within the range of them and them alone. For anyone else to have initiated the end of enslavement would have been accidental—a contrast we can glimpse, it seems, in the British Empire's compromised abolition act in 1833[39]—because to make the event that could truly end it could only find the enslaved peoples in the role of prime mover, the only adequate cause of abolition. Most notably, Du Bois reveals the historical impact less as the result of an interpretation that sews together chaos and more as a preexisting potential finding the means of activation under the right ontological circumstances.

Du Bois's and Sahlins's respective arguments make it clear that when and how interpretation can be an adequate cause of outcomes remains an open question, and that even to appreciate the locality and particularity of history does not require inserting interpretation as an initial state for what we observe. Singularity can be defined in other terms, as we reiterate again in the next section. Linking interpretation with chaos as defined on the above terms also does not mean that interpretation is capable of contingency, and thus of localizing and particularizing effects, all the time. In chaotic situations, with the ontology so described, interpretation is all that can sew or suture the chaos together. But as mentioned in our discussion of Weber's *Protestant Ethic* in chapter 3, interpretation there is treated by Weber as the initial state for a whole range of distant outcomes, most of which are very non-chaotic, in which taking on the interpretation is so symmetrical with outcomes at later stages that one does not need to ever know what the interpretation in question is. Even as non-chaotic a patch as the "steel-hard casing," however, still demonstrates a sewing envisioned first through a series of interpretations.

Abductive and Synchytic Logic

Both Sahlins's and Du Bois's accounts could demonstrate a kind of Bayesian logic. The initially surprising event—the apotheosis of Cook, the General Strike of enslaved people—becomes less surprising as more information updates that original belief, and we see how probable these events are. The same could work for any initially surprising event or case. But a different aspect of the logic is on display here that we can emphasize. Such attention to what is "surprising" about data might recall *abduction*, or what Peirce understood a probabilistic approach to logic to be.

Abduction is distinct from induction and deduction, Peirce thought, because only through abduction do we actually learn anything *new* about the world—that which is not already contained entirely in our categories and concepts or in the small slice of experience available to us. As Iddo Tavory and Stefan Timmermans put it, "abduction is the form of reasoning through which we perceive an observation as related to other observations, either in the sense that there is an unknown cause and effect hidden from our view or in the sense that the phenomenon is similar to other phenomena already experienced and explained."[40] Abduction makes the most out of what surprises us. It places more epistemic value on mismatches with our expectations than on confirmations of them. Abduction departs from Bayesianism, however, on the grounds that more information or more data is not necessarily the route for reducing surprise through probability, because, as the philosophers tell us, we are looking for what will make the surprising observation more *coarse*-grained and thus less particular. The recipe, here, is not for a kind of permanent learning or belief updating ad infinitum.

As Peirce understood, abduction allowed anything to become potential data; we do not have to have a phenomenon in mind and then identify the data we need to represent it. In qualitative sociology, abductive analysis can both agree with grounded theory as a strongly inductive approach to data gathering and analysis, and advocate for "engaging multiple theories" and the necessary role of theoretical priors (or a "background of theorizations") for good qualitative research.[41] Abduction is not Bayesian, however, for the same reasons that lead Peirce to argue that wholes (*continuum*, continuity) objectively exist. In this regard, to engage in abductive reasoning does not simply mean to appraise an original observation as unlikely or not relative to *any* other observation; we do so only relative to what they are both thought to be a part of—a point of continuity or "generality" is found between each particular observation. For our purposes, that continuity or generality is the route to revealing ontological formations of wider scope, inclusive of many observations within the same *habit*.

Abductive logic does not recommend starting our research by defining our main categories and keeping them consistent throughout the research, which is a commonplace recommendation in post-positivist sociology. The recommendation here is similar to a Bayesian logic and how it treats concepts and categories.[42] When concepts and categories are defined too strictly, they have difficulty with what we might call inputs to which they have not been exposed to before, which would certainly include cases that, at least initially, appear surprising or *new* in some substantive respect. A problem of the sort that follows from such a denial of particularity is particularly visible in "model cases" that overdetermine the range of knowledge available about a general phenomenon (the city, urbanism) by tying it to a privileged particular case (Chicago).[43] In abductive logic, categories and concepts seek out new inputs. Unlike in Bayesianism, however, that exposure to new concepts has a secondary goal beyond updating our priors. We can only build the concept by linking cases within the same continuum.

For Peirce, the key to the abductive logic is to invite "chance" (i.e., "first-ness") in via "percipuum," or what we can loosely understand to be a direct encounter with ontology in perception, marking the divide between us and the world that becomes active the moment *after* perception.[44] Continuum here becomes the counterpart to the percipuum as the former organizes chance or pure potential into belief based on links that reach a higher generality. To use a simple example, if it is surprising to us that a grassy meadow is inundated with water when we stumble upon it, we may initially panic and question whether what we have believed "grass" to be is completely mistaken. That process takes us through what Peirce calls "firstness" in the perceptual judgment of wet grass, and "secondness" in the mismatch between *this* (extremely wet) grass and our prior belief. We respond by building our concept further, on a more general plane, on the grounds that grass is usually not *this* wet. We link our observation to a statement about what is currently unobservable, like "that rain must have been a deluge here earlier today." That is not just wild speculation. From what we now believe about grass, it will allow for *both* a state of dryness and a state of wetness.

For his part, Kries offers a comparable logic that, likewise, seeks exposure of concepts and categories to particularity while understanding that there are "no bare particulars."[45] As Kries puts it, "the probability of an outcome increases with the number of cases that have come to be known," but for him, such a claim does not lend itself to the need for large numbers. He has a different rationale in mind. Ideally, in his view, our research would produce synchytic concepts, as we briefly touched upon in chapter 2. A synchytic concept is distinguishable from a synthetic concept. Where the latter fuses particular difference to produce coherence and expectation, a synchytic concept attempts to preserve particular difference and *still* produce coherence and expectation. Some have tracked the notion of "family resemblance" associated with philosopher Ludwig Wittgenstein to Kries's discussion of synchytic concepts.[46] In Kries's view, good examples of synchytic concepts pertain to things "like State, History, Accident, etc."[47] While someone could easily deny that these words "represent concepts" given how widely dispersed the particulars they could apply to, they each nevertheless are simply nominal if we try to define them outside any examples. For Kries, "synchytic concepts can only be explained by means of examples." They are built according to an "impression of belongness" that we cannot anticipate in advance, and which we might not share with everyone else who has (seemingly) the same concept and the same perception. Like abduction, synchysis is rooted in probability. The impression of belonginess arises according to "the degree and type of similarity which the individual cases have to one another, especially the similarity that currently judged cases have to formerly presented cases."[48]

For Kries, too, a basic contact with the world similar to Peirce's percipuum, or a reference to the basic divide required for anything to perceptually "force itself on us as an object," is crucial should we wish to avoid the problems that often arise with synthetic or analytically derived concepts. Both Peirce and Kries deny the validity of psychological measurement or even the very capacity of introspection outside some "object" understood in these perceptual terms. They would tell us, then, to be very skeptical of concepts that largely avoid exposure to the "basic way a subject grasps reality" because they produce meaning via a priori deduction and definition. We might read their recommendation as a recipe for avoiding something that looks like *theory*, if by that we mean general concepts with potential application to lots of particulars. Kries and Peirce do endorse theory, but theory as they endorse it does not emerge from prior definitions of concepts. Synchytic concepts, for instance, draw connections using only what can only be revealed through perception. To clarify this point, Kries makes a distinction between induction and analogy: "The first is a relation from the particular to the particular, the second a relation from the particular to the general."[49] For synchysis, analogy is critical for building a concept iteratively and incrementally, by subsuming new examples according to a probability judgment determined relative to a growing expectation of what is probable among all cases *like* it. Each new addition revises that probability ever so slightly. But we should not expect that the revision will go on ad infinitum, as more like Bayesian approaches. For Kries, a synchytic concept like the color "red" will remain fuzzy and flexible, but it will be definite enough to make reasonably good predictions about what someone else will perceive as "red."

To follow Kries and Peirce through in their logical claims would lend a kind of legitimacy to the sociologist who wishes to study the single case, the single event, or even a single *person*, but not because that is the best way to meet an ideal of locality and particularity. Both Kries and Peirce believe they have found a direct link between the particular and the general that does not have to be forged by frequency counts. Synchysis and abduction are intended to be ways of identifying sources of objective probability, as found in the continuums and concepts formed through synchysis that link particulars together. In both cases, the yield tends to be fuzzy and flexible, not finite. The points of continuity, and the cases gathered through synchysis, have a similarity between them, though not in *every* way.

The logic on display here is different from either the deduction oriented by a strict definition of concepts or what appears recommended by Bayesianism. Contrary to the latter, abduction and synchysis do not recommend a kind of permanent revision. Their appeal to flexibility and fuzziness is, rather, rooted in the idea that objectivity is probabilistic and thus is primarily a reference to ontology, the way definite things exist in relative stability, rather than epistemology. Much as *philosophicus* recommends, we can approach objective probability using a framework that includes initial states and outcomes, which serve to identify ratios of ontological features working for or against a possible outcome within the maximally linked boundaries of a patch. These are ways of avoiding nominalism—the sense that words like "the state" or "social structure" are *just* words rather than concepts. To *not* be nominal, they must loop into ontological formations in the world that exist on some spatiotemporal scale. We must be able to translate them into patches of initial states and outcomes, or what we have referred to above as probability orders or *Chance*.

One problem with forming a concept that ranges beyond particular cases is that it might become invulnerable to revision by *any* future inputs. In probabilistic terms, a researcher might worry that their findings deviate *too* far from what is expected, leading them to disregard those findings no matter how empirically valid they seem. As noted above, the problems of "model cases" in sociology exhibit precisely this failing. More generally, expertise, and the symbolic power that comes with it, is highly vulnerable to the same problem, which is part of the appeal of data science, according to some, to the degree it can offer flexibility (in, say, medical diagnosis) by avoiding the dangers of analytic inflexibility.[50] For our purposes, however, we must be careful. To value particularity or locality for its own sake can carry the same potential for nominalism as can deductive concepts given strict definitions that become their own source of *Chance*. Abductive and synchytic logic offer an alternative, and to the degree that data science employs a similar logic in "neural network" linkages of inputs and outputs that also loop into (or "learn," as they say) objective *Chance* through revision via depth and inclusion, then we can find appeal in it too.[51]

Now, we turn our attention to a key difference between sociology guided by abduction and synchysis and data science guided by the same, and it concerns something that *philosophicus* sketches out in principle, though offering little detail. It is a phenomenon that aligns with some of the terminology introduced above in chapter 5, namely the test and how it can "make" *Chance*, even if ever so fleetingly.

Finding the Chancemakers

Abduction and synchysis are good at finding probabilistic relationships by finding symmetry between particulars—points of continuity, a sense of belongness among seemingly unrelated particular examples. Frequency can also be helpful for finding those relationships and for inferring, at least partially, what joins outcomes and initial states within the same range. For *philosophicus*, objective probability is not conceived as "features of the world that make certain degrees of belief appropriate."[52] It is conceived as objectively configured spaces in the world that *produce* probability. The language of initial states and outcomes, maximally linked in space, provides a way of making sense of objective probability in this ontological sense. In the new image of probability examined above, an initial state treated alone might lead to some outcome of interest, while other initial states seemingly proximate to it led to different and even contradictory outcomes. In such a scenario, we can learn very little from a single case, as it appears unpredictable. But suppose we can find a collection of initial states, all factors leading to that outcome of interest within a not-too-small space and inclusive of many single cases that have a certain repetition or constancy across them. Such links can become legible in relative frequencies in large numbers, using variables, and they also make it possible to augment the range by singling out a "subregion" of the patch, a specific initial state, which we believe could change the outcome having *any* objective probability.

This research strategy is, in a certain sense, the reverse of abduction and synchysis. If, by finding symmetry, abduction and synchysis make the surprising particular more continuous or expected by *linking* it to other particulars and to the general features they share, the goal here is to *unlink* an initial state to reach a point of Laplacean indifference, where the range of possible outcomes approach equality, or equal chance, and where what we could infer as probable based on frequencies now shows no predictable distribution over outcomes. *Philosophicus* sometimes calls this unlinked initial state the "chancemaker," and while we can try to find it by mimicking statistical modeling, to maintain our commitment to objective probability requires that we think differently about what a quasi-experimental design can teach us. Chancemaking, for the probabilist, is not limited to what we would need to *know* in order to translate a probabilistic assessment into an expectation about the future.[53] The difference in question concerns an idea mentioned earlier by both Kries and Peirce, as well as in sociology's rebuttal to the philosophers' association of objective probability and epistemic determinism, in which chancemaking is typically associated with an arbitrary function. If only actors can orient to *Chance*, and if we want our accounts to be ontologically valid, then for the probabilist, chancemakers are not an epistemic construct. We can actually find them in the world, and typically we will find chancemakers in the same place where we find the action. Consider the following example in this regard.

In sociologist Devah Pager's groundbreaking research, the "mark" of a criminal record and race itself—being Black, more precisely—operates as a kind of negative credential on the labor market.[54] Pager begins her argument by pointing to a set of probabilities that sociologists now know well: "Using longitudinal survey data, researchers have studied the employment probabilities and income of individuals after release from prison and have found a strong and consistent negative effect of incarceration."[55] But why is this? Pager's article focuses on the limitations of purely observational survey data to establish this finding. Incarcerated individuals can be different from non-incarcerated ones on an infinity of other (unmeasured, unmeasurable) characteristics. And even if we were to believe a given observational correlation, survey research is unable to "formally identify mechanisms" or the intervening process connecting independent (incarceration status, race) and dependent variables (call back by employer).[56] Pager's results have since passed into sociological lore as prime evidence for the existence and consequences of structural racism.

While, in Pager's study, the mark of a criminal record depressed the chances of being called back for an interview for whites, the surprise comes as the effects of race outweighed those of a criminal record. Specifically, Black testers *without* a criminal record were *less* likely to be called back than white testers *with* a criminal record, and Black testers with a criminal record were doubly discriminated against, having a minuscule probability (5 percent) of receiving a call back. While the criminal record functions as a "negative credential," whiteness serves as a positive credential, rendering criminalized white people more employable than non-criminalized Black people. Whiteness cancels any "error" produced by the perception of official criminalization, while Blackness does the same in the other direction, producing self-fulfilling evidence that in the labor market, to be Black is to be de facto criminalized. The "mark of a criminal record" is comparatively negated for whites in the same way that it is implicitly assumed for Black applicants, whether "marked" on paper or not. Therefore, "discriminatory allocation decisions" are really a systematic reinforcement of distinctly racialized outcomes.

In our view, the influence of Pager's study comes in how an unlinked initial state provides a window onto the chancemaker reflected in frequency counts. Racialized decision-making remains hidden in a veil of ignorance. The decision-maker predicts so as *not* to perceive, canceling discrepancies as they go along. As noted in chapter 6, that is what it means to be oriented to *Chance*. Calling back Black men without a criminal record would effectively amount to a perceptual overload, and so, *not making the call* becomes the adequate cause in this scenario—the cause that links a distribution over initial states with a distribution over outcomes, and without which we could not see the same kind of "patch" of maximal links. Taking the same action on its own, which Pager does by using a comparison of white applicants, shows a kind of equal chance—an initial state that does *not* produce a distribution over an outcome.

The structure that Pager reveals here is the structure of a chancemaker. *Philosophicus* sometimes refers to "Bernoulli distributions" to make sense of chancemaking, or "any two-outcome process in which the outcomes occur with fixed probabilities . . . and in which they are statistically independent."[57] If we could take apart every single case in Pager's dataset, we could describe each as a very small patch of its own, where initial states like incarceration status and applicant's race link to the outcome, specifically of call back, because of the chancemaking employer who confronts the two equally possible outcomes *directly*. The structure of chancemaking, then, puts them in a prime role. We can fill in the context of initial states that form part of these patches—say, in this case, with initial states that pertain to racial structure and racial capitalism, but which do not vary in any significant ratio across the different outcomes. Meanwhile, the employers' action, their confrontation with *Chance*, more directly creates the chances because it contains variability—in their allocation decisions, we can see those more general initial states, with their far-flung frequencies, *activated* (or not). Most importantly, because these employers are the chancemaker, the truth or falsity of the probability statements we make regarding race and employment in this case are ultimately made true or false by *them*, and the kind of "setup" that characterizes their situation as uniquely significant in an ontological sense.

To focus on a chancemaker, then, is akin to focusing on the nature of a *test*, as we mentioned in chapter 5 above. Chancemaking shares the goal of highlighting and foregrounding the "uncertainty haunting situations in social life," where "all powers" are *not* "fixed once and for all,"[58] even in the very ontology of a phenomenon that demonstrates stable frequencies. Notably, for the analyst, chancemaking situations will (epistemically) signal a kind of indifference when we find them, where we cannot judge probability based on our accumulated knowledge of initial states. In such instances, we have entered the region of the patch where equal chance lies waiting. Counting frequencies can help us make a probability judgment in that scenario, but only after we have gathered knowledge of probability of a non-quantifiable kind, specifically initial states and outcomes in a ratio that indicates relatively maximal links. Pager uses the phrase "discriminatory allocation decision" on the part of employers to refer to what resolves this indifference, turns equal chance into distributions, and thus serves as the venue for chancemaking that generates the probabilities that frequency counts register. The idea is not dissimilar from what we mentioned in chapter 1 when discussing Pascal's wager. Likewise, without that allocation decision in the face of equal chance, there would be no inequality. Nonetheless, the structure of chancemaking, or the ontology of the specific situation constant across all employers, means that these employers *have* to make a decision, which they can do even in apparent inaction (i.e., not making the call).

Much as Peirce emphasizes in discussing firstness, or what he sometimes refers to as "chance," or pure potential and possibility, to study chancemaking, we do not presume equality, nor do we presume individuals with the unique propensity to create *Chance* whenever they wish. As *philosophicus* helps us to clarify, there is, in social life, a structure to chancemaking that can be accessed via frequencies. Here, the goal is to translate that structure of chancemaking into a story about "where the action is."[59] The goal is to find action that is consequential, that carries stakes and thus a kind of fatefulness for those doing it. They perceive risk, and that risk could include the risk of perceptual overload depending on what they do (or don't do). This kind of action directly interacts with something approximate to equal chance. It is the action that does the most to link initial states and outcomes and thus *makes Chance* in a way we can measure and conceptualize. While frequency counts can help indicate probability, it takes the deftness of Pager's study—the kind of unlinking it engages in—to indicate it as squarely as this.

Steps Toward a Probabilist Method

As we have argued in this chapter, to do a third-degree monitoring, Bachelard-style, entails reaching into a conceptual space with a well-secured safety rope to pull us back in should we get too close to the brink. It entails questioning the nature of method itself. But there is precedent in what we do, as data science, we claim, has the same effect. To sketch some directions in probabilist method, as we have done, surely pales by comparison to recommendations[60] that have been made on the borderlands of sociology and data science, but that is ok with us. What we seek is not simply new methods to bring into the fold (and perhaps dominate) but more a vision of method not indebted to frequentist probability.

Post-positivist sociology might find itself in a position similar to the one described by the philosopher Alasdair Macintyre in reference to morality. To Macintyre, morality only persists in shards and pieces in the contemporary context. Certain words stick around, faint glimmers of dedication to what once was—"the integral part of morality has to a large degree been fragmented and then in part destroyed."[61] As mentioned in the introduction to this book, the logical-positivist recommendations for science provided a kind of complete picture that has subsequently been "fragmented and in part destroyed." That is a very good thing, in our view, but it leaves us with words and concepts, sets of expectations—"method," "theory," "data"—that float around somewhat mercurially and drift in opposite directions. We have mentioned the supermarket of theory and sui generis method above as evidence of a fragmentation that will only grow further with the advent of data-centricity in sociology. Probabilism sits alongside other efforts sensitive to this plight, among them abductive analysis and Bayesianism. Recent attention to "theorizing" in sociology could also be mentioned.[62] All appear to call for a reformation of sorts through more integration between the disconnected parts of sociological research.

For the probabilist, method is more akin to logic than anything else. To be "methodical" means to monitor, which can include what counts as data as we record it and how we are using data as we analyze it, but particularly in this case, it also means monitoring what we are implying is capable of action. Here we return to our discussion above of Bruno Latour and Isaac Reed, who both make similar recommendations akin to "following the actors" in the context of associations. As highlighted in this chapter in our attention to single-case analysis and chancemaking, there are strict terms of action according to probabilism, and they revolve around adequate causation. Seventeenth-century philosopher Baruch Spinoza informs this idea, as mentioned in part III above, and he draws a contrast between adequate and accidental causation. To act is to be the adequate cause of one's action, which we have resolved into the phrase "being oriented to *Chance*." For the probabilist, the cartographic appeal of data science can be helpful in finding patches, spaces of maximal links between initial states and outcomes, and to do so does not rest upon significance testing. Yet, using data to find out "where the action is" in these patterns requires understanding how action is adequate as it engages with *Chance* and hence loops into the world via expectation.

We return to these points in the next chapter. To close we simply offer the following: Could the standard suite of methods in sociology—from interviews to observations, historical narrative, content analysis, social-psychological experiments, and all manner of statistical techniques—be retained, should method in sociology be revised in a probabilist direction? Of course they should be retained, but the purpose and goal of those methods would be changed, should they be dedicated to the task of finding distinct patches of the social world and, within them, finding the action. Two questions become primary here, with several subsidiary ones: What is the *Chance*? And what actors are oriented to it? To be affected by an orientation to *Chance* does not require that all affected people be oriented to it in the same way. Weber tells us as much in *The Protestant Ethic*, and chancemaking from *philosophicus* suggests the same. But to understand how it is true requires that we reconfigure how we conceptually grasp the social world.

Reconfiguring Our Grasp on the Social World

In the social world, you don't convince anyone by quoting statistics. A scholar can never
have the last word if at a given moment the social truth is stronger than the scientific
truth. I think that this is also extremely important for understanding the peculiar status
of the social sciences.

PIERRE BOURDIEU, *Principles of Vision*

What could the difference be between a social truth and a scientific truth? In
the epigraph to this chapter, sociologist Pierre Bourdieu appears to associate
statistics with "scientific truth" and argues that, should anyone attempting to
study the social world leave their analysis with statistics alone, no one will be
convinced by it.[1] They will always want more of the story. Sociologists know
this, and we have dedicated ourselves to trying to convince others that *more*
is needed than statistics. The problem is that no one really seems to believe
us. Statistics are quoted all the time. But if they furnish a truth that we might
associate with objectivity, perhaps it is an objectivity that remains what it was
for the early frequentists, and thus effectively tantamount to whatever presentation of information is most transferable into a contentious political field
and might sometimes even convince the powers that be. To question probability as frequency typically means moving to Bayesianism, though in most
cases the motivation to do so appears to be simply finding a better version of
statistical truth. More rarely does a concern with truth migrate from statistics
into musings of an entirely different kind.

What kind of truth *could* statistics be? To call it "scientific truth," as Bourdieu does offhandedly, is vague, but maybe he still has a point. As scientific
truth, statistics would seem to comprise *probabilistic* truth, and perhaps the
same could be said of social truth. Probabilistic truth does not appear on
the roster of any philosophically recognized versions of truth that we know
of. If we can speculate, then, probabilistic truth would seem to be a form of

truth based first and foremost on an admission of ignorance. That basis would make it strange enough, but consider further, as we have argued, that to associate an admission of ignorance with a lack of data is misleading. If probabilistic truth is based on a *lack*, it is because of the nature of its object. If that object is probabilistic, then it can make statements about it that are true or false. But to be capable of doing so, and to remain probabilistic not as a function of epistemic ignorance, the object of probabilistic truth must be *real but unknowable in its entirety*. If we had a maximum of allowable data, by the best methods of collection and technologies of storage, it would not be as useful as other data could be for probabilistic purposes. The most useful data would be data on the sources of probability itself, but such data would not confirm our utter certainty; it would only confirm our confidence in the range of possible events.

The philosophers in the last chapter argued that probability statements are made true or false by reality. They would appear to agree with us on the nature of the object of probabilistic truth, though they do not go so far as to speculate on probabilistic truth. What *philosophicus* provides is an image of probability that allows us to study it as an objective reality. In this image, probability is akin to patches of n-dimensional vector space, available to designate as initial states maximally tied to points of outcomes. From the same initial-state space, different outcomes are possible. The same outcomes will not occur all the time but will yield a distribution. This image of probability means that the most local and particular data does not provide us with the best system to understand the world; what we need is a more coarse-grained approach willing to talk about wholes, fields, and spaces—to include complete pictures of the mosaic.

The philosophers argue that we need a different kind of data for the purpose; their image is intended to help define what that data could be. According to them, this different kind of data would, ideally, show us objective properties of the world that generate probability. It could include data about the structure of chancemaking, for example, or the construction of patches in the world that maximally link initial states and outcomes into distinct spaces or fields of probability, though such spaces or fields might only be activated under unique circumstances. The interesting thing, as mentioned in chapter 5, is that this kind of data is not representational in the conventional (positivist) understanding as is common today. Rather, it is more *relational*.[2]

This data consists of stored traces of the world, gathered in many ways that are not as concerned with sampling anymore. It is data that can be put to many uses. It is data that *is* data not because it represents a phenomenon that we define for it, but because of what it could tell us about what transpires in single cases of something more continuous. Single cases fall within a range, but a range of what? What is it that makes the cases that data tells us about *singular*?

All cases are singular, in other words, but they are not singular in the *same* way—they are singular only *within* a patch or space of probability. Whatever relative frequency distribution they might demonstrate, they all track back to a probability order. What the philosophers tell us about constancy tells us that single cases are not particular or local but symmetrical; they overlap with each other, though not entirely. These are essential points of a third-degree monitoring of method. The philosophers do not tell us much about what truth might look like if we take these points seriously. They do tell us that if probability is objective, then whatever makes our probability claims truthful cannot be limited to what might make our statistical claims valid.

Reality ultimately makes true or false any statement that concerns probability (e.g., the likelihood of a blizzard, the risk of a car accident, the chances of having a higher income at age thirty than your parents did). What matters are "facts independent of our state of mind or information." Statistics are valid when they access those facts, but the facts themselves are not statistical. Rather, they concern what *generates* the probability and, as in the last chapter, makes a statement like "There is a high probability of a hurricane" a *physical* and not a frequentist statement. What would these principles mean for social truth, which has for so long been graded by its proximity to statistics?

To attempt to answer that question, our starting point must be that objective probability (*Chance*) takes form as *expectation*—that is, as an embodied model of the world that allows us to reduce surprise by making predictions. Expectations search for environmental probability. The tendency to fall into habit is, here, manifest as the tendency of subjective expectations to match objective chances, in this way becoming bound by probability. The fact of expectation renders statistical truth wanting *and* allows social truth some independence from statistics. The best system for our probability claims would, in this case, include statements that cannot be statistically represented but are, nonetheless, matters of probability—a sense of what is likely to happen. Social truth could turn out to be something akin to evaluating the likelihood of an expectation. Unlike the Bayesians, however, a probabilist does not believe such evaluation is possible only by quantifying those expectations and what they lead us to believe.

A New Linguistic Analogue

The manifest form of probability orders always links to something latent. These are the mechanisms of the *Chance* world, including repetitions,

rhythms, sequences, and durations. It is in these modes that objective probability is available for learning. In chapter 6, we called this dynamic *vertical
capture*. Only by being vertically captured can the error minimization that
maintains *Chance* through action unfold horizontally, or forward in time.[3]
Vertical capture entails the formation of expectation—becoming *bound* by
probability. But far from this loop being the work of the head, it is more what
we might call the work of the body. The body entails a tendency to fall into
habit, to loop in, and to do so in a manner that cannot be subject to much
conscious control. Thus, to orient to *Chance* does not entail action that only
strategizes or appears rational under any description, though it does entail an
orientation to the expectations of others, which are accessible by judging the
probability of one's own action. The kind of recursive and loop-like connections evident here have been a principal focus of our argument so far in this
book, and they are, we believe, integral to any probabilistic reconfiguration of
our grasp on the social world. It is helpful, then, to consider first how we can
bear a modest witness to their tangled operation at work in the probabilistic
reconfiguration of our grasp of the *linguistic* world.

To reframe the foundation of core linguistic concepts like structure and
meaning in probabilistic terms changes what language is understood to be
and how truth can be generated about it. From a probabilist perspective, the
acquired ability to use and understand language does not depend upon innate, "biologistic" traits akin to what the linguist Noam Chomsky famously
called "universal grammar."[4] Neither is language an entirely an objective formation, the sort of structure of syntagmatic concatenations, paradigmatic
substitutions, and binary oppositions famously, and perhaps misleadingly,
linked to Ferdinand de Saussure as *langue*. Language is, rather, reconfigured
here at least as an analytic category along the lines of a corpus of content arranged by probability. When we learn language, we learn words, and we tie
words to cognitive metaphors; but we also learn probabilities, as guided and
reinforced by expectations.[5] Learning language entails learning *probability*,
and as a probability order par excellence, language allows for what we might
call a unique kind of precision guessing.

Thus, a typical language user orients to the place and context of word use.
Their fluency is a cognitive and perceptual habit gained by communicating in
ways that loop into what they've learned interlocutors will expect. Each context, habit, and muscle movement is a bearer of linguistic meaning, though it
remains filtered by a *guess*—what will loop into expectation? Frequency can
be helpful for this task. The easiest route to learn to *make* meaning is what
cognitive linguists call a kind of adaptive loop that takes form as "probability
matching." Thus, "if one wants to *maximize* one's probability of choosing the

right form on a particular test, one should always choose the most likely form given the current cues . . . Unless there are some occasions on which the more frequent form *will not do*, we should all *maximize*, choosing the more frequent form every time."[6] Fluency in a language entails knowing the frequency with which a given word is used in a particular context, and in a way that does to a remarkable extent mirror what we, as analysts, might calculate by simply counting word frequencies. Yet when we use language, we orient not to frequencies but to frequencies as *Chance*—as objective probability and how it serves as a window onto the expectations of others.

For the fluent language speaker, it becomes possible to augment frequency to create meaning: to use a rare word instead of a common one, "utilize" instead of "use," "fastidious" instead of "detailed." The words are not mere synonyms, in this sense, as they are the bearers of different probabilities.[7] Linguistic meaning thus consists, as all probability orders do, of distributions, and a distribution of word frequency becomes an initial state that links to outcomes. Among those outcomes is the meaning of a word as used in context, the response it elicits in relation to expectations. The maximal links between word frequency distribution and meaning supplies the basis of a patch, and as mentioned in the last chapter, patches provide us with an image of what we learn when we acquire expectation. To use a word on a given occasion involves the probability of using it, which loops into expectation. The capacity to use language more generally refers to the capacity to form expectations and to associate meaning via objectively existing probability or, in the more pleasing sense of saying the same thing—via *Chance*.

Language serves as arguably the principal example of what a probabilist might call *duration in action*. Every word used is *singular*; it cannot be interchanged with any other without difference, even though the available words might be of synonymous meaning. It is possible to create new words or give entirely different meanings to old ones (just consider the career of the English word "literally"). On a probabilistic understanding, then, a language is not arrayed by a general structural architecture or even essentially by grammar or syntax. A language is arrayed as a vast series of repetitions, single cases all singular in the same way, but also slightly different, one case not *entirely* the reflection of any other. These cases accumulate. They reveal distributions, which can be looped into in future language use as expectation. Thus, probabilism does not simply offer an update on the idea that "language is use." It means, rather, that every linguistic "trial" is a single case marked by the *Chance* of language.

The probabilistic reconfiguration of linguistic knowledge entails something very different from what we might be accustomed to assuming about language. *Chance* is inaccessible if we get too particular and local; though by studying the single case, what is carried over and constant between *every* single case of language use is accessible. If truth is our concern, then linguistic truth would be probabilistic. It would include what we have mentioned here: distributions, contexts of use, and probabilities reflected in musculature. But it would not treat these linguistic facts in a manner that makes them inaccessible to language users. On the contrary, the core of linguistic truth must remain ontologically credible—it must pertain to what can happen in a single case of linguistic action.

The influence of linguistic analogues in social science, especially in sociology and anthropology, was profound in the twentieth century. The language model at the root of "structuralism" still provides much of the image of structure for human scientists in these fields. "Language is use" has been influential to nearly the same extent, especially for those seeking a way out of structuralism. To find a new linguistic analogue for the social world, then, may offer a critical assist for those attempting, as we are, a reconfiguration of our grasp on the social world. Some might say that social truth is "structural." They are the inheritors of an old linguistic wisdom—so what about the new one?

What Is the Smallest Unit?

Historically in sociology, action once found a similar consideration as a "frame of reference."[8] That was Talcott Parsons's famous phrase, and it consisted of what Parsons considered to be the minimum features that apply to action as the "smallest unit" of a social system.[9] Parsons's instincts here are novel. He worries that a growing scientism will corrupt sociology. It will displace action with a concept like "behavior." The problem is that behavior is *too* small. Among other things, it forbids any connection of the smallest unit to a social system. While Erving Goffman, as we mentioned above, thought Parsons might have missed the key issue at stake, the older sociologist shared the goal of Goffman's Vegas *Theoria* in the sixties. Though his trip was limited to his own recessed thought and the proverbial armchair, Parsons was also trying to find out *where the action is*.

For Parsons, the smallest unit is action that has the ingredients necessary to still make a social system visible to us. His question of smallness is really a question of orientation. We should be able to pick out things that look like ends, means, conditions, and norms of action.[10] The action must be viewed with distance enough to allow us to see something that looks normative and something that looks conditional, with action trying to bring the two together. Finally, the sequence must be framed with enough temporal distance that we can see some time elapse and get a sense of process. For Parsons, examining some events that might look like action from either too close or too far away will lead us to miss these elements, but his reasoning here is not one in search of a kind of interpretive adequacy. The adequacy he is grasping for is different, as he defines the smallest unit. It is more like adequacy as social *truth*, which above all demands a continuism—with action as the smallest unit, we should be able to peer into a social system and bring it right before our eyes.

Parsons's frame of reference has been pilloried over the years—and we join the crowd—but if social truth may carry no apparent validity independent of statistical truth, it might be because, in the wake of Parsons's fall, no good answer has appeared for a basic question: *What is action for?* Parsons answered this question by positing values in the role of both goal and motivator, which he framed along lines of autonomy and resistance to force and arbitrariness. That was the systemic aspect. Action in the smallest unit kept a system as a parcel of autonomy alive in the world. Some action (like scratches, sniffs, and blinks) was *too* small for the task.

Consider, now, another view of action. Without a "metaphysical or epistemological guarantee of success . . . we do not know what 'success' would mean except simply 'continuance.' [For instance,] we are not conversing because we have a goal, but because Socratic conversation is an activity which is its own end . . . [The] conversation which it is our moral duty to continue is merely our project."[11] These are the words of the philosopher Richard Rorty, written many years after Parsons but drawing a different conclusion about the same question. Unlike a frame of reference, there is no sense in which action could be for anything beyond itself. To add such a condition would be to commit to a problematic metaphysics, in Rorty's view, that would open far more questions than it would ever resolve. Thus, in response to the question *what is action for?* we get the following response: *Action is for the continuation of action*, or at most the continuation of a project.

For us, an argument like this one constitutes not so much a theory of action as a different approach to it. If Parsons makes the *inflationary* mistake of saying that action has a certain essence or nature that adds too much to the smallest unit, saddling it with all kinds of unneeded (particularly functionalist) elements, then Rorty's approach provides a *deflationary* alternative, in which action is what allows for its own continuance, like "continuing the conversation" in Rorty's famous revision of philosophy itself as deflationary action.[12] In Giddens's own deflationary approach, action is for "ontological security" needed for a continuance of identity and for constancy of the "surrounding social and material environments of action," a "sense of the reliability of persons and things."[13] More recently, Isaac Reed ties human action to "iterative, nested and overlapping projects,"[14] in which small actions are tied to the realization of larger projects on varying scales—in his example, drinking coffee to be alert, being alert to do well on a job interview, scoring the job to get a paycheck, getting a paycheck to start a family. Action here is for the continuance of these projects, presumably their realization, and the smallest units we can find, we place within larger timeframes and orientations that might end only with the inevitable visit of mortality.[15]

The deflationist option seems to have won, then, in the current era of "posts." Action no longer registers as much of a unique concern on its own, as it becomes more non-topical—interpretively satisfying, to a minimum, while remaining noncommittal about further inferences. To reference something as "action," in this case, is not an attempt to convince anyone of anything, as it was for Parsons, which contributes to a certain paradox. Under a deflationary view, so much could be considered "action" that typically nothing specific is. The concept is omitted far more frequently than it is invoked, as presumably there is not much to be gained by describing an "action" under a deflationary definition. Comparable concepts, like "practice," offer slightly more specificity and insight, but their application remains targeted—practices are typically singular *nouns* rather than elemental to all of social life.[16]

Nothing could be more different from the spirit of Parsons, who in defining a smallest unit attempted to articulate where action could be found, regardless of what specific topic might fall into our empirical focus. By striking a happy medium, Parsons thought action could do this task without being watered down *too* much, losing all definition. It is on this score that Parsons sought what we are calling a social truth, which can be convincing without and even *despite* statistics. Having arrived at action as the core of some version of social truth, one which all social science could unite under in distinct specialties, Parsons would be inspired to continuously refine it, identifying what we could read from action once we found it, as something whose mysteries could even reveal the very truth of "the human condition" to be contained within boxes and arrows.[17]

The two positions have a Scylla and Charybdis quality. The fortunes of inflation and deflation are tied to each other. The latter is shaped, in large part, by a will to avoid the excesses of the former, which are easy to ridicule. The former, meanwhile, contains an ambition entirely foreign to social theory today. The inflationary tendencies that characterized Parsons's faith in action appear emblematic of a Kantian faith that, in this case, action could be extended to its *conceivable* limits, removed of all unnecessary empirical elements. A different inflation might be the Hegelian version, as expressed by the philosopher Alexandre Kojève during lectures given in Paris around the same time Parsons was writing his book in Cambridge. For Kojève, humans are "negating *Action* [*l'Action*], which transforms given Being and, by transforming it, transforms itself." Thus, humans are also therefore "History only in and by *Action* that negates the given, the Action of Fighting and of Work."[18] Both efforts appeared to inflate action in significance in order to reach social truth. But there is an alternative, we believe, to these two options and what we see as their mutual limitations.

As discussed in chapter 6, predictive processing (PP) presents action as its central concept in developing a general theory of perception and cognition. Every key idea that the paradigm shift proposes works through action.[19] Here, action marks the meeting point of the looping architecture that applies to a living organism's engagement with the world. On the one hand, "action is the only way to underwrite an upper bound on the entropy of sensations. On the other hand, perceptual inference is the only way to inform action."[20] There is a loop here, and it serves a very specific purpose in this case. We can illustrate it with a problem that arises in predictive processing called the "dark-room problem."[21]

The problem goes something like this: If cognition is dedicated to the ceaseless reduction of uncertainty, or "free-energy minimization," in anticipating environmental contingencies, why do we not simply flee those contingent environments entirely and seek perpetual solace in a "dark room"—a space characterized by such complete sensory deprivation that nary a contingency is to be perceived? There does not seem to be a great organismic tendency to do such a thing, but why not? For predictive processing, action serves not only as the main route into the world becoming perceptually available to us, but also as the main route by which we can remind ourselves that we are in it. If we do not tend to search for a dark room, it is because, typically, we are not drawn toward such an environment to confirm our own existence in the world. It gives us no sense of being alive (though it does help us fall asleep). We are drawn, rather, to dynamic spaces of probability that *can* do offer us just such a confirmation, which in a PP formulation is vital not for existentialist purposes, necessarily, but for homeostatic integrity.

Thus, a probabilist will certainly say that action is *for* something, and what it is for, apropos of pragmatism, is not something transcendent of action or lacking in practical consequences that require an inflation of terms. However, to equate action with mere "continuance" is deflation gone too far.[22] The assumption that action is *present* and *occurs* remains one of the least questioned among deflationary approaches to action. With so few essential features, deflationary approaches imply that action is present *everywhere* and occurs *the same way*. While their analytic dissection of action can resemble Parsons's action frame of reference, action here is not distinguishable as the "smallest unit" where we can still see traces of something with greater range, like a social system. Action is distinguishable, rather, from what remains when all else has been deflated down (e.g., desire-belief-opportunity, problem-solving, projects), so we can simply plug-and-play the terms.

In our view, a renewed theory of action that pivots from the inflationary views emblematized by Parsons's ambition, but pivots differently than deflation's downward momentum, is needed for the present and future of social science, should social scientists put up a resistance to reductionist tendencies of a data-centric social knowledge. From that perspective, what action seems to be *for* is the collection of data and the building of a record, typically to extract value.[23] How often do you visit a website? How long do you linger? What do you click on? How many times? Of particular importance, too, is the interface with the recording apparatus: How fast do you swipe and type? With what force and pressure of the thumbs and fingers?

The most deflationary view of action would dispute whether these behaviors constitute action; even for that approach, they seem entirely *too* small. The smallest unit in a data-centric definition appears to be whatever constitutes the most localized and particular matters of fact that a machine can record and store. A sociologist partial to deflation might counter the data scientists by suggesting that the data gathered should be a little more coarse-grained to allow for an inference like, what problems might be *being* solved on these website visits? The data scientists might respond with a Laplacean quip: They simply do not need a hypothesis such as "problem-solving" to make the same inferences as the deflationary sociologist. The data itself will tell enough of the story to predict the problems and projects in our lives—like, allegedly in a famous case, whether our child is pregnant, even though they have not told us (and might not know themselves).[24]

Data-centricity, then, constitutes the *ultimate* deflation of action. Our concern is that its definition of "small" is not that distant or different from an approach like "continuance" but requires none of the same conceptual grounding to reach the same insights. As we will argue further below, action for predictive processing holds a promise of renewal beyond inflated and deflated trajectories. What we stand to lose by data-centric deflation can only become clear if we first attend to the most important aspect of action in a probabilist sense; specifically, the nature of *looping*.

Consider the much remarked-upon relationship between AI-generated text and human-generated text. Even if AI can successfully produce a human sentence or an entire undergraduate term paper, human-generated text remains irreducible to it and irreplaceable by it. But why? The best answer is the most obvious one—because humans alone *produce* the text. The machines can do their magic by mimicking that production in an engineered repetition, using embedding vectors, distance metrics between words, and weighted values. An obvious answer is not necessarily a simple answer, however, as in this case it requires that human generators of text do something remarkable—like loop into linguistic *Chance* and produce repetitions both expressive and original, while also *expectable* by their interlocutors. So how does looping work?

Three Kinds of Looping Effect

A loop is simply a shape, but of a unique kind—it is shape in *motion*. It is hard not to identify a loop without either seeing it be created or recreating it in a mental simulation. A loop crosses itself and returns to its starting point; but it returns slightly changed and altered, at the very least because it is now asking to be extended again (if it has not been already) to create another shape, and so on and so on. On its path, a loop may intersect with something else in space and time, and by returning to its starting point, it *connects* the two. The "first" in a loop is a temporal distinction, not a causal one. Whatever is "second" in the loop is what it connects. Altogether, the loop itself stands as a "third" element that appears from their connection. Among the advantages of the architecture of the loop is how it allows for probability. Because loops are active and must be recreated, they are maintained by opening a field of probability with just enough continuity (i.e., a replication proportionally close to 1) in each repetition to create expectation. Here, contingency is absorbed by what is probable, which does not mean that a loop predetermines what *will* happen but only the way it *could* happen within a range of possibility, and that when it *does* happen, it can be expected.[25] More generally, a loop architecture allows for a translation of social formations of all scales into the analytic terms mentioned in the last chapter. A loop produces its effects through initial states, outcomes, and constancy between them.

A non-probabilistic sociology will be empirically "hesitant," Du Bois argues, because it will always create a trap between unpalatable binaries or dualities.[26] By contrast, he sought to be non-hesitant, and not fearful of the physicists, by putting seeming opposites like "Chance" and "Law" under the same umbrella, talking about them both at the same time. A loop architecture is helpful for the purpose. A loop is not a *duality* that links two things understood to exist in different ontological registers and whose relation is, therefore, as arbitrary as water mixed with oil—they never merge but create a kind of liquid layer cake. Duality applies when, for instance, one party to the relation is considered "virtual" and the other "actual." In Du Bois's terms, that would be a recipe for hesitancy, as it delineates a kind of division of academic labor, akin to only talking about law and leaving chance unexplained. A *dialectic* relation gets us closer to looping effects. However, to the extent that one thing stands only as the negation of the other in a dialectic relation, it does not demonstrate a loop architecture, as in every dialectic looping there would be a kind of deformation and remaking of the parts.[27] In a loop, the relating parties *incorporate* each other in a probabilistic or proportional sense. For Du Bois, only by the combination of "Chance" and "Law" is it possible to account for something that loops like a "rhythm" and depends on a ratio of both Chance and Law in every single instance. For the probabilist, a loop creates the basis for *repetition* with a unique ontology, one comprised of single cases or instances that remain symmetrical and analogous to each other. A loop can maintain the singular nature of each *looping-in* as a product of the same range—much as each living organism is a singular product of the same DNA.

We tend to think of formations of great scale and duration like social structures according to interchangeable characteristics. Each part of the structure is made general rather than particular; that is a good way, as we suggested in the last chapter, to explain far-flung frequencies. We can do the same if we attempt to dissect a structure into component parts, like "rules [or schemas] and resources," as demonstrated in first by Giddens in a central problems formulation, and later taken up again and revised by historian William Sewell in a vastly influential framework.[28] That is the standard way to grasp the social world using the concept of structure.

But consider the following distinction that might seem only distantly related: between the echo of a song, which works through repetition, and an exchange of money, which works according to the generality we are describing. The connection of money to what it can buy is perfectly arbitrary. Just compare an actual US ($) dollar with an actual gallon of milk. The two are connected because they have been made equivalent to each other. As Marx describes it, that equivalence is only possible because both money and milk have been rendered "abstract" and interchangeable once shifted into the realm of "exchange-value."[29] Money can adequately cause milk to appear, and it becomes the only thing that will do so. We would not be mistaken in thinking that this process does work by simply following general rules.

The echo, by contrast, retains the same characteristics as its original creation in every single moment it remains perceivable.[30] The sounds it loops together are all sequentially related in a rhythm, rather than arbitrarily set alongside each other. The echo is a good example of a modulation, where the past shapes the avenues down which the future can go. The first sound opens the range for all the others, following a probable path. Whatever is original can become expected; deviations become noticeable. In the case of the echo, as the looping effect from past into future becomes melodic, it must *repeat*, and each repetition regenerates a *potential* for future iterations. A loop does not completely recreate its initial state, however, but retains it in a large enough ratio across its outcomes that the initial state is taken up and made anew. That initial state will fade, however, as the gap or *in*constancy among single loopings grows over time and the echo disappears, or else turns into something else—perhaps by being preserved in audio form as a patch of data points, or in written form as musical notation. Whenever it is repeated, the same looping effects will return.

So where does thinking probabilistically, with repeating looping effects, get us? It might lead us to revise the dualism evident between money and milk, perhaps much as Marx himself did in making the argument that, actually, milk *can* make money appear, and vice versa, when they are both possessive of value and their connection a single case of capitalist accumulation, which must loop and loop and loop, presumably forever.[31] Our suggestion, then, is threefold: (1) There is precedent in theorizing looping effects to grasp the social world, but (2) those prior efforts needs be revisited and read critically to reveal how they are probabilistic, and (3) once we do that, we can come together with predictive processing and take action as our main concern to bring forth a version of probabilistic truth. To make that point relevant to our grasp on the social world, we must first flesh out a few varieties of looping effects as we can observe them in varied forms. The first of these we will call *interpretation* (structures), the second *description* (enclosures), and the third *probability* (modulations).

INTERPRETATION LOOPS

For an interpretation loop, let us take Sewell's framework, which has proven integral to theorizing how social structure constitutes itself. A concentration on "duality" in his formulation features a distinction between schemas and resources, in a slight alteration of Giddens's rules and sources. A "mutually sustaining" loop of schemas and resources resolves them into an adequate relation according to the following influential formula and applied to a theory of structure: "Structures . . . are constituted by mutually sustaining cultural schemas and sets of resources that empower and constrain social action and tend to be reproduced by that action. Agents are empowered by structures, both by the knowledge of cultural schemas that enables them to mobilize resources and by the access to resources that enables them to enact schemas."[32]

Such a loop does suggest a deeper effect, as the very constitution of a set of properties in the world as "resources" is schema-dependent, just as the constitution of "schemas" is resource-dependent. In this case, an interpretation of those properties as resources of a certain kind arises through a process that Sewell compares to "reading" them. A certain reading of these properties as resources will only become enshrined as the right or, indeed, the only one, however, if it does in fact work: if it does, that is, turn those properties into resources. Such a relation has all the hallmarks of a loop that restarts at its own initial state, having been extended into space and time. Sewell puts it as follows, using a poignant example: "When the priest transforms the host and wine into the body and blood of Christ and administers the host to communicants, the communicants are suffused by a sense of spiritual well-being. Communion therefore demonstrates to the communicants the reality and power of the rule of apostolic succession that made the priest a priest. In short, if resources are instantiations or embodiments of schemas, they therefore inculcate and justify the schemas as well."[33]

As we have noted before, interpretation can stabilize a situation in which initial states are highly sensitive, with small changes corresponding to wildly shifting outcomes. It seems that that capability is exercised here. In the case of a scenario like the beginnings of the Catholic Church, such a stabilization is crucial given the broad proliferation of religious practices—at the time and still—and thus the need to establish an authoritative interpretation of liturgy, which can offer this reading of resources but also make them the *only* resources. The problem is to think of this reading as fundamentally a relation between two ontologically different things, like "ideas" and "material properties." That is what causes Sewell (and before him Giddens) to talk about virtual relations that have real effects. That notion is paradoxical, to be sure, but it also means that the relation turns into a generality that can only explain single cases by abstracting from them—it can only explain things nomologically, to use Kries's words.

Authority appears to be the only way a mutually sustaining loop can appear from duality, which ontologically speaking is a further obfuscation. The goal would be to see how reading is more like creating constancy between initial states and outcomes, as opposed to a model of reading that gives meaning to something that is, by nature, chaotic and without meaning. The schemas that interpret resources are those that stabilize the links between initial states and outcomes. In this case, doing so means ensuring that the priestly transformation of the body and blood of Christ are all that will predict a "sense of spiritual well-being," as opposed, say, to a different pathway to the same sense, one involving an unpredictable array of practices. A schema like "exchange-value," for instance, can render new resources by finding that only certain ways of using material properties in the world can predict "value." Capitalism could not exist if not for such a looping effect, of universal and seemingly perpetual extension, capable of eroding all other distinctions that might apply to those material properties. Thus, interpretation secures a basic stability in initial states, anchoring an expectation in what will lead to what, and as it does so, probability distributions appear—of actions, events, changes to physical environments—all as outcomes with constancy, within the same patches, with shared initial states. The result will be a loop that propels itself forward, largely on the grounds of action that can now unfold according to what means what, what signifies what, and what can be expected to *be* what—or the looping effects of interpretation.

Part of the appeal of Sewell's loop is its scalar ability. A structure of a small range (a family tradition) can be explained in the same way as a structure of a large range (global capitalism). We might ask, however, whether anything can be made into a schema/resource loop and exercise looping effects? Such a question draws our attention, again, to the probabilistic aspects of interpretation, that more fundamentally than finding meaning in what is meaningless it consists of a loop architecture connected by probability. We can put a certain schematic stock in the result of a coin toss, for example; we can interpret its results as signifying this or that. On those grounds, we can build a structure according to what is repeated on each toss of the coin. But, as you might be thinking, to do so would indicate something quite peculiar about a coin as a resource—specifically, we cannot control what the results of a given toss will be, unless we rig it, of course—which as we noted above with testing and games, is part of the appeal of sports, though here it makes us consider why something like capitalism is actually not decided by the results of a coin toss, as much as possible, at least for those who stand to benefit the most. The coin is impervious to interpretative and schematic assimilation of its material properties on some level—and we might say the same about the Earth itself relative to a schema like exchange-value—but to appreciate that point requires a framework that finds limitations in *how much* of an outcome a given initial state can remain constant with and therefore predict.

If there is instability in a structure built on the results of a coin toss, it would also indicate that a schema does not read a resource only *once*. To shift from duality to a loop, and to capture the probabilistic aspects of Sewell's framework, repetition must be brought into the fold, and with repetition comes thinking about the singular. Every single iteration of a structure is a singular looping effect. To ignore this point, which is typically the case, means that looping effects are discussed separately from the prevalence of scaled orders and formations, with phenomena of great range typically associated with structures (or institutions) as encompassing containers (or highly general "logics"), with each individual only available to theorize (as we saw in chapter 5 with class structure) as they are contained by the structure and substitutable with every other. They are not considered in a probabilistic sense as a singular product that demonstrates partial but not *entire* overlap with every other. Our point is that without considering duality as a loop, sociologists will have a difficult time distinguishing the effects of structure from, say, laws or rules—which do apply generally, and which allow us to remain effectively oblivious to single cases—or determining how to answer a question about the singularity of a case, how "single" does not mean as local and particular as the data will allow us to get, and what a single case is a case of.

The appeal of Sewell's interpretation loop, then, is enhanced when we consider it probabilistically as a looping effect. A repeating relation consists of an initial state held constant across outcomes in ratio enough to sustain an order or pattern as a probability order, which is produced in every iteration and thus is slightly varied across what the loop establishes as single cases. The looping effect of interpretation is to prevent the small variations in initial states from becoming big variations in outcomes. There is contingency here—one schematic interpretation is interchangeable with another and therefore replaceable—but it is *symmetry* that more accurately describes the contingency. As different initial states, interpretations constitute a more or less one-to-one replacement of each other (e.g., healthcare as a resource that predicts "value" in capitalist terms or as a resource that predicts human dignity and social justice). Symmetry is why interpretation can be the "difference that makes the difference."[34] It is harder to appreciate the gravity of this point without seeing that difference as working through a repeating loop. Another way of creating a loop does not interpretively secure some initial states against chaos but instead links descriptions with scattered empirical traits in a self-sustaining identification.

DESCRIPTION LOOPS

In Ian Hacking's analysis of "looping kinds," there is evidently more attention to a particular looping effect. Loops here emerge via a classification and categorization that feeds a "dynamic nominalism." As Hacking describes them, descriptive looping effects are different from "arid and scholastic forms of nominalism," because they refer to an active process in which "our spheres of possibility, and hence ourselves, are to some extent made up by our naming and what that entails."[35] Hacking's looping kinds have become so popular that they are often treated as synonymous with any mention of "looping effects."[36] But for our purposes, the dynamism of description loops are perhaps undersold if they are not conceived as repetitions, with each instance conceivably modeled as looping-in.

Unlike an interpretation, a description does not alter the properties or traits it describes by reading them in a certain way and giving them meaning and significance. Rather, a description bundles the equivalent of resources together as, instead, being traits that become tautologous with the description—to define what it is requires describing them. In any description loop, then, classifications are made by people as an index of traits and properties. In what we might call more specifically a *Hacking* loop, these traits are given a vertical source in the authority and expertise of those who exercise a kind of total control over the description, but who do not maintain it horizontally themselves; those who are classified horizontally maintain the description, thereby rendering it dynamic.

The classifiers, in this case, "create certain kinds of people that in a certain sense did not exist before." Such a nominal category is legitimized and managed by expertise, elaborated by institutions, and officialized by bureaucracy, all of which reinforces its external and public existence as recognizable and expectable. In one example, Hacking describes the creation of "multiple personalities." At one point, it "was not a way to be a person, people did not experience themselves in this way, they did not interact with their friends, their families, their employers, their counselors, in this way." At least not in 1955. But by 1985, the story had changed. It had become possible "to be a person, to experience oneself, to live in society" with multiple personalities.[37] The intervention of thirty years meant the formulation of this name, the proliferation of knowledge about it, and the accumulation of traits under its heading. But most of all, it entailed people forming a self-identification by looping into "multiple personality disorder" and then turning aspects of themselves into traits ("*this is that*"). While the now-indexed traits might have preceded the name, their prior existence is not Hacking's main concern. As a "way to be a person," rather, a description like "I have multiple personality disorder" becomes an enclosure within the category by looping into its index and using these traits as a way of indexing *oneself* ("*that is me*"), which more specifically means making inferences about one's experience (*this is that* ↔ *that is me*) and more generally forming expectations about what those traits mean, what the future will probably bring, and how other people will likely (or in some cases, should) treat you.

The initiating category can become standardized, rationalized, and increasingly externalized. In such cases, a descriptive looping effect can become highly predictive of those who loop into it. To be a certain type of person, to live in society as that person, to be interacted with as that person, and most importantly, to experience oneself as that person—these identifications can occur in a way that makes one meet clearly defined expectations. For other descriptions, which appear less externalized, the looping effect does not carry the same predictability. It can, rather, be subject to wide variations in what it entails, which can be part of its appeal: The room exists to define it because it does *not* seem so set in stone.

To call looping effects "descriptive," then, is to say that they are *descriptively constructive*. A category or classification is "deep" only in a contingent sense. The loop rests upon empirically available traits made into traits of an indexed property (a disorder, a race, a crime). The dynamic nature of a description becomes visible with what Elizabeth Anscombe once called "action under a description."[38] Externally imposed categories provide plausible descriptions of action, particularly that the action is motivated in some kind of way. We can find it in Michel Foucault's *History of Sexuality*, as a description comes to apply to actions that are "sexuality" and those that are perversion.[39] This description only appears when the *scientia sexualis* constructs and maintains the description according to a "will to truth." This description follows a similar description to the *ars erotica* that does not feature the will to truth. The most significant difference arises between the looping effects of each, with only sexuality leading to a "subjection" and ultimately "subjectivation," because it puts action under a description and attaches normativity to it. There seemingly could not be a better recipe for using a description to create looping effects with high predictability because of the kind of expectations they yield.

When looping effects become uniform because of a description, as they do in the case of sexuality, the aggregate effect is an *enclosure*. In this case, people are enclosed by the description, because their traits and actions are described. The enclosure created by a description could make *all* future examples fall under it. Thus, "multiple personality disorder" simply *is* the traits named as "multiple personality disorder." As the name or category is enacted by someone diagnosed with the disorder, they are now the type of person who has "multiple personality disorder," yet beyond the description and its attachment to them (*this is that = that is me*), there is no further relation between the description and traits, or between the description and the persons it describes.

In our terms, the looping effect of description provides the grounds for looping in each application or in each action that falls under it. Whatever is so described is thereby *expected* to be or to appear a certain way; the description allows for certain inferences to be drawn, which can become stereotypical, strictly nominal. Though, when the description becomes a point of orientation for those whom it describes, not merely for its expert creators, that nominalism becomes dynamic in its looping effect. Different sets of traits could be made to fit the description. Even if the description was meant just to describe, the looping effect creates an enclosure when the description begins to draw out ranges in the world. Without this addition, there is no clear understanding of what it would mean *not* to loop into a description when one is expected to, apart from, perhaps, inviting the violent enforcement of the description and its maintenance on expected terms.

As we have argued, to appreciate both structures and enclosure as looping effects requires a framework of continuous looping-in, which makes each effect or each singular case the products of the same *Chance*, even if they seem highly variable. Schemas and descriptions initiate each loop, and the persistence of resources or traits creates the grounds for expectation that grows with further looping. As this framework might suggest, both looping effects presuppose a further kind. Embedded here is a looping effect that can emerge independently of names, indexed traits, schemas, or resources. Probability can create a looping effect all on its own, in what we will call the construction of a modulating effect. It is this effect that comes to fruition most distinctively in the interface between machine and social learning.

PROBABILITY LOOPS

The shape of a loop, then, for both a structure and enclosure, starts with a kind of arbitrary investment. That investment refers to the interpretation or description. An interpretation has a looping effect when it makes certain material properties meaningful as a resource. Likewise, a description has a looping effect when it makes certain traits fit a certain kind of definition, thus defining what something is in the world. A probability loop is different from both. Not only are probability loops essential to all others, but they also have no need for a contingent starting point. A looping effect can instead emerge as a *modulating* effect, which arises when the logical connection between initial states and outcomes becomes a kind of closed link. When that happens, the future is modulated by the past. As the past accumulates (as data or record), a future becomes increasingly structured and channeled, to the point where all future options come to be reflections of all past ones. For no other reason, those options might be appealing to us because we have learned to *expect* them. Modulation typically exercises a looping effect directly through probability, which means that these loops, above all, can have the most encompassing effects on cognition.

In one version of this loop, the tale is told indicatively as follows: "Acrimonious debates about the calculative abilities of individuals and the limits of human rationality have given way to an empirical matter-of-factness about measuring action in real life, and indeed in real time. The computers won, but not because we were able to build abstract models and complex simulations of human reasoning. They bypassed the problem of the agent's inner life altogether. The new machines do not need to be able to think; they just need to be able to learn. Correspondingly, ideas about action have changed."[40] Here, a proposal for non-intentional action becomes applicable to data-gathering mechanisms, but the index is rather different in this scenario, as it requires no description. Meanwhile, culture becomes more akin to an association than an interpretation; it stands for a history of traces. A theory of action remains, even though there is no inner life to speak of. Because action is stored and recorded as data, data can have a modulating effect on action by "herding" or "funneling"—that is, by targeting some initial states by their link to outcomes, constructing new parameters based on current action, taking these parameters as initial states, feeding action forward into outcomes, and so on. This process is how action can lead us onto a preselected patch.

In a modulation, a certain future becomes programmable as opposed to projected. Possibilities are presented algorithmically and displace what, by comparison, is a "wild" cognition of uncontrolled looping. Control becomes an algorithmic modulation of future possibilities, most evident in the systematic production of "good matches" based on controls exercised from both ends—a production that keeps the loop closed between the objective provision of possibilities and subjective anticipations or guesses, a closure that makes "this matching feel all the more natural because it comes from within—from cues about ourselves that we volunteered, or erratically left behind, or that were extracted from us in various parts of the digital infrastructure."[41]

A modulated looping effect is, therefore, typically more subtle than one initiated by an interpretation or a description. You will know, for instance, when a description no longer applies to you or to the kind of person it describes you to be. The same is true of a structure. It will become readily apparent if you try to actualize a possibility not opened by interpretations that keep stable links between initial states and outcomes (like, say, inventing your own ritual in the middle of a church ceremony). Outside a structure, the very same action will not elicit such a response. Boundaries are less definitive in a modulation, however, as the initial states are immanent to the loop, rather than introduced in arbitrariness as an interpretation or description.

In a modulation, the initial states are more difficult to escape or even notice, though it is through initial states that outcomes become available. A modulation is dynamic and adaptable as a "self-deforming cast that will continually change from one moment to the other, or a sieve whose mesh will transmute from point to point."[42] Thus, the control evident in such a probability loop demonstrates no need for schemas or standards. Initial states are *volunteered* rather than enforced or imposed. Even as an individual becomes a record, however, there is no apparent record-keeping individual ("examiner" or "recorder") to construct and impose categories or descriptions. Rather than being incorporated into a structure through schemas, individuals are made into a code or classification based on what is collected and recorded about them. On these grounds, they are not forced into a mold, as a description loop can do; rather, in a modulation, the effect is to make us *precise*.[43]

In a modulation, individuals are given a future in which to range. It all might seem free. After all, an algorithmic modulation is typically organized by presenting *a lot* of options from which to choose. Individuals loop into *Chance* that looks increasingly like good matches, then, as *Chance* is built according to a past sequence of looping. But there is a catch. To break from a probability loop can produce an experiential manifold a little like the one that characterizes the amnesiac who recovers their memory after a time of memory blankness. In such a scenario, they might exclaim: "My God! What did I do in all those years!?"[44] Now consider that moment of "coming to" after diving down an algorithmically modulated "rabbit hole." A rabbit hole might not last for years—though it could—yet the effect of leaving one is the same, even if the waking moment has a different source. It demonstrates what happens when our cognition, already predisposed to looping into partially predictable environmental cues, catches itself in a reflexive moment, which could simply be boredom, that draws us out and into a different orientation to a different *Chance*.

For interpretation and description loops, most of the *Chance* available in the social world pertains to a materially and symbolically affected being, vertically arranged by a schematic assimilation or classification, to engage with resources and properties or traits within a range of possibility. For probability loops, however, the same passage through a vertical capture is not necessarily contingent on anything serving in a similar role as prior. An interpretation or a description serves as the grounds for expectations of resources and traits; for a probability loop, the past does, but with the caveat that within modulations, only *certain* elements of the past are preserved and maintained as prior.

Significant differences, then, can be found between these loops. The digital technologies that shape so many contemporary action environments lend themselves to the proliferation of modulations far easier than interpretation or description loops and the probability orders they create in the form of structures and enclosures. The latter often seem old by comparison, and they typically are indeed old, as new structures and enclosures, we can assume, are comparatively rare. But the interaction between these probability orders presents a different way of grasping the social world. As we have suggested above, when gender becomes affected by a modulation more than an enclosure or structure, it changes the gender categories typically referenced and used in an analytic sense. Gender modulation, outside its effect as a structure or enclosure, seems to be made possible largely by its presence in a digital space, which among other things preserves a far more varied history than a binary one. To have one's gender identity oriented toward a modulated *Chance* rather than a structured or enclosed one, matters.

As we stress, structure, enclosure, and modulation—these are not "things." They are looping effects. They are, in other words, specific outcomes of looping into the world based on specific kinds of initial states—from interpretations, to descriptions, to priors that preprogram the future. An important front that this understanding opens is in the study of cross-mappings between looping effects: phenomena, like gender, race, and class, organized by all of them. Does one set of looping effects prevail? Have they always? And what happens when new phenomena emerge, as new probability orders, due to the looping effects of either (or all) of these three kinds? While their differences are appealing because they can allow us to ask questions like these, those differences should not lead us to ignore an important commonality among these effects, which is rooted in an essential part of the looping architecture. Across all three examples, we notice the necessity of *twos*. Here we can return to a point that Peirce makes about *chance* (the lowercase-*c* kind).

Anything on its own, according to Peirce, is logically available only as pure possibility or "chance."[45] It will remain that way until we bring ourselves into relation with it and create a relation of *two*. In this dynamic, the *first* thing forces us to acknowledge it; there is always an element of passivity to the relation. That is why, in discussing abduction, Peirce associates secondness with a sense of surprise. A dyadic framework like this one is artificial, however, because we never relate to anything by stopping at just *two*; there is always a *third* involved—specifically, our habitual self-impression (*Interpretant*) that brings how the chancy first affects us, the second, into some kind of continuum, part of a triad—making *its* effect the effect *of* something on *us*. In an interpretation or description loop, the resources and traits are a potential. Schemas and descriptions serve as the continua in which engagement with them unfolds, activating that potential. But as continua, interpretation and description are more arbitrary than they need to be. Because anything single can *only* be a potential, interpretation and description are built upon probability loops, which means that our habitual self-impressions, what the effect of a first is the effect *of* on us, reflects objective probability or patches of *Chance* in the world.

For our purposes, these points are especially relevant not only for answering questions we mentioned above in chapter 5, using the plight of the poor graduate student pondering what their case is a case *of*, but also for explaining a probability loop and the effects it creates. As a modulation, a probability loop requires as little of a *third* as is necessary. An algorithmic modulation, for example, has "content," though that content is typically forgettable and often only peripherally connected to what the modulation needs to exercise a looping effect. Principally, the effect arises because of a looped connection between the past, *any* past, that acts as a control on the future.[46] For Peirce, probability in the relation of *twos* is implied by our action in the world; but in this case, thinking about counterintuitive sequences seems to matter, a point that draws our attention to a larger concern, inching us a little closer to the nature of social truth.

A New Continuity Frame

Suppose we assume that interpretation must come *first* in a sequence of the following kind: *Interpretation → Perception → Action*. We can find this assumption in the argument that schemas are the first step in the formation of structure because they "read" resources,[47] or that a perception can only happen once a description has been given.[48] However, for an account that takes what we have described as the relation of *twos* seriously, the sequence would likely be more like this one: *Action → Perception → Interpretation*. In this case, only through action do we discover what potentials are there in front of us, what is different from us, and toward what we must orient and loop in. It is only in a third movement that we interpret, and we only feel the need to interpret based on what we have perceived. Since action comes first, what we perceive are the differences, what is unexpected and insistent—what, in other words, compels our acknowledgment of it.

A sequence like this one can seem entirely scrambled relative to the more straightforward one. Among other reasons, the straightforward sequence appears to map onto the arrow of time. In the straightforward sequence, the past generates probability about a yet-to-occur future: *Past* → [Present] → *Future*. The present has no apparent role to play, being only a mediating point from which to notice the past and future. Among other things, the absent present means that the present needs its own vocabulary to include things like "lived experience" that can accumulate as memory and be hoped for in the future, but which really live nowhere else but in the present.

A scrambled sequence that puts action first draws on the past to generate a present, but it does so only after having first engaged the world on the basis of a future: *Future* → *Past* → *Present*. This sequence means we have no other option but to engage the world through a kind of guessing that loops into the future. When we do so, the outcome immediately comes back to us, in our initial state, and tells us what it is: how rare it is and what is problematic about it—what we need to notice about it. This sequence does not depend on our knowledge of the past. It does depend, however, on our orientation to *Chance* in the form of the singular (potential) things we loop into in this way and now exist in a field of probability with. Any significant deviation from our initial state becomes apparent to us in the present; it is what we notice. Indeed, that deviation constitutes whatever is *present* for us, in turn dictating how *we* are present.

In scrambling these two sequences, several things become clear about our pursuit of social truth. First, to shift to either of the latter sequences, or preferably both, would serve to demonstrate that whatever else it is, social truth is *not* statistical truth. To be truthful using statistics is to use what happened in the past as a hold on what will happen in the future. Probabilities are always future representations based on past counting. In all such epistemic treatments of probability, "the present" goes missing.[49] Second, the continuity frame we propose, featuring the scrambled sequences, shows us that only in the present can we find perception, and that is important to remember if we are trying to account for single cases. There is nothing more singular than what we are currently perceiving. These perceptions might overlap with others, but they will never overlap *entirely*. In the scrambled sequences, we cannot understand how the present appears to us in perception without these connections of past and future. A Bayesian, we think, would agree. Third, the scrambled sequences tell us why the separation of probability from interpretation at the beginning of the twentieth century has been so consequential. Interpretation assumed priority over the present. It came to seem like the only way to be present is to be interpreted or described, or to be interpreting and describing. Very little is singular about that, however, for the simple reason that such efforts make any two people perfectly interchangeable with each other—little more than particular examples of a general form.

Probabilistic Social Truth

A probabilistic social truth is rooted there—in the future grasped and the present perceived. It is found in expectation—in being bound by probability. It is found, in other words, in being oriented to *Chance*. Statistics is a science of the past. Even Quetelet knew that, and statistics does not actually *predict*, if by that we mean reaching into the future as a region unknown. "To predict something is not to foresee it," the philosopher of science Jean Cavaillès once observed; it is a "rule-governed" synopsis of the past.[50] But that claim is only true of scientific (statistical) prediction. Social truth *is* rooted in prediction, we argue, because the core of social truth is an orientation to *Chance*. We must anticipate "intuitively," as Bourdieu observes; we *must* predict.[51] Only a living being can relate to the future as a region unknown and unknowable.

The primary thing that action does for such a being, according to PP, is provide a sense of being alive, and a sense of being alive means something quite specific from a PP point of view. Consider fidgeting as action under the PP description.[52] As we twirl our hair, bounce our knee, or tap our fingers, we build a generative model in the repetition of easily predictable sensory information. Notably, the data scientists would *not* consider fidgets like these to be action, and not only because they cannot datafy them (yet). It is because this action leads and can *be* led nowhere. A fidget is comforting and anxiety-reducing because it is as close to a *closed* probability loop as we will ever see. Little new information taxes us with inference; we do not feel like a (surprised) second to the potential it brings. The opposite of the fidget, on these terms, would almost certainly be the tickle, which overwhelms us with surprise and perceptual overload. It is worth noting, however, that we cannot do it to *ourselves*. Self-tickling is impossible—a long-standing conundrum for cognitive science.[53] For our purposes, such basic examples as tickling and fidgeting contain a special insight as far as social truth goes. They help us to conceive how, in a probabilistic sense, social truth has everything to do with how people orient to *Chance*. Just as we cannot self-tickle, so we can never experience social truth as anything but a relation of *twos*.

Consider the following vivid description, a stream-of-consciousness portrayal of engaging with a problem, as written by pragmatist thinker George Herbert Mead:

> The kaleidoscopic flash of suggestion and intrusion of the inapt, the unceasing flow of odds and ends of possible objects that will not fit, together with the continuous collision with the hard, unshakable objective conditions of the problem, the transitive feelings of effort and anticipation when we feel that we are on the right track and substantive points of rest, as the idea becomes definite, the welcoming and rejecting, especially the identification of the meaning of the whole idea with the different steps of its coming to consciousness . . . If there ever was a psychical feeling of relation, it is when the related object has not yet risen from the underworld. It is under these circumstances that identities and differences come with thrills and shocks . . . And it is in this phase . . . with its activities of attention in the solution to the problem . . . that the individual has his functional expression or rather *is* that expression.[54]

Much of what Mead describes here is difficult to account for should our attention remain concentrated on only what we have called deflated action; though neither is it inflated into abstractions that never seem to be present to us in our quite *single* lives—even if, in Parsons's view, we are all living out the same human condition. As Mead describes, a strange subpersonal process bubbles up inferences; the entire process feels quite passive. Something is working on us, even though we are fundamentally alone as we grapple with the problem. The "underworld" Mead describes here is a "puzzling through" but it is aligned and linked vertically, as we mentioned in chapter 6, by something continuous at a higher level, where presumably we can meet others (i.e., "generalized others") who are in the same pursuit as we are. This engagement seems to require an equivalent aspect of *prediction* in action, which makes the entire experience as enlivening as Mead clearly wants to convey in his prose.

In line with probability theorists like Bruno di Finetti, it is in the underworld that we can find social truth—in that "bubbling up" from a relation of *twos* as we described above with Peirce, social truth appears in its smallest unit, though by no means does that suggest that the range of social truth is small. As Finetti put it, once "the idol of perfect, eternal and universal science" has fallen, "we see in its place, beside us, a living creature, the science which our thought freely creates. A living creature: flesh of our flesh, fruit of our torment, companion in our struggle."[55] Finetti here was talking about probability. Even in 1931, he saw a positivist edifice crumble, and probability was his alternative. Mead's description above could be as applicable to the scientist on the brink of a revolutionary discovery as it is to one of us in the muck of the world searching for our lost keys. Finetti makes a similar point. To associate probability with how much you'd be willing to bet on the future assuming some specific state is a principle he believes holds in the laboratory as much as it does in life. In both instances, something in the world must pull that willingness to bet or wager out of us. Much as Goffman realized in Las Vegas; to orient to the world as probability, we can only relate to it as a *second*.

Social truth is necessarily probabilistic truth. It is truth about what is real but unknowable in its entirety. It is the interface with *that* kind of thing, a *first* that strikes us with that kind of potential, that a sociological explanation should ultimately strive to reach. A probabilistic truth is not shapeless; but neither is it determinative. It is, most fundamentally, a *range* (*Spielraum*) with tendencies and probabilities—but most objectively, whatever in the world is capable of a probabilistic social truth consists of its *possibilities*. Parsons's ambition was not wrong in this regard. Sociology should try to bring what-ever can make its statements capable of being truthful right before our eyes. Sociology should be able to read it from what is singular and not-too-small, though importantly that does not mean that social truth is equivalent to sub-jective meaning or common sense. As mentioned above in chapter 2, when Alfred Schutz read Weber's probabilism he responded in a way that made "adequacy" convey something like the very opposite of probability, and prob-ability has been lost in the hinterland of statistical method ever since.[56] Yet, to be adequate is to make arguments that are capable of being true. The only way to bring whatever makes sociology truthful right before our eyes—in our sin-gular state of being, in our action, or what Kries refers to as "ontological"—is to make it clear how our engagements with the world are rooted in probabil-ity. Those engagements *must* be rooted in probability—a fixed sense of reality is merely a holding concept for whatever present state the world happens to be in; underneath it is possibility all the way down. Mead's description tells us what it is like to sense that possibility in a relation of *twos*. It can be tumul-tuous and exhilarating—we would expect what activates our sense of being alive to be nothing less than that—even if on a surface level our situation never appears to change.

To orient to *Chance* is to care about something, but not necessarily as a project; it is to be vulnerable to something, but not necessarily because one knows all the consequences. We orient to *Chance* to sense accomplishment or being finished. Only within probability orders, as we have described them, can there be adequate rather than accidental causes. In this perspec-tive, *Chance* is what social truth *already* consists of, and when sociologists are truthful, it is *Chance* that they get closest to revealing. Statistics can be helpful for the purpose, but as we have stressed, quantitative methods provide no royal road to social truth; though neither for that matter do qualitative methods, if by that we mean a grasp on the social world that generalizes the significance of interpretation to all phenomena. *Chance* has been our orientation all along, and thus our recommendation right now is that sociologists reconfigure our grasp on the social world by leaving the Laplacean spirit behind for good. The data scientists can have it. Reconfiguring the world into data of the most local and particular kind technologically allowable, just to activate the will to prediction, has never helped us get closer to *Chance*.

Theory Versus Machines

All attachments are optimistic. When we talk about an object of desire, we are really talking about a cluster of promises we want someone or something to make to us and make possible for us. This cluster of promises could seem embedded in a person, a thing, an institution, a text, a norm, a bunch of cells, smells, a good idea—whatever. To phrase "the object of desire" as a cluster of promises is to allow us to encounter what's incoherent or enigmatic in our attachments, not as confirmation of our irrationality but as an explanation of our endurance in the object . . . Being drawn to return to the scene where the object hovers in its potentialities is the operation of optimism.

LAUREN BERLANT, *Cruel Optimism*

We can learn a lot by studying a promise. Simply to be *oriented* or to have an *orientation* is not unlike being the subject of a promise. As with a promise, we feel like something *ought* to happen—a potential is in store for us in the future. Our forward momentum, our investment, comes not from being oriented toward what is certain to come next but by what *probably* will—like a promise, giving a sense for what *should* happen, and what *could*, a "hovering potential" with no guarantees. The capacity to *expect* so resembles the capacity to make and receive promises that Nietzsche wondered if there are any real differences between the two.[1] To have expectations does not suggest an ex nihilo source we can never know but instead a particular configuration of the world, perhaps a way that we ourselves have configured it—an extension into the future from where we currently stand, things we can loop into on our own terms, as a hope, a fear, a future. A promise is an intervention into the world, creating and constructing probabilities that might never come to be. Probabilities in the strictest sense might not be real, but they maintain an orientation nonetheless.

A promise can remain just that—a *promise*, promissory—in the potential never realized, the bubbling thought that never comes to form, perhaps, or the dream deferred. Nietzsche fails to mention that optimism must accompany such an orientation. As we loop into the world, we can do so according to expected (error-free) states, driven by a form of "intuitive faith."[2] Optimism in its quite literal embodied form becomes clear in predictive processing, the vanguard of probabilistic reasoning today, which suggests how the separation of probability and interpretation makes the disenchanting effects of scientific rationality only that much more consequential. We cannot understand our capacity to make promises, or our optimism, or our faith in constructed orders without drawing in error minimization. We can therefore offer these arguments as interpretive attempts to grasp our action and ultimately our humanity. As historian of science Georges Canguilhem once observed, the only real difference between a machine and life is that "there is no machine monster."[3] Living things have "less purpose and more potentialities" than machines. A machine "verifies the rational norms of identity, consistency, and predictability. Life, by contrast, is experience, that is to say, improvisation," which means above all that "life tolerates monstrosities." We can interpret "monstrosity" here as signifying what exists now just in a very improbable form.

These points assume a heightened significance in the present, should the looping effects we observe via machine interfaces be approached using probabilism. For us, the language of optimism, faith, and promises is important, but anyone who uses these words today must admit that something is working vertically below the level of consciousness, in the underworld, does not have to leave us in a suspicious or disenchanting mood. Pascal would remind us that we are *already* in a game, and we only move forward on the strength of our optimism. We embody better states of being. Even if those states may never occur, even if the odds are stacked against us, we remain oriented to them. Yet, the process can be manipulated. As Weber understood, loops are sites of power and domination. It is because of our cognitive susceptibility to loops, evidenced by the inevitability of having expectations, that the technical capacities of information storage and retrieval—and the construction of "modulation"—become consequential.[4] Machine learning can create optimism; algorithms can make promises. They can operate as a control on both expectation and *Chance*, keeping us within a loop, and thus reliable, regular, necessary—in a word, *predictable*, which for a probabilist is incommensurate with being a subject, or having a subjectivity, at least as this word is typically defined.

On Theory

The origination of theory, as Jurgen Habermas tells the story in 1965, involves a way of likening the body and soul to the "ordered motion of the cosmos."[5]

Theory thereby enters into the "conduct of life." Habermas recounts the break with this *traditional* view of theory in critique and crisis: specifically, the articulation of critical theory by those like Max Horkheimer and the concern addressed about science by those like Husserl in the forbidding 1930s.[6] For Husserl, science could provide no answers to the questions that have gone *unanswered* as a result of its triumph. The disenchantment of the world is contingent on those questions remaining unanswered and, preferably, *unasked*. In its pursuit of theory, science rendered itself from the "problems of life." For Horkheimer, theory in this traditional mold was bankrupt because it had turned its back on theory's calling, rightly conceived: to provide an enriched account of the world and look past the facts constructed by empirical methods into what their possibilities are—what they *could* make possible; indeed, what they *will* make possible given enough time.

Habermas sought a redemption of theory, and he pursued a course that would attempt to reground it in the fulfillment of interests: technical control, meaning, and emancipation. While many tools could be used to appeal to these interests, theory makes a unique contribution, particularly to the grandest human interest of them all: liberation from an otherwise fated existence, arbitrarily defined, decided, and determined.

When philosopher Friedrich Schelling gave his famous lectures in 1802 during the summer semester at Jena, it was full of confidence that he could state: "Only Ideas can lend point and ethical significance to action."[7] These were bold words at the time. They justified and invited the manufacture of "Ideas" (capitalized) with the presumption that whatever consequences came (political change, religious skepticism, moral upheaval) did not matter. All institutions and orders must present the Idea that informs them. Perhaps boldest of all, Schelling's ambitions justified the existence of universities, at the time widely perceived to be antiquated and medieval institutions, useless and corrupt to the core. Schelling said they could be redeemed by becoming the institutional home of new and wholly justified activity: *philosophizing*.[8] For him, theory was of a minor status due to its link to the world and to practice; philosophy stood entirely "unconditional" by contrast. It was only through philosophy that the "whole" or the "absolute" could possibly appear at all. Schelling praises "pure science" for similar reasons. It also finds little obligation to meet things where they are or remain consistent with the maxims of action. Pure science could discover a pristine space.[9] Theory remains the lesser cousin of philosophy and science, as it is of limited possibility. It can only teach us practical lessons. In Schelling's view, theory differs from experience only in being able to describe experience "apart from accidental conditions."[10]

Habermas's effort at redemption finds its lineage here. Theory is disregarded by Schelling for its worldly interests, and Habermas simply turns the tables. But something different is at stake here. For his part, Weber describes the appearance of the "concept" in ancient Greece as heralding a revolution: "Here, for the first time, there seemed to be an instrument with which you could grip someone in a logical vice so that he could not escape without admitting either that he knew nothing, or that this and nothing else was the truth, the *eternal* truth that was unperishable." On these grounds, it "seemed to follow that if you could just find the right concept of beauty, goodness, perhaps of courage, or of the soul . . . then you could also grasp its true essence; and that, in its turn, seemed to show the way toward knowing and teaching how to act rightly in life."[11] In their Platonic definition, concepts did lead to power, as famously portrayed in the "Allegory of the Cave."[12]

The ambition evident here shares the Idealist ambition, but notably, as Weber continues, if concepts, or *Ideas* for Schelling, make the absolute and ultimate (the unconditioned) possible, they also make authority of rationalization possible, opening up the dialectic of enlightenment. Pure science is what Husserl would speak of so fearfully a little over a decade after Weber's "Science as a Vocation" lecture. It is what happens when "science loses meaning for life" and stands disconnected. For Habermas, accompanying this trend is a resistant hermeneutic tradition that is also plagued by an "objectivist self-understanding . . . [defending] sterilized knowledge against the reflected appropriation of active tradition and [locking] up history in a museum."[13]

Schelling's ambitions, at the heart of the research university and its modern charisma, seemed to have failed by the early twentieth century. Habermas arrives in the aftermath of World War II, his expectations and hopes for theory looped into its destructiveness and oblivion as a sign, just as for Adorno.[14] For Habermas, the problems ultimately stem from severing "the connection of knowledge and interest." The problem may be one of severance and division, but not from human interest or the "negative" in Adorno's case. If concepts seem remote or result in philosophy and science as twin forms of authoritative knowledge, they are severed from probability, which is the antithesis of authority, as the fully predictable absolute, with that predictability being the potential of power.

Theory, however, is different. In the exploration of *Chance* as opposed to *Ideas*, theory finds in action an orientation to possibilities beyond the observable, the countable or the recordable. Ignoring this orientation, we *will* get a "state philosophy" sooner or later, as various attempts at authoritatively grasping the world come forward with a frame or system that asks or demands to be maintained in action.[15] Unlike Adorno's despair at their incapacity to not simply *identify*, and thereby become mythical, theory can provide "substance in cognition"—but only probabilistically.[16]

Habermas is right about the "methodological prohibitions" that restrict theory. The restriction applies by forbidding theory to play any but a secondary role in probabilistic reasoning. The *hope* of theory, particularly among those who find hope in critique, is lost when the prohibition on theory concedes the ground to method and data, and now presumably to data science. The idealist revolution would be surpassed by natural science. Technology became the conceit of liberation.[17] What remains unchanged, however, is that, regardless of the mode of engagement, the point of study, and specifically what *is* studied, we are left with objective possibility all the way down.

Despite all the changes to social theory over the last several decades, theorists only superficially engage in probability without approval by methodologists. Words are a secondary aid to the numbers game. Yet probability is not simply our accounting tool. We can find its concretization in the flows, rhythms, and distributions that mark social life, in the construction of new objective possibilities, and in the finer shades of expectation revealing the production of subjects. To figure out the social effects of probability requires an interpretive social science, one for which a spatial imagination surpasses the hermeneutic. A probabilist finds no equivalent of "social action as text," for example, nor do they transpose themselves into horizons or landscapes that do not take form as *expectations* and *anticipations*, as loops into the real but unknowable.[18] What they find are people oriented by beacons linking past and future, moving forward on paths that focus attention and create motivation via optimism. Promises, however endangered, find *confidence* in better states of being that, once lived, can be lived again.

There is nothing closely comparable in this framework to the idealist tradition that shapes the heritage of philosophy still to this day.[19] Perhaps, like Habermas but for different reasons, we should not treat this lack of connection, and the departure we propose, as a significant loss. After all, the idealist turn that began full of possibility would culminate, perhaps inevitably, in paternalistic authority. The founding of the University of Berlin in 1809 would have as its goal the "spiritual and moral training of the individual," to be achieved "by deriving everything from an original principle," thus "relating everything to an ideal" and "unifying this principle and this ideal in a single idea." The end product of such an institution would be "a fully legitimated subject of knowledge and society."[20] Whatever else this goal is, it is a story of fixing certain possibilities in place, constructing a range—"the single Idea" at its head, which some at the time confused with the state itself—with the very definition of authoritative knowledge found in the impossible legitimacy of anything else.

Interpretivists worry about authoritative knowledge, particularly as they find it hidden in critical theory's imputations of interests and capabilities, which removes variability from the dappled world and theorists' capacity to bring recognition to it. But the nomadic traits of probabilistic reasoning introduce more symmetry into this analysis. Whether an interpretation fixes possibilities, or whether it is an idea associated with universality and accompanying authority—these are all attempts to loop into *Chance*. The idealist, for their part, acknowledges that "lawless will is no will at all,"[21] and, probabilistically understood, law is among the most effective ways of constructing objective possibilities because of the assurance they appear to lend to a subjective looping-in. Yet any law begs the question of its *own* objective possibility (its own "Chance," in Du Bois's terms), specifically the possibility of giving and asking for reasons, and how that possibility could rely on anything other than itself for normative authority. In the self-legislating effects of giving reasons, what is reconstructed is the collectivity itself: the "we" included in participation.[22]

What we find here is law (or rule) probabilistically understood. What possibilities does it contain? And what else does such a question contain but a *test*?[23] Law, like interpretation, is a way of specifying *Chance*, even if only as a disguised and hidden repetition. To neglect this possibility is to assume the authority of interpretation or lawgiving as linked to no outcomes other than those available from the theorists' own definition of them. Action does not, then, matter in this perspective—nothing new can appear from it. Theory removed from probability appears like a coin toss in that respect, though with not even two possibilities as its range. Yet in this critique, and in its unique way of selecting and affirming as opposed to negating, we can find hints of a new turn in contemporary social theory. The present-day prospects of AI and machine learning, to put a finer point on it, cannot be left to the data scientists *or* to the philosophers.

On Machines

The data frontier is, according to some, poised to upend received knowledge practices and inferences. However, data science in its present form is not radically new in the *longue durée* of the philosophical discourse on probability. It marks a methodological engagement with the *Chance* world that, with assistance from computing technology, has managed to surpass the limits of statistical practice. Outside the relatively controlled sphere of structured data, data science promises to tabulate single events without needing to make them examples of classes or particular examples of unwieldy general categories. The science of the past was data-poor by comparison, and what counted as methods can now be appreciated as ways of coping with data poverty, maximizing the nature of what could count as significant, because it was more likely that nothing was. For some, the new condition of data wealth heralds a "transformation of contemporary economy and society . . . a much wider shift that makes everydayness qua data imprints an intrinsic component of organizational and institutional life."[24] Yet, beyond the technological prowess to accumulate data points, achieving a *continuity* like "everydayness" or structural mimicry like "form-searching," data science essentially remains a brand of frequentism that can render action probabilistic, as it *always already* is, only by transforming it first into a data vector.[25]

Whether data science makes for better social science can only be answered if we are *also* prepared to ask whether action can and should be datafied as digital traces. If data science can outflank sociology, as some fear (or hope), it can do so mainly because sociologists' current conception of action remains disconnected from probability, and thus it cannot put up any resistance. Those who remain unconvinced that theorists will ever find an adequate theory of action recommend that sociologists focus on policy-relevant data analysis instead, using our pedagogy and research to equip ourselves with tool kits now necessary to provide access to the objective dimensions of the social world.[26] If probability is entirely external to action, so this argument goes, then turning to probability is *per force* a turn away from action.

Yet data science could not guarantee such an analytic breakthrough if it did not already contain a theory of action. In this theory, data extraction, or the datafication of action, comes before predictive behavioral modulation. In the case of credit scores, objective possibilities consist of possible futures classified by risk potential. Algorithmic digital capitalism can make "good matches" between people and products, news stories, or social media posts, based on information flows "extracted from us in various parts of the digital infrastructure."[27]

A probabilistic sociology identifies definite arrangements in relation to *ranges* of possibility. It is on these grounds that we pursue continuums and analogies. Novel comparisons of the presence or absence of objective probability in different times and places, specifying historically emergent factors creating pockets of predictability, and the different orientations that can loop into these formations, shaping expectations and anticipations—if all social formations consist of possibilities repetitively made definite, then sociologists can abstract from this interface in specific examples, analogizing between single cases. The challenge is to theorize social constructions as a version of prediction in action, not in an algorithm.

Consider that Bourdieu's "anticipation of classification" works in a similar modulated manner as prediction using behavioral data and machine learning's own attempt to make our action horizontally continuous rather than veering off-course. Among the most familiar encounters with digital infrastructure are those that come when we interface with a digital thing found to have rich predictive signals. As a data vector, our interface with this thing requires that artificial intelligence modulate the equivalent of an avatar, reassembling it according to what are now singled out as key attributes.[28]

But the process requires an expropriation of what we *already* do using digital control. Because actors always already predict, predictive analytics can hijack this capability. If human actors did not already predict, we should not assume the profit potential of "human futures" to be so vast. The predictions of data science, to steal a Schutzian turn of phrase, are "second-order" predictions that piggyback on the "first-order" predictions actors produce as they make their way through the world.[29] Presumably, if we understand the predictive capability that we already exercise as actors, it can provide a basis from which to resist a digital architecture that targets this capability and works to expropriate a *means of prediction*.

The power of prediction becomes observable as a power over a classificatory *pattern recognition* and over predictive *pattern completion*. Power in this form eludes many contemporary accounts, as it seems to operate not via the well-worn formula of "constraint and enablement" but via *repetition and control*, based on the possibilities of data to create what approximates what we might refer to as a *singular cognitive authority*.[30] Some scholars have described this authority as a potential return of information asymmetries not seen since the pre-Gutenberg era, when cognitive authority had not yet diffused by print and literacy.[31] The effect is a channeling or canalizing of action that would not otherwise occur if prediction were allowed to happen "in the wild." Thus, replacement of the *Chance* that we confront, loop into, and use for action appears as the exercise of a novel form of power. The anticipations made *by* actors, in this case, compete with predictions made *about* them. The goal? To breach the data/action barrier and narrow the predictability divide between people and their data-derived avatars.[32]

Accordingly, much is at stake in the struggle over and around prediction. As control over the future, algorithmic prediction can be used to exercise power over the present based on the patterns that it finds in the past. We can find different uses of this prediction: profit prediction, social-policy prediction, epistemic prediction, and a host of others, about us and our planetary future, all of which, we *predict*, will only become even more consequential. Probabilism makes visible a missing variety of prediction in action, one overlooked or explicitly dismissed by scholars since the early twentieth century. Uncovering prediction in action at the heart of these other varieties helps us understand the full scale of their implications. But this move demands that power be understood as operating on this front rather than on those that are more familiar—through immanent *matching* rather than an exogenous disciplinary standard or overt violence.

Designer and theorist Benjamin Bratton remarks, in his study of software sovereignty *The Stack*, that he noticed his design students shifting strongly away from theory sometime in the late 1990s, replacing this interest—and all its accompanying *human* interests—with software as their primary tool for thought.[33] Questions that required theory to answer or even to ask and envision can now be answered without any mention of it. Learning *via* machine, suitably programmed, its user with the right aptitude, can provide for both question and answer. But Bratton observes that as technical "analysis" has replaced conceptual "synthesis," a certain uniformity has coincided. While the number of options available in the market for software and its degree of consolidation might make the tech universe appear wide open, it is more trapped by convention than ever before.

On Fate and Fatedness

The contingency of human existence is not a new idea, and the range of inferences we can make here is far from limited by the narrow terms with which we have presented it.[34] We can use an example far more wide-ranging, as it deals with contingent existence, and more specifically *fate*, using techniques of probabilism. In 523 CE, Roman statesman Anicius Manilus Severinus Boethius wrote a book from his prison cell. He was awaiting his execution. *The Consolation of Philosophy* would become a widely read text of the European Middle Ages, and for good reason it seems. Written as a dialogue between Boethius and another he calls "Lady Philosophy," the *Consolation* unfolds as a richly stylized treatise on a heavy subject: *chance* or *fortuna*, the very possibility of the accidental and unexpected event, and the reasons why. Boethius has reason to know a lot about the subject matter. He has been wrongly imprisoned on a false accusation and knows that a safe resolution to his predicament is unlikely. He writes as a man condemned to a fate. He is not interested in how this condemnation happened—he knows the causes all too well. He is interested in how it could have *possibly* happened. His interlocutor, Lady Philosophy, teaches him that while his imprisonment and impending doom may appear as a misfortune, they are really the results of an ever-changing fortune, and the spinning *rota di fortuna* (wheel of fortune) will continue on and on:

> You should have recognized that it was never in your control and that the visit of the unreliable goddess is a sure sign of misery to come. You should never confine your attention to what is before your eyes at the moment but consider too what the future is likely to bring. You knew the mutability of Fortune and you should have inured yourself against her constant threats of betrayal that too often inspire fear and flattery from those she has momentarily graced. If you submit your neck to her yoke, you cannot then complain about what happens to you or how the mistress you have yourself chosen is treating you badly. You can no longer bargain with her, tell her what is fair, or how long she should stay, or under what circumstances she may depart from you. If you spread your sails before the wind, then you must go where the wind takes you and not where you might wish to go. You want to try farming and sow your seeds on the earth, then you must expect barren years as well as years of abundance. If you worship her, then you are her slave and cannot question her. Would you presume to stop that wheel of hers from turning? If you could do that, it would no longer be the wheel of Fortune (*rota di Fortuna*), would it?[35]

The wheel of fortune attempts to grasp a providential structure where human-bound notions of time and sequence do not signify. For Boethius, even figuring out causal sequences leaves out a divine knowledge that seems to foretell events.[36] What Boethius faintly glimpses here is not essentially different from the highest ambitions of data science. There, too, we find the hope of discerning a system that creates the appearance of inevitability in time. Though, as Boethius realizes, inevitability is merely *one* way of orienting to *Chance*.

There is insight in simply linking this sort of eternal question to what, through digital loops, rapidly takes shape as a higher formal unity. Boethius learns in his own engagement with fate and the harsh outcome constructed for him that eternity is non-time, and everything there is "One" or self-identical. There are no differences, just as there are no instants that contain twists of fate. Words like "eternity" and "One" are simply cheap imitations of the inexpressible. We do not know them intimately. What we know are movement, action, and time, or the finite and profane opposites of what exists absolutely—unity, quiescence, immobility, eternity. Finite beings cannot truly "be." Each eruptive instant, each contingency and unexpected consequence, forbids a true identity. Yet contingency and accident can still serve a purpose—only they lead to understanding. Boethius comes to this realization in contemplation of his harsh fate. Our finite world of non-eternity, in which time exists, in which we must act, and which confronts us constantly by things external to us (Peirce's "objects"), is a world that *must be*, as only through experience can the soul, which is all that persists across *these* tests, have its needed odyssey. Only from what is conditional can we reach what is absolute or necessary.

Boethius does not understand his fate because it seems to be completely disconnected, out of the ordinary, coming from nowhere. He comes to understand it by making it *continuous*, by seeing how it *could* be expected once he accounts for the eternally rotating wheel of fortune. Equivalents to wheels of fortune always do the same; they make events come *next* in a continuous sense, as extensions of a range of possibilities. The events in question do not *necessarily* follow, but this does not mean they are *contingent*; they are instead a real *potential*. Explanations of this sort could be called the *Boethian*.

Like Boethius, we could come up with causes for surprising events, but doing so would not mean we would know how these events are *possible*. For our purposes, this limitation introduces a different task to science. The *rota di fortuna* might seem to be an almost perfect demonstration of what Cassirer calls "mythical thought."[37] This style of reasoning cannot admit chance (of the lowercase-*c* kind). It instead gives everything a purpose: "All the forces of nature are for myth nothing other than expression of a demonic or divine will." But, as Cassirer suggests, any strict separation of mythical thought from "theoretical thinking" on these grounds cannot be assumed so easily. For theoretical thinking must encounter chance all the time too, in the form of the accidental. Though, when it does it takes the opposite tack: "To 'understand' an event means nothing else than to reduce it to universal conditions, to subordinate it to that universal complex of conditions we call 'nature.'"

Both mythical and theoretical thinking constitute something very different from how Boethius responds to his tribulations. He does so by constructing an image of *Chance* that he can loop into and by which he can have expected his cruel fate, but also expect that the wheel will keep turning and something else will be on the horizon. The symmetry between the *rota di fortuna* and the proprietary uses of data to create the future shows that the only real difference between digital and non-digital looping is how possibilities are selected and affirmed. The power that comes from controlling the loop is its covertness and concealability. Bourdieu always wants to attend to the doxic blinders that keep things peripheral and invisible. It is those blinders that make possible or, even more apparently, *probable*, what can only be destroyed practically, when a loop breaks and expectations and chances mismatch. What we have remained blind to forces itself abruptly into our attention space.[38] We can finally see the range of possibility responsible for what we expected as probable or even necessary, and it is only at this time, when the spell is broken and we lose the perceptual and cognitive fluencies we once had, that we can engage in creative and potentially democratic social action, subjecting a range of possibility to tests of inclusion, participation, and justice.

To lock into a data-driven loop captures the possibilities that we can infer from the source, because it derives from *us*. We are driven forward by an optimism found in our past engagements, and in the loop we embody the promise of more. The better states that we embody find this specific recognition in the absence of a particular content as what we seek to rectify. The task is not fundamentally different from the idealist task and the purpose of theory. Theory, too, can be a source of hope found in states of better being, leading us to misrecognize and misfigure what appears before us. We loop into a transcendental sphere, fully clarified only in thought. How did the range of possibility come to be constructed? We can ask this question of anything that attempts a vertical capture, and how such capture makes action the horizontal movement through time adequately caused by something other than consciously chosen beliefs and desires. The framework presents us with an urgent question of fate.

We remain subjects in relation to the law because we can break it. As Weber emphasizes, we can probabilistically judge when it is *possible* to break the law without the expected consequence. Are we capable of the same subjectivity in a digital loop? For this loop, we are neither consumers nor users; we are more like component parts. *Our* action, as our engagement with *Chance*, transforms into *its* data, as a machine engagement with the same, in an exchange of information. We cannot judge when the loop applies, or when our action is *only* action and not also data. We cannot tell the difference between what we exchange and what we are given. The better states that we embody are what we seek as we correct errors. In the data stream, "content" defines that range of possibility and demonstrates a progressive increase in the proportion of a *constant* capital.[39] It acts as a control on the future by ensuring our continuous engagement in the loop.

We do not really roll the dice, then, as there can be no true outcomes in the digital loop. The tests that create analogies and similarities are united by us, though they do not promise self-understanding as do the Boethian odyssey and its vale of tears. In the data stream, it can seem as if we pass through a similar world of time, a world without eternity, a world of constant change, yet we find no culmination at the end. The loop, seemingly, cannot be broken, as we cannot locate ourselves in such a probability order and question its unity. It cannot seem exterior to us. When the means of prediction have been fully expropriated, when the loops are entirely modulated constructs, we bear fates or destinies that tell us nothing about ourselves, in which we cannot find our own reflection. Just think of the opaque fate of "going viral."

In the "The Social Psychology of the World Religions" and "Religious Rejections of the World and Their Directions," two essays that Weber published after his 1913 *Logos* essay, we find a proposal for the core of religion in what Weber describes as the "incongruity between destiny and merit."[40] He takes it as a point of focus for the comparative study of religion. Destiny implies courses of events that are impersonal and irrational in a subjective sense, yet also something that cannot be avoided—the certainty of death comes to mind. Merit can be defined only in relation to destiny. It finds a connection to a right, legitimate, or meaningful destiny; a life in which "meritorious actions and intentions correspond to the way in which the world is 'really' ordered."[41] If a destiny is "merited," then no other outcome *should* have been possible.

If Boethius tells us of *Chance* as divine knowledge, this point has bearing on the incongruity, as divine knowledge stands in relation to our experience as *deus absconditus* ("the hidden God") which, according to Weber, serves as the most effective means ever invented for resolving the incongruity by attributing an unknowable divinity at work in destinies that can find no merit. Yet the historical breaking of this religious totality ruptures with any reliance on unknowable divine processes at work. In the wake, politics can appear as a solvent, as capable of directing destiny in line with doctrine that promises order and mobilizes through a cause or project. In bureaucracy, an overlap of destiny and merit becomes achievable, as the bureaucrat has the capacity to adjust their inner convictions to whatever destiny might choose. They can make order regardless of the directions they are given, which is why, so often in modernity, social justice must ultimately pass through bureaucracy's state of exception.[42] This is one reason why Weber found bureaucracy so alienating yet so indestructible. Bureaucrats are the most successful order-making creatures to ever exist. They can make order without reconciling merit and destiny in the world at large. Politics may try to suffice in place of an unknowable divine while confronting tests, say, on the battlefield and making death in that site a destiny *independent* of meaning. A soldier can believe she dies for a cause as a destiny created by the polity, but that destiny must remain unquestioned—a perfect demonstration of order-making effects of the polity.

Transcending the limits of bureaucracy, charisma appears in the gap of merit and destiny that remains. It is uniquely capable, in Weber's assessment, of shifting orientations entirely, by creating new merits directed at new destinies. But charismatic flashes in the pan, by and large, cannot last long in the face of overwhelming incongruity. If those who are situated closer to rationalizing centers ("intellectuals") search for consistency in the face of destinies that come like fate, those who are more distant from such centers ("the masses") tend to desire just compensation for what has been done to them, which also conflicts with the formalism of rule-following demonstrated by those less peripheral to a rationalizing center, and who are oriented by rules and not concepts.

For Weber, science cannot be a replacement for the collapse of divine knowledge and its own reconciliation of merit and destiny. Still, Weber preferred "science as a vocation" under the circumstances, because science alone could "force an individual to give an account of the ultimate meaning of his own conduct." It could pose the very question of the incongruity of destiny and merit, falsely representing an approaching destiny, revealing how a "merited" order really isn't, and inspire accounts of this incongruity with none of the conciliation of *deus absconditus*.

The fragmentation of a religious totality results in a dappled world, a proliferation of independent probability orders propelled "towards making conscious [their] internal and lawful autonomy." In each of these orders, an overlap of merit and destiny becomes objectively possible. Outside distinctive pockets of predictability, we encounter a passage of time without sequence, instants without durations, and outcomes that come like fate with no account of having to be meaningful. Within a probability order, a fate *could* be merited and destiny *could* be made explicable by way of what all-too-human concepts *can* signify. Weber found the probabilistic dynamics of the "erotic sphere" to be particularly noteworthy as an exception that proves this rule: "no erotic communion will know itself to be founded in any other way than through the mysterious destination for one another: *fate*, in the highest sense of the word."[43] Even if a partner appears entirely unexpectedly, as a result of obscure machinations impossible to rationalize, for eroticism this unexpectedness is not incongruous but the source of the sacred meaning of the bond itself. Merit cannot be admitted: "Rarely does life grant such value in pure form. He to whom it is given may speak of fate's fortune and grace—not of his own 'merit.'"[44]

In a fully digital world, there will also be no opportunities for merit, though not exactly because we will be forbidden from ever having *Chance*. On the contrary, it can seem like we have *every Chance*; the range of possibilities can seem limitless. Yet Boethius's fraught path will no longer be available, as there will be no engagement with lowercase *chance* and therefore with fate.[45] And why would there be? To invite *that* kind of chance in would result in the opposite of a fully "modulated," fully *predictable* subjectivity.[46] It could spark an entire new universe—Peirce himself thought it *had* before.

Merit and destiny incongruities cannot be interpreted independently of expectations. The significance of erotic partnership is directly connected to the expectation of an improbability, not by a causal sequence that we could diagnose but by reference to the same real but unknowable realm for which Boethius's *rota di fortuna* has its application, to be called upon in times of need. Destiny attempts to signify that realm, and the intervention of merit is equivalent here, too, to attempts to find sequences that our concepts can signify. Weber's larger point gives attention to *Chance* as what has been constructed from Boethius's mysterious space of divine machination, which we can never understand fully. It nevertheless remains a source of meaning in the world.

Glossary

action: Any engagement with the world that assumes the form of a forward-feeding trial and reaction of learning and looping. We engage as *parte subjecti*, of expectations and habits, within a real but unknowable world, or as *parte objecti* with its potential and probabilities. Action generates sensory inputs through which we can learn these probabilistic environments. Action within a loop can make objective possibilities actual within a given range and mediate between the initial conditions and outcomes of probability orders, maintaining them through repetition. In action, we find an orientation to *Chance*.

active inference: The basic cognitive mechanism that maintains a loop into *Chance*. The neural tendency to form generative models allows for a predictive interface with incoming sense data. Thereby, the generative model partially configures a probabilistic environment, allowing for meaningful interfaces that are also characterized by diminished perception.

adequate cause: Relations of initial conditions and outcomes that occur in ways conducive to expectations. This definition indicates that they are adequately connected within a relatively coherent probability order rather than relating only through accidental causation.

Chance: Objective probability as subject to a judgment in action. *Chance* is the most direct interface with constituent patches in the world. Combined with expectation, it is also the most direct indicator of objective probability.

chance mechanisms: Events unmarked by expectation or objective probability. They might be objectively possible but to this point have remained unknown. Because they are unordered, they are the source of chance causation that can be threatening to the coherence of probability order.

chaos: When there is extreme sensitivity to small variations in initial conditions linked to outcomes, and expectations cannot form. A chaotic order is surprising (and is expected to be so) because we cannot judge single-case probability; we cannot loop in.

expectation: Judgment of probability that yields perception of *Chance*. Action as guided by expectation shows evidence of loops. Expectations are not arbitrary or subjective. They show evidence of the past that feeds into the future and create perceptions in the present. Expectations are only possible relative to objective probability. Otherwise, the forward feeding in action is more akin to a perpetual guess.

horizontality: Action as it moves through time. In a pure sense, horizontality would be composed of unrelated instants. Yet because of vertical capture and the dispositional formation of habits through learning, instants of time are bound together in a repeating connection, allowing for order to be generated and maintained through action.

horizontal project: A forecasting of action, either individual or collective, that must find subpersonal mechanisms to be maintained, as it counts primarily on perception. It does so because any such project can only move forward in time through error minimization.

initial states: Analytically defined, temporally prior phenomena that, in a line of action or in a statistical analysis, find a persistent link to some outcomes, thus binding time and allowing for expectations and/or analytically devised correlations or predictions. A probability distribution applies to initial conditions even outside of frequency counts, as it can designate aspects of a *Spielraum*.

interpretation: What can stabilize a chaotic order through an intervention in initial conditions that lend a contingent (i.e., symmetrical to other possible interpretations, with no adequate relation to what it interprets) meaning and significance to them.

looping: A persistent and repeating connection between *Chance* and expectation, such that orders can be constructed as predictable and action becomes less like a test to form expectations. Previously formed expectations can be relied upon. All loops are probabilistic in this sense, though some may rely on descriptions or interpretations to form expectations.

objective possibility: The real but unknowable constituent potentials of the world. These exist in time and space as durations and ranges. We learn objective possibility by testing it, via action-reaction flows that take the form of expectations or in statistical methods based on frequency counts. Neither of these options creates complete knowledge of objective possibility; it can only asymptotically approach it. Also known as "potential" or Aristotelian *dynamis*, ability/capacity.

objective probability: What objective possibility looks like as we try to know it. Takes the form of repeating, durational patterns, sequences, correlations, and rhythms. Such patterns are actually existing tendencies that we loop into via expectations.

outcomes: Analytically defined, temporally subsequent phenomena that, in a line of action or in a statistical analysis, find a persistent link to some initial states, thus binding time and allowing for expectations and/or analytically devised correlations or predictions. A probability distribution applies to outcomes even outside frequency counts, as it can designate aspects of a *Spielraum*.

personal, the: A level of analysis characterized by semantically accessible beliefs and desires— explicitly stated projects consisting of goals. An explanation that remains entirely at this level is autonomous, or self-contained, yet it allows for no chance for belief and desire, instead presuming their presence, suggesting a purely nominalistic ("in name only") significance.

probability order: Constructed of loops between expectations and *Chance*, the repeating connection of which yields relatively coherent spaces of social action. A typology (fields, apparatus, games of chance) can allow us to compare and analogize between probability orders. Probability orders differ according to how much they leave to chance ("invite it in") and how much they control it ("tame chance"). Probability orders, whether by design or not, allow for adequate causation.

prediction error: Sense information that a generative model cannot predict and that is the basic information content of perception. We perceive what we cannot predict, in other words.

single-case probability: Probability learned without ("in the long run") frequency counts, often through knowledge of what can be analytically defined as initial conditions. It can reveal certain tendencies in a *Spielraum*. As opposed to contingent probabilities, these probabilities can be the source of expectations.

social action: Any engagement with a probabilistic social order as an orientation to *Chance*. Social action is marked, most of all, by expectations formed via the expectations of other actors.

State, the: The most fundamental source of objective probability in a modern probability order. This circumstance arises in large part because the state can authorize interpretations capable of fixing the meaning and significance of initial conditions and outcomes.

subpersonal, the: A level of analysis characterized by semantic inaccessibility. This inaccessibility can contribute to an autonomous explanation focused purely on physiological or cognitive mechanisms, with no apparency in perceptions. Yet, continuism suggests linkages to the personal that allows its terms to be more than nominal but by no means local and particular.

tests: Action that engages with objective possibility and allows for learning (particularly by finding persisting links of initial conditions and outcomes) through reaction to it, thus absorbing its uncertainty. This process can also be designed and administered for the purpose of creating controlled spaces of adequate causation, in which case we find *tests* that channel engagement with an objective potential, limiting the distribution of possible outcomes. Tests mimic statistical testing rooted in frequency counts by allowing for a modeling of real but unknowable probabilistic environments.

vertical capture: When expectation-generating capabilities are captured by a higher-level order than a single individual, orienting action toward certain *Chance*. Action thus fulfills, at the levels of groups and institutions, the same maintenance of a probability order through correction of related prediction errors.

will to prediction: A concept that refers to the dispositional tendency to loop into *Chance*. It can be manifest as interpretation, expectation, desire. Typically, it renders especially the latter from a fluid to a stable state by translating probabilities into our qualitative experience.

Notes

Introduction

1. Karl Marx, *Capital: Critique of Political Economy*, vol. 1 (Princeton University Press, 2024 [1867]), 295–96; Emile Durkheim, *Rules of Sociological Method* (Free Press, 1982 [1895]), 91ff; Max Weber, "Some Categories of Interpretive Sociology," *Sociological Quarterly* 22, no. 2 (1981): 151–80; Max Weber, *Economy and Society: A New Translation*, trans. Keith Tribe (Harvard University Press, 2019[1921–1922]); W. E. B. Du Bois, "Sociology Hesitant," *boundary 2* 27, no. 3 (2000 [1905]): 37–44.

2. Andrew Abbott, "Transcending General Linear Reality," *Sociological Theory* 6, no. 2 (1988): 169–86.

3. For philosopher Nelson Goodman, this process makes perfect sense, as in his famous analysis of worldmaking, the core process is to bring "temporally diverse events together under a proper name. . . . Repetition as well as identification is relative to organization. A world may be unmanageably heterogeneous or unbearably monotonous according to how events are sorted into kinds." See *Ways of Worldmaking* (Harvester Press, 1978), 8–9.

4. Collins was thinking in particular of the multivariate structural-equation modeling methods popular at the time; see "Statistics Versus Words," *Sociological Theory* 2 (1984): 329–62.

5. Ernst Cassirer, *Determinism and Indeterminism in Modern Physics* (Yale University Press, 1956), chap. 1.

6. Philip K. Dick, "The Minority Report," *Fantastic Universe* (January 1956): 4–37.

7. David Donoho, "50 Years of Data Science," *Journal of Computational and Graphical Statistics* 26, no. 4 (2017): 745–66, at 746; see also John Tukey, "The Future of Data Analysis," *Annals of Mathematical Statistics* 33, no. 1 (1962): 1–67.

8. David Blei and Padhraic Smyth, "Science and Data Science," *Proceedings of the National Academy of Sciences* 114, no. 33 (2017): 8689–92.

9. See especially Carl Hempel, "On the Logical Positivists' Theory of Truth," *Analysis* 2, no. 4 (1935): 49–59.

10. On this front, as the hypothetico-deductive foundation of "theoretical science," see Nancy Cartwright, *How the Laws of Physics Lie* (Oxford University Press, 1983), 100ff.

11. Ian Hacking, *The Emergence of Probability: A Philosophical Study of Early Ideas About Probability, Induction and Statistical Inference* (Cambridge University Press, 1975), 36.

12. Jules Desai, David Watson, Vincent Wang, Mariarosaria Taddeo, and Luciano Floridi, "The Epistemological Foundations of Data Science: A Critical Review," *Synthese* 200, no. 469 (2022): 468–95.

13. Sabrina Leonelli, *Data-Centric Biology: A Philosophical Study* (University of Chicago Press, 2016), chap. 6.

14. While many strands coalesce into data science, the computer scientist Jim Gray, working for Microsoft, is often credited with first envisioning its potential to the fullest extent. See Tony Hey, Stewart Tansley, and Kristin Tolle, "Jim Gray on eScience: A Transformed Scientific Method, Based on a Transcript of a Talk Given by Jim Gray to the National Research Council, Computer Science and Telecommunications Board, January 11, 2007," in *The Fourth Paradigm: Data-Intensive Scientific Discovery*, eds. Tony Hey, Stewart Tansley, and Kristin Tolle (Microsoft Research, 2009), xvii–xxxi. The provocative 2008 article by the editor of *Wired*, Chris Anderson, entitled "The End of Theory" (June 23, https://www.wired.com/2008/06/pb-theory/), is also treated as a touchstone, in addition to the popular book by Viktor Mayer-Schonberger and Kenneth Cukier, *Big Data: A Revolution That Will Transform How We Live, Work and Think* (Harper Collins, 2013). For an overview, see, Wolfgang Pietsch, *Big Data* (Cambridge University Press, 2021); Netta Avnoon, "The Gates to the Profession Are Open: The Alternative Institutionalization of Data Science," *Theory and Society* 53 (2024): 239–71; Rob Kitchin, "Big Data, New Epistemologies, and Paradigm Shifts," *Big Data and Society* (April–June 2014): 1–12.

15. Leonelli, *Data-Centric Biology*, 77ff.

16. The first person to propose an idea of "consilience" seems to have been the nineteenth-century philosopher William Whewell, in his book *The Philosophy of the Inductive Sciences* (John Parker, 1840), indicating that there existed enough discipline-like specialization at that time to require an approach to unity. Whewell rooted this approach in induction: consilience "takes place when an Induction obtained from one class of facts, coincides with an Induction, obtained from a different class" (xxxix). As we discuss below, Whewell was an influence on probabilism via his influence on Charles Sanders Peirce. For a more recent argument, see Edward Wilson, *Consilience: The Unity of Knowledge* (Random House, 1999). The term "two cultures" was coined by the British chemist and novelist C. P. Snow in 1959 to refer to the difference between scientists and "literary intellectuals." See C. P. Snow, "The Two Cultures," *New Statesman*, October 6, 1956.

17. Much of this history is recounted in Donald Mackenzie, *Statistics in Britain, 1865–1930: The Social Construction of Scientific Knowledge* (Edinburgh University Press, 1981); Theodore Porter, *The Rise of Statistical Thinking, 1820–1900* (Princeton University Press, 1986), chap. 9; Theodore Porter, *Karl Pearson: The Scientific Life in a Statistical Age* (Princeton University Press, 2004), chap. 9; Tukufu Zuberi, *Thicker Than Blood: How Racial Statistics Lie* (University of Minnesota Press, 2001), chap. 3.

18. Daniel Benjamin, James Berger, Magnus Johannesson, et al., "Redefine Statistical Significance," *Nature Human Behavior* 2 (2018): 6–10. This article features seventy-two coauthors from a wide variety of fields, including sociology. For the American Statistical Association's own position on statistical significance as the generally interpreted $p \leq 0.05$ value, see Ronald Wasserstein and Nicole Lazar, "The ASA Statement on p-Values: Context, Process and Purpose," *American Statistician* 70, no. 2 (2016): 129–33; see also Stephen Ziliak and Deirdre McCloskey, *The Cult of Statistical Significance: How the Standard Error Costs Us Jobs, Justice and Lives* (University of Michigan Press, 2008).

19. What goes by the name of "Bayesianism" today is a kind of synthesis or peaceful coexistence between a more data-driven version, exemplified in American physicist Edwin Jaynes's text *Probability Theory: The Logic of Science*, and a more personalist version, with Italian actuary Bruno de Finetti being a key theorist.

20. Aubrey Clayton, *Bernoulli's Fallacy: Statistical Illogic and the Crisis of Modern Science* (Columbia University Press, 2021).

21. Bruce Western, "Bayesian Thinking About Macrosociology," *American Journal of Sociology* 107, no. 2 (2001): 353–78.

22. Judea Pearl, *Probabilistic Reasoning in Intelligent Systems* (Morgan Kaufman Publishers, 1988), 34ff.

23. An example is a statistical measure that has become commonplace to assess performance in baseball: Wins Above Replacement (or WAR). WAR is calculated by taking a prior estimate—treated as the performance standard of an "average" player—and calculating how much a given individual player surpasses or falls below it. Rather than being a counting stat (like how many hits or strikeouts a player has), WAR is conditional on a prior estimate, namely the average level of performance in a given season, and it can be updated by new data in perpetuity. See Christopher Phillips, *Scouting and Scoring: How We Know What We Know About Baseball* (Princeton University Press, 2019).

24. Iddo Tavory and Stefan Timmermans, *Abductive Analysis: Theorizing Qualitative Research* (University of Chicago Press, 2012); Monika Krause, *Model Cases: On Canonical Research Objects and Sites* (University of Chicago Press, 2021).

25. David Lewis, "A Subjectivist's Guide to Objective Chance," in *Studies in Inductive Logic and Probability II*, ed. Richard Jeffrey (University of California Press, 1980), 263–95.

26. Rudolf Carnap, *Logical Foundations of Probability* (University of Chicago Press, 1950).

27. David Lewis, *On the Plurality of Worlds* (Blackwell, 1986).

28. Lewis, "Subjectivist's Guide to Objective Chance," 270.

29. David Lewis, *Philosophical Papers II* (Oxford University Press, 1986), viiii.

30. Jean-Francois Lyotard, *The Postmodern Condition: A Report on Knowledge*, trans. Geoff Bennington and Brian Massumi (University of Minnesota Press, 1984), 14.

31. Lyotard, *Postmodern Condition*, 51.

32. Susan Athey, "Beyond Prediction: Using Big Data for Policy Problems," *Science* 355 (2017): 483–85, at 484.

33. Athey, "Beyond Prediction," 484.

34. Here we are thinking of Google Flu Trends; see David Lazer, Ryan Kennedy, Gary King, and Alessandro Vespignani, "The Parable of Google Flu: Traps in Big Data Analysis," *Science* 343, no. 6167 (2014): 1203–5.

35. Lorraine Daston, *Rules: A Short History of What We Live By* (Princeton University Press, 2022).

36. David Hume, *An Enquiry Concerning Human Understanding* (Clarendon Press, 1975/1748), 90.

37. Albert Hirschman, *The Passions and the Interests: Arguments for Capitalism Before Its Triumph* (Princeton University Press, 2013/1977), 66ff.

38. For more on "normic laws" and how they must be practically reliable (or "ontological," as we say), see Pearl, *Probabilistic Reasoning in Intelligent Systems*, 477ff.

39. Hume, *Enquiry Concerning Human Understanding*, 21.

40. Compare, say, a painting like Georges Seurat's *A Sunday on the Island of La Grande Jatte* (1884) with Mark Rothko's *Multiform* (1948).

41. Our argument here has much in common with the heterodox probability theory of George Spencer-Brown, particularly his idea of a "chance-machine." Our idea of the probability order is comparable. As Spencer-Brown puts it: "Thus a chance-machine is allowed by the properties we ascribe to it to give results which fall only within a certain range. If they fall outside this range, we at once cease to call it a chance-machine." See his *Probability and Scientific Inference* (Longmans, Green, and Co., 1957), especially 39–40, 100ff.

42. See Pierre Bourdieu, "The Economy of Linguistic Exchanges," in *Language and Symbolic Power* (Harvard University Press, 1991); Vsevolod Kapatsinski, *Changing Minds Changing Tools: From Learning Theory to Language Acquisition to Language Change* (MIT Press, 2018), 41ff.

43. See Keith Tribe, "'Chance' in Max Weber's Later Writings," in *History as a Translation of the Past*, ed. Luigi Alonzi (Bloomsbury Academic, 2023), 107-21.

44. Ralf Dahrendorf, "Max Weber's Concept of 'Chance,'" in *Life-Chances: Approaches to Social and Political Theory* (University of Chicago Press, 1981 [1979]), 62-74.

45. Kari Palonen, *A Political Style of Thinking: Essays on Max Weber* (ECPR Press, 2017); Andreas Anter, *Max Weber's Theory of the Modern State: Origins, Structure, and Significance* (Palgrave, 2014 [1995]), esp. 88-95.

46. Carl Schmitt, *Legality and Legitimacy*, trans. Jeffrey Seitzer (Duke University Press, 2004 [1932]), 135-36.

47. Schmitt, *Legality and Legitimacy*, 36.

48. Schmitt, *Legality and Legitimacy*, 136.

49. Du Bois, "Sociology Hesitant."

50. Pierre Bourdieu, *Pascalian Meditations* (Stanford University Press, 2004), 216.

51. Charles Sanders Peirce, "Lessons from the History of Philosophy," *Collected Papers of Charles Sanders Peirce*, vol. 1, eds. Charles Hartshorne and Paul Weiss (Harvard University Press, 1931), 26.

52. Charles Sanders Peirce, *Reasoning and the Logic of Things*, ed. Kenneth Laine Ketner (Harvard University Press, 1992 [1898]), 247.

Chapter 1

1. See, for instance, Stephen Stigler, *The History of Statistics: The Measurement of Uncertainty Before 1900* (Harvard University Press, 1990); Alain Desrosières, *The Politics of Large Numbers: A History of Statistical Reasoning* (Harvard University Press, 2002); Theodore Porter, *The Rise of Statistical Reasoning, 1820-1900* (Princeton University Press, 1986).

2. In many ways, Hacking not only borrows a method from Foucault but picks up a loose thread in his account of the shift from what he (Foucault) calls the "Classical" episteme to what he calls the "modern" one. For Foucault, Thomas Hobbes and the *Port-Royal Logic* were seventeenth-century intimations of modern probability: "It is . . . possible to define the instruments laid down for the use of Classical thought by the sign system. It was this system that introduced into knowledge probability, analysis, and combination, and the justified arbitrariness of the system." See Michel Foucault, *The Order of Things: An Archaeology of the Human Sciences* (Vintage, 1994 [1966]), 63.

3. Ian Hacking, *The Emergence of Probability: A Philosophical Study of Early Ideas About Probability, Induction and Statistical Inference* (Cambridge University Press, 1975), 9.

4. Hacking, *Emergence of Probability*, chap. 5.

5. See especially Stefania Tutino, *Uncertainty in Post-Reformation Catholicism: A History of Probabilism* (Oxford University Press, 2018), chap. 2.

6. See especially Aristotle's *Prior Analytics*, trans. Robert Smith (Hackett Publishing, 1989 [c. 354 BCE]), 102ff; see also Edward Madden, "Aristotle's Treatment of Probability and Signs," *Philosophy of Science* 24, no. 2 (1957): 167-72; John Dudley, *Aristotle's Concept of Chance: Accidents, Cause, Necessity and Determinism* (SUNY Press, 2012), 152. Some classicists have found support for the idea that Aristotle's *Poetics* are rooted in constructing "dramatic probability." In Aristotle's

words, "the task of the poet is not to tell of what has happened, but what might happen, and what is possible according to probability or necessity." See Neil O'Sullivan, "Aristotle on Dramatic Probability," *Classical Journal* 91, no. 1 (1995): 47–63, at 47.

7. See, for instance, Pierre Bourdieu, *Outline of a Theory of Practice* (Cambridge University Press, 1977 [1972]), 168.

8. Hacking, *Emergence of Probability*, 17.

9. Hacking, *Emergence of Probability*, 17.

10. For an overview, see Colin Koopman, "Foucault's Historiographical Expansion: Adding Genealogy to Archaeology," *Journal of the Philosophy of History* 2 (2008): 338–62.

11. This concern is most apparent in Foucault's famous essay on method, "Nietzsche, Genealogy, History," in *The Foucault Reader* (Pantheon, 1984), especially 82–83.

12. Here we build from Michael Baxandall's art history, especially *Painting and Experience in 15th Century Italy* (Oxford University Press, 1972) and Pierre Bourdieu's discussion of Baxandall in *The Rules of Art: The Genesis and Structure of the Literary Field* (Stanford University Press, 1995), especially 320–21.

13. See chapter 4 below. Here we draw from philosopher Friedrich Nietzsche, not only to coin a phrase but also for lessons in naturalism, or providing an account of probability consistent with our best assessment of the kind of beings that humans naturally are. For Nietzsche (*Daybreak: Thoughts on the Prejudices of Morality* [Cambridge University Press, 1997 (1881)], 130), the best route to naturalism is to ponder the nature of will or willing: "We laugh at him who steps out of his room at the moment when the sun steps out of its room, and then says: 'I will that the sun shall rise'; and at him who cannot stop a wheel, and says: 'I will that it shall roll'; and at him who is thrown down in wrestling, and says: 'here I lie, but I will lie here!' But, all laughter aside, are we ourselves ever acting any differently whenever we employ the expression 'I will'?" Nietzsche's point of course is that the will does exist; it just does not exist as Christian morality (and Kant) thinks it does, as the vector of moral responsibility. See Brian Leiter, *Moral Psychology with Nietzsche* (Oxford University Press, 2019), for a defense of reading Nietzsche as a thoroughgoing naturalist.

14. See Rachel Friedman, *Probabilistic Justice: Risk, Insurance, and the Welfare State* (University of Chicago Press, 2020).

15. For a recent Peirce scholar who stresses this point, see Paul Forster, *Peirce and the Threat of Nominalism* (Cambridge University Press, 2011).

16. Elements of this story are surely apocryphal. For one, the Chevalier was not a "Chevalier" (or knight in French). He was a commoner and writer by the name of Antoine Gombaud who happened to have gone to school in the small French town of Méré. It is not clear whether he was a game player, let alone a bad one.

17. Lorraine Daston, "How Probabilities Came to be Objective and Subjective," *Historia Mathematica* 21, no. 3 (1994): 330–44.

18. See Blaise Pascal and Pierre de Fermat, "Fermat and Pascal on Probability," in *A Source Book in Mathematics*, ed. David Smith (Dover Publications, 1899 [1654]), 5. One theorist who did notice this phenomenon is one we'll discuss at length below, Johannes von Kries; see *Principles of the Probability Calculus: A Logical Investigation*, trans. Keith Niall (Springer 2024 [1886]), 161ff.

19. Hacking, *Emergence of Probability*, 68ff.

20. We refer here to Pascal's famous "wager." As he puts it, "One is compelled to wager; it is not voluntary, you are in the game . . . [When] there is such an infinite life of infinite happiness to be won, one chance of winning against a finite number of possibilities for a loss . . . [This]

eliminates all choice . . . one must give all." See Blaise Pascal, *Pensées* (Oxford World Classics, 1995 [1657]), 126.

21. Here we cite the 1714 English translation of Huygens's text *The Value of All Chances in Games of Fortune: Cards, Dice, Wagers, Lotteries & etc., Mathematically Demonstrated* (Keimer and Woodward, 1714 [1657]), which had been in wide circulation in its original Latin version prior to this point. While there is no evidence that Huygens met Pascal or Fermat, he was certainly aware of their correspondence, having visited Paris in 1655.

22. Huygens, *Value of All Chances*, 1-2.

23. Huygens, *Value of All Chances*, 2. The broadly probabilistic enterprise, linked in particular to the activation of belief and desire, in which Huygens engages can be clarified by the "advertisement" for the book: "As all Mathematical studies are unaccountably bewitching and delightful to those that are once happily engaged in them; so that part which considers and estimates how Expectations of Events that are in themselves uncertain, and depend entirely on Chance and Hazard, cannot fail of giving a particular Pleasure and Satisfaction. To reduce the inconstant and irregular Proceedings to blind Fortune to certain Rules and Limits, and to set a definite Value upon her capricious Favors and Smiles, seem to be Undertakings of so chimerical a Nature, that here is no Body but must be delightfully surprised with that Art which discovers them both really possible, and with a little Application easily practicable."

24. Hacking situates Huygens's arguments in this way; see *Emergence of Probability*, chap. 8.

25. For an overview, see Jeff Jordan, *Pascal's Wager: Pragmatic Arguments and Belief in God* (Oxford University Press, 2006), chap. 4.

26. See similar suggestions made by Goldmann, *Hidden God*, especially chap. 15; and Ernest Coumet, "La théorie du hasard est-elle née par hasard?," *Annales. Histoire, Sciences Sociales* 25, no. 3 (1970): 574-98.

27. Lorraine Daston, *Classical Probability in the Enlightenment* (Princeton University Press, 1988), chap. 2.

28. For his part, Pascal arguably had a more democratic penchant than his colleagues, which he gained through fervent opposition to hierarchical Catholic "probabilism" and how it leveraged testimonial authority above all. See Hacking, *Emergence of Probability*, 78-79; Tutino, *Uncertainty in Post-Reformation Catholicism*.

29. Thomas Bayes, "An Essay Toward Solving a Problem in the Doctrine of Chances: By the late Rev. Mr. Bayes, F. R. S. communicated by Mr. Price, in a letter to John Canton, A. M. F. R. S," *Philosophical Transactions of the Royal Society* 53 (1763): 370-418, at 376.

30. Others have made similar arguments; see William Jeffreys and James Berger, "Ockham's Razor and Bayesian Analysis," *American Scientist* 80, no. 1 (1992): 64-72.

31. Bayes, "Essay Toward Solving the Doctrine of Chances," 385ff.

32. Jacob Bernoulli, *The Art of Conjecturing, Together with a Letter to a Friend on Sets in Court Tennis*, trans. Edith Dudley Sylla (Johns Hopkins University Press, 2006 [1713]).

33. Bernoulli, *Art of Conjecturing*, 328.

34. Bernoulli, *Art of Conjecturing*, 327.

35. Pierre-Simon Marquis de Laplace, *A Philosophical Essay on Probabilities*, trans. Andrew Dale (Springer, 1995 [1814-1825]).

36. Laplace, *Philosophical Essay on Probabilities*, 3.

37. Laplace, *Philosophical Essay on Probabilities*, 4.

38. Laplace, *Philosophical Essay on Probabilities*, 6.

39. Laplace, *Philosophical Essay on Probabilities*, 6.

40. According to Laplace, if we can know anything at all, then there must be something

determinate about the world, and that something *could* be known, but not by us. In Laplace's philosophy, it is only because we (humans) cannot know all that could possibly happen that probability becomes a crucial epistemic tool for us; but as a tool it remains just that—*epistemic*.

41. Laplace, *Philosophical Essay on Probabilities*, 6.

42. Here Laplace repeats a formula he developed in the early 1770s and which some argue marked a rediscovery of Bayes's principle; see Stephen Stigler, "Laplace's 1774 Memoir on Inverse Probability," *Statistical Science* 1, no. 3 (1986): 359–63.

43. See Stigler, *History of Statistics*, 90ff.

44. Laplace, *Philosophical Essay on Probabilities*, 10.

45. Laplace, *Philosophical Essay on Probabilities*, 61.

46. Laplace, *Philosophical Essay on Probabilities*, 62.

47. See Madeleine Mazars-Chadeau, "The Savant, Society, and Politics: On Laplace's *Philosophical Essay on Probabilities*," *Année sociologique* 36 (1986): 75–92.

48. Adolphe Quetelet, *A Treatise on Man and the Development of His Faculties*, trans. Richard Knox (Cambridge University Press, 2013 [1835]). The original French version has the title *Sur l'homme et le développement de ses faultés, ou, Essay de physique sociale*.

49. The imagery of the body is taken quite literally by Quetelet in his non-reticence to shift from method to metaphysics: "[The social body] subsists in virtue of conservative principles, as does everything which has proceeded from the hands of the Almighty: it also has its Physiology . . . we find laws as fixed as those which govern the heavenly bodies: we return to the phenomena of physics, where the freewill of man is entirely effaced, so that the work of the Creator may predominate without hindrance. The collection of these laws, which exist independently of time and of the caprices of man, form a separate science, which I have considered myself entitled to name social physics." See Quetelet, *Letters on the Theory of Probabilities, as Applied to the Moral and Political Sciences*, trans. Olinthus Downes (Charles Edwin and Layton, 1849 [1845]), 178.

50. Ian Hacking, "Biopower and the Avalanche of Printed Numbers," in *Biopower: Foucault and Beyond*, eds. Vernon Cisney and Nicolae Morar (University of Chicago Press, 2015), 65–82.

51. Quetelet has the occasion to brag, for instance, about his ability to predict how many potential criminals are acquitted, and even more specifically, how many will be acquitted by a jury trial.

52. Ernst Cassirer, *Determinism and Indeterminism in Modern Physics: Historical and Systematic Studies of the Problem of Causality* (Yale University Press, 1956), chap. 1 and 2.

53. Buckle's book is sprinkled with explicitness: "It is surely an astonishing fact that all the evidence we possess respecting [suicide] points to one great conclusion, and can leave no doubt on our minds that suicide is merely the product of the general condition of society, and that the individual felon only carries into effect what is a necessary consequence of preceding circumstances. In a given state of society a certain number of persons must put an end to their own life. This is the general law; and the special question as to who shall commit the crime depends of course upon special laws; which, however in their total action must obey the large social law to which they are all subordinate. And the power of the larger law is so irresistible, that neither the love of life nor the fear of another world can avail anything towards even checking its operation." See Henry Thomas Buckle, *History of Civilization in England* (Routledge, 1904 [1857]), 15–16.

54. For the relation of Marx to Quetelet, see Julian Wells, "Of Fat Cats and Fat Tails: From the Financial Crisis to the New Probabilistic Marxism," in *Contradictions: Finance, Greed, and Labour Unequally Paid*, ed. Paul Zarembka (Emerald Group, 2013), 197–228.

55. Theodore Porter, "Statistical and Social Facts from Quetelet to Durkheim," *Sociological Perspectives* 38, no. 1 (1995): 15–26.

56. John Venn, *The Logic of Chance* (Macmillan, 1888 [1866]), 164.

57. Venn, *Logic of Chance*, 240.

58. The neo-Kantian philosopher Wilhelm Windelband aptly summarized the tenor of fear and paradox provoked by statistical regularity: "Soul, freedom of will and whatever became without further ado things that are simply not existent." Windelband quoted in Fredrik Beiser, *The Genesis of Neo-Kantianism, 1796–1880* (Oxford University Press, 2014), 520.

59. See Venn, *Logic of Chance*, xviii. Venn mentions Johannes von Kries as one whom he finds himself "in closer agreement than with most others, in respect of his general conception and treatment of Probability."

60. Martin Neumann, "The Ontological Science of Collective Terms: Johannes von Kries in Social Statistics," in *The Range of Science: Studies in the Interdisciplinary Legacy of Johannes von Kries*, ed. Gerhard Wagner (Harrassowitz Verlag, 2019), 112.

61. Tarde points to the adoption of the telephone in the US as something that seems both to demonstrate such a phenomenon and potentially to create it—by making a large number of cases into "repetitions" or "imitations" of each other (e.g., cases of the same thing). See Gabriel Tarde, *The Laws of Imitation*, trans. Elsie Parsons (Henry Holt, 1903 [1890]), 114ff.

62. Richard von Mises, *Mathematical Theory of Probability and Statistics*, ed. Hilda Geiringer (Academic Press, 1964), 19–20.

63. Notably, Mises mentions this example after distinguishing his approach to probability from the approach of Johannes von Kries, whom we discuss below.

64. Mises, *Mathematical Theory of Probability and Statistics*, 21.

65. Mises, *Mathematical Theory of Probability and Statistics*, 2–3.

66. Kolmogorov's axioms include the concept of elementary events, a subset of which are random. Thus, we must posit a "field" of these sets, which Kolmogorov defines as follows: "A system of sets is called a field if the sum, product, and difference of two sets of the system also belong to the same system." Within the proper field, then, a set is capable of bearing a nonnegative real number. The entirety of events in the set must equal to 1, and if two sets of events share nothing in common except that they are part of the same field, then their separate probabilities must sum to their combined probabilities. Any bit of reasoning satisfying all of these axioms Kolmogorov calls a "field of probability." See Andrey Kolmogorov, *Foundations of the Theory of Probability*, trans. and ed. Nathaniel Morrison (Chelsea Publishing Company, 1956 [1933]), 2–3.

67. Mises, *Mathematical Theory of Probability and Statistics*, 10. Mises took Bayes's principle seriously, but he made it conditional on frequency by arguing that a prior probability estimate would reduce Bayesians' subjectivist insistence on "lack of knowledge . . . if the number *n* of observations" used to calculate it "is large" (342).

68. See Donald Mackenzie, *Statistics in Britain 1865–1930: The Social Construction of Scientific Knowledge* (Edinburgh University Press, 1981), 59–60.

69. Mises takes note of this confusion, preferring the term "collective." Mises, a Jew who fled Nazi Germany in 1933, even penned a satirical paper lampooning the Nazis' eugenics policies. Those policies drew inspiration, in particular, from the Galton Society of America. See Mises, *Mathematical Theory of Probability and Statistics*, 12; see also Reinhard Siegmund-Schultze and Sandy Zabell, "Richard von Mises and the 'Problem of the Two Races': A Statistical Satire in 1934," *Historia Mathematica* 34, no. 2 (2007): 206–20.

70. These approaches arguably only returned to at least partial favor with the publication of Leonard Savage's textbook *The Foundations of Statistics* (Dover, 1954).

71. Philosopher Ernst Cassirer refers to this view as part of the "Laplacean spirit"; see his *De-*

terminism and Indeterminism in Modern Physics: Historical and Systematic Studies of the Problem of Causality (Yale University Press, 1956), 4–5.

72. The contrast on this point is particularly observable in the difference, particularly on a "parallel theory of association" or correlation, between Udny Yule (deeply skeptical of eugenics) and Pearson; see the discussion in Mackenzie, *Statistics in Britain*, 173ff.

73. Theodore Porter, "Quantification and the Accounting Ideal in Science," *Social Studies of Science* 22, no. 4 (1992): 633–51, at 644.

74. Aubrey Clayton, *Bernoulli's Fallacy: Statistical Illogic and the Crisis of Modern Science* (Columbia University Press, 2021), 14; see also Porter, *Rise of Statistical Reasoning*, 303.

75. Ronald Fisher, *Statistical Methods and Scientific Inference* (Oliver and Boyd, 1956), 33, emphasis original.

76. Fisher, *Statistical Methods and Scientific Inference*, 44.

77. See discussion in Stigler, *History of Statistics*, 275ff.

78. As Galton himself put it, "Order in Apparent Chaos. I know of scarcely anything so apt to impress the imagination as the wonderful form of cosmic order expressed by the 'Law of Frequency of Error.' The law would have been personified by the Greeks and deified, if they had known of it. It reigns with serenity and in complete self-effacement amidst the wildest confusion. The hunger of the mob, and the greater the apparent anarchy, the more perfect is its sway. It is the supreme law of Unreason." See Francis Galton, *Natural Inheritance* (Macmillan, 1889), 66.

79. Physicist Robert Jahn, onetime dean of the School of Engineering at Princeton, and psychologist Brenda Dunne drew upon similar principles as Galton's quincunx in an effort to see whether and how human minds could interact with machine intelligence, using the normal distribution as an indicator of that intelligence. Establishing the controversial PEAR lab (or Princeton Engineering Anomalies Research) in 1977, they compiled a "massive database of tens of millions of experimental trials in which human subjects sought to influence the workings of various devices merely by thinking, wishing, visualizing, or praying." See D. Graham Burnett, "Games of Chance: Testing at the Limits of the Normal," *Cabinet* (Summer 2009): 59–65, at 63.

80. John Maynard Keynes, *A Treatise on Probability* (Macmillan, 1921), 101.

81. Keynes, *Treatise on Probability*, 101.

82. Keynes, *Treatise on Probability*, 4.

83. Harold Jeffreys, *Theory of Probability* (Clarendon Press, 1961 [1939]), 406. For the sometimes-caustic dispute between Jeffreys and Fisher, see David Howie, *Interpreting Probability: Controversies and Developments in the Early Twentieth Century* (Cambridge University Press, 2002), especially chap. 5.

84. E. T. Jaynes, *Probability Theory: The Logic of Science* (Cambridge University Press, 2003), 373.

85. Jaynes, *Probability Theory*, 88.

86. Leonard Savage, *The Foundation of Statistics* (Dover, 1954), 3.

87. Savage, *Foundation of Statistics*, 51.

88. This point was also echoed by Frank Ramsey, whom we discuss below; see his "Truth and Probability," in *The Foundations of Mathematics and Other Logical Essays* (Kegan, Paul, Trench, Trubner, and Co., 1931 [1926]), 158–59.

89. Bruno de Finetti, "Probabilism: A Critical Essay on the Theory of Probability and on the Value of Science," *Ekrenntnis* 31 (1989 [1931]): 169–233, at 195.

90. Bruno de Finetti, *Theory of Probability*, vol. 1 (Wiley, 1974 [1933]), xix.

91. Richard Berk, Bruce Western, and Robert Weiss, "Statistical Inference for Apparent Populations," *Sociological Methodology* 25 (1995): 421–58.

92. Michael Strevens, "Dynamic Probability and the Problem of Initial Conditions," *Synthese* 199 (2021): 14617–39, at 14620.

93. See Peter Hedström and Richard Swedberg, eds., *Social Mechanisms: An Analytic Approach to Social Theory* (Cambridge University Press, 1998).

94. Venn, *Logic of Chance*, 149.

95. See Edi Karmi and David Schmeidler, "On the Uniqueness of Subjective Probabilities," *Economic Theory* 3, no. 2 (1993): 267–77.

96. See Jacob Hacker, *The Great Risk Shift: The Assault on American Jobs, Families, Healthcare and Retirement and How You Can Fight Back* (Oxford University Press, 2006).

97. The basic idea here is that a market can have better "expectations about probabilities" than either people or data analysts. See Justin Wolfers and Eric Zitewitz, "Prediction Markets," *Journal of Economic Perspectives* 18, no. 2 (2004): 107–26. Present examples of prediction markets include Polymarket and Augur.

98. Savage, *Foundations of Statistics*, 12. For his part, Poincaré (*The Foundations of Science* [University Press of America, 1982 (1903)], 32) observed that "every probability problem involves two levels of study . . . the first—metaphysical, so to speak—justifies this or that convention; the second applies the rule of calculus to these conventions."

99. Henri Poincaré, *Science and Hypothesis* (Walter Scott Publishing, 1907 [1903]), 187–88.

100. Jan von Plato, "The Method of Arbitrary Functions," *British Journal for the Philosophy of Science* 34, no. 1 (1983): 37–47.

101. For a dispatch from the front lines, and one that recommends a very different prognosis than our own, see Deborah Mayo, *Statistical Inference as Severe Testing: How to Get Beyond the Statistics Wars* (Cambridge University Press, 2018).

Chapter 2

1. Lorraine Daston, "How Probabilities Came to be Subjective and Objective," *Historia Mathematica* 21, no. 3 (1994): 330–44; see also Lukas Verburgt, "The Objective and the Subjective in Nineteenth-Century British Probability Theory," *Historia Mathematica* 42, no. 4 (2015): 468–87.

2. Technically, for Kant, the subjective and the objective were both their own form of synthesis and thus always epistemic. Yet the connection to probability has seemingly been underestimated. However, philosopher of science Hans Reichenbach would take note (and use the connection to reject Kries's views) in his doctoral dissertation, *The Concept of Probability in the Mathematical Representation of Reality*, trans. Frederick Eberhardt and Clark Glymour (Open Court, 2008 [1915]), 54–55.

3. Immanuel Kant, *Lectures on Logic*, trans. and ed. Michael Young (Cambridge University Press, 1992 [1770s]), 114.

4. Kant, *Lectures on Logic*, 275–76.

5. On these grounds, Kant rejected the metaphysical hypothesis directed at the existence of God or the soul because both were objects that, as far as we know, have no real possibility. Theories are not perfectly arbitrary in relation to these objects; and because they are not, a theory about them cannot acquire probability. See also Jacob Rosenthal, "Probabilities as Ratios of Ranges in Initial-State Spaces," *Journal of Logic, Language and Information* 21, no. 2 (2012): 217–36.

6. See, for instance, Johannes von Kries, *Immanuel Kant und seine Bedeutung für die Naturforschung der Gegenwart* [Immanuel Kant and his Significance for Contemporary Natural Science Research] (TP Verone, 2016 [1926]), 89.

7. See Guido Fioretti, "Analogies, Conventions and Expert Systems in Medicine: Some Insights from a XIX Century Physiologist," *Studies in Multidisciplinarity* 3 (2005): 131–45.

8. Johannes von Kries, "Conventions of Measurement in Psychophysics," in *Principles of the Probability Calculus* (Springer, 2008 [1882]), 219–40.

9. See the account in Joseph Brent, *Charles Sanders Peirce: A Life* (Indiana University Press, 1998), chap. 2.

10. Fechner is also the discoverer of the "Weber law," which he named after his mentor Ernst Weber and which also involved a logarithmic connection of perception to differences in the world. Give a test subject two boxes of slightly different weights and see if they can tell the difference. The difference between 2 pounds and 10 pounds is much more noticeable than that between 100 and 108. See Michael Heidelberger, *Nature from Within: Gustav Theodor Fechner and His Psychophysical Worldview* (University of Pittsburgh Press, 2004), chap. 6.

11. See especially Charles Sanders Peirce, "The Materialistic and Conceptualistic Views of Probability," in *Collected Papers of Charles Sanders Peirce*, vol. 2, eds. Charles Hartshorne and Paul Weiss (Harvard University Press, 1931–1935), 676.

12. See, for example, Peirce and Joseph Jastrow, "On Small Differences in Sensation," *Memoirs of the National Academy of Sciences* 3 (1885): 73–83; see also Thomas Cadwaller, "Peirce as an Experimental Psychologist," *Transactions of the Charles S. Peirce Society* 11, no. 3 (1975): 176–86.

13. For a discussion, see Jimena Carles, *A Tenth of a Second: A History* (University of Chicago Press, 2010), chap. 2.

14. Kries, "Conventions of Measurement in Psychophysics," 225.

15. See Peirce, *Collected Papers*, vol. 2, 171ff; Johannes von Kries, *Logik* (J. C. B. Mohr, 1916), 11ff; see also Guido Fioretti, "Kries on Cognition," in *The Range of Science: Studies on the Multidisciplinary Legacy of Johannes von Kries*, ed. Gerhard Wagner (Springer, 2019), 65–77.

16. Gestalt psychologist Karl Bühler promoted the utility of synchysis but disputed Kries's understanding of it. After Bühler, however, the concept seems to have more or less disappeared outside of rhetoric. See Bühler's *Theory of Language: The Representational Function of Language* (John Benjamins, 2011 [1934]), 247ff.

17. See John Sheriff's attempt to redeem guessing as legitimate mode of understanding, in his book *Charles Peirce's Guess at the Riddle: Grounds for Human Significance* (Indiana University Press, 1994).

18. Peirce, "The Architecture of Theories," *Collected Papers of Charles Sanders Peirce*, vol. 6, eds. Charles Hartshorne and Paul Weiss (Harvard University Press, 1931–1935), 10.

19. Kries, quoted in Fioretti, "Analogies, Conventions, and Expert Systems in Medicine," 139–40.

20. See Andreas Kamlah, "Probability as a Quasi-Theoretical Concept: J.V. Kries' Sophisticated Account after a Century," *Erkenntnis* 19, no. 1 (1983): 239–51; Mauricio Suárez, "Propensities and Pragmatism," *Journal of Philosophy* 110, no. 2 (2013): 61–92.

21. Kries, *Principles of the Probability Calculus*, 86–87, 172.

22. Kries, *Principles of the Probability Calculus*, 84.

23. Kries, *Principles of the Probability Calculus*, 186.

24. Kries, *Principles of the Probability Calculus*, 59.

25. Kries, *Principles of the Probability Calculus*, 24ff.

26. Kries, *Principles of the Probability Calculus*, 95.

27. Kries, *Principles of the Probability Calculus*, 95.

28. We return to this point below, leveraging Bourdieu's claim that games of chance are the only occasion where "equality of opportunity" can be said, with legitimacy, to apply.

29. Kries, *Principles of the Probability Calculus*, 96.

30. Kries, *Principles of the Probability Calculus*, 99.

31. Kries, *Principles of the Probability Calculus*, 96, 100.

32. Kries, *Principles of the Probability Calculus*, 193.

33. Kries, *Principles of the Probability Calculus*, 262.

34. Kries, *Principles of the Probability Calculus*, 199.

35. Peirce, "On the Probability of Synthetic Inferences," in Hartshorne and Weiss, eds., *Collected Papers*, vol. 2, 685.

36. Peirce, "The Fallibility of Reasoning and the Feeling of Rationality," in Hartshorne and Weiss, eds., *Collected Papers*, vol. 2, 160.

37. Peirce, "On the Probability of Synthetic Inferences," 686.

38. Mauricio Suárez, "Propensities and Pragmatism," *Journal of Philosophy* 110, no. 2 (2013): 61–92, at. 67.

39. See John Levi Martin, "Peirce and Spencer-Brown on Probability, Chance and Lawfulness," *Cybernetics and Human Knowing* 22, no. 1 (2015): 9–33, at 31.

40. Charles Sanders Peirce, "Notes on the Doctrine of Chances," in *Collected Papers*, vol. 2, 664.

41. Charles Sanders Peirce, "Synechism," in Hartshorne and Weiss, eds., *Collected Papers*, vol. 6, 170.

42. Charles Sanders Peirce, *Reasoning and the Logic of Things: The Cambridge Conferences Lectures of 1898* (Harvard University Press, 1992), 262–63.

43. As Kries puts it, we would not say that it is objectively possible for a human body to immediately sink when placed in water, as such an effect would involve "altering nomological determinants . . . by changing things that are actually inalterable" (*Principles of the Probability Calculus*, 54).

44. To take another example from baseball: To gather data of revolutions per minute (RPM) of a thrown baseball is to capture data of the same thing, say, as a curveball but at a different Range, which means gathering more data points than the eye could ever catch. Motion creates the range of outcomes; for instance, it creates the difference between a ball that curves a lot versus a ball that curves very little. This is because, at a sufficiently finely grained level, the descriptor "curve" refers *only* to the motion. Baseball pitchers can be taught to throw while remaining oriented toward RPMs, as doing so will help them engage in action like throwing a *good* curveball; see Ben Lindbergh and Travis Sawchik, *The MVP Machine: How Baseball's New Nonconformists Are Using Data to Build Better Players* (Basic Books, 2019), chap. 8.

45. See Charles Sanders Peirce, "Subjective and Objective Modality," in *Collected Papers*, vol. 5, eds. Charles Hartshorne and Paul Weiss (Harvard University Press, 1931–1935), 456–57; "The Doctrine of Necessity Examined," in Hartshorne and Weiss, eds., *Collected Papers*, vol. 6, 47ff.

46. Peirce quoted in Paul Forster, *Peirce and The Threat of Nominalism* (Cambridge University Press, 2010), 61.

47. Charles Sanders Peirce, "The Percipuum," in *Collected Papers of Charles Sanders Peirce*, vol. 7, ed. Arthur Burks (Harvard University Press, 1958), 642–43; see also Richard Bernstein, "Peirce's Theory of Perception," in *Studies in the Philosophy of Charles Sanders Peirce*, eds. Edward Moore and Richard Robin (University of Massachusetts Press, 1964), 165–90.

48. See Peirce, "Architecture of Theories," 32ff.

49. Kries, *Principles of the Probability Calculus*, 67.

50. Kries, *Principles of the Probability Calculus*, 53–54.

51. Stephen Turner and Regis Factor, "Objective Possibility and Adequate Causation in Max Weber's Methodological Writings," *Sociological Review* 29, no. 1 (1981): 1–28, at 9.

52. See, for instance, Jacob Rosenthal, "The Natural-Range Conception of Probability," in *Time, Chance, and Reduction: Philosophical Aspects of Statistical Mechanics*, eds. Gerhard Ernst and Andreas Huttemann (Cambridge University Press, 2010), 71–90; Michael Strevens, "Dynamic Probability and the Problem of Initial Conditions," *Synthese* 199, nos. 5–6 (2021): 14617–39; Rani Lill Arjun and Stephen Mumford, *Causation in Science and the Methods of Scientific Discovery* (Oxford University Press, 2018), chap. 19; Suárez, "Propensities and Pragmatism."

53. Alongside Kries and Peirce, we could, in a lesser sense, place Kries's contemporaries Hermann Lotze and Wilhelm Lexis as proposing heterodox probability theories that are typically treated as a minor branch of logic. British information theorist George Spencer-Brown, as mentioned above, would be another.

54. William James, "The Dilemmas of Determinism," in *The Will to Believe and Other Essays in Popular Philosophy* (Longmans, Green and Co., 1907 [1884]), 149.

55. James, "Dilemmas of Determinism," 151.

56. James, "Dilemmas of Determinism," 180.

57. George Herbert Mead, "The Objective Reality of Perspectives," in *Proceedings of the Sixth International Congress of Philosophy*, ed. Edgar S. Brightman (Longmans, Green and Co., 1926), 83. As Mead continues, "the possibility is there in nature, for it is made up of actual structures of events and their contents." To perceive a possibility is to make a "mental or working hypothesis." Uncertainty is absorbed only "upon the accomplishment of the act" (84).

58. John Dewey, *Logic: The Theory of Inquiry* (Henry Holt, 1938), 179.

59. John Dewey, *Experience and Nature* (Dover, 1958), 100ff.

60. Dewey, *Experience and Nature*, 101.

61. Dewey, *Experience and Nature*, 102.

62. Dewey, *Experience and Nature*, 129.

63. Dewey, *Experience and Nature*, 107.

64. Dewey, *Logic*, 296.

65. Arthur Burks, *Chance, Cause and Reason: An Inquiry into the Nature of Scientific Explanation* (University of Chicago Press, 1963), 321.

66. John Maynard Keynes, *A Treatise on Probability* (Macmillan, 1921). Keynes would write much of this text in 1907 in an attempt to obtain a fellowship at King's College. It didn't work.

67. Keynes, *Treatise on Probability*, 93–94.

68. For a more extensive listing of those influenced by Kries, see Bernd Buldt, "Johannes von Kries: A Bio-Bibliography," *Journal for General Philosophy of Science* 47, no. 1 (2016): 217–35.

69. Michael Heidelberger, "Origins of the Logical Theory of Probability: Von Kries, Wittgenstein and Waisman," *International Studies in the Philosophy of Science* 15, no. 2 (2001): 177–88; see also Fioretti, "Kries on Cognition," for parallels between Kries's synchysis and Wittgenstein's "family resemblance."

70. Ludwig Wittgenstein, *Tractatus logico-philosophicus* (Kegan Paul, 1922), 123, 139.

71. Frank Ramsey, "Truth and Probability," in *The Foundations of Mathematics and Other Logical Essays* (Kegan, Paul, Trench, Trubner, and Co, 1931 [1926]), 158–59. Ramsey argues that the probability of "recovery from smallpox" can be rendered numerically as a frequency, but he specifies an alignment with Keynes's adoption of Kries's principle of *Spielraum*. While the probability of recovery is a "degree of belief," a certain proportion of initial states (smallpox) remain constant with that outcome (recovery).

72. Clare Hay, "Probability in Wittgenstein's *Tractatus*," *Philosophical Investigations* 45, no. 2 (2022): 130–45, at 133.

73. Savage, *The Foundations of Statistics* (Dover, 1954), 80ff.

74. Ramsey, "Truth and Probability," 173–74.

75. Stumpf served as Lewin's adviser, while Brunswik worked early on with Karl Bühler, who was himself an assistant in Kries's laboratory, shortly after Kries published his *Principles of the Probability Calculus* (see Buldt, "Johannes von Kries: A Bio-Bibliography").

76. Edward Tolman and Egon Brunswik, "The Organism and the Causal Texture of the Environment," *Psychological Review* 42, no. 1 (1935): 43–77.

77. Tolman and Brunswik, "Organism and the Causal Texture of the Environment," 75.

78. See, for instance, Egon Brunswik, "Probability as a Determiner of Rat Behavior," *Journal of Experimental Psychology* 25, no. 2 (1939): 175–97; "Organismic Achievement and Environmental Probability," *Psychological Review* 50, no. 3 (1943): 255–72.

79. Maurice Merleau-Ponty, *Phenomenology of Perception* (Routledge, 2005 [1945]), 513–14.

80. For a discussion, see Robert Nichols, *The World of Freedom: Heidegger, Foucault, and the Politics of Historical Ontology* (Stanford University Press, 2014), 62ff.

81. Carlos Lobo, "Husserl's Logic of Probability: An Attempt to Introduce in Philosophy the Concept of 'Intensive' Possibility," *Meta: Research in Hermeneutics, Phenomenology, and Practical Philosophy* 11, no. 2 (2019): 501–46.

82. Edmund Husserl, *Logical Investigations*, ed. Dermot Moran (Routledge, 2001 [1901]), 147–48; see also Edmund Husserl, *Early Writings in the Philosophy of Logic and Mathematics*, trans. Dallas Willard (Kluwer, 1993 [1890–1895]), 271ff.

83. For example, in Heidegger's *Being and Time* (SUNY Press, 1998 [1927], 136) we can find original phrases like "*Der Entwurf ist die existenziale Seinsverfassung des Spielraums des faktischen Seinkönnen.*" This is translated as: "Project is the existential constitution of being in the realm of the factical potentiality of being." That last phrase strongly resembles Kries's earlier use of *Spielraum*, though Heidegger never appears to draw this connection. Nor does he in this passage from his important "On the Essence of Ground" (in *Martin Heidegger: Basic Writings* [Harper, 1998 (1930)], 133) essay: "Every accounting for things must move within a sphere of what is possible [*Spielraum*] . . . In accordance with its essence, such grounding always necessarily provides a given range of what is possible [*Spielraum*]."

84. Max Planck, "The Origin and Development of the Quantum Theory," trans. H. T. Clarke and L. Silberstein (Clarendon Press, 1922 [1918]), 13.

85. Ernst Cassirer, *Determinism and Indeterminism in Modern Physics* (Yale University Press, 1956 [1936]), 118.

86. Gaston Bachelard, *The New Scientific Spirit* (Beacon Press, 1984 [1934]), 125.

87. Bachelard, *New Scientific Spirit*, 126–27.

88. Karl Popper, *The Logic of Scientific Discovery* (Routledge, 1959 [1934]), 134.

89. Karl Popper, "The Propensity Interpretation of Probability," *British Journal for the Philosophy of Science* 10, no. 37 (1959): 25–42.

90. Popper, "Propensity Interpretation of Probability," 26.

91. Popper, "Propensity Interpretation of Probability," 28.

92. Popper, *Logic of Scientific Discovery*, 108.

93. Popper, *Logic of Scientific Discovery*, 108.

94. Jennifer Platt, *A History of Sociological Research Methods in America, 1920–1960* (Cambridge University Press, 1999), chap. 2.

95. See Jani Erola, "Why Probability Has Not Succeeded in Sociology," *Sociology* 44, no. 1 (2010): 121–38.

96. Scott Lynch and Bryce Bartlett, "Bayesian Statistics in Sociology: Past, Present and Future," *Annual Review of Sociology* 45 (2019): 47–68.

97. For an early example of this filtering, see Paul Lazarsfeld and Anthony Oberschall, "Max Weber and Empirical Research," *American Sociological Review* 30, no. 2 (1965): 185–199.

98. Roscoe Hinkle, "Antecedents of the Action Orientation in American Sociology Before 1935," *American Sociological Review* 28, no. 5 (1963): 705–15.

99. Hinkle, "Antecedents of the Action Orientation in American Sociology Before 1935," 713.

100. Hinkle, "Antecedents of the Action Orientation in American Sociology Before 1935," 714.

101. Talcott Parsons, *The Structure of Social Action* (McGraw-Hill, 1937), 248ff.

102. Parsons, *Structure of Social Action*, 53.

103. Ralf Dahrendorf, *Life Chances: Approaches to Social and Political Theory* (University of Chicago Press, 1979), 62.

104. Keith Tribe, "Translator's Introduction," in Max Weber, *Economy and Society: A New Translation*, trans. Keith Tribe (Harvard University Press, 2019 [1920–1921]), 65.

105. Max Weber, *Theory of Social and Political Organization*, trans. Talcott Parsons and Alexander Henderson (Oxford University Press, 1948), 100n21.

106. Weber, *Theory of Social and Political Organization*, 100.

107. Weber, *Economy and Society*, 88, bold and italics in the original.

108. John Heritage, *Garfinkel and Ethnomethodology* (Polity Press, 1984).

109. Alfred Schutz, *The Phenomenology of the Social World* (Northwestern University Press, 1967 [1932]), 151–52.

110. Schutz, *Phenomenology of the Social World*, 153.

111. Schutz, *Phenomenology of the Social World*, 237.

112. See, primarily, Kari Palonen, *A Political Style of Thinking: Essays on Max Weber* (ECPR Press, 2017).

113. Stephen Turner, "Weber on Action," *American Sociological Review* 48, no. 4 (1983): 506–19; Stephen Turner and Regis Factor, "Objective Possibility and Adequate Causation in Weber's Methodological Writings," *Sociological Review* 29, no. 1 (1981): 5–28.

114. See, especially, Iddo Tavory and Stefan Timmermans, *Abductive Analysis: Theorizing Qualitative Research* (University of Chicago Press, 2014).

115. Some contemporary sociologists have argued that sociologists *should* predict, particularly if they are to survive in an era that so strongly associates rationality with prediction, as a data-centric one does; see Duncan J. Watts, "Common Sense and Sociological Explanations," *American Journal of Sociology* 120, no. 2 (2014): 313–51.

116. Daniel Kahneman and Amos Tversky, "On the Psychology of Prediction," *Psychological Review* 80, no. 4 (1973): 137–51; Amos Tversky and Daniel Kahneman, "Availability: A Heuristic for Judging Frequency and Probability," *Cognitive Psychology* 5, no. 2 (1973): 207–32. These articles laid the groundwork for their wildly influential piece "Judgment Under Uncertainty: Heuristics and Biases," *Science* 185, no. 4157 (1974): 1124–31.

117. This narrowness is, in part, what psychologist and historian of probability Gerd Gigerenzer objected to in the work of Kahneman and Tversky. See his "On Narrow Norms and Vague Heuristics: A Reply to Kahneman and Tversky," *Psychological Review* 103, no. 3 (1996): 592–96.

118. This is in part what Bayesian scholars believe when they critique Tversky and Kahne-

man's argument; see Michelle McDowell and Perke Jacobs, "Meta-Analysis of the Effect of Natural Frequencies on Bayesian Reasoning," *Psychological Bulletin* 143, no. 12 (2017): 1273–312.

119. See Milton Friedman, "The Methodology of Positive Economics," in *Essays in Positive Economics* (University of Chicago Press, 1966), 3–16, especially 14.

120. Hungarian philosopher Georg Lukacs is another theorist who should be mentioned, though eventually he would leave his probabilism behind. Like Schutz, Lukacs was a German-language reader, as well as a part of the Weber circle for a time that Weber and Marianne Weber hosted in Heidelberg. It is no surprise, from this vantage, that Lukacs would notice key categories like "objective possibility" and *"Chance"* in Weber's work, and it is even more interesting that Lukacs helps himself to them. He does so in what remains his most influential concept: the concept of standpoint. Consider how Lukacs puts it in his most famous essay: "The capitalist process of rationalization based on private economic calculation requires that every manifestation of life shall exhibit this very interaction between details which are subject to laws and a totality ruled by chance." As he elaborates, he draws a distinction between the ontological and the nomological, which is required as "chances" becomes an objectively existing thing, in Lukacs's argument, as do "laws of probability." Thus, "chances of exploitation, the laws of the 'market' must likewise be rational in the sense that they must be calculable according to the laws of probability. But they must not be governed by a law in the sense in which 'laws' govern individual phenomena." For Lukacs, those individual phenomena are not "rationally organized through and through"—they are not predictable, in other words. As the standpoint of the whole is destroyed by the division of labor, more particular standpoints become real things, as evident in a distribution of chances. In a critique of "bourgeois thought," Lukacs argues that the laws of probability it yields are inapplicable to the scenarios of the proletariat because they only focus on the chances of exchange. The standpoint of the proletariat is ontological in relation to them: particular and singular. As Lukacs explores the nature of objective possibility, he frames his exploration with a key question: "How far is it *in fact* possible to discern the whole economy of a society from inside it?" It is possible, he concludes, from the standpoint of those whose chance overlaps with the "objective possibility" of a different order. See Georg Lukacs, "Reification and the Consciousness of the Proletariat," in *History and Class Consciousness* (MIT Press, 1968 [1922]), 51ff, 102ff.

121. David Levering Lewis, *W.E.B. Du Bois, 1868–1919: Biography and Race* (Henry Holt, 1993), 91ff.

122. For Schmoller in particular, the solution was clear: There simply was no statistical law, like Quetelet argued, because there could be no material cause of action; there could only be ethical causes of action. Historian Axel Schafer ("W.E.B. Du Bois, German Social Thought, and the Racial Divide in American Progressivism, 1892–1909," *Journal of American History* 88, no. 3 [2001]: 925–49) contends that Schmoller's historicist and moral critique of statistics, in particular, "left a deep imprint" on Du Bois.

123. Aldon Morris, *The Scholar Denied: W.E.B. Du Bois and the Birth of Modern Sociology* (University of California Press, 2015).

124. W. E. B. Du Bois, "Sociology Hesitant," *boundary 2* 27, no. 3 (2000 [1905]): 37–44.

125. W. E. B. Du Bois, "My Evolving Program for Negro Freedom," in *What the Negro Wants*, ed. Rayford Logan (University of Notre Dame, 2012 [1944]), 31–70 quotation is on 58.

126. Du Bois, "Sociology Hesitant," 38; see also José Itzigsohn and Karida Brown, *The Sociology of W.E.B. Du Bois: Racialized Modernity and the Global Color Line* (New York University Press, 2020), 53.

127. Du Bois, "Sociology Hesitant," 42.

128. In this unpublished sketch from 1946, we can find an early version of a book Du Bois

tentatively entitled "Prolegomena to a Science of Human Action"; in it, he includes a chapter outline with several indicative titles: "The Working Hypothesis," "The Assumed Truth," "Welcoming Error and Rearranging Hypotheses," and "The Limits of Chance." We would expect such titles to appear in a book on statistics, perhaps, rather than one on human action. See W. E. B. Du Bois, "Steps Toward a Science of How Men Act," ca. 1946, *W.E.B. Du Bois Papers* (MS 312), Special Collections and University Archives, University of Massachusetts Amherst Libraries.

129. As we argue below, a good application of this idea can be found in Du Bois's account of "the general strike" in his magisterial *Black Reconstruction in America: An Essay Toward a History of the Part Which Black Folk Played in the Attempt to Reconstruct Democracy in America, 1860–1880* (Harcourt, Brace and Co., 1935).

Introduction to Part II

1. Johannes von Kries, *Immanuel Kant und seine Bedeutung für die Naturforschung der Gegenwart* [Immanuel Kant and his Significance for Contemporary Natural Science Research] (TP Verone, 2016/1926).

2. Joseph Brent, *Charles Sanders Peirce: A Life* (Indiana University Press, 1993), 66–67.

3. We owe the initial discussion of this link of Spinoza to Kries (and on to Weber) to Michael Heidelberger, "From Mill via von Kries to Max Weber: Causality, Explanation and Understanding," in *Historical Perspectives on Erklären and Verstehen*, ed. Uljana Feest (Springer, 2010), 241–65, especially 249.

4. Baruch de Spinoza, *Ethics: Proved in Geometric Order*, trans. Michael Silverthorne and Matthew Kisner (Cambridge University Press, 2018 [1667]), 78.

5. Spinoza, *Ethics*, 95.

6. See David Levering Lewis, *W.E.B. Du Bois, 1868–1919: Biography of a Race* (Henry Holt, 1993), 102.

7. Max Weber, "Objective Possibility and Adequate Causation in the Historical Causal Approach," in *Max Weber: Collected Methodological Writings*, trans. Hans Henrik Bruun, eds. Hans Henrik Bruun and Sam Whimster (Routledge, 2012 [1906]), 177.

8. Johannes von Kries, "Ueber den Begriff der objektiven Möglichkeit und einige Anwendungen desselben" [On the Concept of Objective Possibility and Some Applications of it], *Vierteljahresschrift für wissenschaftliche Philosophie* 12 (1888): 179–240, 287–323, 393–428. We thank Kathrin Breuer for help translating this article.

9. Kries, "Ueber den Begriff der objektiven Möglichkeit," 201; see also John Stuart Mill, *A System of Logic: Rationative and Inductive* (University of Toronto Press, 1974 [1843]).

10. As Kries puts it, "the specificity of the case lies only in the fact that, because of the very special and not foreseeable configuration, an action that is generally suited to the highest degree to lead to a certain outcome did not produce it. . . . No causal connection is interrupted, but the culpable act has not fully developed its causal effectiveness in the usual way, because of the special formation of the singular case" (Kries, "Ueber den Begriff der objektiven Möglichkeit," 210).

11. Jonathan Israel, *Radical Enlightenment: Philosophy and the Making of Modernity, 1650–1750* (Oxford University Press, 2001).

Chapter 3

1. Alan Sica, *Weber, Irrationality and Social Order* (University of California Press, 1988), 78.

2. For more on the idea of "model systems" in the social sciences see Monika Krause, "West-

ern Hegemony in the Social Sciences: Fields and Model Systems," *Sociological Review* 64, no. 2 (supplement, 2016): 194–211.

3. Isaac Reed, *Interpretation and Social Knowledge* (University of Chicago Press, 2011), 143; Clifford Geertz, *Interpretation of Cultures* (Basic Books, 1973), 5, 131, 171.

4. See also Monika Krause, "Interpretation and Critical Classification: Geertzism and Beyond in the Sociology of Culture," *Sociologica* 18, no. 1 (2014): 87–93; Richard Biernacki, "Method and Metaphor in the New Cultural History," in *Beyond the Cultural Turn*, eds. Victoria Bonnell and Lynn Hunt (University of California Press, 1999), 62–95.

5. Clifford Geertz, *The Interpretation of Cultures* (Basic Books, 1973), 46.

6. For more on this reading of Geertz, see Bradd Shore, *Culture in Mind: Cognition, Culture, and the Problem of Meaning* (Oxford University Press, 1996), 33ff.

7. Ann Swidler, *Talk of Love: How Culture Matters* (University of Chicago, 2001).

8. Geertz, *Interpretation of Cultures*, 50; see also Michael Strand, "Cognition, Practice and Learning in the Discourse of the Human Sciences," in *Handbook of Classical Sociological Theory*, eds. Seth Abrutyn and Omar Lizardo (Springer, 2021), 651–70.

9. This failure of fruition came about in no small part due to suspension of the project during the height of World War I and acrimonious legal wranglings concerning the connection of the *Grundriss* to the older *Handbuch der politicschen Okonomie*, edited by Gustav von Schonberg. In part, the title *Sozialökonomik* was arrived at to create a distinction from the earlier text, and also because Weber strongly preferred it on intellectual grounds. Things got so bad that Weber even set the date for a duel with a particularly unscrupulous interloper; see Keith Tribe, "Introduction to Max Weber's *Economy and Society*," in Max Weber, *Economy and Society: A New Translation*, trans. Keith Scribe (Harvard University Press, 2019), 20.

10. Edith Hanke, "'Max Weber's Desk Is Now My Altar': Marianne Weber and the Intellectual Heritage of Her Husband," *History of European Ideas* 35, no. 3 (2009): 349–59.

11. Tribe, "Introduction," 27.

12. Tribe, "Introduction," 2.

13. Stephen Turner, "The Origins of 'Mainstream Sociology' and Other Issues in the History of American Sociology," *Social Epistemology* 8, no. 1 (1994): 41–67.

14. Max Weber, quoted in Tribe, "Introduction," 57.

15. Weber, *Economy and Society: A New Translation*, 56.

16. All quotes from Kari Palonen, *A Political Style of Thinking: Essays on Max Weber* (ECPR Press, 2017), 126–27.

17. Thomas S. Eberle, "The Concept of Adequacy in Sociology: Johannnes von Kries, Max Weber and Alfred Schutz," in *The Range of Science Studies on the Interdisciplinary Legacy of Johannes von Kries*, ed. Gerhard Wagner (Harrassowitz Verlag, 2019), 119–37.

18. Stephen Turner and Regis Factor, *Max Weber: The Lawyer as Social Thinker* (Routledge, 1994), 179.

19. Max Weber, "Some Categories of Interpretative Sociology," *Sociological Quarterly* 22, no. 2 (1981): 151–80, at 168.

20. Learning "an average" without frequency counts or real numbers might have seemed implausible to past attempts to make sense of Weber's probabilism, though it aligns with learning mechanisms now proposed by proponents of the "predictive turn" in cognitive science, as we discuss in chapter 5.

21. Weber, "Some Categories," 177, emphasis added.

22. Weber, *Economy and Society: A New Translation*, 112.

23. Weber, "Some Categories," 161.

24. Weber, "Some Categories," 160.

25. Weber, "Some Categories," 168.

26. The role of "effort" in action is a central postulate in Parsons's normativist functionalism. Here, a probabilistic reading of Weber shows that it is unnecessary. See also Daniel Silver, "The Moodiness of Action," *Sociological Theory* 29, no. 3 (2011): 199–222.

27. Weber, "Some Categories," 161.

28. Weber, "Some Categories," 161.

29. Weber, "Some Categories," 161.

30. Weber, "Some Categories," 177ff.

31. Weber, "Some Categories," 178.

32. Peter Berger and Thomas Luckmann, *The Social Construction of Reality* (Anchor, 1966), 23–24.

33. Weber, "Some Categories," 175.

34. Weber, *Economy and Society: A New Translation*, 111.

35. Weber, "Some Categories," 178.

36. Weber, "Some Categories," 178.

37. Weber, "Some Categories," 178.

38. Weber, "Some Categories," 178.

39. Weber, "Some Categories," 177.

40. Weber, *Economy and Society: A New Translation*, 107ff.

41. Weber, *Economy and Society: A New Translation*, 386, 443–44; Max Weber, *Sociology of Religion* (Beacon Press, 1993 [1920]), chap. 1.

42. Max Weber, *The Protestant Ethic and the Spirit of Capitalism*, trans. Stephen Kalberg (Oxford University, 2011 [1904–1905]).

43. Scott Hendrix, *Martin Luther: Visionary Reformer* (Yale University Press, 2015), 53.

44. Weber, *Protestant Ethic*, 17.

45. Weber, *Protestant Ethic*, 120.

46. Weber, *Protestant Ethic*, 124.

47. Weber, *Economy and Society: A New Translation*, 244.

48. Weber, "Some Categories," 178.

49. Richard Lachmann, *From Manor to Market: Structural Change in England, 1536–1640* (University of Wisconsin Press, 1987), 11.

50. Stephen Kalberg, "The Rationalization of Action in Max Weber's Sociology of Religion," *Sociological Theory* 8, no. 1 (1990): 58–84, at 61.

51. Weber, *Economy and Society: A New Translation*, 101, 109ff, 348ff, 386–87, 455–56.

52. See Keith Tribe, "'Chance' in Max Weber's Late Writings," in *History as a Translation from the Past: Case Studies from the West*, ed. Luigi Alonzo (Bloomsbury, 2023), 121–41, especially 116.

53. Weber, "Some Categories," 160–61.

54. For an argument developing this point, see Kari Palonen, "The State as a 'Chance' Concept: Max Weber's De-Substantialisation and Neutralisation of the Concept," *Max Weber Studies* 11, no. 1 (2011): 99–117.

55. Weber, "Some Categories," 178–79; Weber, *Economy and Society: A New Translation*, 386, 443–44; Max Weber, "Science as a Vocation," in *Max Weber: Collected Methodological Writings*, eds. Hans Henrik Bruun and Sam Whimster (Routledge, 2012 [1919]), 350ff.

56. Weber, *Economy and Society: A New Translation*, 107–8.

57. Weber, "Some Categories," 176.

58. Weber, "Some Categories," 178.

59. Weber, "Science as a Vocation," 352.

60. Weber, "Some Categories," 179.

61. Weber, *Economy and Society: A New Translation*, 386, 443–44; Weber, *Sociology of Religion*, chap. 1.

62. Max Weber, "Religious Rejections of the World and their Directions," in *From Max Weber: Essays in Sociology*, eds. and trans. Hans Gerth and C. Wright Mills (Oxford University Press, 1946 [1915]).

63. Weber offers the example of a classical Greek distinction in masculinity, in which "the treatment of erotic experience with women as 'life-fate' . . . would have appeared as almost sophomoric and sentimental." It was only with the "crypto-erotic religiosity" of the Middle Ages that there "began the 'probation' of the man . . . in the face of the erotic interest of the 'lady.'" See "Religious Rejections," 345–46. What Weber attempts to track here, in fleshed-out probabilistic terms, are tests that signal the "erotic sphere" as a realm of adequate cause that can thus be referenced as "proof" of worth. As Weber notes ("Religious Rejections," 349) his point aligns with Nietzsche's *Will to Power* in its account of "transvaluation" via engagement with *force*, which (in addition to the influence of Tolstoy's *War and Peace*) generates a strange commonality between Weber's tests and Bruno Latour's polytheistic "trials." In Latour's trials, whether using words, money, sauces, intimate partners, wounds, and so forth, "we like to do the same things with them—that is, to learn the meaning of strong and weak, real and unreal, associated or disassociated," to make potentials into actualities, in other words, and learn "the meaning of the word 'reality.'" See Bruno Latour, *The Pasteurization of France* (Harvard University Press, 1988), 155ff.

64. Weber, *Economy and Society: A New Translation*, 120.

65. Weber, "Some Categories," 173.

66. Weber, *Economy and Society: A New Translation*, 117.

67. Weber, *Economy and Society: A New Translation*, 134.

68. Though see Palonen, "State as a 'Chance' Concept."

69. Carl Schmitt, *Legality and Legitimacy*, trans. Jeffrey Seitzer (Duke University Press, 2004/1932), at 135–36.

70. Weber, "Some Categories," 168.

71. Weber, *Economy and Society: A New Translation*, 134.

72. Weber, *Economy and Society: A New Translation*, 339.

73. Weber, *Economy and Society: A New Translation*, 105.

74. Weber, *Economy and Society: A New Translation*, 334ff.

75. Ernst Cassirer, *The Philosophy of Symbolic Forms: Mythical Thought*, trans. Ralph Manheim (Yale University Press, 1955), 38.

76. Niccolo Machiavelli, *The Prince* (Penguin, 2006 [1532]), chap. 25. See also Hannah Pitkin, *Fortune Is a Woman: Gender and Politics in the Thought of Niccolo Machiavelli* (University of Chicago Press, 1999).

77. Weber, *Economy and Society: A New Translation*, 135.

78. John Ruggie, "Territoriality and Beyond: Problematizing Modernity in International Relations," *International Organization* 47, no. 1 (1993): 139–74, at 151.

79. Ruggie, "Territoriality and Beyond," 146.

80. Weber, *Economy and Society: A New Translation*, 104.

81. Talcott Parsons, *The Structure of Social Action* (McGraw-Hill, 1937), 658ff.

82. Parsons, *Structure of Social Action*, at 651 and 670, emphasis added.

83. Parsons, *Structure of Social Action*, 111.

84. Weber, *Economy and Society: A New Translation*, 109.

85. Weber, *Economy and Society: A New Translation*, 109.

86. Weber, *Economy and Society: A New Translation*, 111.

87. Here we find inspiration in Tribe's reference to Weber's "relentless use of *Chance*" to describe *E&S* as a whole.

88. Gilles Deleuze, *Difference and Repetition* (Columbia University Press, 1994 [1968]), 153.

Chapter 4

Chapter adapted from Michael Strand and Omar Lizardo, "For a Probabilistic Sociology: A History of Concept Formation with Pierre Bourdieu," Theory and Society 51 (2022): 399–434. Reprinted by permission of Springer Nature.

1. We thank Loïc Wacquant for sharing with us many little-known historical details about Bourdieu mentioned in the following pages.

2. *Outline*, along with *The Inheritors* (coauthored with Jean-Claude Passeron), had already been translated to English by Richard Nice in 1977 and 1979 and published by Cambridge University Press and the University of Chicago Press (respectively) by the time Bourdieu assumed the sociology chair at the Collège. The English translation of *Distinction* would follow shortly after that, also by Nice, published by Harvard University Press in 1984. *Logic*, by contrast, would not see an English translation (again by Nice) until the 1990 publication by Stanford University Press.

3. Pierre Bourdieu, Jean-Claude Chamboredon, and Jean-Claude Passeron, trans. Richard Nice, *The Craft of Sociology: Epistemological Preliminaries* (Walter de Gruyter, 1991 [1968]).

4. Gaston Bachelard, *The Formation of the Scientific Mind* (Clinamen Press, 2002 [1938]), 237.

5. Bourdieu, Chamboredon, and Passeron, *Craft of Sociology*, 57ff.

6. Bourdieu, Chamboredon, and Passeron, *Craft of Sociology*, 69ff.

7. Derek Robbins, "Sociology and Philosophy in the Work of Pierre Bourdieu, 1965–75," *Journal of Classical Sociology* 2, no. 3 (2002): 299–328.

8. For a firsthand account of founding *Actes*, see Luc Boltanski, *Rendre la réalité inacceptable* (Seuil, 2008). *Archives* had been founded by Aron, Ralf Dahrendorf, and Tom Bottomore in 1960. Jean Stoetzel founded *Revue* the same year. Both journals sought to provide a counterweight to Georges Gurvitch's *Cahiers internationaux de sociologie* and its heavily theoretical orientation, with *Archives* tending to have a historical and comparative orientation, and *Revue* a methodological and statistical orientation. *Actes*, by contrast, employed (and still employs) a novel use of empirical documentation (photos, interview fragments, statistical tables), which is visible in Bourdieu's *Distinction*, and with an interdisciplinary and (in contemporary terms) "mixed-methods" focus. More generally, it expressly sought to be "opposed to Parisian fads and intellectual verbalism . . . thoroughly rooted in empirical research while being critically attuned to important questions in both public and scientific debates." See Johan Heilbron, *French Sociology* (Cornell University Press, 2015), 172–73. Earlier (in 1974), Bourdieu had become a founding editor (alongside Randall Collins and Alvin Gouldner) of the American-based journal *Theory and Society*.

9. Derek Robbins, *The Bourdieu Paradigm: Origins and Evolution of an Intellectual Social Project* (Manchester University Press, 2019), 136 n5.

10. Amín Pérez, *Bourdieu and Sayad Against Empire* (Polity Press, 2024), 34.

11. Pérez, *Bourdieu and Sayad Against Empire*.

12. See Pierre Bourdieu, *Sketch for a Self-Analysis* (University of Chicago Press, 2004 [2000]), 73ff.

13. Heilbron, *French Sociology*, 186ff. As Heilbron (120–21) notes, because the Durkheimian tradition that both Halbwachs and Mauss represented had failed to "establish" sociology in

France in coherent form after Durkheim's death in 1917, the national history of French sociology cannot be characterized by a "rise and fall" narrative as much as by multiple inconsistent appropriations and a kind of splintering—between a research and teaching orientation, between the Durkheimians themselves into different camps by the late 1920s (99–100), and between the university presence of Durkheimianism as "neo-idealist philosophy" combined with "secular republican morality" and the 1930s—as it seemed increasingly out place from the belle epoque conditions that gave it birth. Mauss, for instance, was less visible in the broader academic field than the university teachers who rejected Durkheimianism ("not only Durkheimian sociology, but its very aim and style as well"), like Georges Gurvitch and Jean Stoetzel, and (later) Aron. It was their sociologies, along with the Durkheimian apologetics of Georges Davy, that would largely serve to define "sociology" for the postwar generation of students: the time during Bourdieu's (born in 1930) formative academic period.

14. We keep this translation of the title of the lectures, which is what they are referred in their translated form by Polity Press. Arguably, a more apt translation would be "Elements for a genetic sociology." We thank Loïc Wacquant for mentioning this point.

15. Pierre Bourdieu, *Classification Struggles: General Sociology, Volume 1, Lectures at the Collège de France 1981–82* (Polity, 2019 [1981–1982]); Pierre Bourdieu, *Habitus and Field: General Sociology, Volume 2, Lectures at the Collège de France 1982–83* (Polity, 2020 [1982–1983]); Pierre Bourdieu, *Forms of Capital: General Sociology, Volume 3, Lectures at the Collège de France 1983–84* (Polity, 2021 [1983–1984]); Pierre Bourdieu, *Principles of Vision: General Sociology, Volume 4, Lectures at the Collège de France 1984–85* (Polity, 2022 [1984–1985]).

16. Pierre Bourdieu, "Étude sociologique," in *Travail et Travilleurs en Algerie* (Mouton, 1963), 346ff (our translation and italics).

17. Pierre Bourdieu, "Fieldwork in Philosophy," in *In Other Words* (Stanford University Press, 1990), 5.

18. Karl Marx, *Outline of a Critique of Political Economy*, ed. Maurice Dobb (International Publishers, 1859 [1979]), 56.

19. Bourdieu would return to this theme thirty years later in *Pascalian Meditations* (Stanford University Press, 2001 [1997]), 221ff.

20. Pierre Bourdieu, *Algeria 1960: The Disenchantment of the World, the Sense of Honour, the Kabyle House or the World Reversed*, trans. Richard Nice (Cambridge University Press, 1979), vii. Thanks to *Outline*, Bourdieu was better known as an anthropologist than a sociologist in the English-speaking world, part of the then-upstart movement of "practice theory." In fact, Bourdieu appears in this role during his (brief) cameo in Anthony Giddens's *Central Problems in Social Theory* (University of California Press, 1979), 25, 217; see also Sherry Ortner, "Theory in Anthropology Since the Sixties," *Comparative Studies in Society and History* 26, no. 1 (1984): 126–66.

21. Pierre Bourdieu, "Structuralism and the Theory of Sociological Knowledge," *Social Research* 35 (1968): 681–706; Pierre Bourdieu, "The Berber House or the World Reversed," *Social Science Information* 9, no. 2 (1970): 151–70; Bourdieu, Chamboredon, and Passeron, *Craft of Sociology*.

22. Bourdieu, "Structuralism and the Theory of Sociological Knowledge," 704–5.

23. Omar Lizardo, "Beyond the Antinomies of Structure: Levi-Strauss, Bourdieu, Giddens and Sewell," *Theory and Society* 39 (2010): 651–88; Bourdieu would keep this methodological stance all the way through to *Pascalian Meditations*, 176–77.

24. Bourdieu, "Structuralism and the Theory of Sociological Knowledge," 705.

25. Bourdieu, "Structuralism and the Theory of Sociological Knowledge," 705, emphasis added.

26. In these early (pre-1973) writings, Bourdieu operates with an ambiguous (regarding the epistemic/ontic distinction) notion of "objective" (position, relations, etc.) modeled after structuralism, but he will later recast this notion in a less ambiguous ontic manner in terms of objective probabilities qua fields.

27. Pierre Bourdieu and Jean-Claude Passeron, *The Inheritors: French Students Relation to Culture* (University of Chicago Press, 1979 [1964]); Pierre Bourdieu and Jean-Claude Passeron, *Reproduction in Education, Society and Culture* (Sage, 1990 [1970]).

28. Bourdieu and Passeron, *Reproduction*, 156.

29. Pierre Bourdieu, "Intellectual Field and Creative Project," *Social Science Information* 8, no. 2 (1969): 89–119. Translated by Sian France from "Champ intellectuel et projet créateur," *Les temps modernes* (November 1966): 865–906.

30. Mustafa Emirbayer and Victoria Johnson, "Bourdieu and Organizational Analysis," *Theory and Society* 37: 1–44.

31. A rare exception is found in David Swartz, "The Sociology of Habit: The Perspective of Pierre Bourdieu," *OTJR: Occupation, Participation and Health* 22, no. 1 (2002): 61S–69S, see especially 64ff.

32. See Robbins, "Sociology and Philosophy," 32off.

33. Pierre Bourdieu, "Three Forms of Theoretical Knowledge," *Social Science Information* 12, no. 1 (1973): 53–80, at 70, emphasis added.

34. Max Weber, "Some Categories of Interpretive Sociology," *Sociological Quarterly* 22, no. 2 (1981): 151–80, at 159.

35. However, it is possible that Bourdieu had tracked down the essay himself, as he found Freund's translation of Weber's works substandard.

36. Bourdieu, "Three Forms," 64.

37. Bourdieu, "Three Forms," 65, emphasis original.

38. Pierre Bourdieu, "Causality of the Probable and the Future of Class," trans. Michael Grenfell, in *Rethinking Economics*, eds. Asimina Christoforou and Michael Lainé (Routledge, 2014), 247–84, at 235, emphasis added.

39. Bourdieu, "Causality of the Probable and the Future of Class," 260 n7.

40. Pierre Bourdieu, *The Logic of Practice* (Stanford University Press, 1990 [1980]), 63.

41. Bourdieu, *Logic of Practice*, 63.

42. Weber, "Some Categories," 157. Bourdieu would later critique this particular Weberian characterization as an instance of (one version of) the "scholastic" way of defining the chance-expectation loop (characteristic of marginalist economics) while at the same time acknowledging that in deploying the (idealized) notion of average chances, "Max Weber at least had the merit of tacitly taking account of the inequality of chances, which he placed at the center of his theory of stratification" (Bourdieu, *Pascalian Meditations*, 219–20).

43. Bourdieu, *Logic of Practice*, 48–49; Bourdieu, *Pascalian Meditations*. For the argument that *The Logic of Practice* was the underlying theoretical engine of Bourdieu's epoch-making *Distinction* (Harvard University Press, 1984), see Omar Lizardo, "Taste and the Logic of Practice in Distinction," *Czech Sociological Review* 50, no. 3 (2014): 335–64.

44. Edward Tolman and Egon Brunswik, "The Organism and the Causal Texture of the Environment," *Psychological Review* 42, no. 1 (1935): 43–77; Egon Brunswik, "Systematic and Representative Design of Psychological Experiments: With Results in Physical and Social Perception," in *Proceedings of the Berkeley Symposium on Mathematical Statistics and Probability* (University of California Press, 1949), 143–202; F. Attneave, "Psychological Probability as a Function of Experienced Frequency," *Journal of Experimental Psychology* 46 no. 2 (1953): 81–86; Malcolm

Preston and Phillip Baratta, "An Experimental Study of the Auction-Value of an Uncertain Outcome," *American Journal of Psychology* 61, no. 2 (1948): 183–93.

45. Attneave, "Psychological Probability," 81, emphasis original.

46. Attneave, "Psychological Probability," 81.

47. See Vsevolod Kapatsinski, *Changing Minds, Changing Tools: From Learning Theory to Language Acquisition to Language Change* (MIT Press, 2018).

48. While Bourdieu used the category of "field" (*champ*) as early as 1963, in *Travail et travailleurs en Algérie* and, most influentially, in "Intellectual Field and Creative Project" from 1966, he did not link it to habitus until (it appears) *Outline of a Theory of Practice* (Cambridge University Press, 1976) specifically with this statement: "Quasi conscient l'opération que l'habitus réalise sur un autre mode à savoir une estimation des chances supposant la transformation de l'effet passé en avenir escompté, il reste qu'elles se définissent d'abord par rapport à un champ de potentialités objectives" (176). Important to note here is the mention of "potentialités objectives" as part of the habitus/field link. Bourdieu also does not mention "potentialités objectives" explicitly in line with Weber's "objective probability" until 1974. In the 1977 English edition of *Outline*, Richard Nice translates the original "un champ de potentialités objectives" as "a system of objective potentialities" (76). In the "Three Forms of Theoretical Knowledge" essay, this same phrase is translated as "a field of objective potentialities" (64).

49. Pierre Bourdieu, "Séminaires sur le concept de champ, 1972–1975: Introduction by Patrick Champagne," *Actes de la recherche en sciences sociales* 200 (2013): 4–37.

50. Bourdieu, *Logic of Practice*, 48–49. The reference to "deciding to believe" comes from Bernard Williams, "Deciding to Believe," in *Philosophical Papers: 1956–1972* (Cambridge University Press, 1973), 136–51.

51. See also Gerd Gigerenzer, Zwent Swijtink, Theodore Porter, Lorraine Daston, John Beatty, and Lorenz Kruger, *The Empire of Chance*, chap. 3.

52. John Levi Martin, *The Explanation of Social Action* (Oxford University Press, 2011), 84–85; see also Michael Strand, "Sociology and Philosophy in the United States Since the Sixties," *Theory and Society* 49 (2020): 101–50.

53. Derek Robbins, "Theory of Practice," in *Pierre Bourdieu: Key Concepts*, ed. Michael Grenfell (Routledge, 2012), 35.

54. Robbins, "Theory of Practice," 35.

55. It bears mentioning that Bourdieu was evidently aware of this history at the very least from having read (and arranged to translate into French) Ian Hacking's *Emergence of Probability*, a book we engage with in chapter 1.

56. Bourdieu, *Classification Struggles*, 79.

57. Pierre Bourdieu, "What Makes a Social Class? On the Theoretical and Practical Existence of Groups," *Berkeley Journal of Sociology* 32 (1987): 1–17.

58. However, Luc Boltanski and Laurent Thevenot, who at the time were in the midst of distancing their work from Bourdieu, with whom they had both worked closely (particularly Boltanski), retain something of this perspective in their influential "Finding One's Way in Social Space: A Study Based on Games," *Social Science Information* 22, nos. 4–5 (1983): 631–80.

59. Pierre Bourdieu, "Symbolic Capital and Social Classes," *Journal of Classical Sociology* 13, no. 2 (2013 [1978]): 292–302.

60. Bourdieu, "What Makes a Social Class?," 7, emphasis added.

61. Bourdieu, *Logic of Practice*, 54.

62. Loïc Wacquant, "A Concise Genealogy and Anatomy of Habitus," *Sociological Review* 64, no. 1 (2016): 64–72.

63. Bourdieu, *Habitus and Field*, 101.

64. Edmund Husserl, *Cartesian Meditations: An Introduction to Phenomenology* (Martinus Nijhoff, 1960 [1931]), 66ff.

65. Maurice Merleau-Ponty, *Phenomenology of Perception* (Routledge, 2002 [1945]). Merleau-Ponty's analysis of presence and absence clearly informs the *Chance*/expectation loop, as Bourdieu develops this concept further from Weber. For Merleau-Ponty, "the 'sensible quality,' the spatial limits set to the precept, and even the presence or absence of a perception, are not *de facto* effects of the situation outside the organism but represent the way in which it meets stimulation and is related to it" (86).

66. Bourdieu, *Habitus and Field*, 102.

67. Bourdieu, *Habitus and Field*, 134.

68. Pierre Bourdieu, *Sociologie générale* (Editions Seuil, 2016 [1983–1986]), 229, our translation.

69. Bourdieu, *Sociologie générale*, 178ff, 224; Franz Kafka, *The Trial* (Schocken, 1999 [1914]).

70. Bourdieu, *Pascalian Meditations* (Stanford University Press, 2001 [1997]), 237ff.

71. Bourdieu, *Pascalian Meditations*, 229. Bourdieu gives the example of a book publisher deciding to publish a book; such "deciders" are in a "position analogous to that of the judge" in Kafka's story.

72. Bourdieu, *Pascalian Meditations*, 240.

73. Bourdieu, *Principles of Vision*, 20ff; Bourdieu, *Forms of Capital*, 243ff; Bourdieu and Wacquant, *Invitation to Reflexive Sociology*, 119.

74. Bourdieu, *Principles of Vision*, 21.

75. Bourdieu, *Forms of Capital*, 243.

76. Bourdieu, *Habitus and Field*, 125.

77. Shoshana Zuboff, *The Age of Surveillance Capitalism: The Fight for a Human Nature at the New Frontier of Power* (PublicAffairs, 2011); see also epilogue below.

78. Bourdieu, *Forms of Capital*, 244.

79. See Bourdieu, *Logic of Practice*, 57.

80. As Kant put it: "He who lacks wit has an *obtuse* head. As for the rest, where it depends on understanding and reason, he can have a very good head; only we must not demand that he play the poet . . . Lack of the power of judgment without wit is *stupidity*. But the same lack *with* wit is *silliness.*—He who shows judgment in business is *shrewd*. If at the same time he has wit, then he is called *clever.*" Immanuel Kant, *Anthropology from a Pragmatic Point of View*, ed. Robert Loudon (Cambridge University Press, 2006 [1798]), 98–99.

81. Bourdieu, *Pascalian Meditations*, 219.

82. Michael Strand and Omar Lizardo, "The Hysteresis Effect: Theorizing Mismatch in Action," *Journal for the Theory of Social Behaviour* 47, no. 2 (2017): 164–94.

Introduction to Part III

1. Erving Goffman, "Where the Action Is," in *Where the Action Is: Three Essays* (Penguin Press, 1969 [1961]), 105–206.

2. Goffman, "Where the Action Is," 126–27.

3. Goffman, "Where the Action Is," 136.

4. On this point, the city's carefully crafted and marketed slogan—"What Happens Here, Stays Here," or "What Happens in Vegas, Stays in Vegas" (the most recent iteration is "What Happens Here, Only Happens Here")—seems apt.

5. For more on *Theoria*, see Andrea Wilson Nightingale, *Spectacles of Truth in Classical Greek Philosophy: Theoria in Its Cultural Context* (Cambridge University Press, 2004).

6. For more details on the circumstances of Goffman's research, see Richard Handler, "What's Up, Doctor Goffman? Tell Us Where the Action Is!," *Journal of the Royal Anthropological Institute* 18, no. 1 (2012): 179–90; Dmitri Shalin, "Erving Goffman, Fateful Action, and the Las Vegas Gambling Scene," *UNLV Gaming Research and Review Journal* 20, no. 1 (2016): 1–38.

7. Goffman, "Where the Action Is," 150.

8. Natasha Dow Schüll, *Addiction by Design: Machine Gambling in Las Vegas* (Princeton University Press, 2011), 13.

Chapter 5

1. See, in particular, Andrew Abbott, *Processual Sociology* (University of Chicago Press, 2016).

2. George Steinmetz, "Scientific Authority and the Transition to Post-Fordism: The Plausibility of Positivism in US Sociology Since 1945," in *The Politics of Method in the Human Sciences: Positivism and Its Epistemological Others* (Duke University Press, 2005), 275–323.

3. For reflections on this theme, see Nicholas Hoover Wilson and Damon Mayrl, eds., *After Positivism: New Approaches to Comparison in Historical Sociology* (Columbia University Press, 2024).

4. Anthony Giddens, "Positivism and Its Critics," in *A History of Sociological Analysis*, eds. Tom Bottomore and Robert Nisbet (Heinemann, 1979), 238.

5. John Dupré, *The Disorder of Things: Metaphysical Foundations of the Disunity of Science* (Harvard University Press, 1993).

6. Philip Gorski, "What Is Critical Realism and Why Should You Care?," *Contemporary Sociology* 42, no. 5 (2013): 658–70, at 661.

7. Tony Hey, Stewart Tansley, and Kristin Tolle, "Jim Grey on eScience: A Transformed Scientific Method," in *The Fourth Paradigm: Data-Intensive Scientific Discovery*, eds. Tony Hey, Stewart Tansley, and Kristin Tolle (Microsoft Research, 2009). See also Rob Kitchin, "Big Data, New Epistemologies, and Paradigm Shifts," *Big Data and Society* (April–June 2014): 1–12.

8. Cecilia Menjívar, "State Categories, Bureaucracies of Displacement, and Possibilities from the Margins," *American Sociological Review* 88, no. 1 (2023): 1–23; Ellis Monk, "Inequality Without Groups: Contemporary Theories of Categories, Intersectional Typicality, and the Disaggregation of Difference," *Sociological Theory* 40, no. 1 (2022): 3–27.

9. Jenna Burrell and Marion Fourcade, "The Society of Algorithms," *Annual Review of Sociology* 47 (2021): 213–37, at 227.

10. Monk, "Inequality Without Groups."

11. Isaac Reed, "Justifying Sociological Knowledge: From Realism to Interpretation," *Sociological Theory* 26, no. 2 (2008): 101–29.

12. Jeffrey Alexander, "Beyond the Epistemological Dilemma: General Theory in a Postpositivist Mode," *Sociological Forum* 5, no. 4 (1990): 531–44; George Steinmetz, "Positivism and Its Others in the Social Sciences," in *The Politics of Method in the Human Sciences*, ed. George Steinmetz (Duke University Press, 2005), 1–59.

13. See Scott Frickel and Neil Gross, "A General Theory of Scientific/Intellectual Movements," *American Sociological Review* 70, no. 2 (2005): 204–32. Here we can mention the Center for Cultural Sociology at Yale as dedicated to "meaning-centered social analysis," and more generally the Sociology of Culture section in the American Sociological Association, coming to be in the

mid-1980s. The *American Journal of Cultural Sociology* is also linked. From the other end, we can mention the Critical Realism Network and financial support for critical realism by funders like the John Templeton Foundation. The *Journal of Critical Realism* is worth mentioning, though far from limited to sociology. It also bears mentioning that most of the prominent figures in each camp are not marginally placed in American sociology but found in core departments.

14. Stathas Psillos, *Scientific Realism: How Science Tracks Truth* (Routledge, 1999).

15. Gravity, for instance, is accepted as real even though it is not always actual. What is actual are those things affected by gravity, particularly if they are empirically (experientially) available to us. We can imagine or design scenarios where other real mechanisms will counteract gravity, but gravity itself has not disappeared. If it happens to have been neutralized, it still remains real.

16. Roy Bhaskar, *A Realist Theory of Science* (Verso, 1998 [1975]), 33; see also Christian Smith, *What Is a Person? Rethinking Humanity, Social Life and the Moral Good from the Person Up* (University of Chicago Press, 2011); Timothy Rutzou and George Steinmetz, eds., "Critical Realism, History and Philosophy in the Social Sciences," *Political Power and Social Theory* 34 (2018); Douglas Porpora, *Reconstructing Sociology: The Critical Realist Approach* (Cambridge University Press, 2015).

17. Bhaskar, *Realist Theory of Science*, 35. See also Ian Hacking, *Historical Ontology* (Harvard University Press, 2002 [1992]), 33ff.

18. Bhaskar, *Realist Theory of Science*, 34.

19. Alexander, "Beyond the Epistemological Dilemma," 531.

20. Isaac Reed and Jeffrey Alexander, "Social Science as Reading and Performance: A Cultural-Sociological Understanding of Epistemology," *European Journal of Social Theory* 12, no. 1 (2009): 21–41.

21. Roy Bhaskar, *The Possibility of Naturalism: A Philosophical Critique of the Contemporary Human Sciences* (Routledge, 2015 [1979]), 65. See also p. 59 for a discussion of the "compensator" that can draw realism into human science.

22. Reed, "Justifying Sociological Knowledge," 112.

23. See Bhaskar, *Possibility of Naturalism*, 145.

24. "Independent" here can be read as avoiding "conflation"; see Margaret Archer, *Culture and Agency: The Place of Culture in Social Theory* (Cambridge University Press, 1989), 97ff.

25. Dave Elder-Vass, *The Causal Power of Social Structures* (Cambridge University Press, 2010), 73.

26. Porpora, *Reconstructing Sociology*, 177ff.

27. Isaac Reed, *Interpretation and Social Knowledge* (University of Chicago Press, 2011), 10.

28. Elder-Vass, *Causal Power of Social Structures*, 75–76.

29. Christian Smith, *What is a Person? Rethinking Humanity, Social Life and the Moral Good from the Person Up* (University of Chicago Press, 2010). Sometimes this phenomenon is called "the performative contradiction": committing to a theoretical abstraction with a certain ontology (say, of a person) that the theorist refutes in the very act of theorizing. See Andrew Sayer, *Why Things Matter to People: Social Science, Values and Ethical Life* (Cambridge University Press, 2011), 54.

30. This idea derives from philosophical engagements with realism that precede Bhaskar, namely Rom Harre and E. H. Madden, *Causal Powers: A Theory of Natural Necessity* (Basil Blackwell, 1975), 5. The very presence of a "powerful particular" (a person could count, it seems) is enough to make "action causal" in this view; presumably, there are not many of these particulars out there.

31. Reed, *Interpretation and Social Knowledge*, 122.

32. Reed, *Interpretation and Social Knowledge*, 169.

33. See, for instance, Carl Hempel, *Fundamentals of Concept Formation in Empirical Science* (University of Chicago Press, 1952).

34. Hence the concern demonstrated for techniques for proper theory construction; see Arthur Stinchcombe, *Constructing Social Theories* (University of Chicago, 1968).

35. Hernan Mondani and Richard Swedberg, "What is a Social Pattern? Rethinking a Central Social Science Term," *Theory and Society* 51, no. 4 (2022): 543–64.

36. Philip Gorski, "The Poverty of Deductivism: A Constructive Realist Model of Sociological Explanation," *Sociological Methodology* 4, no. 1 (2004): 1–33, at 16; Reed, Interpretation and Social Knowledge, 132; Bhaskar, Realist Theory of Science, 12ff.

37. David Hume, *An Enquiry Concerning Human Understanding*, ed. (Cambridge University Press, 2007 [1748]), 32.

38. Gilles Deleuze, *Empiricism and Subjectivity: An Essay on Hume's Theory of Human Nature* (Columbia University Press, 1993 [1953]), 16.

39. Anthony Giddens, *Central Problems in Social Theory: Action, Structure and Contradiction in Social Analysis* (University of California Press, 1979). Jeffrey Alexander would dub these same trends the "new theoretical movement"; see "The New Theoretical Movement," in *Handbook of Sociology*, ed. Neils Smelser (Sage, 1988), 77–103.

40. For a thorough survey of the history of invoking "problems" to reorient and redefine the practice of philosophy, see Giuseppe Bianco, "The Misadventures of the 'Problem' in Philosophy: From Kant to Deleuze," *Angelaki* 23, no. 2 (2018): 8–30. Giddens might have seized upon a "central problems" focus during his early years at King's College, Cambridge, where philosophers were absorbed in debating the role of problems in "the growth of knowledge." See, especially, *Criticism and the Growth of Knowledge: Proceedings of the International Colloquium in the Philosophy of Science, London, 1965*, eds. Imre Lakatos and Alan Musgrave (Cambridge University Press, 1970).

41. Giddens, *Central Problems in Social Theory*, 5.

42. Anthony Giddens, "Functionalism: *Après la lutte*," *Social Research* 43, no. 2 (1976): 325–66.

43. Andy Clark, "Whatever Next? Predictive Brains, Situated Agents and the Future of Cognitive Science," *Behavioral and Brain Science* 36, no. 3 (2013): 181–204, at 196.

44. Pierre Bourdieu, *Classification Struggles: Lectures at the Collège de France, 1981–1982* (Polity, 2018 [1981–1982]), 83.

45. Anthony Giddens, *The Constitution of Society: Outline of a Theory of Structuration* (University of California Press, 1984), 177.

46. Vivek Chibber, *The Class Matrix* (Harvard University Press, 2022), 122–23.

47. Arthur Lovejoy, *The Great Chain of Being: A Study in the History of an Idea* (Harvard University Press, 1976 [1933]).

48. Bruno Latour, "The Powers of Association," *Sociological Review* 32, no. 1 (1984): 264–80, at 269. Latour (born to the Latour wine family) obtained the equivalent of a PhD in theology from the University of Tours in 1970. He had no prior background in sociology prior to finding his way Côte d'Ivoire to engage in research that would result in *Les idéologies de la compétence en milieu industriel à Abidjan*, a report written for the colonial Office de la Recherche Scientifique et Technique Outre-Mer. The report includes (in nuce) many of the later themes for which Latour would become famous, particularly the attention he gives to "nonhuman" agency. There are good reasons to conclude that Latour could not have had these insights had his path to sociology been more conventional. See Jérôme Lamy, "Sociology of a Disciplinary Bifurcation: Bruno

Latour and His Move from Philosophy/Theology to Sociology in the Early 1970s," *Social Science Information* 60, no. 1 (2021): 107–30.

49. Latour, "Powers of Association," 270.

50. Latour, *Pasteurization of France*, 163. As Latour puts it, the revelation happened at the end of winter 1972, on the road from Dijon to Gray. Tormented by many of the theorists who would help shape the central problems paradigm, he started repeating to himself: "Nothing can be reduced to anything else, nothing can be deduced from anything else, everything may be allied to everything else." For Latour, "this was like an exorcism that defeated demons one by one."

51. Latour, "Powers of Association," 277.

52. Rita Felski, *The Limits of Critique* (University of Chicago Press, 2015); Graham Harman, *Prince of Networks: Bruno Latour and Metaphysics* (re.press, 2009).

53. Isaac Reed, *Power in Modernity: Agency Relations and the Creative Destruction of the King's Two Bodies* (University of Chicago Press, 2020).

54. Bruno Latour, "The Powers of Association," *Sociological Review* 31 (1986): 264–80, at 267.

55. Reed, *Power in Modernity*, 32.

56. Reed, *Power in Modernity*, 33.

57. Maurice Bloch, "Why Religion Is Nothing Special but Is Central," *Philosophical Transactions of the Royal Society* 363, no. 1499 (2008): 2055–61.

58. Reed, *Power in Modernity*, 64.

59. Jeffrey Alexander, *Action and its Environments: Toward a New Synthesis* (Columbia University Press, 1988), 313.

60. Alan Garfinkel, *Forms of Explanation: Rethinking the Questions in Social Theory* (Yale University Press, 1981), 41.

61. Garfinkel, *Forms of Explanation*, 30; Luc Boltanski and Eve Chiapello make a similar point this way, drawing a link between test and *justice*, which we expand on further below: "We may no longer examine the strength of money by means of art, or the strength of reputation or intelligence by money, and so on. To be not only strong but also enjoy high status, it is necessary to commit the kind of strength that is appropriate in the test one is submitting to. To ensure the justice of a test is thus to arrange it and control its performance in such a way as to prevent interference by external forces" (*The New Spirit of Capitalism* [Verso, 1999], 31). Boltanski and Chiapello tend to theorize tests in connection with a "critical capacity," in which case we can only find tests in moments of uncertainty, as part of the effort to resettle them. A probabilist identifies tests in the world, as a mechanism that tames chance, distributes individuals, and—in addition—orients them toward probabilities. Nevertheless, the emphasis among both camps is given voice by Boltanski and Chiapello as follows: "The notion of the test breaks with a narrowly determinist conception of the social, whether based on the omnipotence of structures or, in a culturalist perspective, the domination of internalized norms. From the viewpoint of action, it puts the emphasis on the various degrees of uncertainty haunting situations in social life" (30). See also Luc Boltanski and Laurent Thevenot, *On Justification: Economies of Worth* (Princeton University Press, 2006 [1991]), 133; Bruno Latour, *The Pasteurization of France* (Harvard University Press, 1988), 163–64; Gilles Deleuze, *Difference and Repetition* (Columbia University Press, 1991 [1968]), 207–8.

62. Weber, *Economy and Society: A New Translation*, trans. Keith Scribe (Harvard University Press, 2019), 75.

63. Michel Serres, *The Natural Contract* (University of Michigan Press, 1995), 111–12.

64. There are elements of Jean-Paul Sartre's (see "Paris Alive: The Republic of Silence," *Atlantic* (December 1944): 39–44) informing this thought, particularly Sartre's remark that he was

● "never freer" than under the Nazi occupation of Paris. What Sartre tells reminds one of finding Serres's "sea" in an unexpected place. The torment could come from anywhere, and it did in Sartre's case, all the time; this made it seem as if in walking down the boulevard or having a restful night's sleep, one had passed a test. Nothing was arbitrary. For more conventional "seas" and the pursuit of them, see Jon Krakauer, *Into the Wild* (Anchor, 1997).

65. See Lorraine Daston, *Rules: A Short History of What We Live By* (Princeton University Press, 2022), 120ff.

66. Bourdieu will claim that the more designed and specific tests are, the more directly correlated they are with a sense of injustice, particularly when they allow for a perceivable distribution. See *Principles of Vision: General Sociology, Volume 4, Lectures at the Collège de France 1984–85* (Polity, 2022 [1984–1985]), 24–25.

67. Serres, *Natural Contract*, 113.

68. For a related view, see Noortje Maares and David Stark, "Put to the Test: For a New Sociology of Testing," *British Journal of Sociology* 71 (2020): 423–43.

69. Charles Sanders Peirce, *Reasoning and the Logic of Things: The Cambridge Conferences Lectures of 1898* (Harvard University Press, 1992), 247.

70. Bruno Latour, "From Fabrication to Reality," in *Pandora's Hope: Essays on the Reality of Science Studies* (Harvard University Press, 1999), 113–45, especially 119ff.

71. John Dewey, *Experience and Nature* (Open Court, 1925), 70.

72. George Spencer-Brown, *Probability and Scientific Inference* (Longmans, Green and Co., 1957), 39.

73. See Luc Boltanski and Laurent Thevenot, *On Justification: Economies of Worth* (Princeton University Press, 2006 [1991]); Luc Boltanski and Eve Chiapello, *The New Spirit of Capitalism* (Verso, 1999); Luc Boltanski, *On Critique: A Sociology of Emancipation* (Polity, 2011). Among the range of tests Boltanski, Thevenot, and Chiapello identify are tests of worth, tests of legitimate status, tests of strength, reality tests, existential tests, truth tests, and probably some we are forgetting.

74. Boltanski and Thevenot, *On Justification*, 38f.

75. Boltanski and Thevenot, *On Justification*, 74ff. Boltanski and Chiapello draw from similar criteria to distinguish between tests of strength, which are historically much older, and tests of legitimate status, whose rise to prominence might be one narrative of modernity; see *New Spirit of Capitalism*, 31ff.

76. Boltanski and Thevenot, *On Justification*, 133ff.

77. Spencer-Brown makes a relevant point on this score: "Bias is deviation from an expectation" (*Probability and Scientific Inference*, 84).

78. Anthropologist Claude Lévi-Strauss once observed that games, among certain human groups, could be played as many times "as necessary for both sides to reach the same score." That would appear as a way of settling the socially disruptive *Chance* generated by them. See *The Savage Mind* (Chicago, 1966), 30.

79. Michel Foucault, "Truth and Juridical Forms," in *Power: The Essential Works of Michel Foucault, 1954–1984* (Free Press, 2000).

80. Karl Popper, *The Logic of Scientific Discovery* (Routledge, 1959 [1934]), 77ff.

81. Steven Shapin and Simon Schaffer, *Leviathan and the Air-Pump: Hobbes, Boyle and the Experimental Life* (Princeton University Press, 2011 [1985]).

82. Bruno Latour, *The Pasteurization of France* (Harvard University Press, 1988). In Shapin and Schaffer's words, "solutions to the problem of knowledge are embedded within practical

solutions to the problem of social order, and . . . different practical solutions to the problem of social order encapsulate contrasting practical solutions to the problem of knowledge. *That is what the Hobbes-Boyle controversies were about*" (*Leviathan and the Air-Pump*, 15).

83. See Robert Daly, "The Soteriological Significance of the Sacrifice of Isaac," *Catholic Bible Quarterly* 39 (1977): 45-71.

84. Consider the seeming global presence of a peasantry as emblematic of tests in a kind of mode of production the precedence of which precedes a prevailing capitalism. Chris Wickham, "How Did the Feudal Economy Work? The Economic Logic of Medieval Societies," *Past and Present* 251, no. 1 (2021): 3-40.

85. For an example of a suspension of order leading to a sense of "no order at all," see Christopher Hill, *The World Turned Upside Down: Radical Ideas During the English Revolution* (Viking, 1972).

86. Bourdieu, *Pascalian Meditations* (Stanford University Press, 2001 [1997]), 176-77.

87. Herbert Marcuse associated the dialectic as the core tool of critical theory with the unique capacity of theory to identify exactly such new possibilities and *Chances*. See *Reason and Revolution: Hegel and The Rise of Social Theory* (Oxford University Press, 1941), especially the preface. For an allied though different analysis centered on the potential of concepts to create a sense of randomness, see Gilles Deleuze, *Francis Bacon: The Logic of Sensation* (University of Minnesota Press, 1988), 76ff.

88. Giddens, *Central Problems in Social Theory*, 259.

Chapter 6

1. For two recent summary proposals, see Stephen Turner, *Cognitive Science and the Social: A Primer* (Routledge, 2018); Omar Lizardo, Brandon Sepulvado, Dustin Stoltz, and Marshall Taylor, "What Can Cognitive Neuroscience Do for Cultural Sociology?," *American Journal of Cultural Sociology* 8 (2020): 3-28.

2. Regina E. Fabry, "Betwixt and Between: The Enculturated Predictive Processing Approach to Cognition," *Synthese* 195, no. 6 (2018): 2483-518.

3. Jacob Hohwy, "New Directions in Predictive Processing," *Mind and Language* 35, no. 2 (2020): 209-23. The broad range of ancillary fields in which PP finds influence is striking, including among them clinical psychology, psychiatry, addictionology, plant science, ergonomics, kinesiology, and even literature; see Karin Kukkonen, *Probability Designs: Literature and Predictive Processing* (Oxford University Press, 2020).

4. For an argument against the unificationist perspective, see Colombo, Matteo, and Cory Wright, "Explanatory Pluralism: An Unrewarding Prediction Error for Free Energy Theorists," *Brain and Cognition* 112 (2017): 3-12.

5. For general overviews of predictive processing, with particular attention to its focus on a theory of action, see Andy Clark, *Surfing Uncertainty: Prediction, Action and the Embodied Mind* (Oxford University Press, 2016); Alex James Miller Tate, "A Predictive Processing Theory of Motivation," *Synthese* 198 (2021): 4493-521; Daniel Williams, "Predictive Processing and the Representation Wars," *Minds and Machines* 28, no. 1 (2018): 141-72.

6. Wanja Wiese and Thomas Metzinger, "Vanilla PP for Philosophers: A Primer on Predictive Processing," in *Philosophy and Predictive Processing*, eds. Thomas Metzinger and Wanja Wiese (MIND Group, 2017), 2.

7. For a strong statement for keeping the personal and subpersonal as discontinuous realms

of explanation, see Jennifer Hornsby, "Personal and Sub-personal: A Defence of Dennett's Early Distinction," *Philosophical Explorations* 3, no. 1 (2000): 6–24.

8. Pierre Bourdieu, *The Logic of Practice* (Stanford University Press, 1990 [1980]), 63.

9. In its devious (mis)alignment with *Bildung*, the argument here may appear to pit Helmholtz squarely in a *methodenstreit*, as he makes a claim that does not appear to pay due diligence to the difference (or lack thereof) between knowledge of nature and knowledge of human beings and culture. However, Helmholtz's aspirations (at the time) did not align with what is more familiar in Anglophone contexts of this tension and the boundary-maintenance between the "two cultures." See David Cahan, *Helmholtz: A Life in Science* (University of Chicago Press, 2018), 246ff.

10. Benjamin Steege, *Helmholtz and the Modern Listener* (Cambridge University Press, 2012), 15. See also Hermann von Helmholtz, *On the Sensations of Tone as a Physiological Basis for the Theory of Music* (Cambridge University Press, 2009 [1863]).

11. Hermann von Helmholtz, *Treatise on Physiological Optics, Volume Three: The Perceptions of Vision*, ed. James Southall (Optical Society of America, 1925 [1867]), 10.

12. Helmholtz, *Treatise on Physiological Optics*, 13.

13. Helmholtz, *Treatise on Physiological Optics*, 19.

14. Thus Helmholtz arrives at a kind of pragmatism, but in a slightly different key than American pragmatism. "The tests," in his words, that we employ to strengthen our "conviction of the correctness of the perceptions of our senses" must involve our "movements and actions." Perceptions can, then, only have a "practical truth" as dictated by their "orientation" (*Treatise on Physiological Optics*, 22).

15. Some of the implications have been hashed out as so-called Helmholtz machines or instruments of use in machine learning that leverage Helmholtz's approach to perception. It is possible to create "statistical inference [engines] whose function is to infer probable causes of sensory input. . . . [A] device of this kind can learn how to perform these inferences without requiring a teacher to label each sensory input vector with its underlying causes." See Peter Dayan, Geoffrey Hinton, Radford Neal, and Richard Zemel, "The Helmholtz Machine," *Neural Computation* 7 (1995): 889–904, at 889.

16. Helmholtz, *Treatise on Physiological Optics*, 9.

17. Karl Friston and Klaas Stephen, "Free-Energy and the Brain," *Synthese* 159 (2007): 417–58, at 427.

18. Karl Friston, James Kilner, and Lee Harrison, "A Free Energy Principle for the Brain," *Journal of Physiology-Paris* 100, nos. 1–3 (2006): 70–87, at 70.

19. Elliot Brown and Martin Brüne, "The Role of Prediction in Social Neuroscience," *Frontiers in Human Neuroscience* 6 (May 2012): 147.

20. Elmarie Venter, "Toward an Embodied, Embedded Predictive Processing Account," *Frontiers in Psychology* 12 (2020): 543076.

21. For a sampling, see Maxwell Bennett and Peter Michael Stephan Hacker, *Philosophical Foundations of Neuroscience* (John Wiley and Sons, 2022).

22. Andy Clark, "Busting Out: Predictive Brains, Embodied Minds, and the Puzzle of the Evidentiary Veil," *Nous* 51, no. 4 (2017): 727–53, at 727.

23. This attunement is called "hierarchical predictive coding" and has been shown to provide an empirically plausible model of the workings of the visual cortex; see Rajesh Rao and Dana Ballard, "Predictive Coding in the Visual Cortex: A Functional Interpretation of Some Extra-Classical Receptive-Field Effects," *Nature Neuroscience* 2 (1999): 79–87.

24. Jona Vance, "Action Prevents Error: Predictive Processing Without Active Inference," in *Philosophy and Predictive Processing*, eds. Metzinger and Wiese.

25. We also add the caveat that revision- and action-PEM represent "ideal-typical" ends of an action continuum and not antithetical "types" of activity, as has been the classificatory penchant of standard action theory. Even the most mundane act of perception, cognition, or action leads to some updating of the overall generative world model (at some level of the hierarchy) and is, at the same time, an act geared toward self-fulfilling expectations of future experience derived from the same distributed model by engaging in the requisite experience-sampling activity.

26. PP theorists refer to the process as the principle of "precision weighted prediction error minimization" (Clark, *Surfing Uncertainty*, chap. 2).

27. See Michael Strand and Omar Lizardo, "The Hysteresis Effect: Theorizing Mismatch in Action," *Journal for the Theory of Social Behaviour* 47, no. 2 (2017): 164–94.

28. Williams, "Predictive Processing and the Representation Wars."

29. Evert Boonstra and Heleen Slagter, "The Dialectics of Free Energy Minimization," *Frontiers in Systems of Neuroscience* 13, no. 42 (2019): 1–17. A key difference with Hegelian dialectic would be that reason is not the source generative models that, in our terms, loop in probabilities in the world to predict them; those generative models are built from what works. The absolute would not, then, be freedom in reality removed of all contradiction but in being *without* precepting. See also Catherine Malabou, *The Future of Hegel: Plasticity, Temporality and the Dialectic* (Routledge, 2005).

30. Eviatar Zerubavel, *Social Mindscapes: An Invitation to Cognitive Sociology* (Harvard University Press, 1999). This approach has been taken to task by John Levi Martin as the "grid of perception" argument; see Martin's *Explanation of Social Action* (Oxford University Press, 2011), 112ff.

31. Joe Dewhurst, "Folk Psychology and the Bayesian Brain," in *Philosophy and Predictive Processing*, eds. Metzinger and Wiese, 1.

32. This claim applies to plant life as well; see Paco Calvo and Karl Friston, "Practicing Green: Really Radical (Plant) Predictive Processing," *Journal of the Royal Society Interface* 14, no. 131 (2017): 20170096.

33. José Luis Bermúdez, "Personal and Sub-personal; A Difference Without a Distinction," *Philosophical Explorations* 3, no. 1 (2000): 63–82.

34. Pierre Bourdieu, *Pascalian Meditations* (Stanford University Press, 2000 [1997]), 134.

35. Omar Lizardo and Michael Strand, "Skills, Tools, Contexts and Institutions: Clarifying the Relationship Between Different Approaches to Cognition in Cultural Sociology," *Poetics* 38, no. 2 (2010): 205–28.

36. José Luis Bermúdez, "The Bodily Self, Commonsense Psychology and the Springs of Action," in *The Bodily Self: Selected Essays in Self-Consciousness* (MIT Press, 2018), 267ff.

37. Alina Arseniev-Koehler and Jacob G. Foster, "Machine Learning as a Model for Cultural Learning: Teaching an Algorithm What It Means to Be Fat," *Sociological Methods and Research* 51, no. 4 (2022): 1484–539.

38. Moshe Bar, "The Proactive Brain: Using Analogies and Associations to Generate Predictions," *Trends in Cognitive Science* 11, no. 7 (2007): 280–89.

39. As we alluded to at the end of chapter 2, Du Bois's unpublished essay "Steps Toward a Science of How Men Act" develops this basic idea, drawing attention to the formation of hypotheses in action as being the source of emotional valences and the most integral component of the forward momentum of action in what we have called a horizontal sense. See W. E. B. Du Bois,

"Steps Toward a Science of How Men Act," c. 1946, W. E. B. Du Bois Papers, MS 312, Special Collections and University Archives, University of Massachusetts Amherst Libraries, at 3–4.

40. Jeffrey Alexander, *Action and Its Environments: Toward a New Synthesis* (Columbia University Press, 1988), 312ff.

41. Mustafa Emirbayer and Ann Mische, "What Is Agency?" *American Journal of Sociology* 103, no. 4 (1998): 962–1023; Iddo Tavory and Nina Eliasoph, "Coordinating Futures: Toward a Theory of Anticipation," *American Journal of Sociology* 118, no. 4 (2013): 908–42.

42. Josh Whitford, "Pragmatism and the Untenable Dualism of Ends and Means: Why Rational Choice Theory Does Not Deserve Paradigmatic Privilege," *Theory and Society* 31 (2002): 325–63.

43. Benjamin Dalton, "Creativity, Habit and the Social Products of Creative Action: Revising Joas, Incorporating Bourdieu," *Sociological Theory* 22, no. 4 (2004): 603–22.

44. Daniel Silver, "The Moodiness of Action," *Sociological Theory* 29, no. 3 (2011): 199–222.

45. Helmholtz, *On the Sensations of Tone as a Physiological Basis for the Theory of Music.*

46. For a discussion of the distinction between horizontal and vertical explanations of action and the non-substantiality of the personal/subpersonal distinction, see Bermúdez, "Personal and Sub-personal."

47. Stephen Vaisey and Lauren Valentino, "Culture and Choice: Toward Integrating Cultural Sociology with the Judgment and Decision Making Sciences," *Poetics* 68 (2018): 131–43.

48. Hedstrom, *Dissecting the Social.*

49. John Levi Martin and Alessandra Lembo, "On the Other Side of Values," *American Journal of Sociology* 126, no. 1 (2020): 52–98.

50. Jens Rydgren, "Beliefs," in *Oxford Handbook of Analytical Sociology*, eds, Peter Bearman and Peter Hedstrom (Oxford University Press, 2011), 72–93.

51. Silver, "Moodiness of Action," 205ff.

52. Reed, *Interpretation and Social Knowledge*, 135–36; Hedstrom, *Dissecting the Social*, 38.

53. Why, for instance, do poor Black and Brown women in Philadelphia forgo the security of marriage and have children outside of wedlock at an early age, despite valuing marriage as much as anyone else? See Kathryn Edin and Maria Kefalas, *Promises I Can Keep: Why Poor Women Put Motherhood Before Marriage* (University of California Press, 2005). Why does large-scale racial inequity persist despite de facto equality in the post–civil rights era in the US? See Eduardo Bonilla-Silva, *Racism Without Racists: Color-Blind Racism and the Persistence of Racial Inequality in America* (Rowman and Littlefield, 2006).

54. Colin Campbell, "Distinguishing the Power of Agency from Agentic Power: A Note on Weber and the 'Black Box' of Personal Agency," *Sociological Theory* 27, no. 4 (2009): 407–18.

55. Matthew Norton, "Meaning on the Move: Synthesizing Cognitive and Systems Concepts of Culture," *American Journal of Cultural Sociology* 7, no. 1 (2019): 1–28; Alison Pugh, "What Good Are Interviews for Thinking about Culture? Demystifying Interpretive Analysis," *American Journal of Cultural Sociology* 1, no. 1 (2014): 42–68.

56. Mark Rowlands, *The New Science of the Mind: From Extended Mind to Embodied Phenomenology* (MIT Press, 2010).

57. Gianluca Manzo, "Analytical Sociology and Its Critics," *European Journal of Sociology* 51, no. 1 (2010): 129–70.

58. See Watts, "Common Sense and Sociological Explanation," 327. See also Omar Lizardo, "Foreword," in *Sexual Fields: Toward a Sociology of Collective Sexual Life*, ed. Adam Isaiah Green (University of Chicago Press, 2013), vii–xiii.

59. Adolf Grünbaum, *The Foundations of Psychoanalysis: A Philosophical Critique* (Univer-

sity of California Press, 1985); Paul Ricoeur, *Freud and Philosophy: An Essay on Interpretation* (Yale University Press, 1970), 32ff.

60. Daniel Dennett, "The Part of Cognitive Science That Is Philosophy," *Topics in Cognitive Science* 1, no. 2 (2009): 231–36.

61. Bermúdez, "Personal and Subpersonal."

62. Daniel Dennett, *Content and Consciousness* (Routledge, 2010 [1969]), 93.

63. Arlie Hochschild, *Strangers in Their Own Land: Anger and Mourning on the American Right* (New Press, 2016).

64. Clark, *Surfing Uncertainty*, 294.

65. José Luis Bermúdez, *Philosophy of Psychology: A Contemporary Introduction* (Routledge, 2005), 32; Matteo Colombo, "Constitutive Relevance and the Personal/Subpersonal Distinction," *Philosophical Psychology* 4 (2013): 547–70.

66. Thomas Metzinger, "The Myth of Cognitive Agency: Subpersonal Thinking as Cyclically Recurring Loss of Mental Autonomy," *Frontiers in Psychology* 4 (2013): 931–45, at 937.

67. Zoe Drayson, "The Uses and Abuses of the Personal/Subpersonal Distinction," *Philosophical Perspectives* 26, no. 1 (2012): 1–18, at 3.

68. Dennett, *Content and Consciousness*, 101ff.

69. Tavory and Eliasoph, "Coordinating Futures." As proposed by Isaac Reed's recent framework, actors can form their own projects and also be enlisted as part of the projects of "rectors" (and/or be marginalized and vilified as "others"). Agency is marked by this enrollment, and as distinguishable from action, agency consists of the project-making capacities of additional people *in lieu* of their own potential for projects. Thus, the nation-state consists of such collective agency, or "King's second body," as it can be decomposed as a project of its agents who, even peripherally, act on behalf of the rector. See Isaac Ariail Reed, "Chains of Power and Their Representation," *Sociological Theory* 35, no. 2 (2017): 87–117; Isaac Ariail Reed, *Power in Modernity: Agency Relations and the Creative Destruction of the King's Two Bodies* (University of Chicago Press, 2020).

70. Hae-Jeong Park and Karl Friston, "Structural and Functional Brain Networks: From Connections to Cognition," *Science* 342, no. 6158 (2013): 575–80. The only other action-theoretical construct to behave similarly in the sense of being able to cut across the vertical explanatory hierarchy and to even be applicable to human (and sometimes nonhuman) actants is, indeed, *habit*; see Mark Sinclair, "Ravaisson and the Force of Habit," *Journal of the History of Philosophy* 49, no. 1 (2011): 65–85.

71. This position particularly applies when actors are enrolled into a project, though presumably they are not the only one, and neither is the project personal. This circumstance suggests a vertical arrangement, which does not necessarily mean an arrangement that is "higher" but instead one that works across vertical levels that are typically segmented.

72. This process involves the expectation that an actor be able to give a belief/desire account of what they are currently doing, what they have done, and what they will do. See Kristin Andrews, "The Folk Psychological Spiral: Explanation, Regulation, and Language," *Southern Journal of Philosophy* 53, no. S1 (2015): 50–67.

73. See Daniel Hutto, Shaun Gallagher, Jesús Ilundáin-Agurruza, and Inês Hipólito, "Culture in Mind—An Enactivist Account: Not Cognitive Penetration but Cognitive Permeation," in *Culture, Mind and Brain: Emerging Concepts, Models, Applications*, ed. L. J. Kirmayer (Cambridge University Press, 2020), 163–87. The organic composition of bodies arises from the percepts and affects of which organs become capable. They are constantly subject to vertical capture and may obtain even world-historical significance. See also Alphonso Lingis, "The Society of Dismem-

bered Body Parts," in *Deleuze and the Theater of Philosophy*, ed. Constantin Boundas (Routledge, 1994), 289–303.

74. Daniel Winchester and Kyle Green, "Talking Yourself Into It: How and When Accounts Shape Motivation for Action," *Sociological Theory* 37, no. 3 (2019): 257–81.

75. We should include here our orientation toward our own physiological states and things immediately accessible to us, given how our body happens to be arrayed in physical space (of temperature variability, time of day, and/or distracting influences of one form or another). See Wanja Wiese, "Action Is Enabled by Systematic Misrepresentations," *Erkenntnis* 82 (2017): 1233–52.

76. Mark Miller, Julian Kiverstein, and Erik Rietveld, "Embodying Addiction: A Predictive Processing Account," *Brain and Cognition* 138 (2020): 105495, at 7.

77. Miller, Kiverstein, and Rietveld, "Embodying Addiction," 7.

78. Miller, Kiverstein, and Rietveld, "Embodying Addiction."

79. Miller, Kiverstein, and Rietveld, "Embodying Addiction," 8.

80. Miller, Kiverstein, and Rietveld, "Embodying Addiction," 9.

81. On this score, see Seth Abrutyn and Omar Lizardo, "A Motivational Theory of Roles, Rewards, and Institutions," *Journal for the Theory of Social Behaviour* 53, no. 2 (June 2023): 200–20.

82. Samuel P. L. Veissière, Axel Constant, Maxwell JD Ramstead, Karl J. Friston, and Laurence J. Kirmayer, "Thinking Through Other Minds: A Variational Approach to Cognition and Culture," *Behavioral and Brain Sciences* 43 (2020).

83. Somewhat irreverent acronym for "Good Old Fashioned Action Theory"; see John Levi Martin, *Thinking Through Theory* (Norton, 2015), chap. 5.

84. Clark, *Surfing Uncertainty*, 13ff.

85. Maxwell R. Bennett and Peter Michael Stephan Hacker, *Philosophical Foundations of Neuroscience* (John Wiley and Sons, 2022).

86. It of course bears mentioning that the associations with coffee that Clark mentions are probable, but they do not encompass its range of possibility so far as we know it. Coffee has found an array of medicinal and ritual uses since first spawning from the Ethiopian highlands. See Jonathan Morris, *Coffee: A Global History* (Reaktion, 2019).

87. Sidney Mintz, *Sweetness and Power: The Place of Sugar in Modern History* (Penguin, 1986); see also Marshall Sahlins, "The Sadness of Sweetness: The Native Anthropology of Western Cosmology," *Current Anthropology* 37, no. 3 (1996): 395–428.

88. The formal recipe seems, as mentioned above, logical enough, as (to borrow terms from Gilles Deleuze) it marks repetition in itself: "Repetition is a necessary and justified conduct only in relation to that which cannot be replaced. Repetition as a conduct and as a point of view concerns non-exchangeable and non-substitutable singularities." The loop is what cannot be replaced, in other words; it is singular and non-exchangeable. Those who are subject to the loop, however, *are* exchangeable. See Gilles Deleuze, *Difference and Repetition* (Columbia University Press, 1994 [1968]), 2.

89. Paula Braverman, Susan Ergeter, and David Williams, "The Social Determinants of Health: Coming of Age," *Annual Review of Public Health* 32 (2011): 381–98.

90. Braverman, Ergeter, and Williams, "Social Determinants of Health," 386ff.

91. Looping, here, contradicts an easy distinction like the one proposed by Claude Lévi-Strauss between "hot" and "cold" societies, with the latter attempting to do everything to eliminate "historical factors," while the former makes history the "moving power of their development." To breach this kind of dichotomy, "history" is less at stake than the relative taming or

invitation of chance as different ways of experiencing time. See Claude Lévi-Strauss, *The Savage Mind* (Weidenfeld and Nicholson, 1966), 233–34.

Introduction to Part IV

1. For this narrative, see Mayer Zald, "Sociology as a Discipline: Quasi-Science and Quasi-Humanities," *American Sociologist* 22 (1991): 165–87; Stephen Turner, *American Sociology: From Pre-disciplinary to Post-normal* (Palgrave, 2014), chap. 4.

2. Nancy Cartwright, *How the Laws of Physics Lie* (Oxford University Press, 1983).

3. Ian Hacking used this term frequently in his analysis of science, drawing it from historian A. C. Crombie. A style of reasoning is arguably the most encompassing way to group knowledges, more general than disciplines and even epistemic cultures; see Martin Kusch, "Hacking's Historical Epistemology: A Critique of Styles of Reasoning," *Studies in History and Philosophy of Science Part A* 41, no. 2 (2010): 158–73.

Chapter 7

1. Ian Hacking, *The Emergence of Probability* (Cambridge University Press, 1975), 10.

2. Gaston Bachelard, *Le rationalisme appliqué* (Les Presses Universitaires de France, 1966 [1949]), 97ff.

3. Bachelard, *Le rationalisme appliqué*, 100 (our translation).

4. Bachelard, *Le rationalisme appliqué*, 100.

5. We continue to employ the terms, particularly *philosophicus*, in the following discussion, to refer to a collective view at least partially of our own contrivance, admitted at the sacrifice of subtle differences within it, but we hope justified for the purpose of drawing a contrast.

6. Marshall Abrams, "Mechanistic Social Probability," in *The Oxford Handbook of Philosophy of Social Science*, ed. Harold Kincaid (Oxford University Press, 2012), 186.

7. Jacob Rosenthal, "Probabilities as Ratios of Ranges in Initial-State Spaces," *Journal of the Logic of Language and Information* 21 (2012): 217–36, at 218.

8. Richard Berk, Bruce Western, and Robert Weiss, "Statistical Inference for Apparent Populations," *Sociological Methodology* 25 (1995): 421–58, at 424.

9. Rosenthal, "Probabilities as Ratios of Ranges in Initial-State Space," 224; see also Mauricio Suárez, "Propensities and Pragmatism," *Journal of Philosophy* 110, no. 2 (20130): 61–92.

10. See Michael Strevens, *Tychomancy: Inferring Probability from Causal Structure* (Harvard University Press, 2013); Michael Strevens, "Dynamic Probability and the Problem of Initial Conditions," *Synthese* 199 (2021): 14617–39; Marshall Abrams, *Evolution and the Machinery of Chance: Philosophy, Probability and Scientific Practice in Biology* (University of Chicago Press, 2023); Jacob Rosenthal, "The Natural-Range Conception of Probability," in *Time, Chance and Reduction: Philosophical Aspects of Statistical Mechanics*, eds. Gerhard Ernst and Andreas Huttemann (Cambridge University Press, 2010), 71–91.

11. Rosenthal, "Probability as Ratios of Ranges in Initial-State Space," 226.

12. Rosenthal, "Probability as Ratios of Ranges in Initial-State Space," 226.

13. Michael Strevens, "Objective Probability as a Guide to the World," *Philosophical Studies* 95 (1999): 243–75.

14. A. N. Kolmogorov, *Foundations of the Theory of Probability* (Chelsea Publishing Company, 1950 [1933]), 2–3.

15. Rosenthal, "Natural-Range Conception of Probability," 79.

16. J. Dimitri Gallow, "A Subjectivist's Guide to Deterministic Chance," *Synthese* 198 (2021): 4339–72.

17. Jan von Plato, "The Method of Arbitrary Functions," *British Journal for the Philosophy of Science* 34, no. 1 (1983): 37–47.

18. Pierre Bourdieu, "The Field of Cultural Production," *Poetics* 12 (1983): 311–56.

19. John Levi Martin, "Field Theory and Self-Organization," *Zeitschrift für Theoretische Soziologie* 2 (2016): 158–81; George Steinmetz, "Social Fields, Subfields, and Social Spaces at the Scale of Empires: Explaining the Colonial State and Colonial Sociology," *Sociological Review* 64, no. 2 (2016): 98–123.

20. Abrams, "Mechanistic Social Probability."

21. Abrams, "Mechanistic Social Probability," 188.

22. Johannes von Kries, *Principles of the Probability Calculus: A Logical Investigation* (Springer, 2023 [1886]), 6–7.

23. Charles Sanders Peirce, "The Doctrine of Chances," in *Chance, Love and Logic: Philosophical Essays*, edited by Morris Cohen (Kegan Paul, 1923 [1878]), 69–70.

24. Erving Goffman, "Where the Action Is," in *Where the Action Is: Three Essays* (Penguin Press, 1969 [1961]), 105–206.

25. Charles Sanders Peirce, "The Percipuum," in *Collected Papers of Charles Sanders Peirce*, vol. 7, ed. Arthur Burks (Harvard University Press, 1958), 674.

26. Peirce, "Percipuum," 674.

27. Isaac Ariail Reed, *Power in Modernity: Agent Relations and the Creative Destruction of the King's Two Bodies* (University of Chicago Press, 2020), 31–32.

28. Catherine Gallagher and Stephen Greenblatt, *Practicing New Historicism* (University of Chicago Press, 2000).

29. For the fullest account, see Marshall Sahlins, *Historical Metaphors and Mythical Realities: Structure in the Early History of the Sandwich Islands Kingdom* (University of Michigan Press, 1981); Marshall Sahlins, "Captain Cook at Hawaii," *Journal of the Polynesian Society* 98, no. 4 (1981). For the larger conceptual implications, see Marshall Sahlins, *Islands of History* (University of Chicago Press, 1995), especially chap. 5. See also Isaac Ariail Reed, *Interpretation and Social Knowledge* (University of Chicago Press, 2011), 25ff.

30. On "coincidence" as an analytically independent form of historical temporality and a related analysis of Cook's case, see Simeon J. Newman, "Four Temporalities: Toward a Typology of Narrative Forms," *Sociological Theory* 42, no. 4 (2024): 283–306.

31. Sahlins, *Historical Metaphors and Mythical Realities*, 20.

32. Sahlins, *Historical Metaphors and Mythical Realities*, 22.

33. Sahlins, *Historical Metaphors and Mythical Realities*, 24.

34. Sahlins uses the phrase "mythical reality," echoing Claude Lévi-Strauss, who found it more characteristic of so-called cold societies, which emphasize continuity, as opposed to "hot societies," which are marked by discontinuity. In a probabilistic sense, the different could revolve around the capacity of myth (as Cassirer suggests) for absorbing chance mechanisms. See Claude Lévi-Strauss, *The Savage Mind* (Weidenfeld and Nicolson, 1966), 233–34. Sahlins, *Historical Metaphors and Mythical Realities*, 17ff.

35. Sahlins, *Islands of History*, 149ff.

36. W. E. B. Du Bois, *Black Reconstruction in America, 1860–1880* (Free Press, 1988 [1935]), chap. 4.

37. Du Bois, *Black Reconstruction in America*, 62.

38. Du Bois, *Black Reconstruction in America*, 62.

39. Eric Williams, *Capitalism and Slavery* (University of North Carolina Press, 2021 [1944]).

40. Iddo Tavory and Stefan Timmermans, *Abductive Analysis: Theorizing Qualitative Research* (University of Chicago Press, 2014), 37.

41. Tavory and Timmermans, *Abductive Analysis*, 43.

42. For a good discussion, see Bruce Western, "Bayesian Thinking About Macrosociology," *American Journal of Sociology* 107, no. 2 (2001): 353–78.

43. Monika Krause, *Model Cases: On Canonical Research Objects and Sites* (University of Chicago Press, 2021).

44. Peirce, "Percipuum."

45. Keith Niall, "Translator's Preface," in Johannes von Kries, *Principles of the Probability Calculus: A Logical Investigation* (Springer, 2023 [1886]), x.

46. Guido Fioretti, "Johannes von Kries on Cognition," in *The Range of Science: Studies in the Interdisciplinary Legacy of Johannes von Kries*, ed. Gerhard Wagner (Harrassowitz Verlag, 2019).

47. Johannes von Kries, quoted in Fioretti, "Johannes von Kries on Cognition," 68. See also Johannes von Kries, *Logik* (J. C. B. Mohr, 1916), 10–11.

48. Kries, *Principles of the Probability Calculus*, 17.

49. Johannes von Kries, quoted in Guido Fioretti, "Analogies, Conventions and Expert System in Medicine," *Studies in Multidisciplinarity* 3 (2005): 131–45, at Kries, *Logik*, 403.

50. See, for instance, Eric Topoi, "High-Performance Medicine: The Convergence of Human and Artificial Intelligence," *Nature Medicine* 25 (2019): 44–56.

51. Bernard Mehlig, *Machine Learning with Neural Networks: An Introduction for Scientists and Engineers* (Cambridge University Press, 2022), chs. 7 and 8.

52. Rosenthal, "Probabilities as Ratios of Ranges in Initial-State Spaces," 222.

53. David Lewis makes the epistemic point this way: The chancemaker is "whatever makes it true that the chance of decay is 50% must also, if known, make it rational to believe to degree 50% that decay will occur." See "Humean Supervenience Debugged," *Mind* 103 (1994): 473–90, at 476.

54. Devah Pager, "The Mark of a Criminal Record," *American Journal of Sociology* 108, no. 5 (2003): 937–75.

55. Pager, "Mark of a Criminal Record," 939.

56. Pager, "Mark of a Criminal Record," 939. Pager addresses these challenges using a now-classic experimental audit study. Four men auditors (twenty-three-year-old college students from Milwaukee), two white and two Black, were sent out to apply for job openings to entry-level positions. Working in (same-race) teams of two, testers applied for the same jobs and were matched on all "objective" characteristics listed on their applications (e.g., education, job experience, etc.) except for criminal record status, which shifted between applicants within the team every week of the study.

57. Strevens, "Dynamic Probability and the Problem of Initial Conditions," 14619–20.

58. Luc Boltanski and Eve Chiapello, *The New Spirit of Capitalism* (Verso, 1999), 30, 51.

59. Goffman, "Where the Action Is," esp. 136–37.

60. See, for instance, Jake Hofman, Amit Sharma, and Duncan Watts, "Prediction and Explanation in Social Systems," *Science* 355, no. 6324 (2017): 486–88.

61. Alasdair Macintyre, *After Virtue: A Study in Moral Theory* (University of Notre Dame Press, 1981), 5.

62. Richard Swedberg, *Theorizing in Social Science: The Context of Discovery* (Stanford University Press, 2014).

Chapter 8

1. Pierre Bourdieu, *Principles of Vision* (Polity, 2022 [1984–1985]), 173.

2. Sabina Leonelli, "What Counts as Scientific Data? A Relational Approach," *Philosophy of Science* 82, no. 5 (2015): 810–21.

3. See Andy Clark, "Beyond Desire? Agency, Choice, and the Predictive Mind," *Australasian Journal of Philosophy* 98, no. 1 (2020): 1–15.

4. Noam Chomsky, *Syntactic Structures* (Mouton, 1957). See Vsevolod Kapatsinski, *Changing Minds, Changing Tools: From Learning Theory to Language Acquisition to Language Change* (MIT Press, 2018), 302.

5. Martin Zettersten, "Learning by Predicting: How Predictive Processing Informs Language Development," in *Patterns in Language and Linguistics*, eds. B. Busse and R. Moehlig-Falke (2019): 255–88.

6. Zettersten, "Learning by Predicting," 42.

7. Alina Arseniev-Koehler, "Theoretical Foundations and Limits of Word Embeddings: What Types of Meaning Can They Capture?," *Sociological Methods and Research* (2022): 00491241221140142.

8. Talcott Parsons, *The Structure of Social Action* (McGraw-Hill, 1937), 731.

9. Parsons, *Structure of Social Action*, 731.

10. Parsons, *Structure of Social Action*, 732–33.

11. Richard Rorty, "Pragmatism, Relativism and Irrationalism," in *Consequences of Pragmatism: Essays 1972–1980* (University of Minnesota Press, 1982), 172.

12. Richard Rorty, *Philosophy and the Mirror of Nature* (Princeton University Press, 1979), 373.

13. Anthony Giddens, *The Consequences of Modernity* (Stanford University Press, 1990), 92. Giddens draws ontological security from psychoanalyst R. D. Laing to refer to what patients diagnosed with schizophrenia tend to lack relative to a non-schizophrenic presence in the world. Laing in turn drew the principle from a comparison Lionel Trilling once made between Kafka, Keats, and Shakespeare. See R. D. Laing, *The Divided Self: An Existential Study in Sanity and Madness* (Routledge, 1999 [1964]), 40–41.

14. Isaac Ariail Reed, *Power in Modernity: Agency Relations and the Creative Destruction of the King's Two Bodies* (University of Chicago Press, 2020), 34.

15. See also Ann Mische, "Projects and Possibilities: Researching Futures in Action," *Sociological Forum* 24, no. 3 (2009): 694–704.

16. Stephen Turner, *The Social Theory of Practices* (University of Chicago Press, 1994).

17. See Talcott Parsons, *Action Theory and the Human Condition* (Free Press, 1978), chap. 15.

18. Alexandre Kojève, *Introduction to the Reading of Hegel*, trans. James Nichols (Cornell University Press, 1969 [1933–1939]), 39.

19. Andreas Engel, Alexander Maye, Martin Kuthen, and Peter König, "Where's the Action? The Pragmatic Turn in Cognitive Science," *Trends in Cognitive Science* 17, no. 5 (2013): 202–9.

20. Micah Allen and Karl Friston, "From Cognitivism to Autopoiesis: Towards a Computational Framework for the Embodied Mind," *Synthese* 195, no. 6 (2018): 2459–82, at 2477.

21. Karl Friston, Christopher Thornton, and Andy Clark, "Free-Energy Minimization and the Dark-Room Problem," *Frontiers in Psychology* 3 (2012): 130.

22. Terence McDonnell, Christopher Bail, and Iddo Tavory, "A Theory of Resonance," *Sociological Theory* 35, no. 1 (2017): 1–14.

23. Marion Fourcade and Kieran Healy, *The Ordinal Society* (Harvard University Press, 2024), chap. 2.

24. See Charles Duhigg, "How Companies Learn Your Secrets," *New York Times Magazine,* February 19, 2012.

25. Yuk Hui, *Recursivity and Contingency* (Rowman and Littlefield, 2019), 20.

26. W. E. B. Du Bois, "Sociology Hesitant," *boundary 2* 27, no. 3 (2000 [1905]): 37–44, especially 38. In addition to groups, other binaries include structure as either a "methodological" reference to a continuous and distributional range of objective probabilities, or the foundation of all social reality—a foundation that becomes only partially manifest in mechanisms and experiences; agency as either the autonomy of the mental and the intentional or the fulfillment of structurally derived prerogatives and the power-laden projects of "rectors."

27. See Herbert Marcuse, "A Note on Dialectic," in *Reason and Revolution: Hegel and the Rise of Social Theory* (Beacon Press, 1960 [1941]), xi–xiv.

28. Anthony Giddens, *The Constitution of Society* (University of California Press, 1984), 25; William Sewell, "A Theory of Structure: Duality, Agency and Transformation" *American Journal of Sociology* 98, no. 1 (1992): 1–29.

29. Karl Marx, *Capital,* vol. 1 (Penguin Press, 1976 [1867]), 163f.

30. We draw this example from Gilles Deleuze, *Difference and Repetition* (Columbia University Press, 1994 [1968]), 1–2.

31. Marx, *Capital,* chap. 4.

32. Sewell, "Theory of Structure," at 27.

33. Sewell, "Theory of Structure," 13.

34. Marshall Sahlins, *Culture and Practical Reason* (University of Chicago Press, 1976), 63.

35. Ian Hacking, *Historical Ontology* (Harvard University Press, 2002), 170.

36. Jaakko Kuorikoski and Samuli Pöyhönen, "Looping Kinds and Social Mechanisms," *Sociological Theory* 30, no. 3 (2012): 187–205; Tuomas Vesterinen, "Identifying the Explanatory Domain of the Looping Effect: Congruent and Incongruent Feedback Mechanisms of Interactive Kinds," *Journal of Social Ontology* 6, no. 2 (2020): 159–85.

37. Ian Hacking, "Making Up People: Clinical Classifications," *London Review of Books* 28, no. 17 (August 2006): 78–90, at 80.

38. G. E. M. Anscombe, *Intention* (Harvard University Press, 2000 [1957]); G. E. M. Anscombe, "Under a Description," *Nous* 13, no. 2 (1979): 219–33.

39. Michel Foucault, *The History of Sexuality, Volume 1: An Introduction,* trans. Robert Hurley (Vintage, 1984), part 3. See also Judith Butler, *The Psychic Life of Power* (Stanford University Press, 1997), 3–4.

40. Marion Fourcade and Kieran Healy, "Seeing Like a Market," *Socio-economic Review* 15, no. 1 (2017): 9–29, at 24.

41. Fourcade and Healy, "Seeing Like a Market," 17.

42. Gilles Deleuze, "Postscript on Societies of Control," *October* 59 (1992): 3–7, at 4.

43. The difference, here, is also captured by Gilles Deleuze and Felix Guattari; see *A Thousand Plateaus,* trans. Brian Massumi (University of Minnesota Press, 1987 [1980]), 458.

44. Pierre Bourdieu, *The State Nobility: Elite Schools in the Field of Power* (Stanford University Press, 1996), 385. Here Bourdieu draws from Deleuze, *The Fold: Leibniz and the Baroque* (University of Minnesota Press, 1993).

45. For arguably the best discussion of Peirce's one-two-three, see "The Categories in Detail" and "A Guess at the Riddle," in *Collected Papers of Charles Sanders Peirce,* vol. 1, eds. Charles Hartshorne and Paul Weiss (Harvard University Press, 1931).

46. Kate Eichhorn, *Content* (MIT Press, 2022).

47. Sewell, "Theory of Structure," 17.

48. Isaac Ariail Reed, *Interpretation and Social Knowledge* (University of Chicago Press, 2011), 135.

49. In a sense, this disappearance is what Heidegger seems to notice in what he calls "the ontological priority of the question of being." See *Being and Time*, trans. Joan Stambaugh (SUNY Press, 1996 [1927]), 7ff.

50. Jean Cavaillès, *On Logic and the Theory of Science*, trans. Robin MacKay and Knox Peden (Sequence Press, 2021 [1942]), 123.

51. Bourdieu, *Pascalian Meditations* (Stanford University Press, 2000 [1997]), 214.

52. Kelsey Perrykkad and Jakob Hohwy, "Fidgeting as Self-Evidencing: A Predictive Processing Account of Non-Goal-Directed Action," *New Ideas in Psychology* 56 (2020): 100750.

53. Sandra Proelss, Shimpei Ishiyama, Eduard Maier, Matthias Schultze-Kraft, and Michael Brecht, "The Human Tickle Response and Mechanisms of Self-Tickle Suppression," *Philosophical Transactions of the Royal Society B* (2022): 20210185.

54. George Herbert Mead, "The Definition of the Psychical," in *George Herbert Mead: Selected Writings*, ed. Andrew Reck (University of Chicago Press, 1981 [1903]), 42.

55. Bruno di Finetti, "Probabilism: A Critical Essay on the Theory of Probability and on the Value of Science," *Erkenntnis* 31 (1989 [1931]): 169–223, at 169–70.

56. Alfred Schutz, "Common-Sense and Scientific Interpretation of Human Action," *Philosophy and Phenomenological Research* 14, no. 1 (1953): 1–38.

Epilogue

1. "To breed an animal with the prerogative to promise—is that not precisely the paradoxical task which nature has set herself with regard to humankind? is it not the real problem *of* humankind?" See Friedrich Nietzsche, *On the Genealogy of Morality*, trans. Carol Diethe (Cambridge University Press, 2006 [1887]), 35. Nietzsche poses promise-making against forgetfulness, or what "shuts the doors and windows of consciousness for a while." To explain the distinction further, he introduces concepts that echo a probabilistic style of reasoning worth quoting en extenso: "A world of strange new things, circumstances and even acts of will may be placed quite safely in between the original 'I will,' 'I shall do' and the actual discharge of the will, its *act*, without breaking this long chain of the will. But what a lot of preconditions there are for this! In order to have that degree of control over the future, man must first have learnt to distinguish between what happens by accident and what by design, to think causally, to view the future as the present and anticipate it, to grasp with certainty what is end and what is means, in all, to be able to calculate, compute—and before he can do this, man himself will really have to become *reliable, regular, necessary*, even in his own self-image, so that he, as someone making a promise is, is answerable for his own *future!*" (*On the Genealogy of Morality*, 36, emphasis original).

2. Dustin S. Stoltz and Omar Lizardo, "Deliberate Trust and Intuitive Faith: A Dual-Process Model of Reliance," *Journal for the Theory of Social Behaviour* 48, no. 2 (2018): 230–50.

3. Georges Canguilhem, "Machine and Organism," in *Knowledge of Life*, trans. Stefanos Geroulanos and Daniela Ginsburg (Fordham University Press, 2009), 75–97, at 89–90.

4. For a discussion of "modulation" as a looping effect, see Gilles Deleuze, "Postscript on the Societies of Control," *October* 59 (1992): 3–7; Gilles Deleuze and Felix Guattari, *A Thousand Plateaus*, trans. Brian Massumi (University of Minnesota Press, 1987 [1980]), 456–73.

5. Jurgen Habermas, *Knowledge and Human Interests*, trans. Jeremy Shapiro (Beacon Press, 1968 [1971]), 302.

6. Max Horkheimer, "Traditional and Critical Theory," in *Critical Theory: Selected Essays,*

trans. Matthew O'Connell (Continuum, 1972 [1937]), 188–244; Edmund Husserl, *The Crisis of the European Sciences and Transcendental Philosophy*, trans. David Carr (Northwestern University Press, 1970 [1936]).

7. Friedrich Schelling, *On University Studies*, trans. E. S. Morgan, ed. Norbert Guterman (Ohio University Press, 1966), 72.

8. See Terry Pinkard, *German Philosophy, 1760–1860: The Legacy of Idealism* (Cambridge University Press, 2002), 88ff.

9. Schelling, *On University Studies*, 50.

10. Schelling, *On University Studies*, 14–15.

11. Max Weber, "Science as a Profession and Vocation," in *Max Weber: Collected Methodological Writings*, eds. Hans Henrik Bruun and Sam Whimster, trans. Hans Henrik Bruun (Routledge, 2012 [1919]), 343.

12. See especially Alvin Gouldner, *Enter Plato: Classical Greece and the Origins of Social Theory* (Basic Books, 1965).

13. Habermas, *Knowledge and Human Interests*, 316.

14. Theodor Adorno, *Negative Dialectics*, trans. E. B. Ashton (Continuum, 1983 [1966]), 361ff.

15. See Gilles Deleuze, *Difference and Repetition*, trans. Paul Patton (Columbia University Press, 1994 [1968]), 60–61; Brian Massumi, *A User's Guide to Capitalism and Schizophrenia* (MIT Press, 1992), 4–5.

16. Here we refer to Adorno's famous insight, which, read as probabilistic reasoning, shows a shocking alignment with PP's brain-based insight: "Mythical is that which never changes, ultimately diluted to a formal legality of thought. To want substance in cognition is to want a utopia. It is this consciousness of possibility that sticks to the concrete, the undisfigured. Utopia is blocked off by possibility, never by immediate reality; this is why it seems abstract in the midst of extant things" (*Negative Dialectics*, 56). See also Theodor Adorno, "The Experiential Content of Hegel's Philosophy," in *Hegel: Three Studies*, trans. Shierry Weber Nicholson (MIT Press, 1993 [1963, 1971]), 80ff.

17. Pinkard, *German Philosophy*, 356ff.

18. Paul Ricoeur, "The Model of the Text: Meaningful Action Considered as Text," *Social Research* 38 (1971): 529–55; Isaac Ariail Reed, *Interpretation and Social Knowledge: On the Uses of Theory in the Human Sciences* (University of Chicago Press, 2011), 92.

19. We can say the same about both branches, in the rapidly dating distinction between "analytic" and "continental" alike. See Michael Dummet, *Origins of Analytical Philosophy* (Harvard University Press, 1988).

20. Wilhelm von Humboldt, "On Germany's Educational System," in *The Rise of the Research University: A Sourcebook*, eds. Louis Menand, Paul Reitter, and Chad Wellmon (University of Chicago Press, 2017 [1809]), 105–22, at 118–19.

21. Leszek Kolakowski, *Modernity on Endless Trial* (University of Chicago Press, 1990), chap. 4.

22. See Ernst Cassirer, *Rousseau, Kant and Goethe* (Harper, 1963), 34–35.

23. Our inspiration here is, again, Peirce, particularly his famous pragmatic maxim: "Consider what effects, which might conceivably have practical bearings, we conceive the object of our conception to have. Then, our conception of these effects is the whole of our conception of the object." The maxim is well-known. Less well-known is what Peirce suggests next: "Let us illustrate this rule by some examples; and, to begin with the simplest one possible, let us ask what we mean by calling a thing *hard*. Evidently that it will not be scratched by many other substances. The whole conception of this quality, as of every other, lies in its conceived effects. There is absolutely no difference between a hard thing and a soft thing so long as they are not brought

to the test." Hardness, in this case, is every possibility objectively capable of it, but can only be revealed via tests. See Charles Sanders Peirce, "How to Make Our Ideas Clear," in *Chance, Love and Logic: Philosophical Essays*, ed. Morris Cohen (Harcourt, Brace and Company, 1923 [1878]), 45–46.

24. Ioanna Constantiou and James Kallinikos, "New Games, New Rules: Big Data and the Changing Context of Strategy," *Journal of Information Technology* 30, no. 1 (2015): 44–57, at 48.

25. Mario Carpo, *The Second Digital Turn: Design Beyond Intelligence* (MIT Press, 2017), 40ff; Peter Denning and Matti Tedre, *Computational Thinking* (MIT Press, 2019), 155–56.

26. Duncan Watts, "Common Sense and Sociological Explanations," *American Journal of Sociology* 120, no. 2 (2014): 313–51.

27. Marion Fourcade and Kieran Healy, "Seeing Like a Market," *Socio-economic Review* 15, no. 1 (2017): 9–29, at 17.

28. Alberto Cevolino and Elena Esposito, "From Pool to Profile: Social Consequences of Algorithmic Prediction in Insurance," *Big Data and Society* 7, no. 2 (2020): 1–22.

29. Alfred Schutz, *The Problem of Social Reality: Collected Papers 1*, ed. Maurice Natanson (Nijhoff, 1962).

30. Sociologist of science Barry Barnes describes an ideal-typical case of a "society wherein a specific form of cognitive authority is allocated entirely to a single individual, acting in a recognized role. Such an individual may instantiate a term by fiat. He may be entitled to pronounce any entity an S, or any entity of kind A an S, and thereby make it an S." Such a society is an extreme case, in which knowledge can be "intensely self-referential and completely self-validating." This knowledge is self-validating, meaning that it involves patterns named earlier as specific designations, with every new learner acting as a "confirming instance" of the knowledge. The "sole distributor" need not have a connection to pattern recognition on any other terms than ones she defines. On the other extreme, "there is no clear concentration of cognitive authority." Knowledge will still "retain a self-referring character," yet in circumstances without a cognitive authority, the "simple self-reference," as Barnes calls it, is "replaced by spaghetti junction." Knowledge may still have local validity, and it may even involve reference to assertions or applications of that knowledge; but lacking the weight of cognitive authority, knowledge is vulnerable to a "parallel stream of judgments." More specifically, habituated pattern recognition overcomes any claim to "privileged" pattern recognition. See Barry Barnes, "Social Life as Bootstrapped Induction," *Sociology* 17, no. 4 (1983): 524–45, at 526.

31. Shoshana Zuboff, "Big Other: Surveillance Capitalism and the Prospects of an Information Civilization," *Journal of Information Technology* 30, no. 1 (2015): 75–89.

32. David Lyon, "Surveillance, Snowden and Big Data: Capacities, Consequences, Critique," *Big Data and Society* 1, no. 2 (2014): 1–13.

33. Benjamin Bratton, *The Stack: On Software and Sovereignty* (MIT Press, 2015), xvii–xviii.

34. Boethius, *The Consolation of Philosophy*, trans. David Slavitt (Harvard University Press, 2010).

35. Boethius, *Consolation of Philosophy*, 29–30.

36. Boethius, *Consolation of Philosophy*, 146–48.

37. Ernst Cassirer, *The Philosophy of Symbolic Forms, Volume 2: Mythical Thought* (Routledge, 2020 [1923]).

38. Pierre Bourdieu, *Outline of a Theory of Practice* (Cambridge University Press, 1972 [1977]), 168–69.

39. Kate Eichorn, *Content* (MIT Press, 2022), 85–88.

40. Max Weber, "The Social Psychology of the World Religions," in *From Max Weber: Essays*

in Sociology, eds. and trans. Hans Gerth and C. Wright Mills (Oxford University Press, 1946 [1915]), 267–302, at 275. This essay and "Religious Rejections of the World and Their Directions" (also in *From Max Weber*) were both published in the *Archiv für Sozialforschung* and later collected after Weber's death in the first volume of the *Gesammelte aufsätze zur religionssoziologie* (J. C. B. Mohr, 1922). Notably, the "incongruity" [Inkongruenz zwischen Schicksal und Verdienst] comes as part of Weber's critique of Nietzsche's theory of *ressentiment*, which he introduces by citing the different "*Lebenschancen*" of the disadvantaged. Gerth and Mills translate this term as "life-chances." Despite the apparent centrality of the "incongruity" for Weber's sociology of religion, it has received little scholarly attention. However, see Gershon Shafir, "The Incongruity Between Destiny and Merit: Max Weber on Meaningful Existence and Modernity," *British Journal of Sociology* 36, no. 4 (1985): 516–30. See also Ann Swidler, "Foreword," in Max Weber, *Sociology of Religion* (Beacon Press, 1993), xvi.

41. Shafir, "Incongruity Between Destiny and Merit," 519.

42. Bourdieu's influential analysis of modern education systems finds its focal critique, in a sense, in its demonstration that education systems are almost by design functioning as hosts and propagators of self-perpetuating loops removed of merit, destinies made perfectly contingent as the inheritance of birth.

43. Weber, "Religious Rejections," 348.

44. Weber, "Religious Rejections," 350.

45. Kries argued that mechanical systems were remarkable because they produced closely analogous *Spielraum*, however we divide them into outcomes and whoever is the source of expectation. The comparison to machine interface and digital looping suggests a similar point: Individuals become closely analogous *Spielraum* with fewer individual anomalies. In other words, they become more predictable as they are less individual and less subjective—so powerful can be a machine-based verticality. See Johannes von Kries, "On Probability Theory," in *Principles of the Probability Calculus*, trans. Keith Niall (Springer, 2023 [1916]), 204–5.

46. John Cheyney-Lippold, "A New Algorithmic Identity: Soft Biopolitics and the Modulation of Control," *Theory, Culture and Society* 28, no. 6 (2011): 164–81; Gilles Deleuze, "Postscript on Societies of Control," *October* 59 (1992): 3–7.

Index